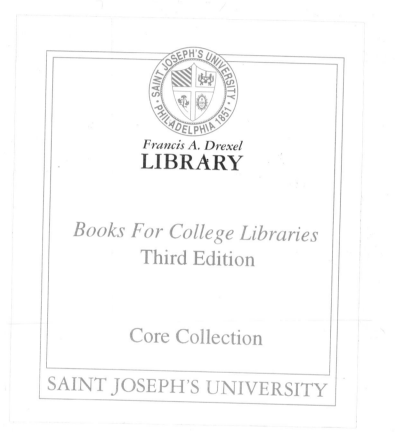

Work & Family

Work & Family

Changing Roles of Men and Women

Edited by Patricia Voydanoff

Mayfield Publishing Company

First edition

Library of Congress Catalog Card Number: 83-061534
International Standard Book Number: 0-87484-576-9

Manufactured in the United States of America
Mayfield Publishing Company
285 Hamilton Avenue
Palo Alto, California 94301

Sponsoring editor: Franklin C. Graham
Manuscript editor: Linda Purrington
Managing editor: Pat Herbst
Art director: Nancy Sears
Text designer: Wendy Calmenson
Cover designers: Wendy Calmenson and Nancy Sears
Production managers: Wendy Calmenson and Cathy Willkie
Compositor: Columbia Phototype
Printer and binder: Bookcrafters

Contents

Preface

The increasing recognition that relationships between work and family are crucial to the understanding of contemporary family life has led to the emergence of work and family issues as a subarea of family studies and to the development of courses on work and family in several academic disciplines. However, this is the first text in this significant and growing subarea of family studies. The book presents a comprehensive analysis of issues important in understanding work/family linkages within a broad, integrated sociological context. It also documents the relevance of the issues to the lives of men and women, both at work and at home. The book examines two major aspects of work and family: (1) the economic roles of men and women and (2) the impact of occupational conditions on family life. This analysis provides the basis for an examination of (1) the ways in which individuals attempt to coordinate the demands of work and family and (2) institutional responses to work/family conflict and economic difficulties among families.

The book is directed to undergraduate and graduate students enrolled in courses in family sociology, sex roles, the sociology of work, and business and management. It is also well suited to interdisciplinary programs in women's studies and courses on social psychology, social problems, and general social science. The interdisciplinary nature of the subject matter makes it relevant to diverse courses and academic programs. In some cases the book can serve as a major text; in others, as a supplementary resource.

The readings were carefully selected, according to several criteria. First, and most important, was the selection of the highest-quality articles available for each topic. The articles also needed to be as current as possible, nontechnical, clearly and concisely written, and of enduring importance to the field. Following these criteria has resulted in a collection of the most significant literature appropriate for graduate and undergraduate students.

In addition to being the first text to focus on work and family, the book is a collection of articles on work and family for professionals and a general audience. Professionals will find an up-to-date and comprehensive source of information on work and family. Men and women in nonacademic settings, as well as students, will find the book relevant to their own experiences in coordinating work and family roles.

Many individuals have contributed to the development and preparation of this volume. I am indebted to the authors and original publishers of the readings for their intellectual contributions and their willingness to make the material available. I would like to acknowledge valuable comments and suggestions on the original outline of the book by Jeanne E. Kohl, Phyllis Moen, Jeylan T. Mortimer, and Joseph H. Pleck. Jeanne Dost and Sharlene Hesse-Biber reviewed the first draft of the text and also gave helpful comments. The generous assistance of Roseanne Engles and Jan Thornton in organizing and preparing the manuscript is greatly appreciated. The staff of Mayfield Publishing Company, especially Franklin C. Graham, Pamela Trainer, and Judith Ziajka, provided considerable expertise and support in the preparation and editing of the manuscript.

P.V.

Work & Family

PART ONE

The Changing Context of Work and Family Roles

Introduction

The past decade has witnessed changing orientations to work and family roles. A belief in the separateness of work and family has shifted to an increased recognition of the interdependence of work and family roles and a desire to better understand the nature and implications of this interdependence.

The belief that work and family roles operate independently of each other, referred to by Kanter (1977) as the "myth of separate worlds," has existed since industrialization. The myth of separate worlds has been reinforced by the Protestant Ethic and traditional sex-role norms. According to the Protestant Ethic, individuals at work are expected to "act as though" they have no commitments other than to work (Kanter, 1977). Traditional sex-role ideology sees men as breadwinners performing a work role outside the home and women as wives and mothers performing family duties inside the home. The examination of issues regarding work and unemployment among men and family issues among women in the social-science literature reflects this approach.

An ambivalence toward the family is embedded in the myth of separate worlds. On the one hand, the family is considered to be a private institution providing a haven from the burdens and responsibilities of work. On the other hand, families are expected to adapt to the conditions of work, to socialize children to become competent workers, and to provide emotional support to workers to enhance their effectiveness. The myth of separate worlds ignores the fact that family functioning depends on the pay, hours, and other demands of work as well as on interactions with other institutions that provide services to families, such as schools and government.

Recent social changes have contributed to a breakdown, partial though it may be, of the myth of separate worlds. The myth was built on the assumption that men worked outside the home to support their families, women were homemakers, and families adapted their pattern of living to the conditions and level of economic rewards associated with the men's work. Strains and tensions were not perceived as issues requiring major changes in work or family life. Today only 7 percent of families fit the traditional model of a man working outside the home, a housewife, and two school-age children. In 1980, 52 percent of women aged sixteen or over were in the labor force, up from 34 percent in 1950. The percentage of women with children under six who are working has increased from 12 percent in 1950 to 45 percent in 1980. The number of single-parent families doubled in the last decade, reaching 21 percent of all families in 1981. Factors associated with the increasing number of two-earner and single-parent families highlight the connections and tensions between work and family roles. Most women in two-earner and single-parent families work because of economic need; many families cannot be supported solely by a man working outside the home. New patterns of work and family roles are necessary for working men and women to meet their obligations in both realms. These range from changing the hours and scheduling of work, reallocating family work among family members, and entering and leaving the labor force over the life course to meet family needs.

In recent years, recognition of these connections has led social scientists to extensively examine work and family linkages. These linkages can be viewed from three perspectives—interdependence of work and family, the impact of work roles on family life, and the influence of family responsibilities on labor force participation and commitment to work.

On an institutional level, interchanges take place between the economy and the family. The economy produces goods and services for consumption by families. Families use income earned in production activities to buy these goods and services. The economy provides jobs to family members while the family supplies skilled workers to the economy. The family is partially responsible for its members entering the labor force with the skills and motivation needed to operate within an industrial and commercial environment.

Interdependence of work and family roles also exists within individual families. Scanzoni (1970) has developed a model of family cohesion based on reciprocity and the exchange of rights and duties. An exchange of rights and duties between husband and wife exists on the instrumental level—that is, economic provision and household work—in which both the husband and wife perform their assigned responsibilities. This exchange on the instrumental level leads to a similar exchange on the expressive level—that is, empathy, companionship, and affection. The mutual performance of expressive activities leads to marital happiness and satisfaction, producing further motivation to maintain the system, thereby leading to stability, solidarity, and cohesion.

This model can be applied to both one-earner and two-earner families. In one-earner families, the instrumental exchange involves the husband working outside the home and the wife performing household duties. When the husband is successful in his occupation and the wife maintains the household, both feel their instrumental rights have been met.

Scanzoni (1972) suggests that the potential for cohesion is greater in two-earner families because wife employment provides additional opportunities for exchanges of instrumental rights and duties between husband and wife. If the wife also performs economic duties and the husband also performs household duties, the expanded performance of instrumental roles provides additional motivation for the husband and wife to engage in expressive activities, which in turn increase marital cohesion. This model challenges Parsons' (1949; Parsons and Bales, 1955) hypothesis that wife employment decreases family cohesion because role differentiation is decreased. According to Parsons, role differentiation prescribes that husbands perform instrumental roles and that wives perform expressive roles, thereby preventing competition and increasing cohesion. The evidence is not sufficient to permit a choice between these contrasting hypotheses. Perhaps each hypothesis holds under certain conditions. For example, families with traditional sex-role norms may be more cohesive with differing instrumental roles for husband and wife.

Much empirical work focuses on the effects of work on family life. These effects are of two types—economic security as a basic requirement for family life and the impact of occupational conditions on families. A minimum level of income and employment stability is necessary for family stability and cohesion. Beyond this minimum, the family's subjective perception of adequacy becomes relatively more important in relation to happiness and stability. In addition to the economic function of work, the conditions associated with performing a work role have pervasive effects on family life. Work-role demands are relatively heavy among families at higher occupational levels in terms of amount and scheduling of work time, job transfers and business travel, and duties expected of corporate wives. Therefore, individuals with middle-level incomes and occupational status may be best able to combine work and family roles: those at the lower end have too few economic resources, and those at the upper end have difficulty performing family roles.

Less recognized, but still significant, are the impacts of family responsibilities on labor-force participation and the commitment to work. Men see the role of economic provider as their primary family role; therefore, family-role responsibilities provide an important motivation for adequate performance in the work role. Men usually coordinate the timing of marriage and career preparation and do not marry until they are able to support a family, either alone or with the support of parents or spouse. In addition, many men moonlight or work voluntary overtime to meet the economic needs of their families.

The family also exerts a major influence on the labor-force participation of other members. Historians of the early stages of industrialization report that the family regulated the labor-force participation of women and children according to economic need and family life-cycle stage. Recent evidence also documents family influence on the extent and timing of women's labor-force participation according to economic need, constraints of the husband's occupation, and family life-cycle stage. Part-time employment among children was a significant response to economic deprivation during the Depression, especially among boys.

These three perspectives, with their varying emphases, illuminate complex interrelationships between work and family life and provide a context for viewing men's and women's changing work and family roles. The limited work done so far, however, raises more questions than it answers about the nature, extent, and direction of changes in work and family roles. Changes in work are occurring that have implications for family life; for example, the development of flexible work schedules that help working parents combine their work and family responsibilities. The shape of work roles in the future will be influenced by a complex mixture of factors, including the level of articulated need for family-oriented personnel policies, technological developments and innovations, the health and vitality of the economy, and the demands of increasingly educated workers for changes in working conditions. Interesting speculations about the future of work are being made; for example, Toffler's (1980) prediction of the emergence of the "electronic cottage" in which many individuals will work at home at their computer terminals.

Recent changes in family life have been rapid and profound. Families are smaller, divorce and remarriage are more prevalent, more children are living with one parent, and more young and elderly live alone. The impact of women's employment on family life has been tremendously important and will continue to be influential in yet undetermined ways. How will two-earner families coordinate their work and family responsibilities? To what extent will men participate in household work and child-rearing activities? Will women continue to alternate between work and child-rearing responsibilities over the life course? Will commuter marriages become more common in response to the vagaries of the job market? These questions regarding changing work and family roles are significant and require further investigation.

Research done so far on work and family roles is limited by its methodology and the lack of variety in family types included in the studies. Initial research generally consists of qualitative studies based on informal interviews with small samples. This is useful for outlining major issues and formulating hypotheses. Now we need more systematic studies with larger, more representative samples to test the provocative hypotheses developed in the preliminary research.

These early studies on work and family roles focus on white middle- and upper-middle-class families. This is partially due to the fact that researchers coping with these issues in their own lives are middle class and that middle-class families are more accessible for research. Studies of lower-class families generally have not included a work/family perspective. Much of the research on black families is limited to the lower class although female employment has been a significant factor in the growth of the black middle class over the past twenty years. Almost no studies exist on work and families among the growing Hispanic population or other ethnic groups with differing values and family patterns. To develop insights and understanding of work/family relationships that are generalizable, it is essential to broaden the base of research to include more class and ethnic diversity.

This book integrates and examines current knowledge on relationships between the work and family roles of men and women. It documents the interdependence of the family and work and the ways in which this interdependence influences the organization of work life and limits the family's ability to nurture children and provide economic and emotional support to its members. It demonstrates the significance of societal trends such as changing sex-role norms and increased female employment for family functioning and stability. The book explores a variety of solutions used by families to accommodate changing work and family roles. At a time of growing recognition that the family is not a self-sufficient institution, this book analyzes the implications of this realization for the development of policies and programs to strengthen families. It builds on the current knowledge base by raising issues for future research and reflection.

This book is based on two major assumptions. The first is that women's employment will continue as a prominent trend in American society. This trend means that a growing majority of families will have no adult in the home full time, making the dilemmas involved in work-family role coordination a major issue in American life. Thus, the issues addressed in the book will have more general application in the future than in the past, even up until the last ten years. The second assumption is that the consideration of work/family linkages must move beyond an examination of women's roles and assume a broader perspective in which work/family issues are recognized as relevant to both men and women. This change involves increased consideration of role sharing, in which men and women assume more equivalent work and family responsibilities.

The first part of the book views work and family roles from the perspective of changing norms and behavior and documents the interdependence of work and family roles.

The second and third parts discuss two major aspects of this interdependence, economic roles and occupational conditions. Economic roles performed by men and women provide access to the financial resources necessary to support family life. Occupational conditions such as time and scheduling of time, job transfers and geographic mobility, and occupational cultures all have a strong impact on the nature and quality of family life.

In Parts Four and Five, implications of economic roles and occupational conditions are developed on two levels—family coordination of work and family roles and social policy. Family role coordination consists of processes through which individuals attempt to deal with the strains associated with work and family roles; for example, staging work and family roles over the life course, creating a more symmetrical division of labor between men and women at home and at work, and developing coping strategies to handle role conflicts. However, in the long run, institutionalized policies are necessary to effectively deal with work/family linkages, including changes in the structure of work and policies to meet the economic needs of families. Taken together, the readings provide a comprehensive view of the basic components of work/family linkages and review the alternative ways in which linkages are handled by individual families and by institutions such as corporations and government.

The two articles in Part One look beyond the myth of separate worlds to map out relationships between work and family roles. Pleck conceives of "The Work-Family Role System" in terms of four roles—male work, female work, female family, and male family—and relationships among the several work/family role combinations. For example, women's work roles influence their family roles in terms of children's psychological well-being, marital satisfaction, marital power, and time spent on family tasks; and men's and women's work roles are characterized by a high degree of occupational segregation relegating men and women to different occupations. Pleck examines the articulation of work and family roles by analyzing two structural buffers between men's and women's work and family roles: (1) sex segregation in labor market activity and family division of labor, and (2) asymmetrical boundaries between work and family roles through which work is allowed to intrude on the family life of men and family responsibilities are permitted to intrude on the work roles of women. These buffers reinforce traditional relationships between work and family roles. New role patterns accommodate female work roles and male family roles and facilitate more equal sharing of work and family roles among men and women.

Mortimer and London's article, "The Varying Linkages of Work and Family," examines the interdependence of work and family roles from a different perspective. They identify several structural dimensions of work and family that contribute to variations in work/family linkages. These variables include (1) occupational status—professional/managerial and blue-collar occupations; (2) family status—two-parent and single-parent families; and (3) employment status of family members—single-provider and dual-worker families. Their analysis documents the importance of each of these work and family statuses separately and in combination for the texture and quality of work and family life. Among single-provider families, for example, differences between the work/family linkages of professional/managerial families and blue-collar families are still extensive.

These articles provide an introduction to the complexity and diversity involved in relationships between work and family—the linkages vary according to the structure of the work role, the sex of the person performing it, and the composition of the family.

1

The Work-Family Role System

Joseph H. Pleck

The study of work and the study of the family have traditionally constituted separate sub-disciplines in sociology. Rapoport and Rapoport (1965) and Kanter (1977), among others, have aptly stressed the need for greater examination of work and family roles in relation to each other. Such joint consideration is necessary to describe how individuals' functioning in either of these spheres is affected by their involvement in the other. Further, the current examination of sex roles brings added impetus to the analysis of work-family interrelationships. A major part of what is usually meant by change in "sex roles" is specifically change in the traditional allocation of work and family roles between men and women. Traditional sex role norms prescribed the specialization of work and family responsibilities by sex, but a new option for each sex to integrate roles in both work and the family is now emerging.

This paper analyzes some aspects of what I term the "work-family role system." The work-family role system is composed of the male work role, the female work role, the female family role, and the male family role. Each of these roles may be fully actualized, or may be only partly actualized or latent, as is often the case with the female work role and the male family role. The analysis of these four roles as a system provides a useful way of organizing research about the relations among these roles, and suggests new relations to be examined. It also makes possible some inferences about the dynamics of future changes in women's and men's roles in work and the family.

Reprinted from Joseph H. Pleck, "The Work-Family Role System," *Social Problems*, vol. 24, April 1977, pp. 417–427.

Analyzing men's and women's work and family roles as components of a role system involves specifying how each role articulates with the others to which it is linked, and how variations in the nature of each role, or whether the role is actualized at all, affects the others. For example, to describe the link between the female work and the female family roles, we consider how the extent of the female work role (ranging from no paid work at all, to the most demanding and highest status full time work) both affects and is affected by the extent of the female family role. These links can be considered at two conceptual levels. They can be analyzed at the level of the individual couple; e.g., the relation between wives' employment status and wives' role performance in the family. Each link can be considered at the aggregate or macrosocial level; e.g., the relation between married women's labor-force participation rate and married women's level of household work and childcare (expressed, for example, in mean hours per day).

FEMALE WORK AND FAMILY ROLES

Let us start with the link between the female work and female family roles, and move clockwise around the figure [Figure 1.1]. Research on the effects of married female employment on the family (see Hoffman and Nye, 1974; Howell, 1973a, 1973b) contains much information relevant to this link. The three major topics in this research have been the effects of wives' employment on children's psychological well-being, marital satisfaction and happiness, and marital power. The consensus today appears to be that when other variables are controlled, wives' employment has no clear positive or negative effect on children's well-being, and when freely chosen, has no negative effect on marital happiness and satisfaction. Most reviews (cf. Bahr, 1974) conclude that wives' employment is associated with some increase in wives' marital

FIGURE 1.1
The Work-Family Role System

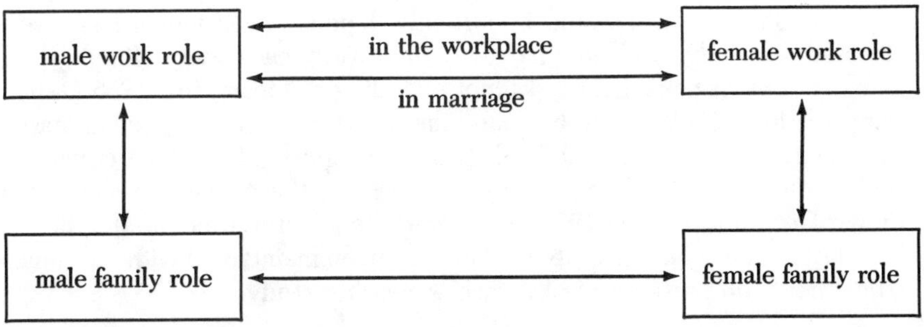

power (primarily assessed by wives' reports of how the couple would make various hypothetical decisions). However, Safilios-Rothschild (1970) has questioned the support for this and other aspects of the "resource" theory of marital power.

The most important aspect of married females' employment in the present analysis is simply its effect on the level of wives' performance of family roles. Blood and Wolfe's (1960) examination of the relation between household division of labor and wives' employment indicated that when wives held paid jobs, they reported doing a lower proportion of the work performed by the couple on eight household tasks (not including childcare). Several analyses of time budget data (Walker, 1969; Meissner et al., 1975; Robinson, Juster, and Stafford, 1976) have likewise shown, predictably enough, that wives holding paid jobs outside the family spend less time performing family tasks than wives not so employed. In Walker's data, for example, wives' average time in family tasks was 8.1 hours per day when not employed and declined, through several intermediate categories of part-time employment, to 4.8 hours per day when the wife was employed thirty or more hours per week.

Two observations should be made about this inverse relationship between wives' performance of work roles and family roles. First, it is not clear as yet whether the composition of wives' family role performance changes when they hold paid work. The various time budget analyses do not indicate a consistent reduction in wives' family work disproportionately greater in some categories than others. But the categories for family tasks used in these analyses may be too broad. Second, it should be emphasized that the overall reduction in employed wives' time in family work is not fully commensurate to their increased time in paid employment. The total burden of work and family roles combined is substantially greater for the employed than the non-employed wife.

FEMALE AND MALE FAMILY ROLES

The first and most obvious feature of the articulation between females' and males' family roles is that women and men generally perform different family tasks.[1] That is, there is a marital division of family labor. There is no single accepted way of quantifying how far family tasks are segregated by sex, and any quantitative index would be strongly dependent on which tasks were selected for study, and how narrowly or broadly each was defined. In an analysis of eight household tasks (not including childcare) in a 1955 Detroit sample, Blood and Wolfe (1960) found that six were performed predominately by one or the other spouse, and only two were performed relatively equally by both spouses. Duncan et al. (1974), replicating these items in a similarly drawn Detroit sample in 1971, concluded the general principle that household tasks should be segregated by sex had been maintained with only slight adjustments on particular tasks since the earlier study.

Ideological support for the traditional division of family labor by sex remains quite strong. Robinson, Yerby, Feiweger, and Somerick (1976) note that in their national sample of married women in 1965–66, only nineteen percent responded "yes" to the question, "Do you wish your husband would give you more help with the household chores?" Repeating the question in a 1973 national survey, the percentage of agreement rose only four points to twenty-three percent. The increase in the percentage of wives wanting more help from their husbands in household work was considerably greater in certain subgroups, however. There was, for example, an increase of twenty-three percent for black women, and twenty percent for women who graduated from college. The increase in these groups may presage a challenge to the traditional division of household labor which will become more widespread in the future.

A second important feature of the link between male and female family roles concerns simply the relation between the overall levels of each. Though no direct analyses of this relation have been located, it can be inferred from the relation between males' family role performance and wive's employment status, since the latter is associated with variations in females' family role performance. Walker's (1970) time budget data indicate that, on average, there is *no* variation in husbands' mean time in family roles (about 1.6 hours per day) associated with their wives' employment status. That is, husbands contribute about the same time to family tasks whether their wives are employed (and doing an average of 4.8 hours of family work per day), or are not employed (and doing an average of 8.1 hours of family work per day). Other time budget studies (Meissner et al., 1975; Robinson, Juster, and Stafford, 1976) confirm Walker's general findings. In Walker's data, husbands' family time does increase slightly, to 2.1 hours per day, when their wives are employed if a child under two is present, but otherwise the independence of husbands' family time from wives' employment status holds true when age and number of children are controlled.

Blood and Wolfe (1960: 62–68) and later studies using their methods (see Bahr, 1974), however, find an increase in the proportion of household work performed by husbands, when their wives are employed. At least two factors may account for the discrepancy between Blood and Wolfe's and the time budget findings. First, Blood and Wolfe's measure sampled only a few household tasks, and expressly excluded childcare. It may be that the particular tasks Blood and Wolfe sampled are ones in which husbands do increase their participation when their wives are employed, but this explanation seems unlikely. The time budget analyses do not indicate any change in the composition of husbands' unvarying family time according to wives' employment status, though the categories of family tasks used in these analyses may be too broad. In small-sample British and American studies, Oakley (1970) and Lein et al. (1974) suggest that husbands of working wives are more likely to increase their participation in childcare than in other household work. But if so, then it is quite paradoxical that Blood and Wolfe's measure, which does not include childcare, shows an increase in husbands' family role performance in response to wives' employment, while the time budget measures, which do include childcare, do not indicate such an increase.

A more likely account for the discrepancy is that the time budget data concern each spouse's contribution to family work in absolute terms, while Blood and Wolfe's measure indicates only the relative division of labor between husband and wife. If the husband's absolute time in family tasks remains constant when his wife is employed, and if his wife spends less time in family work, the husband's *relative* share of family work increases. Thus, Blood and Wolfe's results and the time budget data are not inconsistent.

The two most significant features of the relation between husbands' and wives' family role performance are, then, that family tasks are strongly segregated by sex, and that husbands' time in family tasks does not vary in response to the changes in wives' family work resulting from wives' paid employment. Note that the time budget data indicating that husbands do not increase their family role performance when their wives are employed are cross-sectional rather than longitudinal in nature. It is possible that longitudinal analysis might find changes in husbands' level of family work as their wives enter the labor force, leave it during childbearing, and then re-enter it, in the family life cycle pattern so frequent today. Further, although there is no average increase in husbands' family time when their wives have paid jobs, this average lack of response may conceal subgroups of husbands who do take on a significantly greater family role. If so, there must be subgroups of husbands who actually decrease their family role when their wives work. More needs to be known about the determinants of individual variation in husbands' family role performance, and in their responsiveness to their wives' paid employment.

MALE FAMILY AND WORK ROLES

The effect of the male work role is receiving increasing attention. Scanzoni (1970) notes that functional theory emphasizes how the family is linked to the larger society through the husband-father's occupational role, and how this extrafamilial link affects family relationships. A number of studies and reviews (Aberle and Naegele, 1952; Dyer, 1956, 1965; Miller and Swanson, 1958; Scanzoni, 1965, 1970; Aldous, 1966; Gronseth, 1971, 1972; Pearlin, 1974) have considered how characteristics of the male's occupational role (especially his occupational status) affect the family and particularly the socialization of children.

The most obvious and direct effect of the male occupational role on the family, however, has so far received little analytical attention: the restricting effect of the male occupational role on men's family role. Again using the budget and division of labor measures, data from Walker (1974) and Blood and Wolfe (1960) indicate that role performance in work and family are inversely related to each other for husbands as they are for wives.

While the extent of the husband's role co-varies with the extent of his work role, variation in the extent of the husband's family role occurs around a low baseline *not* accounted for by the demands of his work role. Rather, men's family role varies within the limits imposed by the traditional division of family labor by sex. Though both men's and women's family roles vary according to their employment status, fully employed men still do only a fraction of the family work that fully employed women do—about one-third, according to Walker's data. To put it another way, though employment status has a significant main effect on family work, sex has a stronger effect and accounts for much more of the variance in an individual's time in family work than does his or her employment status.

Thus, it would be misleading to state that men's role work is the primary determinant of the limited family role men typically hold at present. It would be more accurate to say that the objective demands of the male work role are now a latent and secondary constraint, but will emerge as the primary constraint on men's family role if and when ideological support for the traditional division of family labor by sex is weakened. Until then, reduction in the demands of the male work role (for example, shortening the workweek) may not lead to much of an increase in males' family role, as compared to increases in overtime work, the holding of two jobs, and leisure.

Several other aspects of the relation between male work and family roles can be considered. When the methods and assumptions traditionally used in the analysis of married females' employment and its relation to the family are applied to married men, it becomes apparent that many important questions have not yet been asked. For example, economic literature on the "labor supply response" (Mincer, 1962; Cain, 1966) uses slightly different analytic models for husbands and wives. Wives are assumed to allocate time among paid market work, "home market" work (i.e., housework and childcare), and leisure. The parallel analytical equations for men, however, omit "home market" work and include as dependent variables only paid market work and leisure. That is, men's actual participation in family roles is analytically invisible. Such analytical formulations reflect an assumption that men's contribution to family roles is unvarying and of little conceptual significance.[2] For another example, maternal employment has long, and incorrectly, been thought to harm children psychologically. Despite decades of clinical stereotypes about psychologically absent or "weak, passive" fathers, it was rarely asked whether or how *paternal* employment might harm children.

There has been considerable research on the effects of husbands' occupational status and, to a lesser extent, other occupational characteristics, on marital satisfaction and marital power (see Scanzoni, 1970). Of particular note are two recent studies on the effects of a previously overlooked aspect of men's occupational role: the overall salience of men's occupational role in comparison to their family role as a source of satisfaction. Bailyn (1971) classified husbands as oriented primarily to work or to the family, according to their self-rating of which gave them more satisfaction. In marriages where wives held paid employment and valued it positively, marital satisfaction was high if the husband was family-oriented, but markedly low if the husband was work-oriented. Husband's orientation was not associated with marital satisfaction, however, in other marriages. Rapoport et al. (1974), classifying husbands in the same way, found that both husbands and wives reported greater enjoyment of everyday activities with their spouses if the husband was family-oriented than if he was not. Interestingly, both studies noted that husbands' orientation to work or family appeared to have a stronger effect on marital variables than did wives' orientation.

MALE AND FEMALE WORK ROLES

There are two distinct contexts in which male and female work roles articulate with each other: in work environments themselves, and in marriage. In the workplace, the most significant feature of the articulation on male and female work roles is the high degree of occupational segregation by sex (Waldman and McEaddy, 1974; Blaxall and Reagan, 1976), with females concentrated in lower-paying, lower status occupations. Within this overall occupational segregation, two dominant patterns for the articulation of male and female work roles can be distinguished. In the older pattern, typical in much blue-collar employment, women and men work in entirely separate settings, and do not generally interact with each other in their work roles. Females are completely excluded from male workplaces. Males are not completely excluded from female workplaces, since women work under the authority and control of male employers. However, this control is largely administered through a cadre of female supervisors, thus greatly minimizing male-female contact.

A major source of this pattern of occupational segregation historically has been men's desire to exclude women in order to keep their own wages up (Hartman, 1976). This pattern may derive from non-economic sources as well. Caplow (1954) proposed that a fundamental norm that women and men should not interact with each other except in romantic and kinship relationships underlies this sex-segregation of the workplace. Caplow speculatively argued that a major psychological source of this norm is that aggression toward females is severely punished in male childhood socialization, and is therefore highly anxiety-provoking to males. Since interaction with work partners inevitably entails some degree of competition and aggression, Caplow argues, interacting with women in the workplace makes men anxious. We can also note similarities between these traditional norms prescribing complete segregation of male and female work roles and what anthropologists term "pollution ideology" (Douglas, 1970). According to pollution ideology, if certain categories of social objects (e.g., menstrual blood) are not segregated or handled in special ways, the order of the world is disturbed and catastrophe will result. In similar fashion, many miners and seamen in the past have resisted the introduction of women as co-workers because they superstitiously believed that women would be a "jinx" or "bad luck" bringing on mining disasters and shipwrecks.

The more recent pattern for the articulation of male and female work roles, whose ideal type is the modern office, is the integration of women into mixed-sex workplaces, but in roles that are segregated from and clearly subordinate to men's. Thus, women and men do not compete for the same jobs, and do not have to interact with each other as peers. In this pattern, the potential for interacting with members of the other sex, particularly if unmarried, has almost attained the status of a fringe benefit. The shift from the first pattern of work organization to the second has not received sufficient attention. Several studies have examined how certain previously male occupations became female ones (Prather, 1972; Davies, 1974), but that these occupational shifts transformed previously all-male environments into mixed-sex ones has not been adequately analyzed as yet.

The second context for the articulation of male and female work roles is marriage. The critical factor affecting this link is primarily psychological in nature, based on men's investment in their performance of the paid breadwinner role as uniquely validating their masculinity. Yankelovich (1974: 44–45) has suggested that for the large majority of men whose jobs are not inherently psychologically satisfying, daily work is made worthwhile by pride in hard work. The sacrifices made to provide for their families' needs validate them as men. Wives working thus takes away a major source of these men's identity, and is psychologically threatening.

Two dominant patterns for the articulation between male and female roles in marriage are apparent, corresponding to the two patterns noted in the workplace. In the more traditional pattern, husbands cannot tolerate their wives taking or holding any paid employment. Supporting this pattern, in many workplaces married women were ineligible for employment, and single women were dismissed if they married. In the more recent pattern, husbands can accept their wives' employment as long as it does not come too close to, or worse surpass, their own in prestige, earnings, or psychological commitment. The segregation of women in lower paying, lower status occupations helps insure that this limit is not breached. Further, husbands' acceptance of their wives' work in this pattern is conditional on their wives' continuing to meet their traditional family responsibilities.

Taking an overview of the workplace and marriage, the second pattern for the articulation of male and female work roles in each is not necessarily more equitable or less restrictive to women than the first. The emergence of the second pattern was, however, inevitable as the married female labor force has expanded over the course of this century. The question now is whether a third pattern can emerge on a widespread scale in which wives can have work roles of equal or greater status than their husbands' (Rapoport and Rapoport, 1971), and in which female workers can interact with male workers as equals in the workplace.

STRUCTURAL "BUFFERS" IN THE WORK-FAMILY ROLE SYSTEM

What are the more general characteristics of the links in the work-family role system? How do these links affect whether change in one role does or does not lead to accommodating change in the other roles to which it is linked? We consider here two structural "buffers" in the links among these roles, limiting how much change in one role affects the others.

The first kind of buffer is *sex-segregated market mechanisms* for both paid work and family work. A sex-segregated, dual market for paid work means that women and men do not compete for the same jobs. As a result, changes in the level of female employment occur neither at the expense nor to the benefit of male employment. Further, since women are segregated into not only different but inferior jobs, women will rarely have jobs of equal or greater status than men's, psychologically threatening their husbands or co-workers. In these ways, the dual market for paid work insulates the male work role from the changes in the female work role that have occurred so far in our society.

Household work and childcare can likewise be conceptualized as allocated by a sex-segregated, dual market mechanism. This market mechanism is supported by ideology concerning the appropriate household activities of the two sexes as well as by differential training in family tasks. The result is that the husband's family role is generally unresponsive to changes in the wife's family role. If a wife's employment requires her to reduce the level of her family role performance, the husband is unlikely to increase his. He may perceive that family work needs doing, but he will not perceive the kind of work that needs to be done as appropriate or suitable to him. The dual market for household work and childcare thus has insulated men's family role from the changes in the female family role resulting so far from paid employment.

The second kind of structural buffer in the work-family role system is *asymmetrically permeable boundaries between work and family roles* for both men and women. For women, the demands of the family role are permitted to intrude into the work role more than vice versa. Though working mothers try to devise schedules to accommodate the demands of both roles, if an emergency or irregularity arises requiring a choice between the two, the family will often take priority. For example, when there is a crisis for a child in school, it is the child's working mother rather than working father who will be called to take responsibility. This vulnerability of the female work role to family demands is an important part of negative stereotypes about women workers. It is also a major source of stress for women on the job, since the sex role norm that women take responsibility for the family conflicts with the norms of the job role.

For husbands, the work-family role boundary is likewise asymmetrically permeable, but in the other direction. Many husbands literally "take work home" with them or need to use family time simply to recuperate from the stresses they face in their work role. Husbands are expected to manage their families so that their family responsibilities do not interfere with their work efficiency, and so that families will make any adjustments necessary to accommodate the demands of husbands' work roles.

CHANGE IN THE WORK-FAMILY ROLE SYSTEM

As is well known, over the course of this century there has been a major increase in married women's rate of labor force participation (Oppenheimer, 1970). Married women's increased employment has induced a partially accommodating reduction in women's family role, but as yet almost no increase in husband's family role, as indicated by the time budget data considered earlier. In consequence, employed wives face considerable problems of strain and exhaustion in both their work and family roles. As Rapoport and Rapoport (1972) have formulated it, there is a psychosocial lag between the changes occurring for women in the macrosocial world of work and changes in the microsocial world of the family. In their analysis, this psychosocial lag generates transitional problems of adjustment, but these will be resolved as the family "catches up" to changes in the workplace. Young and Willmott (1973) have likewise argued that the family is becoming more "symmetrical," that is, evolving toward a pattern where each marital partner has a significant role in both paid work and in the family. The analysis of the work-family role system developed here makes possible a more specific consideration of the issues these social changes will involve.

First, it is clear that one of the most pressing changes needed in the work-family role system is an end to the traditional norms prescribing the sex-segregated and unequal division of household work and childcare. As noted earlier, however, if and when these norms break down, the demands of the male work role will emerge as the crucial constraint on how much men can increase their family role. Expansion of the scope of the male family role without accommodating changes in the male work role will lead to role strain in men similar to the strains now faced by working wives. While this distribution of strain thoughout the role system will be more equitable than the current one, it will continue to be a source of instability. Husbands who are committed to equal sharing of household work and childcare will find that the demands of their jobs make this quite difficult, and that a diversion of their energy from work into the family will penalize them in the competition for job advancement. The idea of paternity leave—admittedly only beginning to be raised in labor negotiations, and not widely taken advantage of in the few places where it has been implemented—is perhaps the first indication of the kind of workplace practices needed to legitimate a shift of husbands' energies from work to the family.

A second potential future change in the work-family role system is the breakdown of occupational sex segregation. Recent progress toward reducing occupational segregation, when it has been evident at all, has been dishearteningly slow (Waldman and McEaddy, 1974; Blaxall and Reagan, 1976). If occupational segregation is significantly reduced, major adjustments will be required in men's self-conceptions as primary family breadwinners and in the norms governing male-female interaction on the job. In addition, women holding higher-status jobs may give added impetus to the desegregation of family work and the enlargement of the male family role. First, women holding higher-status jobs may require that women's boundary between their work and family roles become more like men's, that is, their work role will more often need to take priority over their family role, and they will be able to do less family work. Second, women holding jobs more equal in status to their husbands' will give greater legitimation to the demand for a more equal sharing of family work. Contrary to these two effects, however, the increased income provided by women's holding higher-status jobs may make it more possible for families to purchase goods and services to compensate for the reduction in women's family role than is possible now where women are in relatively low-paying jobs. If these goods and services are available, purchasing them may be less stressful than trying to increase men's family role.

Third, if the sex segregation of both family work and paid work is significantly reduced, a fundamental change in the nature of the work role may be necessary, not just for men but for both sexes. As the paid work role has evolved in modern society, it has come to call for full time, continuous work from the end of one's education to retirement, desire to actualize one's potential to the fullest, and subordination of other roles to work. This conception of the work role has been, in effect, the male model of the work role. Women, because of the family responsibilities traditionally assigned to them, have had considerable difficulty fitting themselves to this male model of work. To a large extent, it has been possible for men in modern society to work according to his model precisely because women have subordinated their own potential work role and accepted such an extensive role in the family. In doing so, wives take on the family responsibilities that husbands might otherwise have to fill, and in addition emotionally, and often practically, support their husbands in their work role.[3]

In the past, it has been possible for families to function, though not without strain, with one marital partner, the husband, performing according to this male work model. Families have also been able to function, though with even more strain, with one partner conforming to the male work model and with the other partner in a less demanding job role. Though it is stressful, especially for the wife, this kind of two-job family is on the verge of being the statistically dominant pattern (Hayghe, 1976). However, it does not seem possible for large numbers of families to function with *both* partners following the traditional male work model. Such a pattern could become widespread only if fertility dropped significantly further or if household work and child-care services became inexpensive, widely available, and socially accepted on a scale hitherto unknown.[4] In the absence of such developments, greater equality in the sharing of work and family roles by women and men will ultimately require the development of a new model of the work role and a new model for the boundary between work and the family which gives higher priority to family needs.

2

The Varying Linkages of Work and Family

Jeylan T. Mortimer and Jayne London

The recent dramatic increase in the employment of married women has drawn attention to the connections of work and family and has stimulated a rapid expansion of scholarly literature on these linkages. This review is therefore, by necessity, a selective one. In the first section, we consider some general ways that work affects the family, and the family influences work. In the second section, we examine differences in the linkages of work and family, depending on some special features of both work and family contexts. We assess the implications of five such contexts: (1) the blue-collar single-provider family, (2) the professional/managerial single-provider family, (3) the blue-collar dual-provider family, (4) the dual-career family, and (5) the single-parent family. In the last section of this review, we point to new directions for social policy that are indicated by the recent changes in work and family life.

THE INTERRELATIONS OF WORK AND FAMILY

The division of scholarly work, with family scholars and occupational sociologists each attending to their separate domains, has contributed to a "myth of separate worlds" (Kanter, 1977a). But it is now widely recognized that in spite of the institutional separation of work and family, they are linked together and dependent on one another in numerous ways. We have found it useful to divide the influences of work on the family into three categories: (1) socioeconomic resources, (2) time and spatial constraints, and (3) psychological effects. We consider each type of influence with respect to particular work and family contexts.

First, work provides social status and economic resources for the family, and therefore sets limits on its standard of living. It also provides opportunities for social mobility and threats to economic security. Perceived opportunities and threats to economic well-being strongly influence family decision making regarding the employment of its members (Ghez and Becker, 1975). When families are confronted with a disruption in ongoing resources—that is, from layoffs or unemployment or when income from regular jobs is inadequate—the family must alter its activities and sometimes change its entire organization. It might move to another geographical region where employment prospects are better; attempt to find additional jobs for the wage earner (or earners), such as overtime work or moonlighting; or send additional earners into the labor force—most frequently wives, but sometimes also adolescent children. Considerable research has documented the harmful consequences of marginal employment and unemployment for the family (Rubin, 1976; Elder, 1974; Sennett and Cobb, 1972; Steinmetz and Strauss, 1974; Schorr and Moen, 1979). Because work is the only source of income for most families, families undergo sacrifices and strains to meet the demands of employment, even when these accommodations cause deterioration in family relationships (Piotrkowski, 1978).

Second, work sets external constraints on family organization and activities. These constraints include the amount of time spent working and the scheduling of work. Working parents often complain that the demands of their work do not allow sufficient time with their children. The particular patterning of work time may also unduly interfere with, and disrupt, family functioning. In a recent nationwide survey (Quinn and Staines, 1979), the issues surrounding work time and scheduling emerged as highly problematic for working parents. Further constraints on the family are set by requirements for travel and geographic mobility. Although there is evidence that families are balking at some of these demands, such as frequent geographic moves, they often have little choice. They must either meet the requirements of the employer or seek a position elsewhere.

Third, work experiences influence the family by affecting the attitudes, values, and personalities of the working member(s). There may be experiences in the workplace that cause dissatisfaction and stress for the worker, which the family must cope with when the worker returns home. In other cases, the work may be so demanding and involving that the worker has little energy left to become involved with other family members. There has been considerable scholarly debate over whether the responses of workers to their jobs are characterized by processes of segmentation and compensation on the one hand, or by generalization and spillover on the other (Piotrkowski, 1978). According to the first hypothesis, workers segment their lives, blocking out thoughts of work when at home, or attempt to compensate for the dissatisfactions of work by seeking out stimulation and gratification in leisure or family activities. According to the second, the job's effects on the worker "carry over" to nonwork spheres. There appears to be far more evidence for the "generalization hypothesis" than for the segmentation or compensation model. Numerous psychological dimensions have been examined in relation to work experience, including parental values, self-confidence and self-deprecation, intellectual flexibility, authoritarian conservatism (Kohn, 1977; Kohn and Schooler, 1982), self-esteem (Rosenberg, 1979), and the sense of competence (Mortimer and Lorence, 1979). Although most of this research has been restricted to men, similar studies of women have indicated no major differences in their psychological responses to work (Miller et al., 1979; see also Kanter, 1977b).

Let us now consider the effects of the family on work. In most past studies, the family has been viewed as accommodative to work, for only recently has change in the family begun to stimulate changes in work roles and organizational requirements (we will describe some of these changes in a later section). But the family makes vital contributions to the workplace. Of foremost importance, the family socializes each new generation of workers, instilling the most basic attitudes and values concerning the meaning of work (Mortimer, 1975, 1976), which influence vocational preferences and eventual occupational destinations (Mortimer and Kumka, 1982; Spenner, 1981). It is evident that in families where mothers are employed outside the home, new messages are transmitted regarding the legitimacy of employment and nontraditional work roles for women. Adolescent boys and girls in dual-earner households have less traditional attitudes toward gender roles than those in which the mother is a full-time homemaker (Hoffman, 1974, 1980).

Second, the family influences the occupational attainment of its members. Family economic needs provide a major motivation to seek employment and to be successful in the occupational career (Harris, 1981; Piotrkowski, 1978; Sennett and Cobb, 1972; Rubin, 1976). Researchers have directed considerable attention to the limitations to women's occupational attainment associated with marriage and fertility (Havens, 1973; Card et al., 1980; Sewell et al., 1980). At the same time, there is consistent evidence that married men have higher socioeconomic attainment than unmarried men (Duncan et al., 1972: 232–236; Aberles et al., 1980; Mortimer et al., 1982). We give further attention to the family's differential support of its working members in the next section.

Finally, at a more structural level, widespread changes in family organization influence the conditions under which employees are able and willing to work. As we shall see, these changes are beginning to affect the structure of work roles and organizational requirements, as employers attempt to maintain a steady and committed work force.

It must be recognized that the linkages of work and family vary tremendously in character. Important structural dimensions of both work and family provide quite different contexts for their interrelationships. First, the particular demands of professional and managerial occupations, in contrast to those of lower-paid white-collar and blue-collar work, pose very different external constraints for the family, and generate different dynamics of work/family interface. Second, one must consider the features of the family. Is there only one working member, or are there two? Is there only one or are there two parents? These work and family characteristics are important because they set different work opportunities and demands, as well as different family needs and resources, of both an economic and interpersonal character. We will now examine five prevalent work and family contexts.

THE VARYING LINKAGES OF WORK AND FAMILY

THE SINGLE-PROVIDER FAMILY

Single-provider families are a diminishing minority, constituting approximately a third of the husband/wife families (Aldous, 1981). It is important, however, to examine the linkages of work and family in this context. First, because in previous generations single-provider families were the majority, work is often structured as if this traditional family type were still the most prevalent. Requirements of work, particularly at high socioeconomic levels, seem most compatible with the single-provider structure. Second, the study of single-provider families illuminates the stresses of the homemaker role and shows that the husband's occupational role can structure the wife's family role as well. Third, consideration of the dynamics of the single-provider family enhances understanding of the particular stresses facing dual-earner, dual-career, and single-parent families.

The Blue-Collar Single-Provider Family. In examining single-provider blue-collar families, it is useful to consider some unique aspects of their family and work roles. Of foremost importance, traditional sex-role expectations—the husband as provider and the wife as mother/homemaker—are central to conceptions of the "good life" in the working class (Rainwater, 1971; Komarovsky, 1964; Rubin, 1976). Children of blue-collar workers, in comparison to those of the middle class, are raised with clearer distinctions as to their proper sex roles (Lambert et al., 1980). There also appears to be a wider gulf between the activities and interests of spouses in the working class than in the middle and upper classes (Bott, 1971).

Second, to understand the character of work/family linkages in this situation it is necessary to consider the nature of men's blue-collar work, as craftsmen, operatives, nonfarm laborers, and service workers. Many blue-collar jobs require little skill, independent judgment, freedom, or autonomy (Ritzer, 1977). As a result, work experiences may generate alienation (Rubin, 1976) and job dissatisfaction (Rosow, 1971). Furthermore, increasing educational attainment may raise expectations (Seybolt, 1976), creating greater dissatisfaction among younger blue-collar workers with the routine tasks they are asked to perform (Miller, 1971; Schrank and Stein, 1971).

The early work life of young blue-collar male workers is generally unstable. They move from job to job in search of higher wages and better working conditions as well as a sense of dignity in work (Rubin, 1976). Overall, these men can expect little security in their jobs due to the fluctuations and uncertainties in the labor market and economy. Blue-collar men and their families often live with fear of a cutback in their hours, a reduction in overtime pay, or worse, being totally laid off.

But most blue-collar men are effectively "locked in," unable to improve their working conditions and rewards by changing jobs. First, the blue-collar worker is constrained from *intra*organizational mobility. The routine nature of his tasks make it difficult for him to display the ability or initiative that could demonstrate suitability for a better job assignment. White-collar managers may exclude blue-collar workers from promotions partly because such managers feel they can trust only people like themselves—educated middle-, and upper-class men (Kanter, 1977b). Second, *inter*organizational mobility may threaten seniority, retirement, and other benefits, thus constituting a substantial risk to the family. At the same time, the worker's limited skills and education decrease his attractiveness to other employers. As a result, blue-collar men are often stuck in dead-end, low-paying, alienating work.

The financial difficulties of blue-collar families are often compounded by early marriage and pregnancy (Howell, 1971; Rubin, 1976; Sidel, 1978). A common solution is for the husband to work overtime, or to take a second job, either of which results in the husband/father being less physically and emotionally available to the family (Sennett and Cobb, 1972; Piotrkowski, 1978). Another common solution is for the wife/mother to enter the labor market.

In addition to the harmful effects of marginal income on family life, research has demonstrated that blue-collar men's feelings about their jobs influence family interaction (Farrell and Rosenberg, 1981). In Piotrkowski's study (1978), although most blue-collar men contended that their work and family lives were separate, in actuality their relationships with other family members were very much influenced by feelings generated at work. When they were upset, due to their distress on the job, they came home fatigued, irritable, and worried. They attempted to create "personal space" between themselves and other family members, blocking out their wives and children. Under these circumstances, wives tried to help their husbands by keeping the children away and by not bothering them with their own problems. The children, too, learned to distance themselves from the father. Piotrkowski's research disproves the popular notion that blue-collar men, because they are not involved in their work, find compensatory gratification through high involvement in their families. She concludes, "Those who feel assaulted, depleted, and uninvolved in their work have little energy left to invest in their families" (Piotrkowski, 1978:106). Piotrkowski's study also draws attention to the possibility that the traditional function of the family, as an oasis of support replenishing the working member, may occur at some cost to wives and children and to the character of family life in general.

It is evident that the father's work situation likewise affects his parental behavior (Kohn, 1977; Rubin, 1976). Blue-collar men are directive (rather than supportive) in their parenting styles and rely more on physical forms of punishment than on appeals to reasoning or guilt. McKinley (1964) believed that lower-class men more severely discipline and punish their children because of their frustration due to low job satisfaction and work autonomy. Findings of class differences in child-rearing values and behaviors have been replicated in many studies (Kohn, 1977; Gecas, 1979). According to Kohn, when work is routine, closely supervised, and lacks substantive complexity, men place a high value on children's conformity and obedience to authority—behaviors necessary in their work environments. Alternatively, when their work requires independent and complex thought, they value self-direction in their children.

It should be noted that blue-collar wives are largely excluded from their husband's work, either because the men feel that work and family should be separated, or because they think their work is too technical, boring, or self-deflating to speak about (Rubin, 1976; Piotrkowski, 1978). Wives often experience difficulty in crossing the work/family boundary—even in emergencies they may be unable to contact their husbands (Piotrkowski, 1978). This exclusion of the blue-collar wife from her husband's work is quite different from the high absorption (to be described) of middle- and upper-class women in their husband's careers.

The Professional/Managerial Single-Provider Family. In general, as the husband's occupational prestige and income increase, marital satisfaction and stability likewise increase (Scanzoni, 1970). But at the highest status levels, demands on the family may, to a large extent, offset these occupational rewards (Dizard, 1968; Young and Willmott, 1973; Aldous et al., 1979). Professional and managerial families often face the unique pressures of the career, a vertically structured sequence of positions through which individuals expect to move (Wilensky, 1960). Because careers are generally quite demanding and open-ended in their requirements, particularly in their early phases, the career aspirant may feel that work is never finished. The rewards gained through career advancement—both intrinsic and extrinsic—can generate exceedingly high levels of work involvement, drawing men away from their families.

According to the exchange model of family dynamics (Scanzoni, 1970, 1972), the husband in the traditional single-provider family provides economic support to the wife in exchange for her household duties, child care, companionship, and support. But it is apparent that this exchange, in the professional and managerial family, often extends to the wife's support of the husband's career. A decade ago, Papanek (1973) coined the term "two-person career" to describe a prominent pattern in professional and managerial work:

only the husband is officially employed, but there are clear expectations that the wife will engage in a range of activities whose manifest purpose is to enhance the husband's career. The prospects of increasing income and economic security, through advancement in the career, provide incentives for the wife to accommodate, in this way, the excessive requirements of the husband's work (Grieff and Munter, 1980).

In these occupations, heavy time commitments draw the husband away from the family, placing the major burden of family responsibility on the wife (Bailyn, 1971; Pahl and Pahl, 1971; Young and Willmott, 1973, ch. 5). Frequent social obligations, travel requirements, and geographic relocations also require the wife's active support (Renshaw, 1976; Grieff and Munter, 1980). The wife's participation in the "two-person career" has been most extensively studied in the managerial ranks of large organizations (Whyte, 1956; Helfrich, 1965; Handy, 1978; Kanter, 1977a; Grieff and Munter, 1980). But the pattern has been similarly described in other occupational contexts—politics (MacPherson, 1975) and diplomacy (Hochschild, 1969), the military (Goldman, 1973; Finlayson, 1976), academe (Hochschild, 1975; Fowlkes, 1980), medicine (Fowlkes, 1980), and the ministry (Scanzoni, 1965; Douglas, 1965; Taylor and Hartley, 1975). Mortimer (1980) has documented this pattern in a panel of male college graduates, in the early stages of a broad range of professional and managerial careers.

Two recent case studies (Kanter, 1977b; Fowlkes, 1980) have shown how the pressures and opportunities of managerial and professional work mobilize both spouses' efforts. Wives sometimes do work that would otherwise be performed by employees, such as clerical tasks, keeping books in the office, making appointments, editing, attending meetings, and reading. All these contributions increase the husbands' productivity. The wives may also be responsible for extensive entertaining. They are "image builders" for their husbands, because a "good" wife and family connote a stable, trustworthy worker. They serve as community volunteers, while at the same time enhancing the public images of their husbands' employing organizations and making contacts that bolster their husbands' businesses and professional practices.

Wives also provide emotional support, acting as "sounding boards" or informal consultants, soothing their husbands after long, hard days at work. But they often complain that their husbands are psychologically unavailable, inaccessible to family members even when at home (Kanter, 1977b; Machlowitz, 1980; Fowlkes, 1980; Maccoby, 1976). Because of their high degree of "absorption" in their careers (Kanter, 1977a), their husbands have little energy left to become actively involved with wives and children. Under these circumstances, the wives become, in effect, single parents. In addition, fulfilling the requirements of the "two-person career" limits the wife's ability to pursue her own occupational career (Seidenberg, 1973; Mortimer et al., 1978). Research on men shows that they too recognize the problems that professional and managerial work cause in their family lives (Mortimer, 1980).

THE DUAL-PROVIDER FAMILY

When both spouses are employed outside the home, the linkages of work and family are dramatically altered. The dual-provider family is rapidly becoming the most prevalent family pattern. In 1979, 49 percent of married women, with husband present, were in the labor force (U.S. Department of Labor, 1980). The labor-force participation rate was 52 percent for mothers of children under age eighteen, 59 percent for mothers whose children were between six and seventeen, and 43 percent for mothers with children under age six (U.S. Department of Labor, 1980, Table 26). In recent years, increases in maternal employment have been greatest among women who previously had very low rates of employment; that is, among mothers with very young children (Kamerman, 1980).

Employed married women enhance the family's economic resources, contributing, on the average, about one-fourth of the family income, and 40 percent, if employed full time (Hayghe, 1979). But in other ways the family's resources are diminished—no longer is there a full-time homemaker to attend to housework, child care, and to support the husband's occupational role. The employed wife, of course, also lacks support from a full-time homemaker. Who will keep the children away when both spouses come home feeling stressed and exhausted? When parents are working, child care is needed for preschool children, and supervision must be found for children after school. Although couples attempt to streamline housekeeping, the needs of children are less tractable, and time for families to spend with one another, in leisure activities, may radically decline when there are two paid jobs, as well as family work.

Role overload is the key problem for the dual-provider family, particularly the employed mother. Although couples now generally share the provider role, the traditional division of labor in the home has been remarkably tenacious. In most families the unemployed wife remains responsible for most family work, leading to feelings of fatigue and harassment for many employed mothers (Kamerman, 1980). According to Pleck and Rustad's (1980) study of time use, husbands of employed wives only contributed about thirteen hours of family work per week, in comparison to their wives' contribution of about twenty-eight hours. When the husbands of employed women and the husbands of homemakers were compared, the difference in time spent in family work was negligible (only about 15 minutes per week). In comparison to homemakers, wives who were employed outside the home did fifteen hours more work per week (including market and family work) and got a half-hour less sleep per night.

Issues surrounding work time and scheduling, coupled with the difficulties surrounding child care, seem the most problematic stressors in the dual-provider family. In the 1977 Quality of Employment Survey (Pleck et al., 1980), men were more concerned about the amount of time spent working, while women were more concerned with the scheduling of work. This pattern is consistent with working mothers'primary responsibility for their children's needs. It is usually the mother who gets them off to school and makes arrangements for after-school care. Given these responsibilities, women more often have intermittent or part-time employment, express a preference for work close to home, and must cope with the role conflicts arising from children's illnesses and inability to attend school. They must choose between calling in sick themselves, letting the child care for him or herself, or, sometimes, persuading an older child to stay home from school to care for a younger one.

Pleck (1977) has called attention to the differential permeability of work and family boundaries for men and women. Although women are expected to disrupt their work to attend to their families, it is acceptable for men to disrupt their family lives in pursuit of occupational advancement. This normative pattern has important implications for the socioeconomic attainment of men and women (Mortimer et al., 1978).

In effect, employment for most married women does not radically disrupt the core responsibilities of the traditional wife/mother role. Married women have two jobs—one in work and the other in family (Mydral and Klein, 1968; for an excellent literature review on women's work in the home and in the workplace, see Miller and Garrison, forthcoming). They have taken on new positions in the labor force, without relinquishing their traditional functions. Most employed women are in clerical, blue-collar, and service occupations (Howe, 1977; Barrett, 1979). Their work does not usually require frequent travel or overtime work. These job features and the absence of vertically structured careers free most married women to focus on their husbands' and children's needs in their off-work hours. But at the same time, work in female-typed occupations does not offer good prospects for economic reward and advancement—as employed women still earn only about 59 percent of the earnings of men, even when they work full time (Barrett, 1979).

The Blue-Collar Dual-Provider Family. Most detailed qualitative studies of dual-provider families have focused on college-educated professional dual-career families (Fogarty et al., 1971; Holmstrom, 1972). This gap is certainly one of the most problematic in the work and family literature. Although the greatest recent increase in women's employment has been among wives whose husbands have incomes in the upper and middle categories, it is nevertheless true that wives whose husbands have below-average incomes have the highest rates of labor-force participation (Ryscavage, 1979). Moreover, the experiences of dual-career families are not fully generalizable to other dual-provider families due to the differences in their class situations, the nature of the problems they confront, their resources, and the types of solutions they can devise (Rubin, 1976; Hunt and Hunt, 1981).

Working-class women's occupations include traditional blue-collar jobs (crafts, operatives, nonfarm labor, and service), as well as clerical work. Although clerical work is generally categorized as a white-collar occupation, clerical tasks have become closely akin to blue-collar work. As a result of technological change and bureaucratization, clerical work has become increasingly fragmented and closely supervised (Glenn and Feldberg, 1976). The wives of blue-collar men (as well as many wives of white-collar men) tend to be crowded into "the secondary market" (Doeringer and Piore, 1971), characterized by low wages, little or no fringe benefits, poor working conditions, and little opportunity for advancement (see Baker, 1978). Hence most blue-collar employed women are restricted to jobs that are low paying and otherwise unattractive.

In deciding whether to be a working mother, special issues confront women of the working class (Rubin, 1976). An employed wife may seem to reflect negatively on the blue-collar husband who does not feel that he has truly succeeded unless he is able to provide for his family (Baker, 1978). Women, in accord with the same role expectations, have developed traditional self-images that lead them to marry at a young age, and rarely to think seriously, in late adolescence, about the realities of having a long work life.

But although these traditional values inhibit the blue-collar wife's participation and advancement in the labor force, the insufficiency of financial resources for the family draws her into employment. For many of these women, employment is necessary to keep their families above the poverty line (Baker, 1978). Rising inflation increases economic pressure to be continuously employed.

But though the primary motivation for employment among working-class women is undoubtedly economic, it appears that they receive more than merely financial rewards from their jobs (Komarovsky, 1964; Lein, 1979). In spite of the relatively low intrinsic and extrinsic occupational rewards, many feel that having a paid job is more liberating than alienating (Feree, 1976). By being employed, they gain a sense of self-worth and self-sufficiency, while at the same time escaping the drudgery of housework (Walshok, 1979).

But even when they are employed, blue-collar women are almost solely responsible for carrying out the daily time-consuming chores of cooking, cleaning, and laundering (Rubin, 1976; Lein, 1979). Blue-collar and professional women both face problems of time and energy in accomplishing their dual workload. Yet the effect of this role overload varies by social class—due to the differential availability of resources and the differences in acceptance of traditional sex-role stereotypes. Specifically, in contrast to dual-career couples, working-class women lack the financial resources and the egalitarian attitudes that can promote adjustment to dual employment. They must often rely on relatives and/or friends for provision of free child care (Kamerman, 1980), and they do heavy domestic work without the aid of commercial services (Angrist et al., 1976). The adherence to traditional beliefs about "men's work" and "women's work" impedes working-class couples from developing a more equitable reorganization and sharing of family tasks. Husbands' narrow identity as breadwinner ill-equips them emotionally to fully share household work or to nurture children. It also prods men to work overtime or to take on a second job, thus being unavailable to help. Moreover, it is often difficult for the wife to relinquish her traditional chores. Finally, blue-collar male and female jobs are characterized by inflexible work schedules that allow little time off for personal business and often impose forced overtime or rotating shifts on the worker (Baker, 1978:368).

Two recent studies have examined the manner in which blue-collar families cope with family work. Lein (1979) discovered extensive use of split shifts so that one parent is always available to be with the children. This arrangement restricts the jobs that the spouses (especially the wife) can have, and also limits the amount of time that they can have at home together. Kamerman (1980) notes that families rely on diverse modes of child care, orchestrating a complex set of supports to assure the continuity of care. Often parents are required to be at work before school starts and after the school day ends, and have to arrange for babysitters, neighbors, relatives, and child-care centers to fill in the gaps. If the children are of different ages, different types of care and different time schedules have to be developed. Men help to some degree with domestic tasks, although they are apparently much more involved with child care than with housework. In Lein's study (1979), some women expressed resentment over the fact that their husbands were taking over some of the more pleasurable aspects of women's role while leaving them with the bulk of the routine, monotonous chores (see also Piotrkowski, 1978). The issue of housework is thus a source of overt tension in blue-collar dual-provider families.

The Dual-Career Family. The dual-career family, in which both spouses pursue demanding professional or managerial careers, represents a distinctly different situation, due to the special requirements, opportunities, and structure of careers (Mortimer, 1978). In some ways, the dual-career family is highly advantaged, because it has two comparatively high incomes that allow substitution of paid services and products for family work. The woman's career can permit her the kind of personal fulfillment and individualistic achievement that may be less possible in other family contexts. And the commitment to equality prevalent among highly educated, dual-career spouses can serve as a further resource in coping with the demands of work.

But largely because of the unique requirements and opportunities of careers, most research on dual-career families emphasizes the stresses experienced by this family type (Holmstrom, 1972; Rapoport and Rapoport, 1971; Hunt and Hunt, 1977). In fact, some recent commentators (Hunt and Hunt, 1981; Benenson, 1981) reject the dual-career structure as a viable option for many families. Stress results from extreme role overload, simply not enough time available to accomplish the highly demanding work required by the two careers, as well as housework and parenting. When neither partner has a wife to perform the supportive "backup" functions prevalent in the "two-person career," both may feel less competitive and productive than they would otherwise be (Holmstrom, 1972). Demanding career and family roles are basically incompatible, especially when there are young children (Poloma et al., 1981). Excessive work time—the need to work nights and weekends, the travel requirements, the mobility expectations and opportunities, and the intrinsically rewarding character of careers all represent "centrifugal forces" (Turner, 1971) pulling each spouse away from the family. A heavy involvement in career may engender guilt in the working mother, a feeling that there is not enough time with children to ensure their optimal development.

At the same time, the incompatibility of each spouse's occupational demands acts as an additional stressor. Spouses may face pressures to move in opposite directions, or, at the beginnings of their careers, difficulties in securing employment in the same location. A "commuter marriage" may result (Gross, 1980a, 1980b; Pour-El, 1981). The husband and wife may also experience the peak requirements of their careers simultaneously, particularly if they entered the work force at the same time. Family needs may be greatest, likewise, at this time, with young children present, unless the couple has engaged in active planning or "recycling" (Rapoport and Rapoport, 1971), scheduling their children and work in such a manner that will relieve these pressures.

Some dual-career couples complain of a tendency to get too scheduled and routinized. Since most parents feel that their children should be given top priority in "family time," there may be little time left over for their own companionship and recreation, or for friends and relatives. The couple's own relationship may suffer as a result, while social isolation diminishes support from outsiders.

David Rice (1979) has described the special problems and dynamics of the dual-career marriage in coping with the stressors of work. Whereas both spouses need emotional support and encouragement from each other, if each is struggling with the problems of their own careers, and particularly if they face the more extreme demands and career crises simultaneously, they may have little emotional reserve left over to provide support for one another. Tension may be heightened if one spouse is more successful in the career than the other, particularly if the one's success is perceived to be at the expense of the other's. Given the time demands of each spouse's work, the sharing of family tasks becomes of crucial importance. According to Rice, it is important that this sharing be perceived as fair—if not in the short run, at least over the long term.

Although there is almost universal support in our society for the principles of equal opportunity and of equal pay for equal work, traditional attitudes regarding family life are still quite persistent (Mason and Bumpass, 1975; Harris, 1981). Many believe that it is better if the husband is the main breadwinner and the wife is the children's chief caretaker. Children are thought to suffer if their mothers are working, especially in the early years of life. Although the potential for role strain and ambiguity exists for all employed mothers, such ambivalence may be especially heightened in the dual-career context, particularly if it is perceived that the family is not dependent on the wife's income contribution. Although the woman in a traditional, sex-typed "female" occupation is at least available for her family in "off hours," the dual-career woman, along with her husband, may feel pressure to work around the clock, to travel, to be away in the evenings, and so on. This pressure can engender feelings of guilt at being unable to meet all the obligations of traditional and nontraditional roles—or can give rise to valiant attempts to be "superwomen," excelling at everything, with consequent frustration and exhaustion. While the previous generation of dual-career women lessened their occupational involvement in accommodating to the pressures of work and family, the emphasis on equality makes this pattern of adjustment less attractive to young professional and managerial women and increases role strain (Hunt and Hunt, 1981).

The Single-Parent Family. The single-parent family is surely the most limited with respect to resources—money, time, and the personnel to cope with family tasks. Largely because of the increasing divorce rate, but also due to the growing number of illegitimate births, single-parent families are rapidly increasing (Sawhill, 1976). In fact, in 1980 almost one out of five children of school age lived with a single parent. Ten years ago, the figure was one of eight. Among black children, 46 percent lived with one parent and an additional 9 percent with no parents (Glick, 1980). Of children born in the 1980s, it has been estimated that before reaching maturity nearly half will live a period of time with a single parent (Schorr and Moen, 1979).

The central problem of the single-parent family is economic (Kamerman, 1980). About a third of female-headed families (and nine of ten single-parent families are headed by women) are poor; that is, below the government's poverty standard, in 1980 (Rudd, 1981). Divorced women are increasingly considered "liberated" by the courts, capable of supporting themselves and their children without alimony or substantial child support. A recent government publication (U.S. Census Bureau, 1981) reports that in 1978 only 60 percent of divorced mothers were awarded child support. Of these, only half received the full amount they were due. Only 14 percent of divorced and separated women are awarded alimony. However, the economy still treats women as secondary wage earners, crowding them into relatively few, sex-typed areas of work that pay poorly and lack advancement opportunities (Sawhill, 1976; Barrett, 1979; Oppenheimer, 1975). Clearly, issues of wage equity, advancement opportunities, and equal pay for comparable worth are of crucial importance for all working women, but the consequences of inequality are particularly problematic for the single mother.

For the single parent, the problem of role overload—including employment and family work—is also especially severe. Although husbands in other dual-earner families may not contribute much to housework, in terms of hours per day, they still make some contribution, working mainly on traditional male tasks, but also helping with children. The single parent, in contrast, has no one to provide this assistance, unless relatives live nearby or there are close friends willing to help. Limited economic resources make it difficult to purchase services. Furthermore, many single parents complain about the lack of support in child rearing. They must bear the worries and concerns surrounding their children's development on their own (Shorr and Moen, 1979). There may be a general lack of social support, outside of relatives, because of the limited time to cultivate friends in the face of a full-time workload and the full burden of family work (Kamerman, 1980). This social isolation can exacerbate feelings of inadequacy and depression when confronted with the stressors of work.

IMPLICATIONS FOR SOCIAL POLICY

The changing linkages of work and family pose new problems for individual men and women, and new dilemmas for the work organization, for the family, and for the broader society. Clearly, personal adjustments and strategies cannot fully resolve these problems. Social change—in employing organizations, schools, government policy,and families—is necessary to substantially alleviate the pressures on families.

Some very basic dilemmas arise in facing social-policy questions. First, should the employing organization be responsible for its effect on the family? If so, are there "tradeoffs" between the needs of the family and those of the employer? For example, the organization's need for productivity makes it beneficial to have its professionals and managers able to commit themselves to sixty-hour workweeks (or more), without distraction from the family. The organization will benefit if the employee comes equipped with a spouse, ready to step in and do excess work and to take exclusive responsibility for family work. But the "two-person" career pattern is inimical to the individualistic achievement of educated women. Given the rising career aspirations of women, it would seem that this pattern will become increasingly untenable in the future. Conflicts between the work organization and the family in the allocation of time—problems of work time and scheduling—remain crucial dilemmas in all the special contexts we have considered. While employers benefit from the large pool of female wage earners crowded into relatively few, low-paying positions, women (and their families) are increasingly dependent on their wages. But to promote equity and family economic well-being, the sex-segregated character of the labor force must be abandoned; the principle of equal pay for comparable worth must be implemented.

At another level, one might ask, "What will be the costs for the organization if it continues to go on as before?" It appears that organizations are beginning to recognize both some costs of their traditional policies and disruptions in long-term practices. Increasingly, for example, managers are refusing to be relocated when their spouses are employed, even if at substantial cost to their own careers. New programs are being developed to lessen these problems; some corporations have instituted job-relocation services for spouses, or even themselves attempt to give jobs to spouses. Some personnel managers are complaining of increasing lateness and absenteeism, particularly among working parents, and are developing more flexible working hours and leave policies to help parents cope with the conflicting demands of jobs and families. Some firms are providing more opportunities for part-time work, while maintaining acceptable benefit levels, providing options to share jobs, or to bring work home during normal work hours (Polit, 1979). Others are lessening requirements for travel and geographic mobility, and are providing more liberal maternity and paternity leaves, including parental leaves for lengthy childhood illnesses and crises. To help employed women obtain child care, some companies are providing referral information regarding day care facilities, giving child-care vouchers, subsidizing community day care centers, reserving places in centers or in family day care homes, or offering on-site child care. (Kamerman, 1980, documents the modes of caring for the children of working parents in European countries, which could serve as models for the United States.) Employers are increasingly concerned with job dissatisfaction, turnover, and declining productivity. Changes designed to ameliorate the conflicts of work and family may lessen these problems in the future.

The availability of qualified labor is an important factor affecting the willingness of organizations to experiment with new, sometimes costly, arrangements. The baby boom of the 1950s glutted the labor market with relatively highly educated new job seekers in the 1970s. As we move into the 1980s and 1990s, workers seeking entry-level jobs—members of the much smaller cohort born in the late 1960s and 1970s—will be in very short supply. With organizations finding themselves competing for a diminishing supply of workers (Freeman, 1979), the choice of employer may increasingly depend on the organization's level of accommodation to women's—and men's—family lives.

Although change in employing organizations is crucial, other changes are also necessary to accommodate the altered linkages of work and family. Clearly, government tax policy and Social Security regulations are inequitable to working women (Gordon, 1979a, 1979b). Recent changes in welfare policies will make life even more difficult for the single parent. To ease the lives of working parents, schools should develop pre- and after-school programs. Finally, the services necessary for working parents (such as doctors' and dentists' offices, counselors, and children's teachers) should be available when parents are off work.

But until very recently the family has been the more accommodative institution, changing its own organization, in order to sustain and enhance its economic well-being and to meet the requirements of the employing organization. Thus the family, faced with mounting inflation, has added wage earners to the labor force, restricted its fertility, and has attempted to act as a buffer, shielding the worker from the strains suffered in the workplace. However, it would appear that many families are resisting the kind of change in their internal organization—particularly in the division of labor in the home—that would be most responsive to the needs of the employed wife/mother. What is needed is a radical shift in the organization of the family as well, to complement and support the increase in married women's labor-force participation.

Hopefully, the growing attention to the interrelations of work and the family, changing values, and increasing awareness of the problems will encourage actions by employers, government, families, and other organizations, leading to more fully integrated, equitable, and satisfying linkages of work and family in the future.

PART TWO

Economic Roles of Men and Women

Introduction

The interdependence of work and family takes on two major forms—the economic roles of men and women and the impacts of occupational conditions on family life. Economic roles are examined in Part Two, and occupational conditions are explored in Part Three.

Norms associated with the myth of separate worlds prescribe that men perform a work role for pay outside the home and that women perform unpaid family duties inside the home. This division of labor forms the basis of the traditional exchange of instrumental rights and duties in one-earner families referred to in Part One. The husband's work role, if he is successful, provides the financial resources necessary for the existence of stable and cohesive family life. The wife's performance of family duties sustains the ongoing activities of family life by keeping family members fed, clothed, and prepared for their outside activities.

As we shall see in Part Two, these prescriptions oversimplify contemporary economic roles of men and women by ignoring changes over time and by glossing over diversity in how men and women provide economically for their families. Most men do work during their adult years; however, the level of economic rewards varies considerably. Some men experience unstable employment and/or low incomes, making it necessary for other family members, especially wives, to contribute economically to the family. The pattern in which men are economic providers and women make unpaid contributions through housework, child care, and the support of their husbands' careers now represents a minority of American families. In most families, women's economic contributions include a combination of paid employment and unpaid activities with significant economic value.

A broad understanding of the relationships between economic roles and family life is furthered by the concept of the worker/earner role. The joint worker/earner role links the economic system to the family. The worker role in the economy consists of the production of goods and services for economic rewards. The earner role indicates the other component in which income earned in the worker role is used by the family as resources for consumption (Rodman and Safilios-Rothschild, 1983). The social-class status, prestige, and standard of living of families derive from the level of success and achievement in the worker/earner role.

Work is one of the crucial social roles performed by people in any society. Although the structure and nature of work vary immensely within and between societies over time, production through work remains central. In addition to the basic functions of economic production, work has taken on broader meanings to individuals and to society. The performance of a work role is a source of social integration. Studies of retirement and unemployment show that loss of the work role creates difficulties for some people: they may no longer feel part of society in general and may also lose social contacts, structured activities, and a sense of accomplishment. People in different social classes and with various employment histories have similar values regarding the importance of being able to work and the desire to have a worthwhile, productive job. Welfare as a desirable alternative to work is consistently rejected. In addition, in American society, the material and symbolic value of success and achievement have intensified the importance of the work role. Success and achievement in the occupational sphere are considered indices of personal worth.

Men are expected to work during the adult years from the end of schooling until retirement. Work is considered to be the primary role for men in American society. In addition, men are expected to be major providers for their families by providing their wives and children with an adequate standard of living. Men usually coordinate the timing of marriage and child rearing with career preparation and progress. Men with unstable, low-paying jobs find it almost impossible to maintain satisfactory family lives. Adequate performance of the provider role is crucial for family cohesion, family stability, and satisfying husband/wife and parent/child relationships. When men do not provide sufficient resources for their families, family relationships suffer. The problem derives from two sources—the lack of financial resources and the failure of the men to meet strong normative expectations.

Much research has focused on class differences in family behavior that stem directly or indirectly from the performance of the worker/earner role. Measures of class are based on (1) level of occupation, education, and income; (2) patterns of social mobility; and (3) status consistency or inconsistency. These measures are related to several aspects of family life. Indices of marital happiness, adjustment, and satisfaction are directly related to social class. In addition, measures of marital stability—including divorce, desertion, and separation—are inversely related to social class. The resource theory of marital power proposes that the power of the husband relative to the wife is related to the relative economic resources that the man provides to his family. Studies of lower-class families point out the extreme difficulties lower-class males have in playing a satisfactory role in their families. Female-headed families are one result of problems encountered by lower-class males in fulfilling their worker/earner roles.

Interesting variations are also found within broad social-class categories. The phenomenon of the life-cycle squeeze is a good example. In working- and lower-middle-class families with teenage children, the growth in the husband's income levels off at about the time that family responsibilities are greatest. This situation points out the joint importance of income, family size, and life-cycle stage in determining what can be considered an adequate standard of living. In addition, the rate of inflation over the last several years has combined with these and other factors to greatly increase the economic squeeze on families.

In "The Good-Provider Role: Its Rise and Fall," Jessie Bernard examines the traditional worker/earner or good-provider role of men and the changes occurring in the norms and behavior associated with the role. She attributes many of the problems accompanying the good-provider role to the physical separation of work duties from family life during industrialization and the development of a money economy. This separation became associated with a lack of expressivity among men and an all-or-nothing expectation regarding men's success in their worker/earner responsibilities. Bernard deftly illustrates the family difficulties of men who either are extremely successful at work or who fail to live up to the economic expectations of their families. The decline in the good-provider role in recent years is related to increases in wives' employment, which dilutes the rewards associated with men being sole providers and increases the demands on men with employed wives to participate more actively in family tasks. Although the good-provider role is losing influence, a legitimate successor has not yet evolved, creating a state of flux and uncertainty regarding this important role. New directions and developments will be interesting to observe in the coming years.

The significance of the worker/earner role is further illuminated by considering the effects of unemployment on families. The Voydanoff selection, "Unemployment: Family Strategies for Adaptation," indicates that unemployment often, but not always, contributes to family problems and crisis. Families are less likely to experience crisis if they have adaptable and cohesive family systems, egalitarian sex-role norms and authority patterns, and financial management skills. In addition, families that are able to prepare for unemployment, families that don't blame the unemployed member(s) for their situation, and families with some certainty about future employment are better able to avoid crisis. Using these resources in an active coping process also reduces the likelihood of crisis. In spite of these mitigating factors, unemployment with its financial hardships and loss of the provider role remains a severe crisis-producing event in many families. Changes in the occupational structure are necessary to reduce the incidence of unemployment and its impact on family life.

Bernard and Voydanoff make us aware of the pervasive impacts of the worker/earner role on family life. They also document the problems created in families when individuals cannot meet the expectations associated with the worker/earner role.

While men's economic roles have been fairly narrowly defined in terms of the traditional worker/earner or good-provider role, women's economic contributions to families have been considerably more varied.

Over one-half of married women are in the labor force performing a worker/earner role. However, the patterns of women's labor-force participation and earnings differ from those of men. Women are more likely to be working part time and to enter and leave the labor force one or more times during their working lives. Women earn less than men even when they work full time over a period of years. However, earnings from the paid employment of women are critical to the maintenance of an adequate standard of living in many families. Female-headed families are often completely dependent on women's earnings or on government transfer payments such as welfare or Aid to Families with Dependent Children.

Women's economic roles also include several types of unpaid work of economic value to families. The wives of professionals and managers often assist their husbands' careers by entertaining business associates, performing all household tasks to allow husbands more time for work, and making business contacts through volunteer work in the community. These tasks provide career advantages to husbands while restricting wives' development of occupational skills and economic potential. Women, working outside the home or not, have major responsibility for household tasks and child care. They also frequently manage the financial resources earned by themselves and other family members. Many low-income women with sole responsibility for children are able to manage very limited resources through kin-based exchange networks. Gifts of goods, money, and services made over time ensure that a woman will have resources to draw on when she is in need. These activities are significant contributions to the economic status of families.

Rainwater's article, "Mothers' Contribution to the Family Money Economy in Europe and the United States," examines several aspects of women's, especially mothers', labor-force participation in the United States and several European countries. He maps out the complex patterns of women's labor-force behavior, including full- versus part-time work, women's entrances and exits from the labor force over the life course, percentages of family income earned by mothers, and relationships between husbands' earnings and women's labor-force participation. He also attempts to make linkages, however tenuous, between women's labor-force behavior and its meaning to women and families; for example, the effects of women's earnings on spending decisions and on the attitudes of men and women toward women's employment. Recent increases in women's commitment to work should lead to additional changes in the meaning of mothers' employment for family life.

Women's unpaid economic contributions to families vary in content and economic value. The most universal unpaid economic contributions by women are housework and child care. Vanek's article, "Housewives as Workers," documents that, although the tasks associated with housework are changing with technological developments, housework remains a time-consuming activity. Its economic value is difficult to assess, because it is not included in traditional measures of economic production. Two ways of measuring the economic value of housework include replacement costs (the amount it would cost to hire someone to do the work) and opportunity costs (the income not earned by women who stay at home to do housework). These measures focus on different aspects of women's significant economic contribution through housework.

The articles included in Part Two reveal a changing and diverse repertoire of economic roles performed by men and women in contemporary American society. These roles form a link between work and family because work-related activities are required for the maintenance of family life. The adequacy of economic role performance is closely tied with the texture and stability of family life. Recent changes in the roles of men and women suggest that the variety and significance of economic roles will remain and perhaps increase over time.

3

The Good–Provider Role: Its Rise and Fall

Jessie Bernard

The Lord is my shepherd, I shall not want. He sets a table for me in the very sight of my enemies; my cup runs over (23rd Psalm). And when the Israelites were complaining about how hungry they were on their way from Egypt to Canaan, God told Moses to rest assured: There would be meat for dinner and bread for breakfast the next morning. And, indeed, there were quails that very night, enough to cover the camp, and in the morning the ground was covered with dew that proved to be bread (Exodus 16:12–13). In fact, in this role of good provider, God is sometimes almost synonymous with Providence. Many people, like Micawber, still wait for him, or Providence, to provide.

Granted, then, that the first great provider for the human species was God the Father, surely the second great provider for the human species was Mother, the gatherer, planter, and general factotum. Boulding (1976), citing Lee and deVore, tells us that in hunting and gathering societies, males contribute about one fifth of the food of the clan, the females the other four fifths (p. 96). She also concludes that by 12,000 B.C. in the early agricultural villages, females provided four fifths of human subsistence (p. 97). Not until large trading towns arose did the female contribution to human subsistence decline to equality with that of the male. And with the beginning of true cities, the provisioning work of women tended to become invisible. Still, in today's world it remains substantial.

Reprinted from Jessie Bernard, "The Good Provider Role: Its Rise and Fall," *American Psychologist*, vol. 36, no. 1, January 1981, pp. 1–12.

Whatever the date of the virtuous woman described in the Old Testament (Proverbs 31:10–27), she was the very model of a good provider. She was, in fact, a highly productive conglomerate. She woke up in the middle of the night to tend to her business; she oversaw a multiple-industry household; *her* candles did not go out at night; there was a ready market for the high-quality linen girdles she made and sold to the merchants in town; and she kept track of the real estate market and bought good land when it became available, cultivating vineyards quite profitably. All this time her husband sat at the gates talking with his cronies.

A recent counterpart to the virtuous woman was the busy and industrious shtetl woman:

> The earning of a livelihood is sexless, and the large majority of women . . . participate in some gainful occupation if they do not carry the chief burden of support. The wife of a "perennial student" is very apt to be the sole support of the family. The problem of managing both a business and a home is so common that no one recognizes it as special. . . . To bustle about in search of a livelihood is merely another form of bustling about managing a home, both are aspects of . . . health and livelihood. (Zborowski & Herzog, 1952, p. 131)

In a subsistence economy in which husbands and wives ran farms, shops, or businesses together, a man might be a good steady worker, but the idea that he was *the* provider would hardly ring true. Even the youth in the folk song who listed all the gifts he would bestow on his love if she would marry him—a golden comb, a paper of pins, and all the rest—was not necessarily promising to be a good provider.

I have not searched the literature to determine when the concept of the good provider entered our thinking. The term *provider* entered the English language in 1532, but was not yet male sex typed, as the older term *purveyor* already was in 1442. Webster's second edition defines the good provider as "one who provides, especially, colloq., one who provides food, clothing, etc. for his family; as, he is a good or an adequate provider." More simply, he could be defined as a man whose wife did not have to enter the labor force. The counterpart to the good provider was the housewife. However the term is defined, the role itself delineated relationships within a marriage and family in a way that added to the legal, religious, and other advantages men had over women.

Thus, under the common law, although the husband was legally head of the household and as such had the responsibility of providing for his wife and children, this provision was often made with help from the wife's personal property and earnings, to which he was entitled:

> He owned his wife's and children's services, and had the sole right to collect wages for their work outside the home. He owned his wife's personal property outright, and had the right to manage and control all of his wife's

> real property during marriage, which included the right to use or lease property, and to keep any rents and profits from it. (Babcock, Freedman, Norton, & Ross, 1975, p. 561)

So even when she was the actual provider, the legal recognition was granted the husband. Therefore, whatever the husband's legal responsibilities for support may have been, he was not necessarily a good provider in the way the term came to be understood. The wife may have been performing that role.

In our country in Colonial times women were still viewed as performing a providing role, and they pursued a variety of occupations. Abigail Adams managed the family estate, which provided the wherewithal for John to spend so much time in Philadelphia. In the 18th century "many women were active in business and professional pursuits. They ran inns and taverns; they managed a wide variety of stores and shops; and, at least occasionally, they worked in careers like publishing, journalism and medicine" (Demos, 1974, p. 430). Women sometimes even "joined the menfolk for work in the fields" (p. 430). Like the household of the proverbial virtuous woman, the Colonial household was a little factory that produced clothing, furniture, bedding, candles, and other accessories, and again, as in the case of the virtuous woman, the female role was central. It was taken for granted that women provided for the family along with men.

The good provider as a specialized male role seems to have arisen in the transition from subsistence to market—especially money—economies that accelerated with the industrial revolution. The good-provider role of males emerged in this country roughly, say, from the 1830s, when de Tocqueville was observing it, to the late 1970s, when the 1980 census declared that a male was not automatically to be assumed to be head of the household. This gives the role a life span of about a century and a half. Although relatively shortlived, while it lasted the role was a seemingly rocklike feature of the national landscape.

As a psychological and sociological phenomenon, the good-provider role had wide ramifications for all of our thinking about families. It marked a new kind of marriage. It did not have good effects on women: The role deprived them of many chips by placing them in a peculiarly vulnerable position. Because she was not reimbursed for her contribution to the family in either products or services, a wife was stripped to a considerable extent of her access to cash-mediated markets. By discouraging labor force participation, it deprived many women, especially affluent ones, of opportunities to achieve strength and competence. It deterred young women from acquiring productive skills. They dedicated themselves instead to winning a good provider who would "take care of" them. The wife of a more successful provider became for all intents and purposes a parasite, with little to do except indulge or pamper herself. The psychology of such dependence could become all but crippling. There were other concomitants of the good-provider role.

EXPRESSIVITY AND THE GOOD-PROVIDER ROLE

The new industrial order that produced the good provider changed not so much the division of labor between the sexes as it did the site of the work they engaged in. Only two of the concomitants of this change in work site are selected for comment here, namely, (a) the identification of gender with work site as well as with work itself and (b) the reduction of time for personal interaction and intimacy within the family.

It is not so much the specific kinds of work men and women do—they have always varied from time to time and place to place—but the simple fact that the sexes do different kinds of work, whatever it is, which is in and of itself important. The division of labor by sex means that the work group becomes also a sex group. The very nature of maleness and femaleness becomes embedded in the sexual divison of labor. One's sex and one's work are part of one another. One's work defines one's gender.

Any division of labor implies that people doing different kinds of work will occupy different work sites. When the division is based on sex, men and women will necessarily have different work sites. Even within the home itself, men and women had different work spaces. The woman's spinning wheel occupied a different area from the man's anvil. When the factory took over much of the work formerly done in the house, the separation of work space became especially marked. Not only did the separation of the sexes become spatially extended, but it came to relate work and gender in a special way. The work site as well as the work itself became associated with gender; each sex had its own turf. This sexual "territoriality" has had complicating effects on efforts to change any sexual division of labor. The good provider worked primarily in the outside male world of business and industry. The homemaker worked primarily in the home.

Spatial separation of the sexes not only identifies gender with work site and work but also reduces the amount of time available for spontaneous emotional give-and-take between husbands and wives. When men and women work in an economy based in the home, there are frequent occasions for interaction. (Consider, for example, the suggestive allusions made today to the rise in the birth rate nine months after a blackout.) When men and women are in close proximity, there is always the possibility of reassuring glances, the comfort of simple physical presence. But when the division of labor removes the man from the family dwelling for most of the day, intimate relationships become less feasible. De Tocqueville was one of the first to call out attention to this. In 1840 he noted that

> almost all men in democracies are engaged in public or professional life, and . . . the limited extent of common income obliges a wife to confine herself to the house, in order to watch in person and very closely over the details of domestic economy. All these distinct and compulsory occupations are so many natural barriers, which, by keeping the two sexes asunder, render the solicitations of the one less frequent and less ardent—the resistance of the other more easy. (de Tocqueville, 1840, p. 212)

Not directly related to the spatial constraints on emotional expression by men, but nevertheless a concomitant of the new industrial order with the same effect, was the enormous drive for achievement, for success, for "making it" that escalated the provider role into the good-provider role. De Tocqueville (1840) is again our source:

> The tumultuous and constantly harassed life which equality makes men lead [becoming good providers] not only distracts them from the passions of love, by denying them time to indulge in it, but it diverts them from it by another more secret but more certain road. All men who live in democratic ages more or less contract ways of thinking of the manufacturing and trading classes. (p. 221)

As a result of this male concentration on jobs and careers, much abnegation and "a constant sacrifice of her pleasures to her duties" (de Tocqueville, 1840, p. 212) were demanded of the American woman. The good-provider role, as it came to be shaped by this ambience, was thus restricted in what it was called upon to provide. Emotional expressivity was not included in the role. One of the things a parent might say about a man to persuade a daughter to marry him, or a daughter might say to explain to her parents why she wanted to, was not that he was a gentle, loving, or tender man but that he was a good provider. He might have many other qualities, good or bad, but if a man was a good provider, everything else was either gravy or the price one had to pay for a good provider.

Lack of expressivity did not imply neglect of the family. The good provider was a "family man." He set a good table, provided a decent home, paid the mortgage, bought the shoes, and kept his children warmly clothed. He might, with the help of the children's part-time jobs, have been able to finance their educations through high school and, sometimes, even college. There might even have been a little left over for an occasional celebration in most families. The good provider made a decent contribution to the church. His work might have been demanding, but he expected it to be. If in addition to being a good provider, a man was kind, gentle, generous, and not a heavy drinker or gambler, that was all frosting on the cake. Loving attention and emotional involvement in the family were not part of a woman's implicit bargain with the good provider.

By the time de Tocqueville published his observations in 1840, the general outlines of the good provider role had taken shape. It called for a hard working man who spent most of his time at his work. In the traditional conception of the role, a man's chief responsibility is his job, so that "by definition any family behaviors must be subordinate to it in terms of significance and [the job] has priority in the event of a clash" (Scanzoni, 1975, p. 38). This was the classic form of the good-provider role, which remained a powerful component of our societal structure until well into the present century.

COSTS AND REWARDS OF THE GOOD-PROVIDER ROLE FOR MEN

There were both costs and rewards for those men attached to the good-provider role. The most serious cost was perhaps the identification of maleness not only with the work site but especially with success in the role. "The American male looks to his breadwinning role to confirm his manliness" (Brenton, 1966, p. 194).[1] To be a man one had to be not only a provider but a *good* provider. Success in the good-provider role came in time to define masculinity itself. The good provider had to achieve, to win, to succeed, to dominate. He was a bread*winner*. He had to show "strength, cunning, inventiveness, endurance—a whole range of traits henceforth defined as exclusively 'masculine' " (Demos, 1974, p. 436). Men were judged as men by the level of living they provided. They were judged by the myth "that endows a money-making man with sexiness and virility, and is based on man's dominance, strength, and ability to provide for and care for 'his' woman" (Gould, 1974, p. 97). The good provider became a player in the male competitive macho game. What one man provided for his family in the way of luxury and display had to be equaled or topped by what another could provide. Families became display cases for the success of the good provider.

The psychic costs could be high:

> By depending so heavily on his breadwinning role to validate his sense of himself as a man, instead of also letting his roles as husband, father, and citizen of the community count as validating sources, the American male treads on psychically dangerous ground. It's always dangerous to put all of one's psychic eggs into one basket. (Brenton, 1966, p. 194)

The good-provider role not only put all of a man's gender-identifying eggs into one psychic basket, but it also put all the family-providing eggs into one basket. One individual became responsible for the support of the whole family. Countless stories portrayed the humiliation families underwent to keep wives and especially mothers out of the labor force, a circumstance that would admit to the world the male head's failure in the good-provider role. If a married woman had to enter the labor force at all, that was bad enough. If she made a good salary, however, she was "co-opting the man's passport to masculinity" (Gould, 1974, p. 98) and he was effectively castrated. A wife's earning capacity diminished a man's position as head of the household (Gould, 1974, p. 99).

Failure in the role of good provider, which employment of wives evidenced, could produce deep frustration. As Komarovsky (1940, p. 20) explains, this is "because in his own estimation he is failing to fulfill what is the central duty of his life, the very touchstone of his manhood—the role of family provider."

But just as there was punishment for failure in the good-provider role, so also were there rewards for successful performance. A man "derived strength from his role as provider" (Komarovsky, 1940, p. 205). He achieved a good deal of satisfaction from his ability to support his family. It won kudos. Being a good provider led to status in both the family and the community. Within the family it gave him the power of the purse and the right to decide about expenditures, standards of living, and what constituted good providing. "Every purchase of the family—the radio, his wife's new hat, the children's skates, the meals set before him—all were symbols of their dependence upon him" (Komarovsky, 1940, pp. 74–75). Such dependence gave him a "profound sense of stability" (p. 74). It was a strong counterpoise vis-à-vis a wife with a stronger personality. "Whether he had considerable authority within the family and was recognized as its head, or whether the wife's stronger personality . . . dominated the family, he nevertheless derived strength from his role as provider" (Komarovsky, 1940, p. 75). As recently as 1975, in a sample of 3,100 husbands and wives in 10 cities, Scanzoni found that despite increasing egalitarian norms, the good provider still had "considerable power in ultimate decision-making" and as "unique provider" had the right "to organize his life and the lives of other family members around his occupation" (p. 38).

A man who was successful in the good-provider role might be freed from other obligations to the family. But the flip side of this dispensation was that he could not make up for poor performance by excellence in other family roles. Since everything depended on his success as provider, everything was at stake. The good provider played an all-or-nothing game.

DIFFERENT WAYS OF PERFORMING THE GOOD-PROVIDER ROLE

Although the legal specifications for the role were laid out in the common law, in legislation, in legal precedents, in court decisions, and, most importantly, in custom and convention, in real-life situations the social and social-psychological specifications were set by the husband or, perhaps more accurately, by the community, alias the Joneses, and there were many ways to perform it.

Some men resented the burdens the role forced them to bear. A man could easily vent such resentment toward his family by keeping complete control over all expenditures, dispensing the money for household maintenance, and complaining about bills as though it were his wife's fault that shoes cost so much. He could, in effect, punish his family for his having to perform the role. Since the money he earned belonged to him—was "his"—he could do with it what he pleased. Through extreme parsimony he could dole out his money in a mean, humiliating way, forcing his wife to come begging for pennies. By his reluctance and resentment he could make his family pay emotionally for the provisioning he supplied.

At the other extreme were the highly competitive men who were so involved in outdoing the Joneses that the fur coat became more important than the affectionate hug. They "bought off" their families. They sometimes succeeded so well in their extravagance that they sacrificed the family they were presumably providing for to the achievements that made it possible (Keniston, 1965).[2]

The Depression of the 1930s revealed in harsh detail what the loss of the role could mean both to the good provider and to his family, not only in the loss of income itself—which could be supplied by welfare agencies or even by other family members, including wives—but also and especially in the loss of face.

The Great Depression did not mark the demise of the good-provider role. But it did teach us what a slender thread the family hung on. It stimulated a whole array of programs designed to strengthen that thread, to ensure that it would never again be similarly threatened. Unemployment insurance was incorporated into the Social Security Act of 1935, for example, and a Full Employment Act was passed in 1946. But there proved to be many other ways in which the good-provider role could be subverted.

ROLE REJECTORS AND ROLE OVERPERFORMERS

Recent research in psychology, anthropology, and sociology has familiarized us with the tremendous power of roles. But we also know that one of the fundamental principles of role behavior is that conformity to role norms is not universal. Not everyone lives up to the specifications of roles, either in the psychological or in the sociological definition of the concept. Two extremes have attracted research attention: (a) the men who could not live up to the norms of the good-provider role or did not want to, at one extreme, and (b) the men who overperformed the role, at the other. For the wide range in between, from blue-collar workers to professionals, there was fairly consistent acceptance of the role, however well or poorly, however grumblingly or willingly, performed.

First the nonconformists. Even in Colonial times, desertion and divorce occurred:

> Women may have deserted because, say, their husbands beat them; husbands, on the other hand, may have deserted because they were unable or unwilling to provide for their usually large families in the face of the wives' demands to do so. These demands were, of course, backed by community norms making the husband's financial support a sacred duty. (Scanzoni, 1979, pp. 24–25)

Fiedler (1962) has traced the theme of male escape from domestic responsibilities in the American novel from the time of Rip Van Winkle to the present:

> The figure of Rip Van Winkle presides over the birth of the American imagination; and it is fitting that our first successful home-grown legend

> should memorialize, however playfully, the flight of the dreamer from the shrew—into the mountains and out of time, away from the drab duties of home . . . anywhere to avoid . . . marriage and responsibility. One of the factors that determine theme and form in our great books is this strategy of evasion, this retreat to nature and childhood which makes our literature (and life) so charmingly and infuriatingly "boyish." (pp. xx–xxi)

Among the men who pulled up stakes and departed for the West or went down to the sea in ships, there must have been a certain proportion who, like the mythic prototype, were simply fleeing the good-provider role.

The work of Demos (1974), a historian, offers considerable support for Fiedler's thesis. He tells us that the burdens thrust on men in the 19th century by the new patterns of work began to show their effects in the family. When "the [spatial] separation of the work lives of husbands and wives made communication so problematic," he asks, "what was the likelihood of meaningful communication?" (Demos, 1974, p. 438). The answer is, relatively little. Divorce and separation increased, either formally or by tacit consent—or simply by default, as in the case of a variety of defaulters—tramps, bums, hoboes—among them.

In this connection, "the development of the notorious 'tramp' phenomenon is worth noticing," Demos (1974, p. 438) tells us. The tramp was a man who just gave up, who dropped out of the role entirely. He preferred not to work, but he would do small chores or other small-scale work for a handout if he had to. He was not above begging the housewife for a meal, hoping she would not find work for him to do in repayment. Demos (1974) describes the type:

> Demoralized and destitute wanderers, their numbers mounting into the hundreds of thousands, tramps can be fairly characterized as men who had run away from their wives. . . . Their presence was mute testimony to the strains that tugged at the very core of American family life. . . . Many observers noted that the tramps had created a virtual society of their own [a kind of counterculture] based on a principle of single-sex companionship. (p. 438)

A considerable number of them came to be described as "homeless men" and, as the country became more urbanized, landed ultimately on skid row. A large part of the task of social workers for almost a century was the care of the "evaded" women they left behind.[3] When the tramp became wholly demoralized, a chronic alcoholic, almost unreachable, he fell into a category of his own—he was a bum.

Quite a different kettle of fish was the hobo, the migratory worker who spent several months harvesting wheat and other large crops and the rest of the year in cities. Many were the so-called Wobblies, or Industrial Workers of the World, who repudiated the good-provider role on principle. They had contempt for the men who accepted it and could be called conscientious objectors to the role. "In some IWW circles, wives were regarded as the 'ball and chain.' In the West, IWW literature proclaimed that the migratory worker, usually a young, unmarried male, was 'the finest specimen of American manhood . . . the leaven of the revolutionary labor movement' " (Foner, 1979, p. 400). Exemplars of the Wobblies were the nomadic workers of the West. They were free men. The migratory worker, "unlike the factory slave of the Atlantic seaboard and the central states, . . . was most emphatically 'not afraid of losing his job.' No wife and family cumbered him. The worker of the East, oppressed by the fear of want for wife and babies, dared not venture much" (Foner, 1979, p. 400). The reference to fear of loss of job was well taken; employers preferred married men, disciplined into the good-provider role, who had given hostages to fortune and were therefore more tractable.

Just on the verge between the area of conformity to the good-provider role—at whatever level—and the area of complete nonconformity to it was the non-good provider, the marginal group of workers usually made up of "the under-educated, the under-trained, the under-employed, or part-time employed, as well as the under-paid, and of course the unemployed" (Snyder, 1979, p. 597). These included men who wanted—sometimes desperately—to perform the good-provider role but who for one reason or another were unable to do so. Liebow (1966) has discussed the ramifications of failure among the black men of Tally's corner: The black man is

> under legal and social constraints to provide for them [their families], to be a husband to his wife and a father to his children. The chances are, however, that he is failing to provide for them, and failure in this primary function contaminates his performance as father in other respects as well. (p. 86)

In some cases, leaving the family entirely was the best substitute a man could supply. The community was left to take over.[4]

At the other extreme was the overperformer. De Tocqueville, quoted earlier, was already describing him as he manifested in the 1830s. And as late as 1955 Warner and Ablegglen were adding to the considerable literature on industrial leaders and tycoons, referring to their "driving concentration" on their careers and their "intense focusing" of interests, energies, and skills on these careers, "even limiting their sexual activity" (pp. 48–49). They came to be known as workaholics or work-intoxicated men. Their preoccupation with their work even at the expense of their families was, as I have already noted, quite acceptable in our society.

Poorly or well performed, the good-provider role lingered on. World War II initiated a challenge, this time in the form of attracting more and more married women into the labor force, but the challenge was papered over in the 1950s with an "age of togetherness" that all but apotheosized the good provider, his house in the suburbs, his homebody wife, and his third, fourth, even fifth, child. As late as the 1960s most housewives (87%) still saw breadwinning as their husband's primary role (Lopata, 1971, p. 91).[5]

INTRINSIC CONFLICT IN THE GOOD-PROVIDER ROLE

Since the good-provider role involved both family and work roles, most people believed that there was no incompatibility between them or at least that there should not be. But in the 1960s and 1970s evidence began to mount that maybe something was amiss.

De Tocqueville had documented the implicit conflict in the American businessman's devotion to his work at the expense of his family in the early years of the 19th century; the Industrial Workers of the World had proclaimed that the good-provider role which tied a man to his family was an impediment to the great revolution at the beginning of the 20th century; Fiedler (1962) had noted that throughout our history, in the male fantasy world, there was freedom from the responsibilities of this role; about 50 years ago Freud (1930/1958) had analyzed the intrinsic conflict between the demands of women and the family on one side and the demands of men's work on the other:

> Women represent the interests of the family and sexual life; the work of civilization has become more and more men's business; it confronts them with ever harder tasks, compels them to sublimations of instinct which women are not easily able to achieve. Since man has not an unlimited amount of mental energy at his disposal, he must accomplish his tasks by distributing his libido to the best advantage. What he employs for cultural [occupational] purposes he withdraws to a great extent from women, and his sexual life; his constant association with men and his dependence on his relations with them even estrange him from his duties as husband and father. Woman finds herself thus forced into the background by the claims of culture [work] and she adapts an inimical attitude towards it. (pp. 50–51)

In the last two decades, researchers have been raising questions relevant to Freud's statement of the problem. They have been asking people about the relative satisfactions they derive from these conflicting values—family and work. Among the earliest studies comparing family-work values was a Gallup poll in 1940 in which both men and women chose a happy home over an interesting job or wealth as a major life value. Since then there have been a number of such polls, and a considerable body of results has now accumulated. Pleck and Lang (1979) and Hesselbart (Note 1) have summarized the findings of these surveys. All agree that there is a clear bias in the direction of the family. Pleck and Lang conclude that "men's family role is far more psychologically significant to them than is their work role" (p. 29), and Hesselbart—however critical she is of the studies she summarizes—believes they should not be dismissed lightly and concludes that they certainly "challenge the idea that family is a 'secondary' valued role" (p. 14).[6] Douvan (Note 2) also found in a 1976 replication of a 1957 survey that family values retained priority over work: "Family roles almost uniformly rate higher in value production than the job role does" (p. 16).[7]

The very fact that researchers have asked such questions is itself interesting. Somehow or other both the researchers and the informants seem to be saying that all this complaining about the male neglect of the family, about the lack of family involvement by men, just is not warranted. Neither de Tocqueville nor Freud was right. Men do value family life more than they value their work. They do derive their major life satisfactions from their families rather than from their work.

It may well be true that men derive the greatest satisfaction from their family roles, but this does not necessarily mean that they are willing to pay for this benefit. In any event, great attitudinal changes took place in the 1960s and 1970s.

Douvan (Note 2), on the basis of surveys in 1957 and 1976, found, for example, a considerable increase in the proportion of both men and women who found marriage and parenthood burdensome and restrictive. Almost three fifths (57%) of both married men and married women in 1976 saw marriage as "all burdens and restrictions," as compared with only 42% and 47%, respectively, in 1957. And almost half (45%) also viewed children as "all burdens and restrictions" in 1976, as compared with only 28% and 33% for married men and married women, respectively, in 1957. The proportion of working men with a positive attitude toward marriage dropped drastically over this period, from 68% to 39%. Working women, who made up a fairly small number of all married women in 1957, hardly changed attitudes at all, dropping only from 43% to 42%. The proportion of working men who found marriage and children burdensome and restrictive more than doubled, from 25% to 56% and from 25% to 58%, respectively. Although some of these changes reflected greater willingness in 1976 than in 1957 to admit negative attitudes toward marriage and parenthood—itself significant—profound changes were clearly in progress. More and more men and women were experiencing disaffection with family life.[8]

"ALL BURDENS AND RESTRICTIONS"

Apparently, the benefits of the good-provider role were greater than the costs for most men. Despite the legend of the flight of the American male (Fiedler, 1962), despite the defectors and dropouts, despite the tavern habitué's "ball and chain" cliché, men seemed to know that the good-provider role, if they could succeed in it, was good for them. But Douvan's (Note 2) findings suggest that recently their complaints have become serious, bone-deep. The family they have been providing for is not the same family it was in the past.

Smith (1979) calls the great trek of married women into the labor force a subtle revolution—revolutionary not in the sense of one class overthrowing a status quo and substituting its own regime, but revolutionary in its impact on both the family and the work roles of men and women. It diluted the prerogatives of the good-provider role. It increased the demands made on the good provider, especially in the form of more emotional investment in the family, more sharing of household responsibilities. The role became even more burdensome.

However men may now feel about the burdens and restrictions imposed on them by the good-provider role, most have, at least ostensibly, accepted them. The tramp and the bum had "voted with their feet" against the role; the hobo or Wobbly had rejected it on the basis of a revolutionary ideology that saw it as enslaving men to the corporation; tavern humor had glossed the resentment habitués felt against its demands. Now the "burdens-and-restrictions" motif has surfaced both in research reports and, more blatantly, in the male liberation movement. From time to time it has also appeared in the clinicians' notes.

Sometimes the resentment of the good provider takes the form of simply wanting more appreciation for the life-style he provides. All he does for his family seems to be taken for granted. Thus, for example, Goldberg (1976), a psychiatrist, recounts the case of a successful businessman:

> He's feeling a deepening sense of bitterness and frustration about his wife and family. He doesn't feel appreciated. It angers him the way they seem to take the things his earnings purchase for granted. They've come to expect it as their due. It particularly enrages him when his children put him down for his "materialistic middle-class trip." He'd like to tell them to get someone else to support them but he holds himself back. (p. 124)

Brenton (1966) quotes a social worker who describes an upper-middle-class woman: She has "gotten hold of a man who'll drive himself like mad to get money, and [is] denigrating him for being too interested in money, and not interested in music, or the arts, or in spending time with the children. But at the same time she's subtly driving him—and doesn't know it" (p. 226). What seems significant about such cases is not that men feel resentful about the lack of appreciation but that they are willing to justify their resentment. They are no longer willing to grin and bear it.

Sometimes there is even more than expressed resentment; there is an actual repudiation of the role. In the past, only a few men like the hobo or Wobbly were likely to give up. Today, Goldberg (1976) believes, more are ready to renounce the role, not on theoretical revolutionary grounds, however, but on purely selfish ones:

> Male growth will stem from openly avowed, unashamed, self-oriented motivations. . . . Guilt-oriented "should" behavior will be rejected because it is always at the price of a hidden buildup of resentment and frustration and alienation from others and is, therefore, counterproductive. (p. 184)

The disaffection of the good provider is directed to both sides of his role. With respect to work, Lefkowitz (1979) has described men among whom the good-provider role is neither being completely rejected nor repudiated, but diluted. These men began their working lives in the conventional style, hopeful and ambitious. They found a job, married, raised a family, and "achieved a measure of economic security and earned the respect of . . . colleagues and neighbors" (Lefkowitz, 1979, p. 31). In brief, they successfully performed the good-provider role. But unlike their historical predecessors, they in time became disillusioned with their jobs—not jobs on assembly lines, not jobs usually characterized as alienating, but fairly prestigious jobs such as aeronautics engineer and government economist. They daydreamed about other interests. "The common theme which surfaced again and again in their histories, was the need to find a new social connection—to reassert control over their lives, to gain some sense of freedom" (Lefkowitz, 1979, p. 31). These men felt "entitled to freedom and independence." Middle-class, educated, self-assured, articulate, and for the most part white, they knew they could talk themselves into a job if they had to. Most of them did not want to desert their families. Indeed, most of them "wanted to rejoin the intimate circle they felt they had neglected in the years of work" (p. 31).

Though some of the men Lefkowitz studied sought closer ties with their families, in the case of those studied by Sarason (1977), a psychologist, career changes involved lower income and had a negative impact on families. Sarason's subjects were also men in high-level professions, the very men least likely to find marriage and parenthood burdensome and restrictive. Still, since career change often involved a reduction in pay, some wives were unwilling to accept it, with the result that the marriage deteriorated (p. 178). Sometimes it looked like a no-win game. The husband's earlier career brought him feelings of emptiness and alienation, but it also brought financial rewards for the family. Greater work satisfaction for him in lower paying work meant reduced satisfaction with life-style. These findings lead Sarason to raise a number of points with respect to the good-provider role. "How much," he asks, "does an individual or a family need in order to maintain a satisfactory existence? Is an individual being responsible to himself or his family if he provides them with little more than the bare essentials of living?" (p. 178). These are questions about the good-provider role that few men raised in the past.

Lefkowitz (1979) wonders how his downwardly mobile men lived when they left their jobs. "They put together a basic economic package which consisted of government assistance, contributions from family members who had not worked before and some bartering of goods and services" (p. 31). Especially interesting in this list of income sources are the "contributions from family members who had not worked before" (p. 31). Surely not mothers and sisters. Who, of course, but wives?

WOMEN AND THE PROVIDER ROLE

The present discussion began with the woman's part in the provider role. We saw how as more and more of the provisioning of the family came to be by way of monetary exchange, the woman's part shrank. A woman could still provide services, but could furnish little in the way of food, clothing, and shelter. But now that she is entering the labor force in large numbers, she can once more resume her ancient role, this time, like her male counterpart the provider, by way of a monetary contribution. More and more women are doing just this.

The assault on the good-provider role in the Depression was traumatic. But a modified version began to appear in the 1970s as a single income became inadequate for more and more families. Husbands have remained the major providers, but in an increasing number of cases the wife has begun to share this role. Thus, the proportion of married women aged 15 to 54 (living with their husbands) in the labor force more than doubled between 1950 and 1978, from 25.2% to 55.4%. The proportion for 1990 is estimated to reach 66.7% (Smith, 1978, p. 14). Fewer women are now full-time housewives.

For some men the relief from the strain of sole responsibility for the provider role has been welcome. But for others the feeling of degradation resembles the feelings reported 40 years earlier in the Great Depression. It is not that they are no longer providing for the family but that the role-sharing wife now feels justified in making demands on them. The good-provider role with all its prerogatives and perquisites has undergone profound changes. It will never be the same again.[9] Its death knell was sounded when, as noted above, the 1980 census no longer automatically assumed that the male member of the household was its head.

THE CURRENT SCENE

Among the new demands being made on the good-provider role, two deserve special consideration, namely, (a) more intimacy, expressivity, and nurturance—specifications never included in it as it originally took shape—and (b) more sharing of household responsibility and child care.

As the pampered wife in an affluent household came often to be an economic parasite, so also the good provider was often, in a way, a kind of emotional parasite. Implicit in the definition of the role was that he provided goods and material things. Tender loving care was not one of the requirements. Emotional ministrations from the family were his right; providing them was not a corresponding obligation. Therefore, as de Tocqueville had already noted by 1840, women suffered a kind of emotional deprivation labeled by Robert Weiss "relational deficit" (cited in Bernard, 1976). Only recently has this male rejection of emotional expression come to be challenged. Today, even blue-collar women are imposing "a host of new role expectations upon their husbands or lovers. . . . A new role set asks the blue-collar male to strive for . . . deep-coursing intimacy" (Shostak, Note 4, p. 75). It was not only vis-à-vis his family that the good provider was lacking in expressivity. This lack was built into the whole male role script. Today not only women but also men are beginning to protest the repudiation of expressivity prescribed in male roles (David & Brannon, 1976; Farrell, 1974; Fasteau, 1974; Pleck & Sawyer, 1974).

Is there any relationship between the "imposing" on men of "deep-coursing intimacy" by women on one side and the increasing proportion of men who find marriage burdensome and restrictive on the other? Are men seeing the new emotional involvements being asked of them as "all burdens and restrictions"? Are they responding to the new involvements under duress? Are they feeling oppressed by them? Fearful of them?

From the standpoint of high-level pure-science research there may be something bizarre, if not even slightly absurd, in the growing corpus of serious research on how much or how little husbands of employed wives contribute to household chores and child care. Yet it is serious enough that all over the industrialized world such research is going on. Time studies in a dozen countries—communist as well as capitalist—trace the slow and bungling process by which marriage accommodates to changing conditions and by which women struggle to mold the changing conditions in their behalf. For everywhere the same picture shows up in the research: an image of women sharing the provider role and at the same time retaining responsibility for the household. Until recently such a topic would have been judged unworthy of serious attention. It was a subject that might be worth a good laugh, for instance, as when an all-thumbs man in a cartoon burns the potatoes or finds himself bumbling awkwardly over a diaper, demonstrating his—proud—male ineptness at such female work. But it is no longer funny.

The "politics of housework" (Mainardi, 1970) proves to be more profound than originally believed. It has to do not only with tasks but also with gender—and perhaps more with the site of the tasks than with their intrinsic nature. A man can cook magnificently if he does it on a hunting or fishing trip; he can wield a skillful needle if he does it mending a tent or a fishing net; he can even feed and clean a toddler on a camping trip. Few of the skills of the homemaker are beyond his reach so long as they are practiced in a suitably male environment. It is not only women's work in and of itself that is degrading but any work on female turf. It may be true, as Brenton (1966) says, that "the secure man can wash a dish, diaper a baby, and throw the dirty clothes into the washing machine—or do anything else women used to do exclusively—without thinking twice about it" (p. 211), but not all men are that secure. To a great many men such chores are demasculinizing. The apron is shameful on a man in the kitchen; it is all right at the carpenter's bench.

The male world may look upon the man who shares household responsibilities as, in effect, a scab. One informant tells the interviewer about a conversation on the job: "What, are you crazy?" his hard-hat fellow workers ask him when he speaks of helping his wife. "The guys want to kill me. 'You son of a bitch! You are getting us in trouble.' . . . The men get really mad" (Lein, 1979, p. 492). Something more than persiflage is involved here. We are fairly familiar with the trauma associated with the invasion by women of the male work turf, the hazing women can be subjected to, and the male resentment of admitting them except into their own segregated areas. The corresponding entrance of men into the traditional turf of women—the kitchen or the nursery—has analogous but not identical concomitants.

Pleck and Lang (1979) tell us that men are now beginning to change in the direction of greater involvement in family life. "Men's family behavior is beginning to change, becoming increasingly congruent with the long-standing psychological significance of the family in their lives" (p. 1). They measure this greater involvement by way of the help they offer with homemaking chores. Scanzoni (1975), on the basis of a survey of over 3,000 husbands and wives, concludes that at least in households in which wives are in the labor force, there is the "possibility of a different pattern in which responsibility for households would unequivocally fall equally on husbands as well as wives" (p. 38). A brave new world indeed. Still, when we look at the reality around us, the pace seems intolerably slow. The responsibilities of the old good-provider role have attenuated far faster than have its prerogatives and privileges.

A considerable amount of thought has been devoted to studying the effects of the large influx of women into the work force. An equally interesting question is what the effect will be if a large number of men actually do increase their participation in the family and the household. Will men find the apron shameful? What if we were to ask fathers to alternate with mothers in being in the home when youngsters come home from school? Would fighting adolescent drug abuse be more successful if fathers and mothers were equally engaged in it? If the school could confer with fathers as often as with mothers? If the father accompanied children when they went shopping for clothes? If fathers spent as much time with children as do mothers?

Even as husbands, let alone as fathers, the new pattern is not without trauma. Hall and Hall (1979), in their study of two-career couples, report that the most serious fights among such couples occur not in the bedroom, but in the kitchen, between couples who profess a commitment to equality but who find actually implementing it difficult. A young professional reports that he is philosophically committed to egalitarianism in marriage and tries hard to practice it, but it does not work. He even feels guilty about this. The stresses involved in reworking roles may have an impact on health. A study of engineers and accountants finds poorer health among those with employed wives than among those with nonemployed wives (Burke & Wier, 1976). The processes involved in role change have been compared with those involved in deprogramming a cult member. Are they part of the increasing sense of marriage and parenthood as "all burdens and restrictions"?

The demise of the good-provider role also calls for consideration of other questions: What does the demotion of the good provider to the status of senior provider or even mere coprovider do to him? To marriage? To gender identity? What does expanding the role of housewife to that of junior provider or even coprovider do to her? To marriage? To gender identity? Much will of course depend on the social and psychological ambience in which changes take place.

A PARABLE

I began this essay with a proverbial woman. I close it with a modern parable by William H. Chafe (Note 5), a historian who also keeps his eye on the current scene. Jack and Jill, both planning professional careers, he as doctor, she as lawyer, marry at age 24. She works to put him through medical school in the expectation that he will then finance her through law school. A child is born during the husband's internship, as planned. But in order for him to support her through professional training as planned, he will have to take time out from his career. After two years, they decide that both will continue their training on a part-time basis, sharing household responsibilities and using day-care services. Both find part-time positions and work out flexible work schedules that leave both of them time for child care and companionship with one another. They live happily ever after.

That's the end? you ask incredulously. Well, not exactly. For, as Chafe (Note 5) points out, as usual the person is also political:

> Obviously such a scenario presumes a radical transformation of the personal values that today's young people bring to their relationships as well as a readiness on the part of social and economic institutions to encourage, or at least make possible, the development of equality between men and women. (p. 28)

The good-provider role may be on its way out, but its legitimate successor has not yet appeared on the scene.

4

Unemployment: Family Strategies for Adaptation

Patricia Voydanoff

Ralph Brown was numb, barely able to comprehend that after ten years, he was suddenly indefinitely laid off from his job. Sure, he heard rumors of impending layoffs, but he had reasoned that certainly ten years of seniority would prevent him from being affected. Soon he would have to face his family with the word. What would happen to all of their plans—the addition he was going to build on the house, skis for his daughter, camp for his son, the new freezer for his wife? How could he explain that he had no job, no plans for getting one, and no knowledge as to whether or when he would be called back to his old job. What would they think? What would they say? Of course, they know times are tough. Several friends and neighbors have already been laid off. But that's different. What would happen to *him, his* family? What if his wife is laid off too?

Sudden, unpredictable unemployment has devastating effects on individuals and families. It introduces a set of stressors into an individual's life situation and family system with no opportunity for preparation, either psychological or financial. This lack of preparation intensifies an already stressful situation for individuals and families—unemployment of any kind.

Research on unemployment since the 1930s reveals effects on the mental and physical health of individuals and on family relationships and stability. Many studies show strong relationships over several decades between unemployment rates and indicators of mental and physical health, including

Reprinted from Patricia Voydanoff, "Unemployment: Strategies for Family Adaptation." Chapter 9 in C. R. Figley and H. I. McCubbin (eds.), *Stress and the Family, Volume II: Castastrophic Stressors*.

state mental-hospital admissions, suicide, homicide, total mortality, and cardiovascular-renal disease mortality (Brenner, 1973, 1976, 1977). More qualitative research indicates less severe psychological effects, e.g., lowered self-esteem, anxiety, and psychophysiological distress (Cohn, 1978; Krause and Stryker, 1980; Powell and Driscoll, 1973; Schlozman and Verba, 1978).

In addition, unemployment affects other family members and the functioning of the family as a system. In his analysis of work experience and family life, Furstenberg (1974: 355) states that "economic uncertainty brought on by unemployment and marginal employment is a principal reason why family relations deteriorate." Unemployment is related to family instability and family functioning in the areas of marital power, family violence, spending behavior, division of labor, and parental authority and discipline (Voydanoff, 1978).

What are the sources of stress for the suddenly unemployed and his or her[1] family? What resources are available to families to deal with these stressors? What are the effective as well as ineffective methods families use to cope with sudden unemployment? These and other questions are considered in this chapter.

SOURCES OF STRESS FOR INDIVIDUALS AND FAMILIES[2]

Unemployment, sudden or otherwise, is a complex event occurring in varying contexts with differential impacts according to sex, race, age, and occupational-skill level. Unemployment rates vary over time and industry and geographic region. Unemployment in these various contexts is accompanied by several potential hardships. The number and type of hardships associated with an individual's unemployment experience influence the likelihood and extent of individual and family stress.

FINANCIAL HARDSHIP

Financial hardship frequently results from the unemployment of a family earner. The extent of hardship has been defined in two ways: (1) an income level insufficient to meet family needs and (2) economic deprivation, i.e., the loss of at least 30 percent of the income earned before unemployment (Elder, 1974; Moen, 1980). These hardships may occur independently of each other; both are related to patterns of family functioning (Elder, 1974).

The magnitude of individual and family financial hardships depends upon eligibility for Unemployment Insurance and other benefits, the length of unemployment, and prior income level. Company and union policies also influence the extent of financial hardship associated with layoffs and plant closings. Short-term financial hardship is reduced by policies such as the continuation of fringe benefits, especially health insurance; severance pay based on length of service; and the vesting of pensions.

Financial hardship resulting from the unemployment of a major family earner is associated with a shift in the family work effort (i.e., the pattern of labor-force participation and earnings among family members) (Ferman and Gardner, 1979). Spouses may become employed outside the home or increase their level of labor-force participation from part-time to full-time. Children, especially adolescents, may take part-time jobs to reduce the level of financial hardship in the family (Elder, 1974).

Financial hardship is extended to the community when a company laying off workers or closing a facility is the major employer in the community. The lack of alternative sources of employment results in widespread long-term unemployment. High unemployment in a company employing a substantial percentage within the community can have a ripple effect, creating financial hardship in other sectors (e.g., among those providing goods and services that unemployed workers can no longer afford to buy).

LOSS OF THE EARNER ROLE

Hardships associated with unemployment extend beyond the financial to the social and psychological. The loss of work involves more than the loss of income. This is rather obvious in our case example of Ralph Brown. It also means the loss of a major role, a role that is considered desirable, socially valued, and even essential for men with rigid, traditional values, or for either men or women whose identity is part of their profession (e.g., police officer, fire fighter). Work is a major source of social integration, it structures the way people spend their time, and it provides a sense of accomplishment and purpose. The sudden loss of this role can result in a period of shock, lowered self-esteem, and anxiety and depression. Work also determines the amount of time spent with the family and the structure and pattern of family activities. When a family member becomes unemployed and spends substantially more time at home, family routines are disrupted and tensions increase (LeMasters, 1975). The psychological effects on the unemployed lead to strain and concern among other family members (Root, 1977). Children of the unemployed also are at higher risk of illness (Margolis and Farran, 1981).

In addition, plant closings, which are often sudden, have another effect on integration that does not occur in other types of unemployment. Victims of plant closings report a feeling of separation and loss comparable to the death of a relative (Slote, 1969). A plant closing usually consists of several stages: economic difficulties and uncertainty, announcement of closing, anticipation, staged terminations, and final closing. Workers report several emotions during this process including anger, denial, acceptance, and anxiety. The knowledge that the plant is not continuing after the worker has left creates a sense of grief and loss among workers with high seniority and attachment.

MEDIATING FACTORS

Before considering how families cope with unemployment and its associated stress, it is important to examine factors that, under certain conditions, can reduce the level of family stress associated with sudden unemployment. The likelihood that unemployment-related hardships will produce high levels of family stress depends on two major mediating factors: the family's definition of the event and family resources.

FAMILY DEFINITION OF THE EVENT

Suddenness. Sudden, unpredictable unemployment is more likely to result in stress than expected or routine unemployment (e.g., layoffs for automobile changeovers or unemployment among construction workers in bad weather). When unemployment is perceived as normal or manageable (e.g., when it has occurred before, when it has a specified duration, or when there is a period of anticipation and preparation), it is less stressful for individuals and families (Angell, 1936; Bakke, 1940; Cavan, 1959; Powell and Driscoll, 1973). Although the length of time that an event is anticipated is related to a family's definition of the event as non-crisis-producing (Burr, 1973; Hansen and Johnson, 1979), the period of anticipation can be stressful. In their study of a plant closing, Cobb and Kasl (1977) found the anticipation period to be the most detrimental to the mental and physical health of the workers. However, this period may have reduced the stress that otherwise would have occurred *after* unemployment by providing a time for psychological and financial preparation.

Responsibility. A second aspect of a family's definition of the event is the extent to which the unemployed person is considered to be responsible for unemployment, including the worker's sense of blame from the family. During the Depression of the 1930s, many workers and family members blamed the unemployed person (Bakke, 1940; Komarovsky, 1940). This tendency now exists mainly among the long-term unemployed (Briar, 1978; Calavita, 1977; Cobb and Kasl, 1977; Greenwald, 1978). Self and family blame for unemployment are related to family stress and limit adjustment to unemployment (Burr, 1973; Furstenberg, 1974; Hill, 1958; Rainwater, 1974).

Sense of Failure. In addition, even if a worker is not blamed for being unemployed, he or she may be seen as failing in the role as family provider. This may be especially troubling for men, since the role of economic provider is perceived to be the primary family responsibility of men by both husbands and wives (Bernard, 1981; Cazenave, 1979; Lein, 1979; Nye, 1974). The loss of the provider role was a key element in those families where the husband lost his authority in relation to his wife and adolescent children during the Depression (Komarovsky, 1940). The sense of failure may be intensified when wives and adolescents take jobs or when family members hold rigidly traditional sex-role norms (Anderson, 1980; Angell, 1936; Cavan, 1959; Voydanoff, 1963). With the emergence of egalitarianism within the family, however, such sex-specific findings may not be as pervasive today (see Perrucci and Targ, 1974).

FAMILY RESOURCES

In addition to a family's definition of unemployment, several family resources mediate between unemployment and its hardships and individuals' and family reactions. These include financial resources, family-system characteristics, and social supports.

Financial Resources. Unemployed earners with financial resources to draw upon, e.g., savings, home ownership, and lack of debts, are protected from financial hardship for a period of time and have higher morale (Voydanoff, 1963). The level of family financial resources is dependent upon family size and composition and the family's life-cycle stage. These factors determine the number of earners available to the family as well as the number and ages of dependents. For example, families with young children must support dependents with limited earning resources, especially among single-parent families (Moen, 1979). Families with adolescent children are more likely to have a mother and/or teenagers working to supplement family income (Elder, 1974). Women heading families are especially vulnerable to stress because they are less likely to have financial resources, other available earners in the family, or marketable job skills and experience.

Family-System Characteristics. Several characteristics of the family system as it was operating prior to unemployment influence the level of stress occurring during unemployment, especially adaptability, cohesion, and authority patterns. The extent of change in authority patterns during unemployment is related to the type of authority existing before unemployment (Anderson, 1980; Komarovsky, 1940). During the Depression, unemployed husbands were most likely to lose authority based on love and respect (Komarovsky, 1940). Research during the Depression also found that integrated and adaptable families remained so during unemployment, while previously disorganized families became more disorganized (Angell, 1936; Cavan and Ranck, 1938). These data support the circumplex model of family systems, which hypothesizes that families with moderate levels of adaptability and cohesion are best able to respond satisfactorily to stressors (McCubbin et al., 1980).

Social Support. A third significant resource for the families of the unemployed is instrumental and expressive support from friends, relatives, and neighbors. Limited research indicates that help from friends and neighbors contributes to family stability and that social support, especially from other family members, mediates the effects of unemployment on individual mental and physical health (Cobb and Kasl, 1977; Gore, 1977, 1978; Kasl and Cobb, 1979).

These mediating factors influence the extent of stress resulting from the unemployment of a major earner. Unemployment is less stress producing when preparation occurs, when the unemployed husband is not blamed for the unemployment, and when he is not perceived as a failure in his provider role. Family stress is also reduced by the existence of financial resources, adaptive family-system characteristics, and social supports.

COPING WITH SUDDEN UNEMPLOYMENT

The concept of mediating factors suggests that families differ in the number and combinations of characteristics available to resist or limit family stress following unemployment. However, families are also able to manipulate these characteristics in a more active fashion to prevent or handle family stress. Coping is an active process in which families take direct action to use other resources to deal with unemployment and its associated hardships. McCubbin and Patterson (Note 1) conceptualize coping as follows:

> Although family resources and perceptions have been studied independently and offer investigators a gauge of family capabilities used to meet demands, these same observations suggest that we could improve upon our understanding of family adaptation to crises by looking at these two variables simultaneously along with what families do to cope with the situation. Coping appears to be a multifaceted process wherein resources, perception, and behavioral responses interact as families try to achieve a balance in family functioning. (p. 10)

In this context, coping is what families *do* with their resources and perceptions to meet the demands of unemployment as a stressor. Coping may reduce the vulnerability of the family to the stressor, may strengthen or maintain family-system characteristics, may reduce or eliminate stressor events and their hardships, and may alter the environment by changing social circumstances (McCubbin et al., 1980).

Coping with unemployment is a process that occurs over time. The process begins before unemployment if there is a period of anticipation and continues after reemployment as individuals and families adjust to new, sometimes less desirable, jobs. During a period of unemployment, coping strategies must accommodate to changes in the extent of hardships, the level of resources and support, and family definitions. Several formulations of the adjustment process are similar in basic structure (Bakke, 1940; Eisenberg and Lazarsfeld, 1938; Powell and Driscoll, 1973; Zawadzki and Lazarsfeld, 1935). Bakke's formulation serves as a good example. He outlined the following stages of family adjustment to unemployment: momentum stability, unstable equilibrium, disorganization, experimental readjustment, and permanent readjustment. Each stage is characterized by a complex pattern of family functioning and coping in the areas of financial management, family work effort, family division of labor, authority and discipline, and use of social support.

EFFECTIVE COPING METHODS

Family Work Effort. During a worker's unemployment, other family members frequently increase their participation in the labor force to provide financial resources to the family. They either take jobs outside the home or increase their work effort from part time to full time. Children, especially adolescents, take on part-time employment to help out. Although individually wives and children usually earn less than husbands, families may approach their former income level by everyone seeking some work and contributing a large percentage to the household (Ferman, 1979). This realigning of the family work effort provides financial resources and reduces anxiety about the future.

Financial Management. Effective financial management is an important aspect of family relationships at all times; its significance grows during unemployment as resources shrink and family tensions increase. Handling financial resources is often stressful for families and is a major source of family disagreements. Working together as a family to manage limited resources effectively is an important coping mechanism both for practical purposes and as a means of maintaining family cohesion. A consistent strategy for budgeting and bill-paying is crucial for the efficient management of limited resources, especially when it is uncertain when unemployment will end.

The types of cuts in expenditures vary with the duration of unemployment. Early research shows that during the first weeks cuts are limited to recreation, luxuries, and social-contact expenses. Later, some essential items are replaced with less expensive alternatives, clothing is not replaced, and recreation is severely limited (Bakke, 1940). The use of credit attenuates the severity of cuts for several months. More recently, studies show that families make cuts in housing, food, clothing, transportation, and recreation (Briar, 1978; Nicholson and Corson, 1976; Rosenfield, 1977; Sheppard, Ferman, and Faber, 1959). Housing costs are reduced by moving to less costly quarters or sharing quarters with friends or relatives. Many goods and services are obtained more inexpensively through the irregular economy, e.g., purchasing or trading items and services with friends and neighbors. Garage sales and moonlighting plumbers and carpenters are examples of this type of activity. The unemployed with a variety of skills often earn some income by providing services to others on a cash or barter basis (e.g., housekeeping, carpentry, painting).

Quality of Family Relationships. Attempts by family members to maintain and strengthen the adaptability and cohesiveness of the family unit are essential coping strategies among the families of the unemployed. It is important for the family to be flexible enough to reorganize the roles performed in the family and remain a cohesive family unit. Maintaining cohesion through communication, empathy, and joint activities is a second important element. These coping mechanisms are important ways of sustaining family relationships during unemployment.

The Use of Social Supports. Isolation among the unemployed is detrimental to individual and family well-being. It is crucial for unemployed workers and their families to maintain contacts with friends, relatives, neighbors, and former co-workers who have been helpful as emotional supports in the past. In addition, supports are useful in more concrete ways, such as giving job leads and job-seeking advice, providing transportation to job interviews, and caring for children.

Definitional Coping. Definitional coping can decrease stress by altering the perceptions of family members toward unemployment (e.g., by reducing blame, supporting flexible family-role definitions), and perceiving unemployment as an opportunity. It is helpful for the unemployed man and other family members to recognize that most unemployment is structural and not the fault of the unemployed person. A recent study of a plant closing reveals that the level of self-blame is relatively low immediately after the closing; however, it is substantially higher six months later. Thus it is necessary for the long-term unemployed to maintain their perspective on the social context of unemployment.

Regarding traditional views of sex roles, it is also important for family members to have a flexible view of the contributions of husbands and fathers to the family. Unemployed men with traditional sex-role ideologies have lower morale (Voydanoff, 1963). Families perceiving husbands and fathers as more than economic providers and supporting alternative value contributions to the family during unemployment (e.g., housework and child rearing) can develop a more effective and less stressful pattern of family functioning during unemployment. This is especially important if other family members are employed outside the home.

Some families facilitate coping by perceiving unemployment as a challenge, a growth experience. This is particularly likely among dissatisfied workers who use unemployment as an opportunity to get into a more desirable occupation or job situation (Little, 1975; Root and Mayland, 1978).

Certain combinations of definitional coping and family resources can create a situation in which unemployment is relatively unstressful. For example, in a recent study a majority of wives thought that unemployment following a plant closing had been "generally good for their family" (Root, 1977). This perception was much more likely, however, among wives from families with the following characteristics: substantial family resources, including wife employment, high income, and family cohesion; the definition of unemployment as an opportunity; and the perceived ability to make plans. We would expect that the same would be true for workers displaced by plant closings.

INEFFECTIVE METHODS OF COPING

Recent work on family stress indicates that coping strategies themselves can become sources of further stress (McCubbin et al., 1980). Coping mechanisms effectively meet some needs while at the same time creating new problems. For example, shifting the family work effort from the unemployed member to other family members is effective in coping with reduced financial resources. However, it can lead to stress in family relationships if either the unemployed or other family members feel resentment, or if it appears that the unemployed has failed as a provider. Tensions can result from wife employment when men are unwilling to assume household chores (Powell and Driscoll, 1973). The same phenomenon may apply to unemployed wives reluctant to assume or resume the homemaker role her employment once freed her from. These shifts have implications for the entire fabric of family relationships, in some cases undermining the cohesion of the family unit and the quality of husband-wife and parent-child relationships.

The use of social supports and cutting expenditures for recreation may also have mixed results. Social supports effectively mediate between unemployment and mental and physical health and the quality of family relationships. However, the expected loss of support from those in their family, community, and workplace contributes to a reluctance to move to another area with better job prospects. Reducing expenditures for recreation helps families manage limited financial resources; however, it also limits the use of social supports and increases isolation and boredom (Rapoport, 1981). In situations such as this, tradeoffs exist between the costs and benefits associated with various coping strategies.

Another form of ineffective coping includes generally dysfunctional methods of dealing with stress (e.g., alcohol and drug abuse, withdrawal from interaction with others, and lashing out in violence against family members).

IMPLICATIONS

POLICY INTERVENTIONS

What can be done about the Ralph Brown families of tomorrow? The analysis of mediating factors and coping strategies suggests several types of intervention to reduce the level of family stress and to assist recovery from crisis. The most direct approach would eliminate unemployment and economic uncertainty through increased economic stability. Uncertainty regarding the onset and expected length of unemployment influences a family's ability to deal with unemployment. In this context, it is important for families to have a period of preparation before unemployment occurs. Controversy surrounds proposed plant-closing legislation requiring notification before closing. Time requirements for notification vary from a month to a year or more. In his study of a plant closing, Cobb concluded that two years was too long a period. He recommended two or three months as optimal for preparation without drawing out the process longer than necessary and creating additional stress (Slote, 1969). This period may need to be extended, however, when management and workers attempt to negotiate alternatives to closing, e.g., employees purchasing the plant.

Unemployment Insurance and other benefits (e.g., Supplemental Unemployment Benefits) have reduced the financial hardships associated with unemployment. However, many unemployed family members do not qualify for UI and SUB, and most workers still lose health insurance and pensions. These hardships can be alleviated by severance pay and the maintenance of pensions and medical and life insurance. Reduced work time and job sharing can spread out limited employment opportunities and reduce unemployment. When layoffs are necessary, a flexible schedule can facilitate individual planning and reduce community impact (Teague, 1981).

Recession-related unemployment is often accompanied by cutbacks in the programs and services most needed by the unemployed, e.g., mental-health programs. These programs lose government and private support as part of the same economic processes that create unemployment. Policy initiatives that cannot reduce unemployment should at least be able to limit the cuts in programs needed to cope with unemployment.

IMPLICATIONS FOR PROFESSIONALS

Several approaches by professionals can be helpful in increasing the coping abilities of families during unemployment. First, many unemployed workers have not been in the job market for several years and need assistance and support in looking for a job. Companies laying off workers or closing plants can serve as a focal point for efforts in this area, e.g., providing job-placement services, job-seeking skills and advice, and information about community resources. Family-service programs and individual and family counseling can be important in sustaining or improving individual mental health and family functioning and cohesion as well as in encouraging the development and use of social supports. Often, community services appropriate for the unemployed are available; information about these services needs to be available in a compact package of resource and referral material. A critical need for many unemployed is financial counseling and financial management skills. The availability and awareness of credit-counseling centers and programs to build skills in family money management is a crucial first step in coping with unemployment.

These services need to be provided within a context that emphasizes that structural unemployment is not the fault of unemployed family members. This perspective is most important for the long-term unemployed and for those who are among the last rehired after a recession or plant closing. An understanding of labor-market dynamics is important for professionals and the unemployed in clarifying that age, local unemployment rate, and demands for specific job skills are significant, yet impersonal, factors in the timing of reemployment.

To increase understanding of unemployment, coping strategies, and family-oriented policies and programs to deal with unemployment, further research is needed. Much of the current research base was developed during the Depression of the 1930s. It is important to update this research to account for the vast social and economic changes since that time. For example, the increases in female labor-force participation have not been accompanied by research on the individual and family effects of unemployment among women. This is a major deficit which must be redressed immediately.

CONCLUSION

As illustrated by the case study at the beginning of this chapter, sudden unemployment affects families in different ways because of variations in the circumstances associated with unemployment and with family structure and functioning. Family stress theory clarifies these sources of variation. The presence of hardships influences the potential for family stress. In addition, families vary in the nature and extent of resources available to deal with unemployment. Lastly, the coping strategies families are able to mobilize and use effectively influence the ways in which families are affected by unemployment.

These coping strategies include realigning the family work effort by having other family members take on employment; learning techniques for managing limited financial resources; maintaining strong and healthy family relationships; and developing and using social supports to alleviate stress and provide concrete help in family problem solving. However, the use of coping strategies is complicated by the fact that some coping strategies are effective in meeting certain needs, while at the same time creating difficulties in other areas. For example, employment by the unemployed spouse helps financially while changing the balance of and supplementing family roles. This dilemma points out the complexities involved in dealing with external stressors such as unemployment. The family is truly a system interacting with other systems. It is not possible to introduce a sudden stressor like unemployment into these complex interrelationships without expecting multiple repercussions.

Our knowledge in this area is quite unsophisticated. We have data on the effectiveness of individual coping strategies; however, we know very little about the interactions among strategies and their combined effects on family relationships. Examples presented here are just the beginning of knowledge about these complex interrelationships.

5

Mothers' Contribution to the Family Money Economy in Europe and the United States

Lee Rainwater

One of the most striking social changes in the twentieth century has been a steady growth in the proportion of women who are wage earners as well as home producers. In the first half of this century the proportion of wives in the labor force increased from around five percent to almost a quarter. In the next quarter century the proportion increased to nearly one-half of all wives. This amounts to a reasonably steady three percent per-year increase. The participation rates of mothers have increased much more rapidly. This article deals with the contribution of mothers, as wives and single heads, to family income.

Scattered evidence suggests that most of the change in the labor market role of wives has been in the proportion of their participation rather than their contribution to the family exchequer. There is suggestive evidence that in the early part of the present century, as today, wives who worked contributed about 25 percent of family money income (Hayghe, 1976). Although more and more women have worked, in those families in which wives did work, there may not have been a significant increase in their average contribution to family income.

A great deal of scholarly work must be done if we are to understand the social significance for families and for society of the dramatic shift in the labor force participation by women,and mothers in particular. Investigation of its significance (as opposed to documentation of trends) is only beginning. We really know very little about what effects this social change has had. One

Reprinted from Lee Rainwater, "Mother's Contribution to the Family Money Economy in Europe and the United States," *Journal of Family History*, vol. 4, Summer 1970, pp. 198–211.

might assert that mothers' increasing participation in the labor force has really had very little social effect. It could be argued that wives always contributed importantly to families' economic well-being (by their home production) and that the gradual shift to market participation does not signify any significant change in women's roles, their sense of identity, definitions of sex roles, and the like. At the other extreme, one might assert that the participation of women in the labor force signifies a major and permanent change in the nature of the family as a social organization, with repercussions not only on women's roles and identities but also on the roles, identities, and life experiences of men and children.

The central questions need to be whether, in marriage, women are becoming full partners with men in the production of family money income and whether the increased viability of women's labor market roles portends a sharp increase in the number of mother-headed families. There certainly is a great deal of ambivalence in Europe and the United States concerning such possibilities. Some major social and economic policy challenges could flow from such a development (Land and Parker, 1978).

To begin to answer these questions, it is necessary to tease apart a variety of issues often combined under the overall rubric of labor force participation.

The first is that of labor force participation in the conventional sense. There is a great deal of descriptive information about women's labor force participation in the United States and in most other industrial nations. It is possible to know what proportion of women are labor force participants and how this varies by life cycle and family situation. But labor force participation is a very mixed category. Much more information is needed describing the exact character of participation—in terms of hours worked (full-time vs. part-time work) and in terms of the proportion of the year worked. If most are part-time participants, then one can expect the effects of that participation to be very different than if they were full-time participants.

Even more important, and unfortunately even less well described, is the question of the permanence of the labor force involvement by mothers. If most mothers who participate at all move in and out of the labor force fairly frequently during the life course, then one would expect much less change in the traditional role definitions of women than if this involvement is more that of a "work career." (cf. Fried, 1966, for a very useful typology in men's involvement in work and career.)

Finally, there is the question of the actual income earned. This has two components: time worked and wages. Achieving a better understanding of the wage differentials between men and women has an important role here (Corcoran and Duncan, 1978).

These aspects of women's labor force participation—hours worked when working, proportion of the year worked, and wages—together produce the total income earned by women and, thereby, their contribution to family income.

Understanding the social consequences of mothers' labor force participation involves working out effects on patterns of interaction and social meaning from this more complexly defined reality of labor force participation.

The most common social effect which commentators have dealt with is that of the effect on so-called family power structure of women's employment. Most of this research, however, is extremely primitive because it deals with labor force participation in a dichotomous way. We know little about the effects on the woman's influence on family affairs of part-time vs. full-time participation or of high vs. low earning capacity.

One important social implication of women's work has to do with the effect of increased family income on the standards individuals perceive to be advantaged and disadvantaged levels of living. We know that there is a surprisingly high degree of consensus in society about the relative incomes associated with being poor, rich, or comfortable (Rainwater, 1974). These conceptions are related to average levels of economic well being at any given time. If women's working increases families' average incomes and thereby changes conceptions of what represents comfort or prosperity or income deprivation, then the increasing frequency of two-earner families can have important effects on the sense individuals have of how successful they are at achieving mainstream (or more prosperous) styles of life. One-earner families, whether male- or female-headed, could perceive themselves at an increasing disadvantage vis-à-vis two-earner families. If, on the other hand, wives' earnings are relatively invisible, one might expect that increasing participation of women in the labor force would not have a major effect on public conceptions of different levels of living.

Then there is the question of the effect of mothers' earnings on the economic well being of their families. To what extent is the wife's income contribution consumed to increase the family's sense of economic well being? To what extent does the mother's contribution have an effect on the major status-related statements families make about their lifestyles? To what extent, instead, are mothers' earnings spent for a range of discretionary items outside the family's presentation of status? To what extent is home production lost due to the wife's involvement in the labor force?

More centrally, what are the effects of greater labor force participation on mothers themselves? The non-pecuniary effects—the effects simply of having a job or a career—have been much discussed but little researched. This is unfortunate because, as I will argue below, the economic contributions of a great many working women have been so small that it is difficult to believe that these contributions constitute the primary purpose of working. (For all that, their answers to sample survey questions suggest the primacy of financial motivation.) We need to know much more about how women think about their work in terms of their life course, identity, and needs for social participation. Barbara Garson's recent book does an excellent job of suggesting some of the ways that even dull, monotonous, alienating jobs can be important to women for much more than just the money they earn (Garson, 1978).

A great deal may also be learned about the internal family economy from studying what women do with their earnings. To the extent that wives' earnings are not treated as part of the general family pot, we learn something about the internal dynamics of family economy, but this requires that we go beyond simple-minded notions of unitary family decision making.

All of these factors need to be looked at as they vary from one social class to another. The meaning and significance of jobs and earnings in the upper and middle class world must be different in important ways from their meaning and significance in the working class. Finally, we need to understand more precisely the interaction between labor force participation (actual and potential) and marital stability. This article does not provide answers to all of these questions, but our awareness of the importance of these issues has guided the research program I describe below.

In this paper I summarize findings from comparative studies of mothers' labor force participation and their contribution to family income carried out at the Joint Center for Urban Studies. These studies suggest very partial answers to some of the questions raised above.

MOTHERS' LABOR FORCE PARTICIPATION IN EUROPE AND THE UNITED STATES

First, a review is needed of the extent of labor force participation by women with children in several European countries and the United States. We have chosen sample years which, depending on the country, range from 1968 to 1975. These data are from four different sources, so it is not possible to compare them in very precise ways.[1]

For Sweden, Great Britain, and the United States, we are able to explore the family economic circumstances of people in the 25–54 year old range using three rather comparable national surveys conducted between 1968 and 1973. Our indication of labor force participation is taken not from what a woman is doing at the particular time of the interview, but rather from whether she had any earnings at all during the previous year. We find that labor force participation by wife/mothers is not particularly different in the three countries—55 percent of Swedish wives and mothers were labor force participants, 56 percent in Britain, and 50 percent in the United States. Among mothers who headed their own families, Britain has a rather lower figure (61 percent) compared to the United States (73 percent) and Sweden (90 percent). Perhaps more interesting is the fact that in Sweden whether or not a woman in the 25–54 year old age group has children has much less effect on her labor force participation than in the other two countries. In Sweden female heads without children are not much more likely to be labor force participants, whereas in Britain and the United States, those without children are 20 to 29 percent more likely to be participants. Among wives there are no marked differences among the countries. Overall, wives without children are about a third more likely to be participants than are those with children.

Our data for the countries of the European Community are based on a different measure, that of current labor force participation.[2] There are important differences among the countries in the Community in labor force participation. Controlling for age and family characteristics, I find that women's participation ranged from highs of 64 percent (of all women in the age range of 18–64) for Germany, 62 percent for Great Britain, and 58 percent for Denmark to lows of 30 percent in Ireland, and 24 percent in the Netherlands, France, Italy and Belgium were in between with 40 percent participation.

One could discern a general "north-south" split in participation, and so detailed analysis was made of the effects of marital status, presence of children, and age for three "northern" (Germany, Denmark, and Great Britain) and three "southern" countries (France, Belgium/Luxembourg, and Italy). Overall, the northern countries had higher labor force participation. Among married mothers with children in the age range of 18–54, I find 55 percent in the northern countries participating in the labor force compared to only one-third in the southern countries. Among single, separated, and divorced mothers I find 76 percent labor force participants in the northern countries compared to 66 percent in the southern countries, a much smaller difference between the two regions.

Interestingly, in the European Community sample, the number of children, given that a woman has some children, does not seem to affect labor force participation. Women with two or three young children (under the age of 8) were as likely to be labor force participants as women with only one. Contrary to what might be expected, women with older children were less likely to work than women with younger children (even with age and marital status controlled). Overall I found that, controlling for age, family characteristics, and nation, 58 percent of women with no children, 45 percent of women with some younger children, and 35 percent of women with only older children, were labor force participants in Europe.

FULL VS. PART-TIME WORK

The European Community survey allows us to characterize women as full-time workers (30 or more hours per week) or part-time workers (8 to 29 hours per week). I find that it is the frequency of part-time work that accounts for the fact that more women in the three "northern" countries are labor force participants than in the three "southern" countries. Thus, among married women with children, two-thirds of the employed women were part-time workers, whereas in the "southern" countries only 20 percent were part-time workers. Overall, more wives in the "southern" countries were full-time workers (26 percent) than in the "northern" countries (16 percent). Part-time work was an important factor only for married women, fewer than 10 percent of the female heads with children were part-time workers.

These results suggest that the availability of jobs that require fewer than 30 hours per week can be a crucial factor in the level of women's labor force participation.

We do not have data that is quite comparable for the United States. One analysis does allow us to determine the proportion of part-time mothers in the age range of 18–44 in 1975 (Bane, 1977). Slightly over a quarter of both married mothers and the solo mothers were employed part-time. Thus, the United States would seem to stand between the "northern" European pattern of frequent part-time work and the "southern" European pattern of rare part-time jobs. Among solo mothers, more Americans seem to be employed part-time than in either the "northern" or "southern" European countries.

MOTHERS' FINANCIAL CONTRIBUTION TO FAMILY INCOME

The financial contribution of women to family income is highly varied. We find that, on average, working married mothers contribute 22 percent of family income in the United States, 18 percent in Great Britain, and 21 percent in Sweden. The comparable proportions for their husbands are 69, 70, and 66 percent. Government transfers are a small but presumably valued portion of family income in Britain and Sweden (averaging 4 percent and 7 percent); in the United States, on average, only 0.2 percent of the family income of working wives comes from government transfers. In the United States relatively few families are the beneficiaries of government transfers (19 percent) compared to Britain (71 percent) and Sweden (97 percent). Child allowances and other social benefits result in the majority of couples having some transfer income in those two countries. In the United States, however, the few families benefited by government transfers are more dependent on them. Among the 19 percent of American couples who receive transfer income, some 12 percent of family income comes from transfers, compared to only 5 percent and 7 percent for Britain and Sweden.

It is in the families headed by solo mothers that we find the greatest combination of women's earnings and government transfers. Among solo mother workers we find that, on average, over half of the family's income comes from the woman's earnings (51 percent in the United States and Britain, and 58 percent in Sweden). In all three countries about ten percent of the family's income comes from the earnings of other people in the family.

Among families in which the solo mother has earnings, on average 28 percent of family income comes from government transfers in the United States, 26 percent in Britain, and 16 percent in Sweden. In Sweden virtually all such families receive government transfers; 85 percent of the British solo mothers receive government transfers. In the United States the proportion is 58 percent.

Even more strikingly than with married couples, it is in the United States that the solo mother beneficiaries are most dependent on government transfers—they receive on average 40 percent of their family income from transfers, compared to 32 percent in Britain and 16 percent in Sweden. Thus, one must understand the income world of solo mothers as one in which income is packaged from a variety of sources. In all three countries government transfers can play a crucial role.

WELFARE AND WORKING MOTHERS

Consider a particular policy preoccupation of the United States—welfare. Even here one finds the mix between women's earnings and transfers very important. Among the few married couples in the United States who receive means-tested transfers (welfare and food stamps), we find that the wife works in 29 percent of the cases—the comparable figures are 41 percent in Great Britain and 35 percent in Sweden. The wife's contribution is on average 15 percent in the United States, 17 percent in Britain, and 15 percent in Sweden.

Among solo mothers receiving means-tested benefits we find, of course, a much higher proportion in the labor market. In the United States 55 percent are employed. The comparable figures for Britain and Sweden are 48 percent and 89 percent. In the United States 30 percent of the family income of these mothers comes from their own earnings. In Britain the comparable figure is 40 percent and in Sweden it is 48 percent.

Thus, for female-headed households, one observes that the group of women earners and the group of beneficiaries of "charity" overlap considerably. To the extent that social policy does not take this overlap into systematic account, it is highly unrealistic.

THE INFLUENCE OF SPOUSE'S EARNINGS

Contrary to much economic theory, there does not seem to be a strong effect of husband's earnings on wife's earnings or vice versa (Schwartz, 1978). In the United States, although wives are somewhat less likely to work the higher their husbands' incomes (the correlation is −.128) husband's earnings, wages, and hours have almost no relation to own earnings, wages, and hours for wives who work. This suggests that wives' decisions to work are not heavily influenced by their husband's economic circumstances, but rather are related to the woman's own goals and interests and, perhaps, to the social as opposed to economic dynamics of family relationships.

The fact that there is no association between the earnings of husbands and wives is produced by a somewhat complex pattern in which husbands' and wives' wages are highly correlated (.5) and the wife's hours are negatively related to the husband's hours. The husband's earnings are thus fairly strongly correlated with the wife's wage (.27) and negatively correlated with her hours (−.12). The result is an essentially zero correlation between their respective earnings for all couples, and a slight positive correlation in two-earner families.

Thus we find, and this holds in Britain and Sweden, as well as in the United States, that disproportionately high-income families are ones in which the wife is a labor force participant—that is part of why the family is in a high-income group. In each of the three countries, we divided the sample into equal sixths of the population (when combined by twos, we have the low, middle, and high thirds of the family income distribution). In each country the labor market participation of married mothers in the low-income third is much lower than in the highest income third. In the United States somewhat less than 40 percent in the lowest income third are labor force participants compared to a little over 50 percent in the middle income third and slightly over 60 percent in the highest income third. For Britain the comparable percentages are around 45 percent in the lowest, 65 percent in the middle and 72 percent in the highest income thirds, while in Sweden around 33 percent of married mothers in the lowest income third are labor force participants, a little over 60 percent in the middle income third, and not quite 75 percent in the highest third of the family income distribution.

On the other hand, their proportionate contributions to family income do not differ by sextile if they are labor force participants. In all of the sextiles, mothers in the United States contribute on average close to one quarter of family income, while in Britain and Sweden they average two or three percentage points lower. (By 1975 the overall level of mother's contribution in the United States had not changed nor had the pattern of no relation of her proportionate contribution to level of total family income.) Thus, a reasonable rule of thumb is that in all three countries, at all family income levels, the mother's average contribution is between a fifth and a quarter of family income. One would expect, therefore, that the family dynamics governing the choice of whether or not to work, and how much, are in some sense independent of the income level and even the social class of the family.

THE FAMILY EFFECTS OF MOTHER'S EARNINGS

Or it could be that this relatively constant result is produced by somewhat different dynamics at different class levels. In one exploration, a comparison was made of families in which wives did and did not contribute significant proportions of the family income (Coleman, 1978). In working-class families in which wives did not work (often despite quite low incomes on the part of the husband), it seemed that their highly traditional role definitions played a part. Husbands were often not at all accepting of the idea of the wife working. The consumption patterns of the family often showed a considerable degree of masculine domination (multiple cars and trucks, much hunting and fishing activity, and the like).

In such families the conception of family life and roles is such that husbands are strongly resistant to their wives working; they feel that their own prerogatives would be undermined. Often the wife has no particular desire to work in these situations, but sometimes she finds it frustrating that she is not allowed to participate in raising the family's standard of living.

In those working class cases where the wife does work, evidence of masculine domination is not so apparent. The family's life revolves more around common home-based activities, and husbands seem to dominate decision-making less. (There is, perhaps, somewhat of a chicken and an egg problem here, since it is not readily apparent whether role definitions, and particularly the husband's concern to operate his family in a highly masculine way, determine whether or not the wife works. Or perhaps we are seeing instead the effects of the wife's working on the family's psychosocial patterns.)

It seemed in Coleman's analysis that, in general, wives' earnings are not built into the family's basic standard of living (particularly that connected with choice of neighborhood and housing) *unless* the wife is defined as more or less steadily in the labor market. In that case, the family seemed likely to "live up to" the wife's income. In other cases it seemed understood that the wife was not going to be working regularly and, therefore, not making a regular contribution of a fifth or a third or whatever of the family income. In these cases the income contributed by the wife during the times in which she worked tended not to be spent on core, status-related consumption, but either saved for some particular future purpose or spent in ways that were individually meaningful to the wife.

In middle class families, the difference between families in which the mother works and those in which she does not is not so apparent in terms of the husband's traditional role definitions and highly obvious masculine involvements. It is possible that in the middle class the decision to work is much more an effect of the wife's choices and much less determined by the husband's preferences and demands. Middle class husbands feel threatened less often than working class husbands by a working wife, at least so long as the contribution to the family income is not too great. But in the middle class, wives' earnings are also often not built into the family's basic standard of living. So long as the couple do not define themselves as a two-career family, they tend to base their standard of living on the husband's expected earnings. The wife's earnings are used for special purposes, such as clothing for herself, saving for a child's education, sometimes for a special purpose which when satisfied causes the woman to leave the labor market, sometimes to help toward acquiring a luxury item like a vacation home. The most general conclusion that can be drawn from this study is that for a great many families in which the mother is a labor force participant, her earnings have a special role in the family economy and in no sense function to keep the family consumption up to a particular level. If this tentative conclusion is correct, then we should expect that the level of mothers' participation in the labor force has not had a major effect on people's conceptions of levels of living in the United States. That is, mothers' earnings have not served to inflate the consumption standards of adequacy, or poverty, or comfort which the public holds.

Much of the way in which families seem to use the income that wives contribute suggests the primacy of non-pecuniary motives. It is as if for many women the money were almost a by-product of a more important social and psychological gain sought from work, rather than essential to the work choice.

A similar exploration of the experience that female heads have in the labor market underscores the complexity of labor market participation for women (Anderson-Khlief, 1977). For solo mothers, there is no question about the importance to the family's well being of the consumption which earnings allow. But the many cases in which women work, despite the fact that their family incomes would be about as high from welfare alone, suggest that even here the matter is not simple.

Many solo mothers enter the labor market in a highly tentative and marginal way, particularly those who have not worked previously. Their lack of labor market experience, and to some extent their lack of self-conception as regular workers tends to direct them toward marginal jobs—waitress, clerical work, secondary labor market jobs in general. Their earnings are generally low. This, in turn, leads to the very common mix of earnings and government transfers.

Work is important to these women as a way of maintaining "self-respect" and of giving themselves a sense of a future and security. On the one hand, the demands of their children are often great enough that it proves very difficult to allow the work role to become a dominant one in their lives. Often women must change jobs in order to deal with family pressures of one kind or another. They often settle for jobs that pay less well or have poorer working conditions than they might otherwise have because of the press of other responsibilities. For example, if a woman must be concerned about being able to reach her children quickly if they become sick at school or if the babysitter suddenly becomes unavailable, she may accept an inferior job close to home rather than the better one farther away. In short, the centrality of the family role for the solo mother often makes it very difficult to treat the work role as important as the woman might like.

Of course, for many working class women the conception of a career is not particularly attractive anyway. It is more among middle class mothers that the frustration of the choice between primacy for the mother role and heavy investment in the work role is most apparent. Many middle class women seek to avoid these conflicts by acquiring training for one or another professional or technical job which carries with it working conditions and flexibility that allow her to be more successful in avoiding conflicts between the two roles.

When one looks at solo mothers' experience over a few years' time, one is impressed that for many of them working serves simply to provide just enough income for the family to get along when put together with other sources—child support and alimony, help from relatives, earnings of other members of the family, or government transfers.

The woman's responsibilities at home are very often such that she feels things have to be this way, that she cannot effectively commit herself to a career, and indeed, that it is not so important to do so as long as the family can live modestly by combining a number of different income sources.

Solo mothers quickly learn to have reduced expectations about their standard of living compared to those of families with male earners. Once having accepted that as a fact, and presumably having negotiated acceptance by those who are close to them (relatives, friends, children), the incentive for heavy commitment to work is much lower. For many solo mothers the real concern for the future is not developing a career that pays well but remarrying. American society would have to be differently organized in terms of child care and children's environments for most solo mothers to be able to make other kinds of definitions of their situation.

WORK IN THE TRANSITION FROM WIFE TO SOLO MOTHER

In the United States it seems likely that well over a third of mothers will spend some time in the future as sole heads of their families. As noted above, most of them will make use of earnings as a central, often *the* central, element in the family's total income package. It becomes an interesting question, then, what effect a woman's labor market experience during her years as a wife has on her income-getting strategy as a solo mother.

In one exploration we have sought to understand something of the dynamics of this transition (Farley-Marieq, 1979). This study examines families in which the mothers became the head. We were particularly interested in the mother's labor market experience and use of welfare as these have been influenced by the income status of the husband and by the woman's work experience while a wife.

We find strong effects on both the mother's labor force participation and her utilization of welfare, her husband's income level, and her own labor market participation as a wife.

We were interested in the development of the wife's income experience as a solo mother—specifically, the probability of her working in the first, second, third, and fourth year of solo motherhood and the probability in each of those years of her being on welfare. At the beginning of her period as a head, these mothers worked about two-thirds of the time. By the third and fourth year of their solo mother experience, about 80 percent of them had earnings.

The trend is contrary to that for welfare. A quarter of these women go on welfare in the first year in which they are female heads; by the fourth year only a fifth are on welfare. Since many of those who go on in the first and second year stay on welfare, this means that on average the probability of going on welfare drops rapidly as the woman establishes herself as a female head.

Both the husband's economic level and the wife's labor market experience have important effects on the probability of her working while a female head and on her probability of being on welfare. Almost all of those women who had worked at least half of each year in the three years from 1967–1969 continued to work as female heads. Amost none of them went on welfare. Those women who had worked at least half of each year for one or two (but not all three) years were also very likely to continue to work. For these women, the higher the husband's income, the more likely they were to have earnings and the less likely they were to go on welfare.

It is the women who worked less than half of the year in any year, or did not work at all, who were least likely to be labor market participants once they become female heads. This was particularly the case if their husbands were low earners. It is only among wives who did not work for a full year at some point and whose husbands had low incomes that we find a probability of working at less than 50 percent.

We find, as would be expected, that it is women from low income families who are most likely to go on welfare, particularly if they have not had regular work experience in the period just before the marriage broke up. Interestingly, among women from middle-income families, wives who had a pattern of part-of-the-year work are also quite likely to make use of welfare.

One gets a picture, then, of quite different situations of women moving into the solo mother situation depending on social class and personal work experience.

These results would suggest that to the extent that wives become more regular labor force participants they increase their possibility of having a stable and somewhat higher income situation should they become heads of their own families. For example, by the fourth year that they headed their own families, women who had regular work experience before becoming female heads had family incomes equal to 80 percent of their average family income while a wife. Women who had not worked at all had incomes slightly less than half that of their last married years.

WOMEN'S LATENT DEMAND FOR JOBS

The proportion of women who enter the labor force is to some extent a function of the number and kind of jobs that are available. If we wish to assess, therefore, women's interest in labor market participation, we cannot be content merely to look at what women do. We must ask what they would prefer to do. The European Community survey discussed above allows us to do this. There is some, though not quite comparable, information for the U.S. as well.

In Europe the proportion of women not in the labor force who would prefer to work is very high. Overall 57 percent of European Community women not in the labor force preferred to have paid work—77 percent of the single, separated, and divorced women, 55 percent of the married women, and 46 percent of the widows.[4]

Clearly the most dynamic influence of the preference factor is in connection with the desire to work on the part of those women who are not in the labor force. The survey does not tell us why, in fact, they were not in paid employment. We would expect that some are not working because they can't find jobs; they are "discouraged workers." Others are not working because they are concerned about problems of child care. As we shall see, a good number also have to contend with opposition from their husbands.

Overall, we do not find marked variations in the proportion of women who would prefer to enter paid employment by the number or age of their children, or by their own age. There are, however, important differences from one country to another.

"Labor force participation" status involves a considerable element of self-definition. A person who is not employed has the option of defining himself as unemployed or as "not in the labor force." Asking women who do not define themselves as "unemployed" if they would prefer paid work can be regarded as systematizing this issue of self-definition. We can think of three different categories:

1. Those who are not working and who would prefer not to work. We can say that in some sense they choose not to be in paid employment and are satisfied with that choice;
2. Those who are not working but would prefer to work. They are in some way constrained to remain out of the labor market;
3. Those who find themselves unemployed.

These latter two categories could be considered to represent "latent" and "overt" unemployment.[5]

Only 14 percent of Italian women were not in paid employment *and* preferred it that way. Germany and Great Britain and France come next with around a fifth of women 18 to 64 years of age in the not-working-by-choice category. At the other extreme, 42 percent of women in the Netherlands are in that category. For the European Community as a whole, the proportion is 18 percent.

Italy, France, and Ireland had high proportions of women who were not working but who said they would prefer to work—an average of almost 40 percent. This was true of fewer than 15 percent in Germany and Denmark. Overall, about 25 percent of European women seem to be in this category; an additional six percent declare themselves to be unemployed.

These figures give a rather different impression of national differences than we get when we look at the more traditional labor force attachment categories. From the latter it would seem that women in Italy, France, Belgium, and Luxembourg are not particularly attached to the labor force. But we find that in Italy and France there is a very large group of women who say they would like to have jobs.

I have combined the "unemployed" and "would prefer paid work" categories to get an overall measure of "unemployment." Italy, France, and Ireland are high with over 40 percent of all women in this category and Denmark and Germany are on the low end with only 16 percent.

One can also ask what proportion of all women who indicate an interest in employment in fact do not have jobs. Ireland had the highest proportion of unemployed women by this measure—61 percent. France and Italy were next with slightly over 50 percent; the Netherlands is fourth with 50 percent. Belgium/ Luxembourg and Great Britain are next with 42 and 38 percent. Germany and Denmark were at the low end with 19 and 22 percent.

It now is possible to characterize different types of labor market situations for women in these countries. In Germany and Denmark there was a high proportion of women interested in labor force participation (84 and 73 percent) and a very high proportion of them in fact had jobs (81 and 78 percent). In Italy, France, and Great Britain there was an equally high proportion of women interested in labor force participation (86, 80, 79 percent) but far fewer of them had jobs (48, 62, 47 percent). The Netherlands was at the other extreme with a relatively low proportion of women who were interested in labor force participation (58 percent) and relatively low proportion of those who in fact had jobs (50 percent). Ireland and Belgium/Luxembourg are somewhere in between with slightly higher proportions of women interested in labor force participation (67, 66 percent). Of those who are interested, the women in Belgium and Luxembourg do better at finding employment (58 percent) whereas those in Ireland who want work are the worst off in their ability to find it (39 percent).

I do not have data using an exactly comparable preference question for the United States. However, there are data for mothers in the 14–45 year age range who did not have a job and did not say they were looking for one, responding to a question asking whether or not they wanted a job (Bane, 1977).

Only 8 percent of married mothers and 22 percent of solo mothers who were not in the labor force indicated that they wanted a job. It is possible that differences in the phrasing of questions produced higher responses in Europe and lower responses in the United States, but it seems unlikely that the magnitude of the difference could be accounted for in this way. Married mothers in Europe were almost six times more likely to say they would prefer to get a job than comparable women in the United States. European solo mothers were over three times more likely to say they would prefer to get a job. If these differences are not a product of the different survey approaches, they are very intriguing. They suggest that in Europe the unmet demand for jobs by women is much greater than in the United States.

HUSBANDS' PREFERENCES AND WIVES' CHOICES

Obviously, it would be a very complex task to untangle the various factors involved in the fact that some women who say they want employment are not working. Traditional cultural and religious factors probably play a part in interfering with the realization of their desires. On the other hand, economic problems also play a part.

The one factor we can assess systematically is the opposition of husbands to their wives' desire to enter paid employment. The European Community survey asked women whether their husbands would or would not prefer them to be in paid employment. Among wives who were not in the labor force though they wish to be, 47 percent believed their husbands were opposed to their having a job.[6]

Countries vary in how often husbands are believed to be opposed to a wife's desire to enter paid employment. Though 72 percent of Italian wives who were not in the labor force would have liked to have jobs, they were opposed by their husbands over half of the time. The pattern was rather similar in France (48 percent opposed). In Ireland, on the other hand, where there was a high proportion of women who would have liked to go to work, far fewer (28 percent) believed that their husbands were opposed. Similarly, in the Netherlands, where a much smaller proportion would have liked to get a job, few perceived their husbands as opposed (24 percent). Ireland and the Netherlands stand out as countries with more accommodating husbands. In the other countries, over 40 percent of women who would like to find jobs believed that their husbands were opposed to their doing so.

We might well believe that husbandly opposition to wives' working serves as an important brake on their efforts to find jobs and, therefore, as a factor which tends to reduce the measured unemployment rate of women. In countries like Great Britain, Germany, and Denmark, the movement toward women working when they want to has proceeded fairly far along, and therefore, the level of latent demand on the economic system for women's jobs is fairly small. In Italy, France, and Ireland, on the other hand, that latent demand is great. The fact that in Italy and France, at least, such a high proportion of husbands are opposed to their wives working probably serves to reduce the demands on the economic system for women's jobs. If husbandly opposition is gradually diminishing in those countries, we can expect that in the future the pressure for positions for women will increase greatly.

CONCLUSIONS

Overall, our results suggest that (with the possible exception of the United States) there is still a large unmet demand for jobs on the part of women. It would not be unreasonable to conclude from much of the material present here that this demand is not motivated primarily by a demand for increased family income, but rather by a desire for the non-pecuniary gains which women can find in work. Having an income may be symbolic of these gains, but its instrumental significance is probably much less than we commonly assume.

Examining qualitatively the patterns over time of labor force participation by working women suggests that for many women, working at a job does not have the same significance that it has for most men. A minority of women in the United States, at least so far, seems to define their work as a central and continuing part of their social, personal, and family identity. Similarly, few women who are wives and mothers seem to contribute a high proportion of the economic resources used to establish their family's basic life-style and social status presentation to the rest of the world. The longitudinal data for the United States indicate that only nine percent of women who were wives and mothers for the nine years from 1968–1975 earned as much as twenty percent of the family income in at least eight of the nine years, and only three percent earned one-third of the family income in at least eight of the nine years. Three-quarters of these mothers were employed at some time during the nine years; their median contribution to the family's nine-year income was 10 percent.

One can conclude that there are two major transformations in women's roles, one involving the simultaneous participation by most women, at least from time to time, in both childrearing and work roles, and another just now beginning involving the deepening and intensification of work roles and identities. It is the minority of women who have made this second transformation that has attracted the most attention and commentary in the past few years—that the minority is visible should not make us overlook the fact that for the great majority of women workers, jobs are still a much less central part of their sense of identity than is the case with men.[7]

6

Housewives as Workers

Joann Vanek

Housewives are women who are or have been married and who have the responsibility of running a home. For some it is a full-time occupation; others also work in the labor force. In total, more American women are in this occupation than in any other single type of work. In 1974, 32 million women were not employed in the labor force because of their responsibilities at home.[1] In addition 20 million employed wives[2] and an unknown number of the nearly 7 million employed widowed, divorced, and separated women also worked as housewives.

Since the qualifications for this work are only a person's sex and marital status, there is a great deal of diversity among the women in this occupation. Their ages range from the teens through the years of normal retirement from work. They represent all social strata. They have different skills, training, and interests. And the families they serve differ in size and composition. Yet housewives also share important similarities, although not always the similarities people believe they share.

There are several important misconceptions about housework. People often think that housewives work fewer hours, at a slower pace, and less strenuously than other workers. Many believe that housework has little productive value. And some believe the present assignment of tasks between husband and wife is equitable.

Do housewives work less than others? They clearly use many labor-saving

Reprinted from Joann Vanek, "Housewives as Workers," in *Women Working*, ed. Ann H. Stromberg and Shirley Harkess (Palo Alto, Calif.: Mayfield Publishing Co., 1978), pp. 392–414.

goods and services, and they no longer produce as many goods for the family as they once did. Moreover, many married women have full-time paid jobs in addition to being housewives. These observations suggest that housekeeping in modern society must not be very time consuming. But facts contradict these surface impressions. The majority of housewives, particularly those not employed, continue to work as many hours at the job as women did fifty years ago.

Does housekeeping have productive value? It is not figured in national accounting systems and does not receive monetary rewards. Since no price is put on housework, people overlook its value. But housewives do contribute in important ways to both their families' economy and total economic output, although this contribution is not represented by the pricing system. . . .

Is the assignment of tasks between husband and wife equitable? In theory, although husband and wife work in different spheres, the labor of both is necessary to the family. The modern housewife, however, neither produces goods nor earns money, and her less tangible contribution to the family is often not recognized. This lack of appreciation creates strains on several levels: in a woman's self-esteem, in the relationship between husband and wife, and in the distribution of economic rewards.

This chapter considers how the occupational role of housewife has evolved during this century, what housewives do, and their status in relation to other workers.

TRENDS AFFECTING THE HOUSEWIFE'S WORK

Housekeeping has been changed by several modern developments: labor-saving devices, commercial goods and services, and urbanization. Housewives have had opportunities to reduce the length of their working day. If they do not now work shorter hours, are they illustrating Parkinson's law: Do women stretch out *the same work* to fill the time available to complete it? Undoubtedly housewives are no more immune to the Parkinson effect than other workers, but real additions have occurred in a housewife's workload. Many researchers have shown that housewives continue to work long hours because new tasks and new standards have been added to their job.[3]

Certainly the housewife's role at the turn of the century was quite different from what it is today.[4] Although her day started with preparation of breakfast for the family, she began by refueling and lighting the cookstove and carrying water from a tap outside the house. Whether breakfast was a hearty meal of meat and potatoes or a simple one of coffee and bread, the food was homemade.

After doing the breakfast dishes, the housewife turned to the family upkeep chores of the day. If it was Monday, she washed the clothing and linens by hand and hung them out to dry. On another day she ironed them with heavy irons heated on the kitchen stove. She had to filter the oil lamps and trim their wicks daily. The lamp chimneys and shades required washing every other day. She made the beds and fought to keep the house free of vermin. She emptied ashes from the cookstove and the water pan under the icebox. In addition, there were routine cleaning tasks that are still common today: dusting, sweeping, scrubbing, and emptying garbage.

If a family lived in the city and did not have an icebox, shopping for food was a daily task. The housewife cooked three meals a day, baking her own bread, cakes, and pies. After the evening meal, she turned to mending and sewing. Although most men's clothing was purchased, she made dresses and underwear for herself and her children. She also hemmed curtains and sheets and knitted scarfs, sweaters, caps, and stockings.

This routine was augmented by special tasks. For spring and fall cleaning, she had to wash windows, clean cupboards and closets, wash and iron curtains and drapes, take up and beat rugs and carpets and lay them down again. She also cared for the sick and the elderly among family members, neighbors, and boarders. Robert Smuts points out that these nursing tasks were far more extensive in the past than they are today.[5] Diseases such as diphtheria, malaria, and pneumonia occurred frequently in 1900, and without drugs illnesses lasted longer. Hospitals and homes for the aged were not reasonable alternatives for care; they were used only as a last resort by people without families or by the poor.

Changes in household technology have reduced the burdens of housekeeping enormously. In 1900 homes lacked electricity and running water; by 1930 about 60 percent of the nation's homes had electricity,[6] and by 1940 about 70 percent had indoor plumbing.[7] In the 1930s mechanical refrigerators, laundry appliances, gas and electrical cooking ranges, and a variety of canned and processed foods became widely available. In the 1950s automatic washing machines began to replace wringer-type machines. Automatic dryers and wash-and-wear fabrics were introduced in the 1960s.[8]

Where large rooms had been needed for cumbersome wood-burning stoves and metal washtubs, new appliances were more compact and allowed more flexible use of space. As Siegfried Giedion put it, homes in the 1920s and 1930s took on a streamlined appearance as bathrooms and kitchens became smaller, kitchen appliances were located in a compact space, and work areas combined continuous surfaces and easy-to-clean materials.[9] Modern households were consciously designed to save labor.

The migration from farms to cities also changed a housewife's work. In 1920 one-third of the nation's families lived on farms. Early farm families produced most of the goods they used. For example, in the 1920s they produced approximately two-thirds of the food they consumed.[10] Thus in earlier decades farm women tended gardens, kept poultry, gathered eggs, killed and plucked chickens, canned and preserved fruits and vegetables, cured meats, and made lard, cheese, and butter.[11] Urbanization removed these primary production tasks from the housewife's routine.

As the number of people living in the home declined, the housewife's work was reduced. In the early decades of the century, many families took in lodgers who added to the wife's burdens of cooking, cleaning, and laundry. As recently as 1930, 10 percent of the nation's families had at least one boarder.[12] Elderly relatives and adult children, even if they were married, often remained at home. Little by little these living patterns changed, and the "extra" adults left the family home.

Declining fertility also reduced women's work in the home. This trend was interrupted by the baby boom following World War II. But even during those years a change in childbearing occurred that reduced women's child-care and housekeeping responsibilities. Women began to concentrate childbearing into fewer years, spacing their children closer and often completing their families by age thirty. This new pattern together with the increased life expectancy for women meant that a smaller proportion of a housewife's life was devoted to caring for children.[13]

All these developments transformed a housewife's work, but the result did not always save labor. Although goods were no longer homemade, modern equipment was used, and people lived in cities, many new tasks took on importance. Shopping, servicing household equipment, and travel to do household errands became more time-consuming. Children could not be left to play unattended on city streets as they could on a farm. The smoke and grime of the city forced housewives to do laundry and housecleaning more frequently.[14]

The modern housewife had labor-saving equipment, but she was less likely to have paid help than her early counterpart. Between 1900 and 1970, the number of paid domestic workers dropped from one hundred to twenty-five for every thousand households.[15] Women were leaving jobs as domestics to take higher-paying jobs in industry.[16] . . .

Attitudes about what a housewife should do were also changing. As machines eliminated drudgery, housekeeping could be more challenging and presitigious. Women were urged to raise their standards of home and family care, to provide for more than the basic needs of their families. Importance was put on making "homes a place of beauty, culture and spotless cleanliness; on keeping husbands contented and happy and on insuring the sound emotional development of children."[17] These ideas required new work, such as interior decorating, daily cleaning and laundering, planning varied and attractive meals, and supervising, entertaining, and educating children. Housekeeping continued to be a time-consuming job, and it became a great deal more complicated than it had been.

An important force in redefining the housewife's job, according to Barbara Ehrenreich and Deidre English, was the "domestic science movement."[18] In precise terms this was not a social movement. Its only organization was a series of conferences held at Lake Placid beginning in 1899. The meetings were organized by Ellen Richards, a chemist, who, like many professional women of the day, was interested in alleviating the problems of modern family life, particularly the housewife's job. In the early decades of the century there was considerable interest in reformulating housework and educating women to do it well. Men and women in many different fields—academics, domestic science writers, social reformers—pursued this goal with crusading zeal. Their efforts are loosely referred to as the domestic science movement.

Its advocates saw housekeeping as a profession, one that required full-time work and considerable education and skill. They attempted to apply the principles of science and industry to the care of home and family. *Cheaper by the Dozen,* by Frank Gilbreth, Jr., and his sister Ernestine Carey, tells what it was like to be raised in a household organized according to these principles of efficiency.[19] Their parents, Frank and Lillian Gilbreth, were industrial efficiency experts, exponents of scientific management and an ideology called Taylorism that influenced industry in the early twentieth century. Taylorism advocated that managers analyze the work process and its component tasks in great detail and then reorganize jobs and work settings to achieve maximum speed and industrial efficiency from each worker.

The principles of Taylorism and scientific management were applied by the Gilbreths and others to the home. Housewives were urged to manage their homes as if they were modern industrial firms, calculating the most efficient way to do things. For example, they were told to count their steps as they went about daily routines, to measure the energy units expended in certain tasks, or to calculate the "happiness minutes" gained from various activities.[20] It is hard not to smile now at some of these instructions. The procedures did not in fact save labor or increase efficiency to the extent intended, because the household is too small a unit to benefit from a highly specialized division of labor. If the extreme aspects of scientific management did not take hold, others did. Housewives began to do a great deal of planning and record keeping. Today financial and medical records, recipe files, grocery lists, and scheduling of deliveries and repairs are routine work for housewives.

Domestic science also drew on scientific knowledge to improve home and family care. As Wesley Mitchell put it, progress in the art of housekeeping "rests upon progress in science—or rather waits upon progress in science. To secure the better development of our children's bodies we need a better knowledge of food values and digestive processes. . . . To secure the better development of children's minds we need better knowledge of the order in which their various interests waken."[21] Mitchell, whose credentials included the presidency of the American Economics Association, differed from most domestic scientists in that he saw the limits of what science could do for housekeeping. In his view, housework presented many unsolved problems and was often a matter of guesswork: "No doubt the sciences that will one day effect a secure basis of knowledge for bringing up a family are progressing but it seems probable that they will long lag behind the sciences that serve industry."[22]

The crusaders of the movement were determined to spread the principles of domestic science to housewives. The American Home Economics Association successfully lobbied for government money to educate women in principles of health, sanitation, and nutrition. Women's clubs organized centers to give advice to homemakers and to study and apply principles of scientific management.[23] Women's magazines devoted sections to the technical aspects of housekeeping. The popular press told housewives what their new role was and what environment they were to create in their homes. The *Ladies' Home Journal* declaimed:

> Home is a place of abode of persons bound together by ties of affection; a place where affection of parents for each other, for their children, and among all members of the family is nurtured and enjoyed; where genuine personal hospitality is extended; where the immature are protected and guarded. A place where one may have rest, privacy and a sense of security; where one may enjoy his individual kind of recreation and share it with others. A place where one may keep his treasures; where one may satisfy his individual tastes; where fundamental culture, consisting of customs, language, courtesies and traditions is conserved and passed on to the young. A place where regard for others, loyalty, honesty and other worthy character traits are cultivated and enjoyed, a haven, a sanctuary and a source of inspiration.[24]

At a time when technology was reducing many of the traditional housekeeping functions, the domestic science movement provided an ideology that upheld the value of housekeeping and even gave it new importance. But raising the standards of home and family care required women to spend as much time in new housekeeping tasks as they saved by using technological advances.

Certain family-related values still pressure women to spend long hours in housework. The flowery quotation from the 1930 *Ladies' Home Journal* is not out of date in substance to many families. Home is seen as a haven from specialized, routine work outside, a place where family members may satisfy their emotional needs and individual tastes. Thus, the housewife is expected to provide more than the basic food, clothing, and shelter. It is not unusual for a woman to prepare several different menus for a meal: one for the dieter, one low in cholesterol, and one for the children. Nor would a housewife usually complain about the extra work required to entertain her husband's or children's friends. The amount of time she has to spend is considered less important than the goal of giving individual care and attention to family members. Efficient service is not of prime importance in housekeeping.

In the new definition of the housewife role, particular attention was focused on motherhood. Changes in the norms about child care made its duties more important and time consuming than they were in the past. Permissive, rather than programmed, child rearing was popularly advocated in the years after World War II, as Dr. Spock[25] and other experts told mothers not to depend on a set of rules but rather to be sensitive to subtle changes in their children so they could guide them. Children now required a mother's constant attention, and motherhood became more time consuming. Women were told that these efforts were worth the time, since being a mother was a woman's most important role.

Another factor adding hours to housework is our consumer-oriented economy. John Kenneth Galbraith[26] and Staffan Linder[27] point out that consumption is not entirely pleasurable but also requires work. Goods must be purchased, serviced, and maintained. These tasks become more complicated and time consuming as consumption levels increase, and they normally fall to the housewife.

In summary, many different trends have affected the housewife's job. Changes in the structure of society (such as technological development, demographic changes, and urbanization) transformed housekeeping tasks, reducing some and adding others. Moreover, the very definition of a housewife's functions changed. New standards and new areas of care were added. Thus it is not surprising that time-use statistics reveal a uniformity in the time spent in housework for nonemployed women over the past fifty years.

TIME SPENT IN HOUSEKEEPING, 1920–70

Statistics of time on the job are abundant for most workers but not for housewives. Fortunately some information on the daily routine of housewives exists for earlier years as well as today. The early information was compiled by home economists as part of the general attempt, discussed above, to reformulate the housewife's job. Most of the studies were done in the 1920s and 1930s but a few were also conducted in the 1940s, 1950s, and 1960s.[28] The studies were done in land grant colleges under a set of guidelines developed by the Bureau of Human Nutrition and Home Economics of the Department of Agriculture. The other source of data I use here is the "1965–66 United States Time Use Survey," a study directed by John Robinson and Philip Converse of the Survey Research Center of the University of Michigan.

The Robinson-Converse survey is based on a national sample, but the early studies used limited, local populations and primarily rural women. The early data would normally be a weak basis for inferring national patterns, but there are grounds for believing that they can validly be used for such estimates. Even though the studies were dispersed over a wide area and over a forty-year period, the variations (that is, standard deviations) in time spent in housework turned out to be similar from study to study. In addition, since rural housewives worked under much less modern conditions than urban homemakers in their day, the studies with a rural composition could be taken as representing an even earlier period, extending the time span considered.

The records on homemaking activities are time budgets. A time budget is an accounting of everything a person does in some unit of time—a day, a week, or a month. It is difficult to study housework using other methods, such as direct observation of what people do or a woman's own description of her work. Direct observation is impractical because individual researchers would have to invade the privacy of subjects' homes for a long time period. And descriptions by homemakers cannot be controlled for exaggeration of the amount of work done. A time budget is more reliable because, although respondents construct it themselves, it lists all activities of a day, not just homemaking, and together they must total twenty-four hours.

Respondents in the Robinson-Converse survey kept a record of what they did in fifteen-minute intervals for a twenty-four-hour period. In the home economists' studies, logs were kept in five-minute intervals for a full week. I extracted housework from the listing of daily activities. Housework includes all activities connected with the care of a household and its members: food preparation and meal cleanup, clothing and linen care, home care, family care, shopping, household management, and travel connected with household errands. The original data of the home economists' studies are no longer available; only their published tabulations survive. I have compiled the early studies and tabulated the Robinson-Converse data to conform for comparison with the early research. Together these tabulations form a historical series on the time women spend in housework.[29]

The data show that American women continue to work long hours in housework (see Figure 6.1). Full-time housewives (married women with no

FIGURE 6.1
Time Spent in Housework
by Full-Time Homemakers, 1927–66

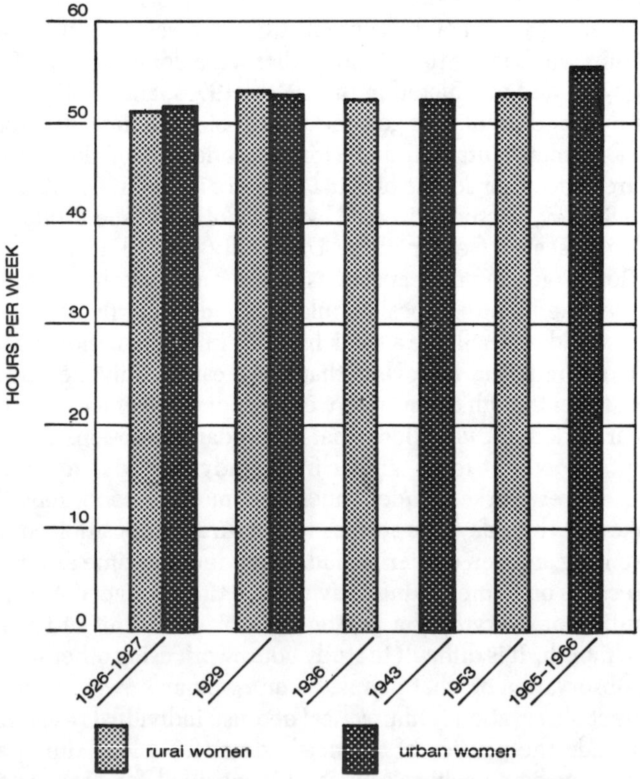

Source: From "Time Spent in Housework" by Joann Vanek. Copyright © 1974 by Scientific American, Inc. All rights reserved.

outside employment) have spent the same amount of time over the past fifty years. In the 1920s they spent about fifty-two hours a week doing housework and in 1966 they spent fifty-five hours. Throughout the period, the time spent has varied only between fifty-one and fifty-six hours.[30] All the changes affecting the household have not caused women to reduce their housework time. To take one specific change, urbanization, Figure 6.1 shows that urban women spent no less time in housework than rural women, even though they worked with more modern equipment and produced fewer of the goods used by their families.

The data show that the nature of housework has changed, however (see Figure 6.2). With labor-saving appliances and commercial products, food

FIGURE 6.2
Distribution of Housework Time by Task for Full-Time Homemakers, 1926–68

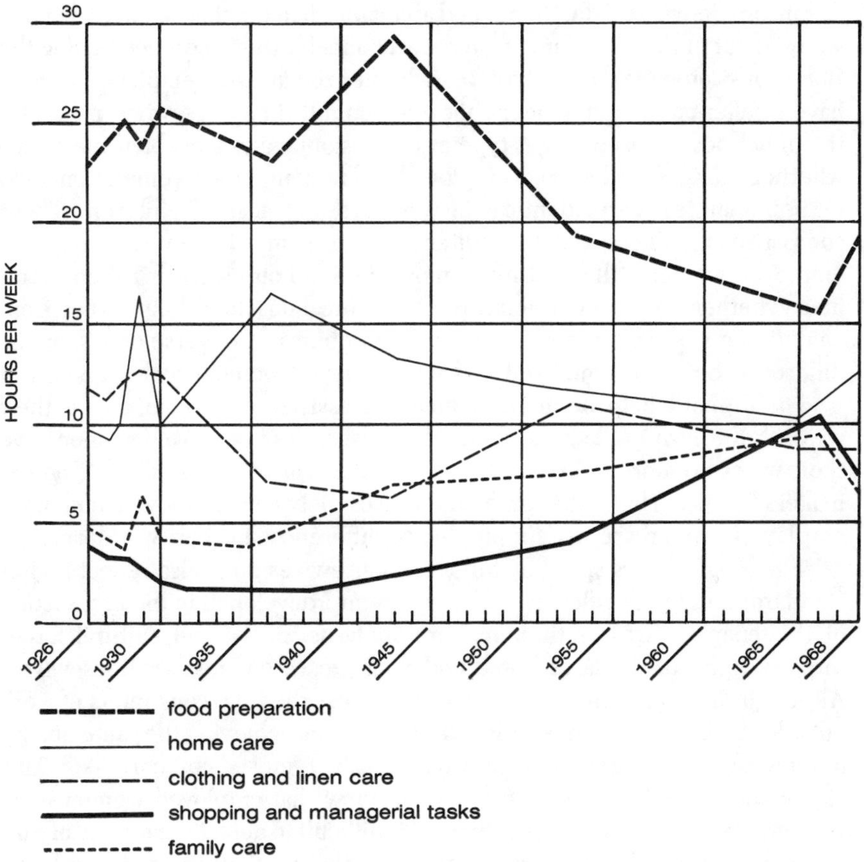

Source: From "Time Spent in Housework" by Joann Vanek. Copyright © 1974 by Scientific American, Inc. All rights reserved.

preparation and cleaning up after meals have become less time consuming. However, because of the consumption of commercial goods, the time spent in shopping and managerial tasks has increased. Time patterns in other tasks indicate higher standards. Housewives now spend more time on child care. An even more dramatic adoption of high standards occurred in laundry work, but this change is muted by Figure 6.2 because it traces the general category of clothing and linen care, which includes sewing and mending as well as laundry. The time spent in sewing and mending has decreased, undoubtedly because relatively cheap commercial clothing is now available. But the amount of time spent in laundry activities has risen even though modern housewives have running water, automatic equipment, and wash-and-wear fabrics. Families have more clothing and linens and wash them more frequently.

Of course, not all married women are full-time housewives. Married employed women spend much less time in housework. According to the Robinson-Converse data, they spend about one-half the time spent by women who are not in the labor force.[31] What accounts for this difference? Using the Robinson-Converse data, I explored whether the fact that employed women have smaller families and older children than full-time housewives makes for this much less housework. A type of regression analysis enabled me to see whether a difference between employed and nonemployed women remained if their families were identical in numbers and ages of children. These comparisons reduced the time differences to some degree, but the nonemployed women still spent much more time in housework.[32] I then examined whether employed women receive more household help either from paid workers or from their husbands. The Robinson-Converse data show no difference between employed and nonemployed women in the amount of paid household help or in the amount of assistance husbands gave their wives.[33] Kathryn Walker also found that husbands of employed women gave their wives no more help with housework than husbands of full-time homemakers.[34] . . . Thus, the time differences between employed and nonemployed women are not simply due to differences in their workloads.

The longer hours spent by full-time housewives must also reflect higher standards and lower efficiency. The argument I developed in the first section of this chapter stresses their higher standards. Social and cultural forces impose high standards of home and family care on modern housewives. Although these pressures affect all housewives, the time constraints of work outside the home prevent employed women from achieving the same quality of housework as nonemployed women. They must "cut corners." This explanation is overlooked in the popular view that employed women work with greater efficiency at home. Since it is difficult to detect the quality of care a woman gives her home and family, people see that married employed women have two jobs, not one, and conclude that they are simply more efficient workers.

THE VALUE OF A HOUSEWIFE'S WORK

Monetary values do not indicate the productive value of housework. Even though housewives are not paid, they contribute to the family economy and to the society's total economic output. A family could not live as cheaply and as well as it does if it did not have the services of the housewife. To purchase cleaning, meal, and child-care services is very costly. To forgo these services drastically lowers the family's standard of living. The work a woman does in the home stretches what the family's income will buy. Ismail Sirageldin estimates that about half of a family's disposable income comes from the unpaid work of its members, primarily the housewife.[35]

Is is commonly recognized that the modern housewife is a consumer rather than a producer of goods, but it is not commonly acknowledged that this contributes to the total economic output. John Kenneth Galbraith asserts "It is women in their crypto-servant role of administrator who make an indefinitely increasing consumption possible. As matters now stand . . . it is their supreme contribution to the modern economy."[36] Galbraith argues that economic growth requires high levels of household consumption. Someone thus has to spend considerable amounts of time "to select, transport, prepare, repair, maintain, clean, service, store, protect and otherwise perform the tasks that are associated with the consumption of goods."[37] Lack of time to do these tasks is one important factor limiting consumption. Usually the costs of maintaining consumption are ignored, because they fall most heavily on an individual whose time is not monetarily valued, the housewife. In Galbraith's term, she is a crypto-servant to her family and the economy, because her economic contribution is not recognized.

A number of researchers have attempted to put a price on the housewife's work. The National Bureau of Economic Research estimated that the value of housewives' services would add an additional one-fourth to the gross national product in 1918, and Simon Kuznets estimated a similar figure for 1929.[38] Calculations of Juanita Kreps for 1960 show that the forgone earnings of married women would raise the gross national product by over one-sixth.[39] Recent figures from the Social Security Administration calculate the value of a housewive's work based on her age. The average value is $4,705 per year.[40]

One basis for these monetary estimates is replacement costs—that is, the cost of buying the housewife's services in the market. Another is opportunity costs—that is, the money a housewife forgoes by working at home rather than in the labor force. Unfortunately both methods give arbitrary unrealistic estimates. The problem, as Carolyn Shaw Bell pointed out, . . . reflects "the basic premise of GNP—that its measuring rod consists of market prices and factor payments. It follows that where production—like housework or child care—occurs within a family rather than in a hotel or nursery school, there is no market price, no meaningful way to estimate one nor any valid wage estimate for the labor involved."[41]

Consider, for example, the replacement cost of a homemaker's services.

This is usually based on the average market wage for persons employed as dishwashers, baby-sitters, seamstresses, maintenance workers, janitors, and the like. But an individual family needs too few hours of each service to hire substitutes easily, particularly at the low market wages it could offer. Moreover, a housewife contributes in intangible ways to her family. The personalized care she gives cannot be purchased.

Estimates based on forgone earnings are also unrealistic. The labor force under present economic conditions could not employ all the housewives who now work full-time at home. Labor statistics classify "women not in the labor force because of household responsibilities" as nonemployed. If this were not so, in 1974 some 30 million women might have joined the already swollen ranks of the unemployed.[42]

Although it is very difficult to determine the real worth of a housewife's services, these services do have productive value. Failure to recognize this value has important consequences for the housewife's self-esteem and for the equitable distribution of economic rewards and work within the marriage.

THE COSTS OF WORKING AS A HOUSEWIFE

If people are esteemed for the kind of work they do, or simply for working, on what basis should society value a housewife? Neither a wage nor a visible product results from her work. In fact housework is noticed more often for its absence than for being done well. Moreover many of the tasks—cleaning, doing laundry, and dishwashing—merit little esteem even when done for pay. Is it surprising, then, that women say, "I'm just a housewife"? The expression, according to women studied by Ann Oakley, implies that housekeeping is trivial and low-status work.[43] Women do not tend to get a sense of accomplishment or competence from working as housewives.

They also are deprived of economic benefits. Housewives are dependent on their husbands for the rewards the economic system routinely provides to workers. Money, Social Security benefits, insurance, and Medicare do not accrue directly to the housewife for her own efforts. Although the modern-day ideal of marriage is a relationship of equality and sharing, the wife's dependence in the important economic sphere is conducive to subordinate, not equal, status. The effects can be felt in family decision making, in the assignment of household work, in the feelings of esteem of family members, and in the distribution of monetary rewards. People commonly believe that a marriage is functioning equitably if husband and wife share income and other economic benefits. When marriages lasted until the death of one partner, this probably was equitable, or closer to it than today. But now divorce is common, and the consequent division of family resources is not always equal under current procedures.

Consider, for example, Social Security. Divorced women may receive Social Security benefits based on the earnings of their former husbands under certain conditions. The conditions, according to Bell, emphasize dependency: "The marriage must have lasted at least 20 years and the man must have been providing at least half the support of the wife when he became entitled to social security."[44] An employed wife can earn her own benefits, but these are usually lower than her husband's. The discrepancy reflects the differences in their employment histories. Generally a woman earns less than her husband and works for fewer years. All the time she has spent working in the home does not count in Social Security calculations.

Another inequality in marriage occurs in the amount of work done. Ideally, husband and wife work equally although traditionally in separate spheres. When the wife enters the labor force the traditional balance is upset. In the 1950s and 1960s many analysts predicted that the employment of married women would change the traditional distribution of household tasks.[45] Equality between the sexes and greater sharing of home duties were expected to result. Research findings by Lois Hoffman[46] and by Robert Blood and Donald Wolfe[47] showed that husbands of employed women were more likely to share housework than those of nonemployed women. As Oakley observed, certainly logic was on this side: one consequence of women's employment *should be* men's increased domestic responsibility.[48]

Recent studies have contradicted the early view, however. Oakley found that housework and child care were still women's responsibilities.[49] Walker's time-budget data showed that husbands averaged about 1.6 hours a day in housework whether or not their wives were employed.[50] My work with the Robinson-Converse data showed no difference in the time spent in housework by husbands of employed and nonemployed women.[51] My tabulations were based on women's responses to the question, "Last week, about how many hours did [your husband] help you with housework?" The question is important because the discrepancy in findings between earlier and more recent studies probably reflects differences in their methods of research. Hoffman and Blood and Wolfe asked respondents about only a few tasks not about a sizable proportion of the household routine. And they gave no detailed information about the frequency of performance. The recent studies asked about "the actual performance of specific tasks over a particular period of time," and this produces the information needed to reach a valid conclusion on the degree of equality.[52]

The recent findings indicate that housekeeping continues to be women's responsibility in the division of labor in marriage. With paid employment, wives take on a second job and compress their housekeeping into fewer hours. Their total workweek averages about sixty-five hours.[53]

While this discussion has dwelt on the negative aspects of being a housewife, there are, of course, some very desirable features of the work. It is not highly regulated and is not competitive. The home is a pleasant work environment, and housekeeping is not segregated from other aspects of daily life. The housewives Helena Lopata studied found these aspects of their work satisfying.[54]

Some women prefer housekeeping to any other type of work. But all housewives confront problems arising from the way their work is rewarded—more precisely from the absence of certain rewards. The employed wife may suffer less from the deprivation of rewards, but the price she pays is holding down two jobs.

CONCLUSION

The role of the modern housewife is shaped by several dilemmas. Housewives work long hours, but they are not rewarded for doing so. Their labor has productive value, but it is very difficult to determine its worth in monetary terms. Solutions for these problems have been proposed for decades. The domestic science movement attempted to redefine the housewife's job, give it high status, and make it professional. In the nineteenth century, Norway and Denmark included the housewife's work (at a very low valuation) in estimates of national productivity,[55] but they did not persist in this policy. In 1924, Dorothea Canfield Fisher's novel *The Homemaker* described a man who exchanged work roles with his wife.[56] It took a physical injury for the husband to stay home legitimately while his wife entered the labor force, even though, in the story, the role reversal benefited every member of the family. Early feminists also attacked the housewife role. Charlotte Gilman, for one, urged communal organization as a way to free women for the pursuit of more valuable and satisfying work.[57]

Although proposals to change the housewife's status are not new, they seem to have a new momentum today. Again efforts are being made to assign a dollar value to housework. Kreps provides one statement of why this is necessary and offers an estimating procedure.[58] Feminist groups such as the National Organization for Women have taken up this cause, and new groups have been organized solely for the purpose of securing "wages for housework."[59] There are proposals for changing the system of allocating the benefits routinely given to workers and for granting Social Security credits for work in the home. Other feminists feel that women's status will not be improved until the housewife role is abolished. For example, Jessie Bernard advocates equal sharing of home and labor market work by husband and wife,[60] and Carolyn Shaw Bell proposes that we create the new occupation of consumer maintenance.[61] By including the services traditionally called housework and child care in the classification of occupations, important changes result. First, the economic contribution made by this work is recognized. Secondly, human and consumer maintenance will no longer be seen as the responsibility of married women alone, but something that must be done by people for themselves and others whatever the family or household type.

Women have worked as housewives for many generations. Modern life has changed this role, but it has not removed all the burdens and inequities.

Certainly part-time jobs for men and women, day-care centers, fuller sharing of family responsibilities by husbands, and a reformulation of Social Security eligibility would benefit housewives. But, as all these proposals indicate, improvements in the housewife's life require considerable change in the economic and legal systems as well as in the family.

PART THREE

The Impact of Occupational Conditions on Family Life

Introduction

Significant issues are currently being raised regarding the work and family roles of men and women. Managers are questioning corporate transfer policies requiring them to move every few years. Interest is growing in more flexible patterns of work such as flextime, job sharing, and the four-day workweek. Two-career families are grappling with the challenges and strains of combining two demanding careers with marriage and family life. Increased paid employment of wives and mothers is precipitating a range of shifts in the expectations and division of tasks associated with the roles of men and women. In this part of the book, we seek to understand the factors and processes underlying these issues. To do so we must look beyond economic roles to the structure and organization of work life and its effects on varied types of families.

In Part Three we examine how the structure and organization of work influence the shape and texture of family life. Time constraints and the physical separation of work from the family limit the nature and extent of family role performance. In addition, the physical effort and psychological involvement required by an occupation affect the amount of energy a worker has for family activities. For example, the emotional stress inherent in police work carries over into family life, causing stress and tension. Professionals and managers working long hours in psychologically demanding work have difficulty performing their family roles. In "Jobs and Families: Impact of Working Roles on Family Life," Kanter discusses several pervasive occupational conditions that affect families. Her analysis underscores the range of factors involved and their diverse effects on families.

In the next three articles, specific occupational conditions are singled out for more detailed attention—occupational self-direction (Kohn), amount and scheduling of time (Hood and Golden), and job transfers and geographic mobility (Gaylord).

Kohn approaches his analysis of the impact of occupational self-direction on families indirectly. He is attempting to explain social-class differences in parental values and practices by discovering the processes through which social class influences these values and practices. His article, "The Effect of Social Class on Parental Values and Practices," summarizes his extensive work in this area over the last twenty years. He begins by noting that middle-class and working-class parents differ in the relative importance they attach to self-direction and conformity as major values to instill in their children. Middle-class parents tend to stress self-direction by valuing responsibility, self-control, and an interest in why and how things happen. Working-class parents generally are more concerned with inculcating values such as obedience, neatness and cleanliness, and honesty.

Kohn explains these social-class differences by examining the conditions associated with the middle- and working-class occupations practiced by parents. Middle-class occupations are more often characterized by self-direction; working-class occupations are more oriented to conformity to external authority. This difference in occupational conditions accounts for social-class differences in parental values and practices. The conditions workers encounter year after year in their work shape their values and behavior as parents. Kohn's sophisticated logic makes his argument especially convincing. His research carefully documents the relevance of occupational self-direction for parental values and practices and indicates that the occupational conditions of men affect the values and behavior of other family members.

The amount and scheduling of work time influence the patterning of family life. The number of hours worked per week is quite long for many workers. Almost half of all workers spend more than forty hours per week on main and secondary jobs combined. Some professionals and managers work exceptionally long hours, often sixty or more per week. Limited evidence suggests that working long hours in paid employment is related to work/family interference and family strain.

It may be, however, that the timing and scheduling of work role activities have a greater effect on family life than the number of hours worked. Those who travel extensively or work evenings and weekends find it difficult to fulfill some aspects of family roles, including companionship with spouse and children, attendance at family and school functions, and participation in household duties. Shift work also has negative effects on family relationships. Husband/wife relationships are most affected among those on the night shift; parent/child relations often become problematic among those working the afternoon shift. In the selection, "Beating Time/Making Time: The Impact of Work Scheduling on Men's Family Roles," Hood and Golden report on two families from a case study of sixteen dual-worker families. In one family, the man's change to an afternoon shift intensifies time pressures and creates problems in his relationship with his five-year-old son. The same schedule has positive consequences for the other man, who is able to care for his two young children during the day while his wife works. Working the afternoon shift creates a closer father/child relationship in one family and increases conflict in the other. This article indicates the complexity of work/family relationships and demonstrates the need to specify the circumstances under which an occupational condition has given effects on family life.

American society has long been characterized by high rates of geographic mobility. Much of this mobility results from attempts to improve occupational status or obtain employment. Frequent moves associated with job transfers are often considered an integral part of moving up the corporate ladder for managers. Family responses to frequent moves vary considerably. In some situations moving is stressful for all family members; in others, families have little difficulty adjusting. It is necessary to consider the conditions under which moving is stressful. Factors that influence adjustment include the number and timing of moves, degree of family cohesion, ages of children, and the extent to which the wife has difficulty making new friends and transferring her credentials and contacts. After many moves, some wives give up trying to become part of yet another community and become isolated and depressed. Gaylord's selection, "Relocation and the Corporate Family: Unexplored Issues," considers a wide range of effects of moving on families. She also notes the limited nature of corporate services for transferred employees and makes a strong argument for greater corporate responsibility in this area.

These articles show us that a diverse set of occupational conditions affects family life. The effects of these conditions on families are also varied. The whole of family life is affected, including husband/wife relationships, parent/child relationships, and family cohesion and stability.

Most of what we know about the effects of occupational conditions on family life is based on studies of men. However, we can expect that these conditions associated with work also influence the families of employed women. It is difficult to assess the similarities and differences because of a lack of information regarding women. Research to date focuses on the effects of women's employment on family life. The studies do not deal with the range of occupational conditions just considered, the reasons for women's employment, the continuity of women's employment over the life course, or the degree of commitment women have toward their work. The next step in the research on women's employment and family life is to tease out the effects of these various dimensions of women's employment on families. The increasing continuity of women's employment and a growing commitment to work make these issues especially salient to the understanding of how women's employment is affecting and changing family life.

The existing literature is ably reviewed by Moore and Sawhill in "Implications of Women's Employment for Home and Family Life." They examine the economic independence associated with women's employment in relation to (1) the probability and timing of marriage and (2) the strength of husband/wife relationships. Economically independent women are less likely to marry and to stay married for economic reasons; the strength of the husband/wife bond derives from the quality of the relationship rather than from economic need. Changes are reported in the balance of power between husbands and wives, time spent by husbands and wives in household tasks, and the extent to which men can rely on wives to accommodate their career demands. Moore and Sawhill also document the effects of women's employment on the need for child care, sex-role attitudes and personality traits of children, and family size. They correctly point out the need for information on relationships between family life and specific conditions associated with women's employment.

Among families where both husband and wife are employed, a distinction can be made between two-earner families and dual-career families. The term *dual-career family* refers to families in which both the husband and wife pursue demanding careers. Two-earner families are those in which the husband and wife are engaged in occupations in which the income is lower, less psychological commitment is required, and economic need is relatively more salient. Obviously, the problems of managing work and family roles differ in the two types of families. Two-earner families are generally trying to manage the responsibilities of work and family with few economic resources and little flexibility. Dual-career families are more concerned with balancing extensive time and psychological demands with family obligations. Qualitative research on dual-career families over the past decade provides a fairly well-developed sense of the rewards and strains associated with dual-career families. We need more systematic research on these families, and we need much more information about two-earner families, an area neglected in recent research on work and family.

In some cases, the demands of two careers require that the husband and wife work in separate locations for a period of time, a somewhat extreme example of the effects of occupational conditions on family life. Gross examines a sample of husbands and wives in commuter marriages in "Dual-Career Couples Who Live Apart: Two Types." She points out that husbands' occupations frequently have required separations from the family; for example, among businessmen, politicians, the military, and professional athletes and actors. What appear to be relatively new are long-term separations caused by both husbands and wives pursuing careers. These separations are characterized by a complex mixture of rewards and feelings of guilt and resentment. The lifestyle appears to be least stressful among couples who are older, married longer, free from child-rearing responsibilities, and established in their careers. Although this pattern may be viewed as a logical extension of trends evolving in work and family roles for several years, attitudes and expectations regarding the roles of women at home and at work have not changed to the point that this arrangement is easily accepted, even by many participants.

Linkages between work and family roles go beyond the economic contribution of work to the family's sustenance and standard of living. Part Three documents that the organization and content of work roles also have pervasive effects on the nature and quality of family life. These effects vary according to the occupational status of husband and wife, the family status of workers, and the employment status of women.

7

Jobs and Families: Impact of Working Roles on Family Life

Rosabeth Moss Kanter

I come at the issue of families from a roundabout direction: the factory, the office, the boardroom, the hospital, the shop. It is in these work settings that, to a large, virtually unexamined and often unacknowledged extent, the quality of American family life is decided. If this assertion was true for the past, for the somewhat mythical pairing of breadwinner-husbands and secondary-worker wives, it will be even more apropos in the future, as ever large numbers of young women enter the labor force with the expectation of successfully combining marriage and a career. Thus, an understanding of work settings and occupations, or organizations and public polices may offer as much insight into the stresses, strains and challenges that families of the future will face as all the private decisions made by individuals about their relationships and households.

This is a particularly appropriate time to be looking at the dynamic intersections of work and family life, for many converging trends call attention to the nature of work and work organizations as determinants of the quality of life for individuals and families. In their concern for the increased well-being of citizens, national policymakers have recently focused attention on the impact of the structure and availability of work on the quality of life. At the same time [1978], Vice President Walter Mondale, while in the Senate, and others have turned attention to dilemmas and changes in family structure,

Reprinted from Rosabeth Moss Kanter, "Jobs and Families: Impact of Working Roles on Family Life," *Children Today*, March/April 1978, pp. 11–16. (Article based on an address prepared for the Smithsonian Institution's Sixth International Symposium, "Kin and Communities: The Peopling of America," held June 1977.)

arguing for the creation of a national family policy which would, in turn, consider the effects on family life of governmental legislation and organizational decisions. And a far-reaching investigation of the feasibility of attaching "family impact" statements to legislation is now underway in Washington, D.C.[1]

Such concerns derive from specific recent social changes as well as from a general interest in the quality of life. The women's movement and the increase of women in the paid labor force (especially married women with children) have focused policy attention on the work-family link for women and on the extent to which work systems make it possible to maintain effective participation in both worlds. A rise in the number of single-parent families has similarly directed attention to the question of bridging the two worlds of work and family. And these issues, of course, are of critical interest to those individuals who find themselves bearing major responsibilities in both domains—working mothers or single-parent fathers.

The late 1960s also brought a number of social movements that challenged the usual patterns of middle-class work and family life. There were groups concerned with some of the unfortunate human effects of contemporary economic organization such as pollution, blue-collar occupational diseases, executive ulcers and heart disease. Meanwhile, the development of the "human potential" movement with its focus on personal fulfillment and growth led to a variety of experiments—communes and work cooperatives—in which people tried to connect work and private life in very different ways, giving priority to leisure, personal expression and relationships rather than to career mobility. Indeed, the movements of the past decade gave rise to the common use of the term lifestyle and to awareness of the plurality of American lifestyles.[2]

Other public discussions have tried to promote a turning away from career striving as the dominant measure of individual success, although this is difficult in times of job scarcity and slow economic growth. Similarly, there appears to have been a revaluing of private family life on the part of professionals inside organizations as well as by younger people, particularly as the personal "costs" of overly work-absorbed careers have been made clear. Whether institutional patterns are actually changing in response, which is still unlikely, at least some relevant questions are being asked, and with increasing public legitimacy.

Several recent intellectual trends have also highlighted the importance of studying work and family life together. In sociology and economics, a revival of interest in Marxist theory and research has taken as a first premise that no part of modern life goes uninfluenced by the structure of capitalist institutions. Families as well as schools, in this view, take their own shape from the demands of capitalism for producers and consumers. Thus the family is one of the critical links in the capitalist economy, since it both produces "labor power" and consumer goods and services. Secondly, in psychology, sociology and psychohistory, a concern with the total life cycle has also led to interest in the variety of settings in which adults as well as children spend their lives as both family members and workers. (School is the workplace for children.)

Furthermore, a growing interest in adult development, in the stages of adult as well as childhood growth, naturally leads to questions about the ways in which people are shaped by and manage their multiple involvements in their private and organizational lives. The timing of events in both the work and family worlds has also begun to receive attention in the developmental perspective. (It has also been argued that historical studies of family structure also need to add this developmental focus on the family as "process," unfolding and changing during the life cycle.)

Developments in certain applied fields also pave the way for the examination of work-family linkages. In both organizational and social psychology (applied behavioral science and industrial psychology) and the growing field of family therapy, "open systems theory" has provided a useful perspective. Organization development has concerned itself with integrating social and technical aspects of work, and family therapy has taken as its central premise the notion that the problems of an individual must be seen and treated in the context of the total family system. The "open systems" perspective makes it possible to consider the inputs into each system from others in its environment.

Finally, the evolving character of society as a whole has made this a particularly good time to consider the relationships between work and family life. Growth in the numbers of people employed in white-collar jobs and service institutions and other changes signalling the "postindustrial society" have led such scholars as Daniel Bell to conclude that future economic enterprises will pay more attention to their "sociologizing" (human welfare) functions than to their "economizing" (profit-making) functions. But, of course, people come to work in organizations not just as individuals but also as members of private systems, such as families, that are themselves constrained by the policies and practices of organizations.

It may be that organizations of the future will have to pay attention to their effects on people other than those who work for them—on spouses and children of employees—and allow the needs of families to influence the decisions and shape the policies of the organization. Questions about day care, part-time work, maternity and paternity leave, executive transfers, spousal involvement in career planning and treatment of family dysfunctions—all difficult to raise at present—may become primary considerations for organizations in the future.

HOW WORK CONSTRAINS FAMILIES

One set of themes relating to the constraints work places on families revolves around time and timing—the scheduling of work and the timing of major demands. Especially in highly absorptive occcupations, such as upper-level management, politics or certain professions, which make time demands well beyond the 40-hour week and even draw other family members in as vital players in the occupational world, the limited amount of time left for personal or familial pursuits is a source of strain. Indeed, recent literature has focused on the corporate or political wife as "victim"—drawn into the public arena in a visible way but left to handle family affairs as virtually alone as a single parent.

But even in less absorptive pursuits, the timing of work events can have profound impact on families. The most egalitarian or "companionate" marriages seem to be found among lower-middle-class, white-collar workers, perhaps as a function of the greater temporal availability of husbands to share chores and act as companions to their wives. In other occupational groups, such as professors or executives, the spillover of work into leisure time can generate irritability and lack of attention at home.

Shift workers have other work-family issues to contend with, due to the way their hours affect the expected synchrony between work and nonwork events.[3] One study discovered that each shift carried its own characteristic family problems. There was more friction between husband and wife for night-shift workers and more trouble with the father role for afternoon-shift workers.[4] Shift work, in a study of a large midwestern company, produced added psychological burdens, in that workers could not establish regular eating and sleeping patterns. But for those preferring isolation, shift work relieved them of community and family responsibilities.

Night workers have not been carefully researched, but journalistic accounts and recent research suggest some of the family issues they face. For one night manager of a grocery store, for example, the major cost was the stress engendered by the limited time the family had to spend together and problems with his wife because of their limited social life, especially on Saturday nights when her friends were all going out. On the other hand, night workers may also be able to help with housework, errands and greeting the children when they come home from school. But when night work fosters a strong occupational community, as among craft printers, the family may lose importance as a focus of primary ties. In any case, such families have to organize their lives around the schedule of the night worker.

The examples of shift and night workers make clear that it is not only the *amount* of time available for family and leisure that is an issue but its *timing*. Since other family members have their own priorities and schedules, and since society makes certain events possible only at certain times, timing becomes important in determining the effects of working hours. Two-worker families, especially, must work out their scheduling issues. Husbands who are home during the day can more easily help with child care, even though wives who do the housework may feel they lose their "job autonomy." In one study, fathers with preschool children were reported to prefer the night shift, hoping to change to a day shift when their children began to attend school.[5]

One striking example of issues created by schedule problems is the failure of some experiments with a 4-day week. In 1958 an aircraft parts plant in California provided workers with one 3-day weekend a month, without a reduction in the total hours worked—once a month the workers had a free Monday. Despite initial enthusiasm, the workers voted to discontinue the system after less than a year. Some of their complaints make clear how much the *timing* of free time may have been at fault: the time was used for home chores that could as easily have been done on Saturdays, it was lonely at home on Mondays with everyone else at work or at school, and daytime television was designed for women and children. In other words, a lump of free time out of synchrony with the rhythms of the rest of the family and society may not improve the quality of family life at all.[6] As David Riesman suggested after reporting a 1957 Roper poll indicating some negative feelings about the 4-day week, housewives may not be eager to have their husbands underfoot on one of *their* working days.[7]

A different kind of time experiment, however, also makes apparent the intertwining of work hours and family life, but with more positive effects. The practise of flexible working hours or *flextime* (a word coined by Willi Haller in Germany) is now in widespread operation throughout Europe and is gradually being introduced in some United States companies. Within specified limits, employees choose their own hours. There is already evidence of its positive effects. (Among other benefits, when enough organizations in a community institute flextime, it lessens traffic congestion and cuts down on commuting time.)

In one survey of workers in a Swiss company, 35 percent (including more men than women) used the flextime hours for spending more time with their families. Married women tended to use their flextime hours to provide more time for domestic chores (in keeping with the highly traditional sex role allocation in Switzerland). Almost 95 percent of the 1,500 employees surveyed were in favor of flextime—45 percent because of the way it improved the organization of private life. Not surprisingly, married women with children were the most enthusiastic of all groups.[8]

For working women in traditional kinds of families, single parents with sole responsibility for children, or men who expect to share family tasks, flextime seems to permit a more comfortable synchrony of work and family responsibilities. Social policy as well as scientific knowledge would benefit from further research on the use and effects of flextime.

Work-related travel poses another time issue for families. If executive husbands and fathers have little time left over after their very long working days to be helpers to wives and companions to children, they are available *none* of the time when they travel. One researcher studied 128 managers and wives in a large multinational corporation for which extensive travel was a job requirement.[9] All felt burdened and stressed by the travel except two people—a single female manager and a man who used travel to escape from his family. The problems of the others included disconnected social relations, especially for the men; increasing responsibility for the wives, since virtually no areas of family life could be assigned to the husbands who were away so frequently; guilt on the part of the husbands for "deserting" their families; fatigue stemming from the travel itself; wives' fears of being alone; and extra worry for one another while the spouses were apart.

Other scholars have mentioned additional travel-related problems: infidelity and a growing gap in the knowledge and life experiences of husbands and wives. If fathers are often absent, the family system may begin to close itself off to them, making re-entry difficult. Important events may occur without them, and the person who has been family leader in their absence may not want to give up the role.

One solution to the travel problem would be to increase the work-family connection and find ways for traveling workers to bring their families along.

Another theme involving work and families relates to jobs as sources of reward—material and/or psychic. The rhythm and setting of work may affect its rewardingness, but these are not the variables considered important in linking work to family life. Instead, the important variables have to do with the prestige, money or exchangeable resources generated by the job. This line of reasoning lies behind the large number of studies of income or, even more frequently, of occupational prestige as correlates of lifestyle and family patterns. It is clear, for example, that income levels and unemployment affect marital stability.

Many social class analyses assign a rank or level to the husband-father's occupation and indicate what proportion of people or families in each group exhibits the predicted private behavior and attitudes. (While the groupings tend to be called "classes," the assignment of ranks in prestige as determinants of consumption style is actually closer to the Weberian definition of "status" than the Marxist notion of class as stemming from relationship to the means of production.) Research in this area remains compelling because of the large number of variables that show predictable patterning when gross occupational and income levels are differentiated, even though there is also a striking amount of variation within income classes.

In a dynamic extension of the reward framework, John Scanzoni has developed and tested an exchange theory of the effects on family cohesiveness of income and general location in the economic structure.[10] He argued that economic and psychic income from a job affects the presence or absence of marital tension. The more a man is integrated into the economic opportunity structure (as measured objectively by his occupational status, education and income and subjectively by his alienation or lack of alienation) the greater the cohesiveness of the family and of satisfaction with the husband-wife relationship, since the husband brings status and income into the family to exchange for services and positive feelings. Lack of integration, however, may cause the displacement of economic discontents onto personal relations.

A third way to approach work-family linkages concerns the cultures within occupations, cultures that are brought home to varying degrees. The assumption here is that jobs shape one's outlook on the world and orientation to self and others, that jobs are important socializers and teachers of values. For example, Melvin Kohn differentiated the nature of white-collar and blue-collar work as it might affect one's world view.[11] White-collar work involves the manipulation of ideas, symbols and interpersonal relations and blue-collar work, the manipulation of physical objects, which requires less interpersonal skill. White-collar work may be more complex and require greater flexibility, thought and judgment, with less supervision, while blue-collar work may be more standardized and supervised.

Kohn then predicted that these differences would be associated with childrearing values and practices—that is, white-collar parents would value creativity, self-direction and initiative in children while blue-collar parents would stress conformity and obedience. Many of Kohn's findings have been replicated, although class-based differences in socialization seem to have diminished during the last decades. The difference between fathers in the white- and blue-collar categories seems greater, in some research reports, than the difference between mothers.

The degree to which the gap between blue-collar and white-collar parents is closing is a function of changes in work, with much white-collar work becoming more routinized and machine-oriented, while blue-collar workers are growing into an affluent working class. Other influences outside of working conditions, such as those of the media, also play a role in closing this gap.

How parental values are influenced by jobs is only one question that can be raised about occupational cultures. How people change as they are exposed to occupational outlooks, and what happens when that change is not congruent with those undergone by other family members are others. What happens when occupational cultures are esoteric or mysterious and so help exclude family members from important parts of each other's experiences? Here work organizations play a part in determining the quality and ease of communication in the family, according to the extent to which companies close their doors against the family or attempt to create bridges between the language, technology and culture of work and that of the home.

The extent to which jobs and work form a culture, cultural outlook—and vocabulary—is seldom recognized. When a group of executives' wives at a workshop were asked to list words which their husbands used, and which they did not understand, more than 100 words were cited by the 12 wives present.

A fourth theme is related: the emotional climate of work. This is the way workers come to feel about themselves and their day, the degree of self-esteem or self-doubt they feel and the sense of well-being or tension which they bring home. There is some evidence, for example, that workers in low autonomy jobs are more severe and hostile as parents. There is also evidence of variation in preferences for leisure "release" among men in different occupations: advertising men, for example, need to "blow off steam" from their high pressure, competitive work. Yet, other people also argue that the emotional climate of work is *not* brought home, that people can behave very differently in the two settings.

Clearly the nature of the links between work experience and family life still needs to be explored. Many important questions remain. Does the family world serve *compensatory* functions for emotional deprivations suffered at work, or *displacement-of-aggression* functions? Does the family get the best parts of a working member's energy or commitment when these are not called for at work, as some research hints, or does it get only the parts left over from an emotionally draining job? Do people orient themselves to the family emotionally in the same way they come to approach their work?

The overwhelming tendency in social theory has been to assume that experiences of alienation at work result in negative consequences in personal life. Melvin Seeman has recently challenged this perspective, presenting Swedish data indicating that work alienation has few of the unpleasant personal consequences imagined.[12] Yet other evidence does make a case for the spillover from the emotional connection with work to other areas of life. People with boring work tend to have boring leisure, and people with involving work tend to have higher levels of both leisure and family involvement, even though the latter may work longer hours and bring home more work than the former. Blue-collar workers in similar occupations at the same pay level tend to be more democratic in their politics and more creative in their leisure when their jobs permit more control, participation and self-direction.

Too often in the past we have viewed families in a vacuum, as a realm unto themselves. Only now are we beginning to consider how public policy and such institutions as employing organizations may be responsible for what happens, or does not happen, in private life.

Structural rearrangements that provide people with more flexibility and options may be a first step in helping families. These would include the use of flextime; more flexible leaves and sabbaticals; greater availability of day care; income supports; explicit focus on communication about work events and work culture to workers' families; and reduction in the number of low autonomy low opportunity jobs that create emotional tensions at home. Major changes in the world of work and the structure of work organizations may, indeed, turn out to have more profound effects on the quality of family life than all the attempts to influence individual behavior.

Let us—the professionals—leave people alone to make their own decisions about their relationships. But let us also do what we can do effectively: work to reduce the constraints brought to them by other institutions that bind them to less satisfying, less relationship-enhancing ways of being.

8

The Effects of Social Class on Parental Values and Practices

Melvin L. Kohn

My thesis is straightforward and relatively simple: that there are substantial differences in how parents of differing social-class position raise their children; that these differences in parental practices result chiefly from class differences in parents' values for their children; and that such class differences in parental values result in large measure from differences in the conditions of life experienced by parents at different social-class levels. This essay attempts to spell out this thesis more concretely and explicitly.[1] Without getting into technical aspects of methodology, it also attempts to give some idea of the type of empirical evidence on which the generalizations are based.

SOCIAL CLASS

Since the heart of the thesis is that parents' social-class positions profoundly affect their values and child-rearing practices, it is well to begin by defining *social class*. I conceive of social class as aggregates of individuals who occupy broadly similar positions in a hierarchy of power, privilege, and prestige.[2] The two principal components of social class, according to most empirical evidence, are education and occupational position. Contrary to the impression of most laymen, income is of distinctly secondary importance,

Reprinted from Melvin L. Kohn, "The Effects of Social Class on Parental Values and Practices," in David Reiss and Howard A. Hoffman, eds., *The American Family: Dying or Developing*, pp. 45–68.

and subjective class identification is virtually irrelevant. The stratificational system of the contemporary United States is probably most accurately portrayed as a continuum of social class positions—a hierarchy, with no sharp demarcations anywhere along the line.[3] For convenience, though, most research on social class and parent-child relationships employs a somewhat over-simplified model, which conceives of American society as divided into four relatively discrete classes: a small "lower class" of unskilled manual workers, a much larger "working class" of manual workers in semiskilled and skilled occupations, a large "middle class" of white-collar workers and professionals, and a small "elite," differentiated from the middle class not so much in terms of occupation as of wealth and lineage. The middle class can be thought of as comprising two distinguishable segments: an upper-middle class of professionals, proprietors, and managers, who generally have at least some college training; and a lower-middle class of small shopkeepers, clerks, and salespersons, generally with less education.

It is probably unnecessary to underline education's importance for placing people in the social order, and it is self-evident that level of educational attainment can be treated as a quantitative variable: a college graduate unequivocally has higher educational credentials than does a high school dropout. But it may be less apparent that occupational position is also a major criterion of ranking in this—and in all other—industrial societies. One of the most important and general findings in social science research is the relative invariance of people's ratings of occupational prestige, regardless of which country is studied. This finding is of great theoretical importance in its implication that the stratification system is much the same across all industrialized societies.

As a methodological aside, I want to note that our knowledge of the stability of occupational prestige rankings is the result of a long series of studies by many investigators. The first major work in this area was a 1946 cross-sectional survey of the U.S. population by the National Opinion Research Center.[4] At that time, the American population agreed to a remarkably high degree on the relative prestige of various occupations: regardless of which segment of the population was examined, and regardless of people's own occupational levels, most Americans ranked occupations similarly, in a regular and nearly invariant hierarchy from bootblack to physician. Later studies showed that this pattern remained stable over the next quarter-century and that it applied to various specific subpopulations, even to children as young as 9 years of age.[5] Another major step in the process of discovery was a 1956 reanalysis of studies of occupational prestige in six industrial societies: the United States, Great Britain, Japan, New Zealand, the Union of Soviet Socialist Republics, and the German Federal Republic.[6] Extremely high intercorrelations (mainly in the .90s) were discovered among these countries despite their cultural differences and despite the inclusion in the analysis of a major noncapitalist state. The stratification system thus appears to be much the same in all industrialized societies. More recent studies have extended this finding to many other countries, several of them non-Western, several of them noncapitalist, and some of them nonindustrialized or only partially so.[7] The evidence for the universality or near universality of occupationally based stratification systems is considerable.

These facts are impressive in themselves, and they become even more impressive when we recognize that people's positions in the class system are related to virtually every aspect of their lives: their political party preferences, their sexual behavior, their church membership, even their rates of ill health and death.[8] Among these various phenomena, none, certainly, is more important than the relationship of social class to parental values and child-rearing practices. But it is well for us to be aware, when we focus on this relationship, that it is one instance of a much larger phenomenon: the wide ramifications of social stratification for people's lives. Any interpretation we develop of the relationship between social class and parental values and behavior must be applicable, at least in principle, to the larger phenomenon as well.

Social class has proved to be so useful a concept in social science because it refers to more than simply educational level, or occupation, or any of the large number of correlated variables. It is useful because it captures the reality that the intricate interplay of all these variables creates different basic conditions of life at different levels of the social order. Members of different social classes, by virtue of enjoying (or suffering) different conditions of life, come to see the world differently—to develop different conceptions of social reality, different aspirations and hopes and fears, different conceptions of the desirable.

The last is particularly important for our purposes, because conceptions of the desirable—that is, values—are a key bridge between position in the larger social structure and behavior. Of particular pertinence to our present interests are people's values for their children.

PARENTAL VALUES

By values, I mean standards of desirability—criteria of preference.[9] By parental values, I mean those standards that parents would most like to see embodied in their children's behavior. Since values are hierarchically organized, a central manifestation of value is to be found in choice. For this reason, most studies of parental values require parents to choose, from among a list of generally desirable characteristics, those few that they consider most desirable of all, and, in some studies, those that they consider the least important, even if desirable.[10] Such a procedure makes it possible to place parents' valuations of each characteristic on a quantitative scale. We must recognize that parents are likely to accord high priority to those values that are not only important, in that failing to achieve them would affect the children's futures adversely, but also problematic, in that they are difficult of achievement. Thus, the indices of parental values used in most of the pertinent inquiries measure conceptions of the "important, but problematic."[11]

There have been two central findings from these studies. One is that parents at all social-class levels value their children's being honest, happy, considerate, obedient, and dependable.[12] Middle- and working-class parents share values that emphasize, in addition to children's happiness, their acting in a way that shows respect for the rights of others. All class differences in parental values are variations on this common theme.

Nevertheless, there are distinct differences in emphasis between middle- and working-class parents' values. The higher a parent's social-class position, the more likely he is to value characteristics indicative of self-direction and the less likely he is to value characteristics indicative of conformity to external authority.[13] That is, the higher a parent's social-class position, the greater the likelihood that he will value for his children such characteristics as consideration, an interest in how and why things happen, responsibility, and self-control, and the less the likelihood that he will value such characteristics as manners, neatness and cleanliness, being a good student, honesty, and obedience. More detailed analyses show that the differential evaluation of self-direction and conformity to external authority by parents of varying social-class position obtains whatever the age and sex of the child, in families of varying size, composition, and functional pattern.[14]

This essential finding has been repeatedly confirmed, both for fathers and for mothers. The original finding came from a small study in Washington, D.C., in the late 1950s, but it has since been confirmed in several other U.S. studies, including three nationwide studies, one as recent as 1975. It has also been confirmed in studies in Italy, Germany, Great Britain, France, Ireland, and Taiwan. There are no known exceptions.[15]

The correlations of class with parental valuation of the individual characteristics (e.g., self-control and obedience) are not very large: none is larger than .20. The correlation of class with an overall index of valuation of self-direction or conformity, based on factor analysis, is a more substantial .34. But even a correlation of .34 is, by absolute standards, only moderate. What makes the class differences in parental values impressive is their consistency. It has repeatedly been confirmed that social class continues to be nearly as strongly correlated with parents' valuation of self-direction when all other major lines of social demarcation—national background, religious background, urbanicity, region of the country, and even race—are statistically controlled.[16] Social class, in fact, is as strongly correlated with parental valuation of self-direction as are all these other major lines of social demarcation combined.[17] Thus, social class, even though only moderately correlated with parental values, stands out as the single most important social influence on parents' values for their children.

Parenthetically, it is pertinent to ask whether there have been changes in parental values, especially in parental valuation of self-direction or conformity to external authority, over the few years for which data are available. The evidence, unfortunately, is equivocal. There is no substantial evidence that there have been changes, but also no conclusive evidence that there have not.

In any case, the magnitude of the correlation between social class and parental valuation of self-direction is as strong in the latest available data, a national survey conducted in 1975, as in earlier studies.[18] The class-values relationship is as important for understanding parental values in the mid-1970s as it was in the mid-1950s.

PARENTAL VALUES AND PARENTAL PRACTICES

We would have little interest in parental values but for our belief that parents' values affect their child-rearing practices. The evidence here is much less definitive than on the relationship of class to parental values, but what evidence we do have is altogether consistent. Parents do behave in accord with their values in the two important realms where the question has been studied: in their disciplinary practices and in the allocation of parental responsibilities for imposing constraints on, and providing emotional support for, their children.

DISCIPLINARY PRACTICES

Most early research on class differences in disciplinary practices was directed toward learning whether working-class parents typically employ techniques of punishment different from those used by the middle class. In his definitive review of the research literature on social class and family relationships through the mid-1950s, Bronfenbrenner (1958, p.424) summarized the results of the several relevant studies as indicating that "working-class parents are consistently more likely to employ physical punishment, while middle-class families rely more on reasoning, isolation, appeals to guilt, and other methods involving the threat of loss of love." This conclusion has been challenged in later research.[19] Whether or not it is still true, the difference in middle- and working-class parents' propensity to resort to physical punishment certainly never has been great.

For our purposes, in any case, the crucial question is not which disciplinary method parents prefer but when and why they use one or another method of discipline. The early research tells us little about the when and why of discipline; most investigators had relied on parents' generalized statements about their usual or their preferred methods of dealing with disciplinary problems, irrespective of what the particular problem might be. But surely not all disciplinary problems evoke the same kind of parental response. In some sense, after all, the punishment fits the crime. Under what conditions do parents of a given social class punish their children physically, reason with them, isolate them—or ignore their actions altogether?

Recent studies have shown that neither middle- nor working-class parents resort to punishment as a first recourse when their children misbehave.[20] It seems instead that parents of both social classes initially post limits for their children. But when children persist in misbehavior, parents are likely to resort to one or another form of coercion. This is true of all social-class levels. The principal difference between the classes is in the specific conditions under which parents—particularly mothers—punish children's misbehavior. Working-class parents are more likely to punish or refrain from punishing on the same basis of the direct and immediate consequences of children's actions, middle-class parents on the basis of their interpretation of children's intent in acting as they do.[21] Thus, for example, working-class parents are more likely to punish children for fighting than for arguing with their brothers and sisters and are also more likely to punish for aggressively wild play than for boisterousness—the transgression in both instances being measured in terms of how far the overt action transgresses the rules. Middle-class parents make no such distinction. But they do distinguish, for example, between wild play and a loss of temper, tolerating even excessive manifestations of the former as a childish form of emotional expression, but punishing the latter because it signifies a loss of mastery over self.

To say that working-class parents respond more to the consequences of children's misbehavior and middle-class parents more to their own interpretation of the children's intent gets dangerously close to implying that while middle-class parents act on the basis of long-range goals for children, working-class parents do not. On the contrary, the evidence suggests that parents of both social classes act on the basis of long-range goals—but that the goals are different. The interpretive key is provided by our knowledge of class differences in parental values. Because middle- and working-class parents differ in their values, they view children's misbehavior differently; what is intolerable to parents in one social class can be taken in stride by parents in the other. In both social classes, parents punish children for transgressing important values, but since the values are different, the transgressions are differently defined. If self-direction is valued, transgressions must be judged in terms of the reasons why the children misbehave. If conformity to external authority is valued, transgressions must be judged in terms of whether or not the actions violate externally imposed proscriptions.

THE ALLOCATION OF PARENTAL RESPONSIBILITIES FOR SUPPORT AND CONSTRAINT

The connection between values and punishment of disvalued behavior is direct: punishment is invoked when values are transgressed. There are also less direct but broader behavioral consequences of class differences in parental values. In particular, class differences in parental values have important consequences for the overall patterning of parent-child interaction.

In common with most investigators, I conceive of parent-child relationships as structured along two principal axes: support and constraint. This conception is derived in part from Parsons and Bales's (1955) theoretical analysis of family structure and in part from Schaefer's (1959) empirical demonstration that the findings of several past studies of parent-child relationships could be greatly clarified by arraying them along these two dimensions.

Because their values are different, middle- and working-class parents evaluate differently the relative importance of support and constraint in child rearing. One would expect middle-class parents to feel a greater obligation to be supportive, if only because of their concern about children's internal dynamics. Working-class parents, because of their higher valuation of conformity to external rules, should put greater emphasis upon the obligation to impose constraints. We should therefore expect the ratio of support to constraint in parents' handling of their children to be higher in middle-class than in working-class families. And this, according to Bronfenbrenner (1958, p. 425), is precisely what has been shown in those studies that have dealt with the overall relationship of parents to child:

> Parent-child relationships in the middle class are consistently reported as more acceptant and equalitarian, while those in the working class are oriented toward maintaining order and obedience. Within this context, the middle class has shown a shift away from emotional control toward freer expression of affection and greater tolerance of the child's impulses and desires.

Whatever relative weight parents give to support and constraint, the process of child rearing requires both. These responsibilities can, however, be apportioned between mother and father in any of several ways. Mothers can specialize in providing support, fathers in imposing constraints; both parents can play both roles more-or-less equally; mothers can monopolize both roles, with fathers playing little part in child rearing; and there are other possible, but less likely, arrangements. Given their high valuation of self-direction, middle-class parents—mothers and fathers both—should want fathers to play an important part in providing support to the children. It would seem more appropriate to working-class parents' high valuation of conformity to external authority that fathers' obligations should center on the imposition of constraints.

The pertinent studies show that in both the middle class and the working class, mothers would prefer to have their husbands play a role that facilitates children's development of a valued characteristic.[22] To middle-class mothers, it is important that children be able to decide for themselves how to act and that they have the personal resources to act on these decisions. In this conception, fathers' responsibility for imposing constraints is secondary to their responsibility for being supportive; in the minds of some middle-class mothers, for fathers to take a major part in imposing constraints interferes with their ability to be supportive. To working-class mothers, on the other hand, it is more important that children conform to externally imposed rules. In this conception, the fathers' primary responsibility is to guide and direct the children. Constraint is accorded far greater value than it has for the middle class.

Most middle-class fathers seem to share their wives' views of fathers' responsibilities toward sons and act accordingly.[23] They accept less responsibility for being supportive of daughters—apparently feeling that this is more properly the mothers' role. But many working-class fathers do not accept the obligations their wives would have them assume, either toward sons or toward daughters.[24] These men do not see the constraining role as any less important than their wives do, but many of them see no reason why fathers should have to shoulder this responsibility. From their point of view, the important thing is that children be taught what limits they must not transgress. It does not particularly matter who does the teaching, and since mothers have primary responsibility for child care, the job should be theirs. Of course, there will be occasions when fathers have to backstop their wives. But there is no ideological imperative that makes it the fathers' responsibility to assume an important part in child rearing. As a consequence, many working-class fathers play little role in child rearing, considering it to be their wives' proper responsibility.[25]

Theories of personality development, including Parsons and Bales's (1955) sociological reinterpretation of the classical Freudian developmental sequence, have generally been based on the model of a family in which the mothers' and fathers' intrafamily roles are necessarily differentiated, with mothers specializing in support and fathers in constraint.[26] However useful a first approximation this may be, both middle- and working-class variations on this general theme are sufficiently great to compel a more precise formulation.

The empirical evidence is partly consistent with the mother-supportive, father-constraining formulation, for even in middle-class families, almost no one reports that fathers are more supportive than mothers. Yet, in a sizable proportion of middle-class families, mothers take primary responsibility for imposing constraints on sons, and fathers are at least as supportive as mothers. And although middle-class fathers are not likely to be as supportive of daughters as their wives are, it cannot be said that fathers typically specialize in constraint, even with daughters.

It would be a gross exaggeration to say that middle-class fathers have abandoned the prerogatives and responsibilities of authority in favor of being friends and confidants to their sons. Yet the historical drift is probably from primary emphasis on imposing constraints to primary emphasis on support.[27] In any event, mothers' and fathers' roles are not sharply differentiated in most middle-class families; both parents tend to be supportive. Such division of functions as exists is chiefly a matter of each parent's taking special responsibility for being supportive of the children of the parent's own sex.

Mothers' and fathers' roles are more sharply differentiated in working-class families, with mothers almost always being the more supportive. Yet, despite the high valuation put on the constraining function, fathers do not necessarily specialize in setting limits, even for sons. In some working-class families, mothers specialize in support, fathers in constraint; in many others, the division of responsibilities is for the mothers to raise the children, the fathers to provide the wherewithal. This pattern of role allocation probably is and has been far more prevalent in American society than the formal theories of personality development have recognized.

SOCIAL CLASS, VALUES, AND CONDITIONS OF LIFE

There are, then, remarkably consistent relationships between social class and parental values and behavior. But we have not yet touched on the question: Why do these relationships exist? In analytic terms, the task is to discover which of the many conditions of life associated with class position are most pertinent for explaining why class is related to parental values. Since many of the relevant conditions are implicated in people's occupational lives, our further discussion is focused on one crucial set of occupational conditions: those that determine how much opportunity people have to exercise self-direction in their work.

The principal hypothesis that has guided this line of research is that class-correlated differences in people's opportunities to exercise occupational self-direction—that is, to use initiative, thought, and independent judgment in work—are basic to class differences in parental values. Few other conditions of life are so closely bound up with social class position as are those that determine how much opportunity, even necessity, people have for exercising self-direction in their work. Moreover, there is an appealing simplicity to the supposition that the experience of self-direction in so central a realm of life as work is conducive to valuing self-direction, off as well as on the job, and to seeing the possibilities for self-direction not only in work but also in other realms of life.

Although many conditions of work are either conducive to or deterrent of the exercise of occupational self-direction, three in particular are critical.

First, a limiting condition: people cannot exercise occupational self-direction if they are closely supervised. Not being closely supervised, however, does not necessarily mean that people are required—or even free—to use initiative, thought, and independent judgment; it depends on how complex and demanding is their work.

A second condition for occupational self-direction is that work allow a variety of approaches; otherwise the possibilities for exercising initiative, thought, and judgment are seriously limited. The organization of work must not be routinized; it must involve a variety of tasks that are in themselves complexly structured.

The third and most important determinant of occupational self-direction is that work be substantively complex. By the *substantive complexity* of work I mean, essentially, the degree to which performance of that work requires thought and independent judgment. All work involves dealing with things, with data, or with people; some jobs involve all three, others only one or two of these activities. Work with things can vary in complexity from ditch-digging to sculpturing; similarly, work with people can vary in complexity from receiving simple instructions to giving legal advice; and work with data can vary from reading instructions to synthesizing abstract conceptual systems. Although, in general, work with data or with people is likely to be more complex than work with things, this is not always the case, and an index of the overall complexity of work should reflect its degree of complexity in each of these three types of activity. What is important about work is not whether it deals with things, with data, or with people, but its complexity.

No one of these occupational conditions—freedom from close supervision, nonroutinization, and substantive complexity—is definitional of occupational self-direction. Nevertheless, each of these three conditions tends to be conducive to the exercise of occupational self-direction, and the combination of the three both enables and requires it. Insofar as people are free of close supervision, work at nonroutinized tasks, and do substantively complex work, their work is necessarily self-directed. And insofar as they are subject to close supervision, work at routinized tasks, and do work of little substantive complexity, their work does not permit self-direction.

THE RELATIONSHIP OF OCCUPATIONAL SELF-DIRECTION TO PARENTAL VALUES

Since most of the research on the relationship between occupational self-direction and parental values deals only with men's occupational conditions and men's values, I shall first discuss fathers' values, then broaden the discussion to include mothers' values as well. All three occupational conditions that are determinative of occupational self-direction prove to be empirically related to fathers' values.[28] Men who are free from close supervision, who work at nonroutinized tasks, and who do substantively complex work tend to value self-direction rather than conformity to external authority for their children. This being the case, it becomes pertinent to ask whether the relationship between social class and fathers' values can be explained as resulting from class differences in the conditions that make for occupational self-direction.

It must be emphasized that in dealing with these occupational conditions, we are concerned not with distinctions that cut across social class but with experiences constitutive of class. The objective is to learn whether these constitutive experiences are pertinent for explaining the class relationship. To achieve this objective, we statistically control occupational dimensions that have proved to be related to values and orientation, to determine whether this reduces the correlation between class and fathers' valuation of self-direction or conformity for their children. This procedure is altogether hypothetical, for it imagines an unreal social situation: social classes that did not differ from one another in the occupational conditions experienced by their members. But it is analytically appropriate to use such hypothetical procedures, for it helps us differentiate those occupational conditions that are pertinent for explaining the relationship of class to parental values from those occupational conditions that are not pertinent. In fact, statistically controlling the conditions that make for occupational self-direction reduces the correlation of class to fathers' valuation of self-direction or conformity by nearly two thirds.[29] The lion's share of the reduction is attributable to the substantive complexity of the work, but closeness of supervision and routinization are relevant too. By contrast, though, statistically controlling numerous other occupational conditions has a much weaker effect—reducing the class correlation by only one-third.[30] And controlling both sets of occupational conditions reduces the correlation of class to fathers' values by no more than does controlling occupational self-direction alone. Thus, other occupational conditions add little to the explanatory power of the three that are determinative of occupational self-direction.

These findings come mainly from a cross-national study in the United States.[31] They are confirmed by a smaller-scale study in Turin, Italy.[32] A study in Taiwan failed to confirm these findings, but it is impossible to say whether this is because occupational conditions have different consequences in that partially industrialized, non-Western society, or because methodological problems of the Taiwanese study may have obscured the phenomenon.[33] A number of other pertinent but not entirely comparable studies—in Peru, West Germany, Ireland, and the United States—tend to confirm the original U.S. and Italian findings.[34] But definitive confirmation awaits the completion of studies now in progress in Ireland, Poland, and West Berlin.

Much less is known about the relationship between occupational conditions and mothers' values. My colleagues and I are currently analyzing data on the relationship between employed mothers' occupational conditions and their values for their children.[35] Preliminary results indicate that women's occupational conditions affect their values in much the same way as do men's occupational conditions. We are also investigating the relationship between housework, conceptualized in essentially the same way as any other work, and parental values, but on this issue we do not yet have findings. There is information from a study in Turin, Italy, that men's occupational conditions affect their wives' values; this appears to be particularly the case in the middle class.[36] But these data say nothing about the mechanisms by which men's occupational conditions affect their wives' values—it may be that men's occupational conditions affect their own values and that men influence their wives; it may be that men communicate something of their occupational experience to their wives and that this knowledge affects the wives' value choices; or it may be any of several other possibilities. These questions, too, are currently being studied in research that attempts to unravel the processes by which each spouse's occupational conditions affect the other's values. Clearly, much remains to be learned. But even now, there is every reason to believe that women's values are affected by class-associated conditions of life through processes similar to those operating for men.

Because the relationship between exercising self-direction on the job and valuing self-direction for children is so direct, one might conclude that parents are simply preparing their children for the occupational life to come. I believe, rather, that parents come to value self-direction or conformity as virtues in their own right, not simply as means to occupational goals. One important piece of evidence buttresses this impression: studies in both the United States and Italy show that the relationship between men's occupational experiences and their values is the same for daughters as for sons, yet it is hardly likely (especially in Italy) that most fathers think their daughters will have occupational careers comparable to those of their sons. It would thus seem that occupational experience helps structure parents' views not only of the occupational world but of social reality in general.

THE DIRECTION OF CAUSAL EFFECTS

It could be argued that the empirical interrelationships of social class, occupational self-direction, and parental values reflect the propensity of people who value self-direction to seek out jobs that offer them an opportunity to be self-directed in their work and, once in a job, to maximize whatever opportunities the job allows for exercising self-direction. But we know that occupational choice is limited by educational qualifications, which in turn are greatly affected by the accidents of family background, economic circumstances, and available social resources. Moreover, the opportunity to exercise self-direction in one's work is circumscribed by job requirements. Thus, an executive must do complex work with data or with people; he cannot be closely supervised; and his tasks are too diverse to be routinized—to be an executive requires some substantial self-direction. Correspondingly, to be a semi-skilled factory worker precludes much self-direction. The substance of one's work cannot be especially complex; one cannot escape some measure of supervision; and if one's job is to fit into the flow of other people's work, it must necessarily be routinized. The relationship between being self-directed in one's work and holding self-directed values would thus seem to result not just from self-directed people's acting according to their values but also from job experiences affecting these very values.

This, of course, is an *a priori* argument. But we also have empirical evidence that the most important of the three occupational conditions determinative of occupational self-direction—the substantive complexity of the work—actually does have a causal impact on parental values.[37] This evidence is based on a statistical technique called *two-stage least-squares,* which was developed by econometricians for analyzing reciprocal effects. With this technique, it has been shown that the substantive complexity of work has a causal effect not only on parental values but on people's values and orientation generally, even on their intellectual functioning. These effects are independent of the selection processes that draw men into particular fields of work and independent of men's efforts to mold their jobs to fit their needs and values. Admittedly, cross-sectional data cannot provide definitive evidence of causality—only analyses of longitudinal data measuring real change in real people can be definitive. Nevertheless, these findings do establish a strong *prima facie* case that the substantive complexity of work has a real and meaningful effect on parental values and also on a very wide range of psychological processes.

More definitive, albeit less extensive, evidence comes from longitudinal analyses currently in process.[38] Analyses of longitudinal data are immensely difficult because they require the development of "measurement models" that separate unreliability of measurement from real change in the phenomena studied. Such measurement models have thus far been constructed for substantive complexity and for one facet of psychological functioning: intellectual flexibility. The latter was chosen precisely because it appeared to offer the toughest test: intellectual flexibility is obviously pertinent to job placement, and it might be expected to be one of the most stable psychological phenomena.

Stable it certainly is. The correlation between the men's intellectual flexibility 10 years later, shorn of measurement error, is .93. Nevertheless, the effect of the substantive complexity of work on intellectual flexibility is striking—on the order of one-fourth as great as the effect of the men's earlier levels of intellectual flexibility. Since this analysis is based on men no younger than 26 years of age, who are at least 10 years into their occupational careers, the effect of the substantive complexity of the job on intellectual flexibility is indeed impressive.

The longitudinal analysis demonstrates also something that no cross-sectional analysis could show—that, over time, the relationship between substantive complexity and intellectual flexibility is truly reciprocal. Substantive complexity has a more immediate effect on intellectual flexibility: today's job demands affect today's thinking processes. Intellectual flexibility, by contrast, has a delayed effect on substantive complexity: today's intellectual flexibility has scant effect on today's job demands, but it will have a sizable effect on the further course of one's career. Cross-sectional analyses portray only part of this process, making it seem as if the relationship between the substantive complexity of work and psychological functioning were mainly unidirectional, with work affecting psychological functioning but not the reverse. Longitudinal analysis portrays a more intricate and more interesting, truly reciprocal, process.

Granted, the research has not yet demonstrated that substantive complexity directly affects parental values. Still, because of its remarkable stability, intellectual flexibility offers the crucial test of the hypothesis that the substantive complexity of work actually has a causal effect on psychological functioning. Moreover, intellectual flexibility is intimately related to valuation of self-direction. It is, in fact, an important link between social class and parents' valuation of self-direction or conformity to external authority.[39] Thus, demonstrating the causal impact of substantive complexity on intellectual flexibility gives us every reason to expect substantive complexity to have a causal impact on parental values too. Further analyses will assess this hypothesized causal impact of substantive complexity—and of other determinants of occupational self-direction—on parental values and also on self-conception and social orientation.

THE ROLE OF EDUCATION IN THE RELATIONSHIP BETWEEN SOCIAL CLASS AND PARENTAL VALUES

Education matters for parental values in part because it is an important determinant of occupational conditions. A major reason for looking to such occupational conditions as substantive complexity, closeness of supervision, and routinization as possible keys to understanding the relationship between social class and parental values is that few other conditions of life are so closely related to educational attainment. This explanation has been confirmed in further analyses that have assessed the effects of education on occupational conditions at each stage of career. Education is a prime determinant, for example, of the substantive complexity of the job; and the substantive complexity of the job, in turn, has an appreciable effect on parental values. It is precisely because education is crucial for the very occupational conditions that most strongly affect parental values that education is so powerfully related to parental values.[40]

Education also has important direct effects on parental values, quite apart from its indirect effects mediated through occupational conditions. Education matters, aside from its impact on job conditions, insofar as education provides the intellectual flexibility and breadth of perspective that are essential for self-directed values.[41] Thus education has both direct and indirect effects upon parental values, both types of effect contributing importantly to the overall relationship between social class and parental values.

CONCLUSION

The facts and interpretations reviewed in this paper have many implications for medicine. One set of implications that I have dwelt on at length elsewhere is that these findings may help us interpret the consistent statistical relationship between social class and rates of schizophrenia.[42] They may also help us understand the role of the family in the etiology of schizophrenia. More generally, these findings are pertinent to our conception of what is normal and what is not in family functioning. I have tried in this paper to show that there are considerable variations in normal family functioning and that these variations are to be understood in terms of the actual conditions of life that families encounter. The values and child-rearing practices of American families must be seen in terms of the realities parents face.

9

Beating Time/Making Time: The Impact of Work Scheduling on Men's Family Roles

Jane Hood and Susan Golden

Men's work schedules are the revolving doors through which men leave and enter family relationships. Which and how many hours a man works help to determine not only the length and frequency of family interactions, but also their quality. This paper closely examines the impact of two men's work schedules on their family lives. The men were the same age, worked similar hours, and each had young children and earned similar incomes when interviewed. However, one had a working wife and the other did not. Further, their occupations, social class, and orientations to work and family differ. As we trace the effect of each man's work hours through the complex maze of his family situation, we find that for one, working an afternoon shift has unanticipated negative effects on his family relationships, while, for the other, the same shift has an equally unintended positive effect. However, in the latter case, as the man becomes more involved in his family, work scheduling again becomes an issue.

PREVIOUS RESEARCH

As Rosabeth Kanter (1977, p. 31) notes, little research has examined the effects of work scheduling on families. Although work scheduling has been the

Reprinted from Jane Hood and Susan Golden, "Beating Time/Making Time: The Impact of Work Scheduling on Men's Family Roles," *The Family Coordinator*, vol. 28, October 1979, pp. 575–582.

topic of numerous reports in the 1970's, most of these are handbooks for managers planning a change to either flextime or the four-day work week, and contain little information about possible effects on families (Nollen & Martin, 1978; Wade, 1973; Wheeler, Gurman & Tarnowieski, 1972).

Studies linking the time and timing of work to the quality of family life usually consider one or more of the following: (a) how shift assignments affect family interaction or role performance; (b) how the amount of time allocated to work affects participation in family activities; (c) how work-family priorities and role demands affect the allocation of energy among work and family roles.

SHIFTS AND SCHEDULES

One of the most complete studies of the impact of shift-work on families is Mott, Mann, McLoughlin and Warwick's (1965) survey examining the effects of different shifts on men's family role performance. They found, for example, that afternoon workers reported difficulties with parenting while night workers had more marital problems. This study, however, included primarily one-job families and did not control for the age of children. More recent work suggests that both the wife's employment status and family life cycle stage have a direct bearing on how men's work schedules are likely to affect their family relationships. For example, in Hood's (Note 1) study of 16 two-job families, fathers of preschool children preferred the afternoon shift since it allowed them to care for their children during the day, while fathers of school-aged children preferred to work days or nights so that they could spend evenings with their families. Hood also found that fathers who cared for young children by themselves for several hours during the day were more likely than those who did not to become psychologically involved with their children. This finding is significant because the alternate shift arrangement for child-care is a popular option among dual-worker families. Duncan and Hill (1975) found that 15.7% of the children in 511 two-job families were cared for in this manner. Lein, Durham, Pratt, Schudson, Thomas, and Weiss (Note 2, p. 45), and the Working Family Project (1978, p. 77) report that half of their 14 dual-worker couples followed the same pattern. Conversely, in a recent study of androgynous parenting, DeFrain (1979, p. 242) found that flexible work scheduling was the social change most often urged by couples seeking to share child care equally. The literature leaves little room for doubt that work scheduling has an impact on men's family relationships, but understanding how it is related is more problematic.

TIME, ENERGY AND COMMITMENT

Understanding how the time involved in a man's work affects his family depends a great deal on assumptions made about the relationships between time, energy and commitment. For example, Clark, Nye, and Gecas (1978), who found little relationship between the number of hours a man spent at work and his wife's marital satisfaction, explain their finding by arguing that the same husbands who worked long hours were also likely to place a high priority on marital roles (p. 19). In other words, these men were sufficiently committed to both roles to find time and energy for each. On the other hand, studies of dual career families and the constraints placed on wives by husbands' occupations suggest that there are finite limits to how much time and energy a man can devote to his career before family relationships suffer (Bailyn, 1971; Mortimer, Hall, & Hill, 1978; Poloma & Garland, 1971; Rapoport & Rapoport, 1972). Underlying this debate is the question of how time, energy and commitment interact. In a thoughtful discussion of multiple roles and role strain, Marks (1977) argues that the more committed one is to a role, the less likely it is that role expectations will be experienced as excessive demands on energy. Energy, unlike time, is an expandable resource, and both its use and supply are governed by commitment. In fact, proponents of the expandable energy position argue that adding new roles may, in some cases, actually liberate new sources of energy (Marks, 1977; Sieber, 1974).

Clearly, then, the relationship between time and timing of a man's work and the quality of his family life is not a simple one. In the two case studies which follow, we illustrate how the impact of men's work schedules on families can vary depending on their wives' employment status, other family members' schedules, children's ages, and the priorities given to occupational and family roles. We also attempt to explain what it is about the work-family role system (Pleck, 1977) which forces one man into a vicious cycle of *beating time,* never having enough, and allows the other to find ways of *making time* even when he is working over 60 hours a week.

CASE STUDIES

METHODS

The concepts presented in this paper have been developed in the context of several research projects. Jane Hood, a sociologist, studied the transition to a two-worker family. She used data from extensive taped discussions with sixteen middle and working class couples over a two year period (1975–1976). The wives had returned to work up to five years before the first interview, after having been home full time for from two to twenty years. Susan Golden, a clinical psychologist, used interviews and methods of naturalistic observation in home, work and school settings to study the work-family interface in families with infants and pre-school children. The initial observational study of two contrasting families from urban and rural settings was extended to include data from short term preventive clinical work with fifteen families in a similar developmental stage in a pediatric setting. The names used in this article are pseudonyms.

JOHN WILLIAMS: A YOUNG PROFESSIONAL

This section of the paper explores some of the ways in which the work hours and commitments of a young professional launching his career interact with family needs during the early child-rearing years. When Susan Golden observed the family, John and Deborah Williams were in their early thirties. John was a systems analyst, and Deborah had left her part-time job after the birth of their second child, planning to return in a few years. The children were 5 years and 5 months old at the time of the study.

John's description of his job centers on the theme of "time" and time use. He is disturbed that there is always more work to be done and not enough time. Accomplishments for him are measured in terms of production. At work, John is "beating time, buying time, selling time, losing time, fighting time." The images of aggressive procurement prevail. Time is the currency of management. His credibility and loyalty to the company are established by his willingness to put in more time for the company.

John feels he works between 40 and 60 hours a week for the sake of his family, but since there are only so many hours in the week, time "spent" in work is taken away from the family and vice-versa. When John's work drew him out of the family for prolonged periods of time, Deborah would find herself embroiled in a spiral of increasing conflict with 5 year old Seth. Tense and overloaded by the end of the day, she would greet John in an angry and demanding manner. John, in turn, would withdraw from her.

During a particular period of 4 weeks, John was managing a team of workers attempting to meet a difficult deadline. The project had had more problems than anticipated and they were behind schedule, having difficulty obtaining adequate computer time for their project. As a result, the team went onto a schedule of working from noon to past midnight, in effect, moving to the afternoon shift. John also commuted 45 minutes each way to work. Seth was in nursery school and arrived home after his father had left for work so that they kept missing each other. Deborah did not keep Seth home from school because she needed the break for herself, and John would only be able to spend one hour at most with Seth before he returned to work, if he had the energy to relate to him at all. John also worked throughout most of the weekends. John felt that this was difficult but that it was important for him to stay with his co-workers in order to sustain team support, as well as develop his own expertise.

During this time, Seth became increasingly provocative with his mother; every small issue became a battle, with resulting temper tantrums and tears. His mother's patience was wearing thin. Seth began to sleepwalk at night, carrying piles of paper around, finally falling asleep at the foot of his parents' bed curled up on his "papers." During the day, he would walk around carrying his "papers" and become very upset if anyone interfered with them. To Seth, the papers were the equivalent of the computer print-out his father always carried to and from work. At the same time, Seth also became more and more preoccupied with Spiderman and his special powers. Deborah said, "I feel as if Seth has turned the house into his own fantasy world. Spiderman is in every corner. Traps are everywhere." The living room was indeed strung from corner to corner with web-like string traps.

In an effort to get out of this uncomfortable power struggle with Seth, Deborah decided to ask Seth what was going on. After talking awhile, Seth broke down, crying, "I hate daddy, I hate daddy, where is he?" alternately hitting the pillow and attempting to hit his mother. Things began to make sense. Deborah had not connected Seth's anger at her to the changes in John's work schedule. The anger Seth felt towards his father for disappearing from the family was being displaced onto Deborah, who was bewildered by Seth's rage and in need of support from her absent husband. This was a crucial time in Seth's development when he needed increased distance from his mother and identification with his father. Seth has been doing well with this separation in nursery school. His attempts to be like his father are reflected in his frantic carrying of the "papers." However, this was not sufficient to help him sustain needed distance from his mother.

Shifts in the family's social network at this time left the family with few outside resources, all of which exacerbated the intensity of the troubled, reactive mother-son alignment. The extent of Seth's rage became more frightening for him the longer his father was gone from the family. Seth's school hours, combined with the availability of computer time at night meant that he did not see the reality of his father to temper his fantasies as this superhero reenacted the anger Seth felt towards his father by filling the house with traps and tricks. Deborah then became preoccupied with her relationship with Seth rather than confront John with her anger.

At the same time, Seth's father was at work, trying to beat a deadline, and planning strategies, traps and tricks to procure more interesting work for his department. Moreover, the greater the tension and stress at home, the greater the distance between John and the family, the greater Deborah's hostility towards her husband, the more likely he is to distance himself from the family, feeling pushed into the role of outsider, completing the destructive spiral.

It would be all too easy to blame Seth's "behavior problem," Deborah's depression, or John's distancing rather than look at the work-family conflicts operating here. John says that he is working for his family and that work and family are separate. John explains that work is a "jungle" and home should be a comfortable nest. Despite John's wish for the separation of these two spheres, the frustrations of work are often inappropriately displaced onto the family. In addition, John's absence from his family has set off a chain of shifting alignments and reactions resulting in a home that is even less comfortable than work. While John has an ideological commitment to the importance of family life and would probably rate it as first priority on a survey questionnaire, his 12–14 hour work days leave him without the energy to work out inter-personal issues within the family, or the awareness of the interdependence of events in work and family arenas. Moreover, on those days when John does get home and reinvests himself in the family, he is left with no time alone for himself.

In this case the strain created by the reallocation of John's work time was felt along the lines of stress already present, acting catalytically to intensify and shift problematic alignments in the family. It is as if the increased demands of a developing career can send ripple effects along the family "fault line," or point of weakness, resulting in shifts in the family structure which can have either constructive or destructive consequences for the family system.

John's dilemmas are not his alone, and the pressures he experiences in the dual role of worker and committed father are shared by many young fathers of this generation. The demands of these two roles are frequently in direct conflict with each other. Deborah has been considering returning to work. If she does this, the pressures on John for more role sharing will be even greater. They will have new areas of sharing but increased competition for resources within the family. Either way, the work-family issues are complex, and there is the potential for considerable growth as well as conflict.

JAMES MOONEY: A DAY SHIFT FATHER

Although both rising young professionals and factory workers experience conflicts between work hours and family needs, both the nature of the conflicts and the timing of them differ. While John Williams' wife was home full time, hoping to return to part time work after the children were older, James Mooney's wife went back to work full-time when her youngest was 2. When Jane Hood interviewed them four years later, they had become co-providers and co-parents and were trying, in spite of inflexible work schedules, to make time to be together as a family.

In 1975, James Mooney was 30 and his wife, Jill, 27. They had two boys, Chuck, then 8, and Jimmy, 6. James had been working for the past 9 years as a diemaker in an auto plant and was earning $17,000 a year including overtime pay. Jill, after staying home full-time for 4 years, had gone back to work and had had a variety of unskilled jobs in the past 4 years. At the time, she was doing a routine clerical job in the finance office of a hospital and earning $7,000 a year, about 30% of their gross family income.

Jill remembers the early child rearing years as a nightmare. Their first son, Chuck, had arrived 9 months after their marriage, interrupting an extended honeymoon. Before that, James would take days off from work and borrow his brother's jeep so that they could go riding through the woods. The baby ended all of that, and James gradually withdrew to the basement with a set of model trains. Jimmy was born less than 2 years after Chuck, and Jill did the best she could with an infant and a very active toddler. However, by the time the youngest was 2, Jill had developed a bad case of eczema. "A nervous reaction," she told me. "Me and the children, we get along when they're older, but babies?" At age 19 and 21, neither Jill nor James was ready for "babies."

Jill's eczema got so bad that finally a doctor told her that she would have to get out of the house. Because he had less than 10 years seniority, James was still working the afternoon shift. This meant that Jill could leave the children with him while she worked from 7:00 a.m. to 3:30 p.m. A baby sitter could fill in for the hour between the time James left for work and Jill returned. Not only would she be getting out of the house, Jill reasoned, but also, she would be adding to the family income, and money was more important to her than it was to James.

James agreed to try the new arrangement, and suddenly found himself alone all day with a 2 year old and a 4 year old whom the doctors were now calling "hyperactive." Jill remembers that during this period, James frequently called her at work and complained about the children: "I finally told him to stop calling me at work or I'll just quit and stay home. We used to have a lot of arguments about this."

James did not remember it being as hard for him the first year as Jill had described, although he was ambivalent: "I was, kinda mixed emotions . . . kind of an economic deal . . . in our situation. I imagine, somebody with a doctor for a husband, it would be more or less something to do (for the wife to work). . . . It wasn't that much. You know, I helped out before. Just the first time I had them all to myself all day. It wasn't much of an adjustment. Diapers, I never could get used to that."

We will probably never know what really happened in the Mooney family during that first year, but, when interviewed 5 years later, James had just gotten back from a picnic lunch with Jill and the children at her work place. After the interview, he had an appointment to take Chuck to the doctor at 2:00 p.m. so that he could be back by 3:00 p.m. to let the baby sitter in before going to work. Although their work schedules make it difficult for James and Jill to spend as much time together as they would like, James feels that he is more fortunate than men whose wives do not work: "Yeah, I see situations like that, where the wife doesn't work. It seems the wife is 'the parent.' The father is always working. Whereas, the situation we have . . . I never really thought . . . it might be just the way the situation was out of necessity . . . I was brought closer to my kids." In other words, although neither he nor Jill planned it that way, James became a psychological parent because he worked the afternoon shift and was home alone with the children while they were awake. Now, he says: "Some days you feel like knocking their heads together. I think it's good though. I'm thinking that later in life, when I get older, they'll be closer with me. And I like to be close to my kids. I think there's too many kids that are on their own nowadays. And when they get older, they get in trouble and the parents can't figure out why . . . and I figure it's because the parents weren't there when the kids needed them. Now, when they're young and everything, you should be developing their life." "Developing their life" is a responsibility that James takes so seriously that in the past year he has been going to P.T.A. conferences by himself, allowing *Jill* to remain at work.

Although James is delighted with the way things have worked out for him and his sons, he would like more time with Jill and more time together as a family. When interviewed, he was working 7 day, 66 hour weeks. He explained that it was mandatory and that if he didn't come in, he would be subject to reprimand and then a disciplinary layoff. He does not like having to leave Jill in the middle of a week-end afternoon to go to work when week-ends are the only time they have together. He does have the option of working days now, but hesitates to do this because of the child care problem they would have when the children are home from school in the summer.

While James would like to reduce his work commitment, Jill would like to increase hers. In between interviews, she had moved up a classification and had a job where, as she put it, she had to use her head. She would like to continue to advance, but that would mean working overtime and/or going to school, and further encroachments on the already too small amount of time she and James have as a couple. Thus, becoming a two-job family has had a positive effect on James' relationship with the children and has increased his role-sharing with Jill, but mandatory overtime and inflexible work-scheduling make it difficult for him to be with his family at the times they are free to be with him.

If the Mooneys could shape their work lives to fit their personal and family needs, James would work 30 to 40 hours a week on a flexible schedule which would allow him to adjust to both his children's needs and Jill's work hours. Jill would work and/or get additional training 40 to 50 hours per week, and would earn enough money to compensate for James' reduction in overtime pay. The family could also gain flexibility by developing a more widely based social support system. As it stands, they have few friends, partly because James is, as Jill describes him, "a loner," and partly because their time together is so valuable they don't want to share it with other people. This, however, makes them very dependent on each other. Given an emotional crisis in either of them or in the relationship, they have no outside resources to turn to. Although more flexible work scheduling would not in itself break the Mooney's isolation, it would provide them with more opportunities for doing this themselves.

CONCLUSIONS AND RECOMMENDATIONS

The work/family conflicts experienced by John Williams and James Mooney are not isolated incidents in the lives of the two individuals, but examples of several of the ways work scheduling affects family life. This conclusion will underline some of the important similarities and differences in the two cases, the patterns that emerge from this comparison, and recommendations to family practitioners and policy-makers.

UNINTENDED CONSEQUENCES

In both cases, work schedule changes had unintended consequences for family roles and the quality of family interaction. In the first case, the choice of an afternoon shift had the unintended negative consequence of increasing the family's stress level and intensifying particular problematic relationships within the family. In the second case, a wife's return to work on the day shift had the equally unintended positive consequence of increasing the father's involvement in the family and investment in the father role. These changes then led him to consider negotiating a new work schedule which would allow him to live in accordance with his new priorities.

WORK SCHEDULES: OCCUPATIONS AND CLASS DIFFERENCES

The range of work schedule options available, the overt and covert forces which shape the choices the men in these cases make, reflect differences in their social class and occupational prestige, as well as in the structure of specific occupations. For example, working class men marry early and peak in earning capacity and on-the-job responsibility sooner than do professionals (Rubin, 1976; Aldous, 1969). They are also more likely to work predictable shift work schedules within a seniority system and be subject to explicit mandatory overtime requirements. The progression of shift work cycles is sometimes in conflict with the developmental needs of the children and other family members. For example, a shift worker who does not have enough seniority to move from the afternoon shift when his children are school age will see his children only on weekends, leaving his wife to resolve all their daily problems.

Professional men continue to add new occupational responsibilities in their 30's, becoming more focused on upward mobility, and less on leisure time. In contrast, skilled workers have gone as far as they can without becoming foremen, and must look to other areas of their lives for personal development in their 30's. In each occupational and class group, the peaking of work hour pressures for time, commitment, and involvement intersects differently with the changing developmental needs within the family.

RECOMMENDED CHANGES IN THE WORK PLACE

For working class men such as James Mooney, the inflexibility of work organizations and the link between seniority and work shifts are major problems related to work scheduling. James needs changes in company policy which would allow him to work day shift during the school year, take time off if a child is sick, reduce his work week to forty hours or less, and abolish mandatory overtime. If James works fewer hours, Jill will need more opportunity for advancement on her job and a higher rate of pay. At present, occupational sex segregation keeps women such as Jill in jobs where they earn an average of 57% of what men do (Levitin, Quinn, & Staines, 1970; Griffiths, 1976). Professionals such as John Williams need major changes in the formal and informal standards by which they are evaluated before they can freely choose to spend more time at home. In John's case, the nature of the task to be accomplished and the criterion for maintaining his professional reputation and credibility required that he work during the hours Seth was home. Moreover, by the time he got home after a 12–16 hour work day, he did not have the energy left to relate to Seth or other family members. Hence, men's values and ideals about work-family priorities are often not actualized under the pressure of conflicting expectations and pressures.

FAMILY ISSUES

These work schedule problems also define, in part, the marital issues couples must negotiate. For example, if John Williams continues to commit as much of his time and energy to his work as he has, it will be increasingly difficult for Deborah to do anything but provide the support services necessary to keep the family going (Mortimer et al., 1978). Such a "two person career" can result in the spiral of anger, resentment, and distance described in the Williams family. While the increased demands of John's job may keep Deborah at home, the limitations of James Mooney's earning capacity sent Jill to work. James, in turn, seeks work schedule changes that will support and accommodate Jill's work requirements. In the process, James, who is not a feminist, has become a staunch supporter of role sharing, and John, ideologically egalitarian, has come to support a very unequal division of labor.

Shifts in work schedules are also reflected in realignments of family coalitions and changing patterns of closeness and distance both in and outside of the family. For John and Deborah Williams, this resulted in destructive rifts between Seth and both his parents, and between Deborah and John, and the intensification of dysfunctional triangles in the family. James Mooney developed a closer relationship both with his children and his wife, but because of their complicated schedule, the family has become more isolated from neighborhood and friends.

RECOMMENDATIONS TO FAMILIES AND FAMILY COUNSELORS

We think that it is especially important that the effects each man's commitments and work schedule had on family interaction were unintended and unanticipated. As Renshaw (1976) has found in her consulting work with corporations, work-family problems often go undetected because of the tacit assumption that the two spheres are in fact as separate as John Williams wished they were. The case studies presented in this paper suggest that it is especially important for family counselors to consider carefully the reciprocal relationship between work and family life. Problems experienced by many men within the family are often, in fact, work-family problems which cannot be adequately understood without considering the entire work-family role system.

In conclusion, we invite families in distress and/or their counselors to include the following questions in their problem assessments:

1. What is the present balance of work and family time? How are decisions made about the time and timing of each? Are these decisions implicit or explicit? How do the outcomes affect specific family relationships?
2. If there have been changes in work schedules, how do these changes affect the family's ability to maintain or expand its existing social support system?
3. How do each parent's career ladder choices interact with the developmental needs of every other family member?
4. How clear are the parents about their own and each other's work and family priorities? Are they prepared to re-examine and renegotiate these priorities as family needs change?
5. What is the family's own style of coping, and what pace of change is reasonable to expect during periods of conflict accompanying family re-organization?
6. Which conflicts can be resolved within the family, and which, such as those mentioned in the above discussion on the work place, must be fought in union halls, legislatures, or before governmental commissions?

10

Relocation and the Corporate Family: Unexplored Issues

Maxine Gaylord

People in the United States have always placed a high value on social as well as geographic mobility. According to the U.S. Census Bureau, approximately 40 million Americans—1 out of 5—moved every year during the early 1970s.[1] More than half these individuals, or an estimated 22 million, made moves that were job related. Until the last decade, it was generally believed that most Americans adapted to the geographic moves of contemporary life with relative ease and little anxiety. In reality, however, a substantial number of individuals experience intense suffering when they move, even though many people move each year and experience few, if any, problems. The 1970s have brought the realization to many that the stressful effects of geographic mobility have been underestimated and that a psychosocial problem exists requiring humane and intelligent attention.

Although not primarily concerned with social issues, psychoanalytic literature has always dealt with the consequences of separation and object loss. Until the last decade, however, surprisingly little in the literature dealt with geographic moves and their potential detrimental effects on the individual or family. Also noteworthy is the fact that until approximately five years ago sociological and psychiatric studies focused mainly on the effects of uprooting on immigrants and on geographic moves made by working-class and lower-class subjects. It is toward this gap in the research that the present article is directed, and it will explore the impact of geographic moves on middle-class and upper-middle-class corporate employees and their families.

BACKGROUND

Several factors have recently helped increase the public's awareness of the potential detrimental effects of geographic mobility on corporate employees and their families. Specifically, Packard's *A Nation of Strangers* and Toffler's *Future Shock*, which both describe the trauma of moving, must be given some credit.[2] Toffler describes people in professional positions as the most mobile of all Americans and compares corporate executives who move from city to city to life-size pawns on a chessboard. Although he refers to these executives as the "new nomads," they have also been called "corporate gypsies," and these terms reflect an increasing focus on their problems.[3] "Future shock" is the phrase Toffler uses to refer to the shattering stress and disorientation that is experienced by individuals when they are subjected to too much change—such as too many geographic moves—in too short a time. Packard's general thesis is that although some arguments can always be advanced in favor of moving, the modern trend toward mobility is malignant, and far too much uprooting is taking place in the United States today.

Other factors have significantly affected the willingness of corporate employees to relocate at their company's behest. In the last five years many articles have substantiated a small but growing trend in the reluctance of employees and their families to pull up roots and move.[4] The "man in the gray flannel suit" loyalties apparently do not always hold true any more. Part of the impetus for this change has come from the youth movement of the late 1960s, with its accent on personal values, self-fulfilling life-styles, and questioning of the "establishment's" way of doing things. These attitudes appear to have affected various corporate elders as well as other segments of the population.

The women's movement has also influenced family attitudes toward job-related transfers, even in families where women do not actively support the movement itself. As they become more conscious of the importance for them personally of exercising their own choices regarding their destiny, women are beginning to realize they do not have to move every time their husbands suggest. Popular literature has helped some women by bringing into focus the existential dilemma of the corporate wife who previously assented dutifully and with little complaint to geographic moves initiated by her husband.[4]

In addition, with women constituting over 40 percent of this country's work force, a growing concern about leaving their jobs has arisen among wives who work.[6] As more and more women become committed to professional careers, they are questioning with increasing frequency the wife's traditional priority of moving when her husband's job demands. And although the working wife still generally follows her corporate husband in a geographic move, this may be about to change in the near future. The wife who works may be unable to find employment in her new community, or she may be of professional status and be forced to accept a lesser position because of a move. More than ever before, women are becoming aware of problems such as these. There are a growing number of educated housewives who have been excluded from the process of being socialized into a profession simply because they have not lived in one place long enough.[7]

The public's increasing awareness of the problems related to relocating and the growing realization among corporate employees and their families that choices do exist are positive developments. However, they represent just the beginning of enlightenment. In reality, the factors just discussed are influencing which families move as opposed to how many; they have not led to a decrease in mobility among Americans. The number of employees transferred by their companies in 1977 remained constant from the year before, at a level of 22 percent of all salaried employees.[8]

In addition, a recent study found that the wife's employment is not yet a deterrent to household moves among corporate employees.[9] In other words, even though in some families the husband's automatic acceptance of a job transfer is giving way to consideration of the wife's career needs, the vast majority of employees are still allowing themselves to be uprooted without closely scrutinizing the potential problems or choices before them.

MOBILITY AND THE FAMILY

Looking at the family of the corporate employee and the impact of uprooting, it appears that the husband has the least trouble adjusting to the new environment. The family's move has been made for the sake of his upwardly mobile career and usually increased status, and despite being in a new office he remains in a relatively familiar business situation. It is true that at this time of transition other employees can be somewhat naive and insensitive regarding the demands placed on someone who has been transferred. In addition, the individual in an executive position is often under stress to the degree that he feels he must prove himself each time he is promoted and relocated. Nevertheless, in reality, his recent move places a much greater hardship on his wife and children.

Mounting evidence indicates that the wife pays the greatest price for a family's move.[10] This is not to deny that individuals may have a wide range of possible responses and that, for some, moving can be a blessing rather than a burden. The point to be made, however, is that even though one formula cannot be applied to everyone, very few women do not suffer some losses as the result of a family move. These may include giving up friends, community, a sense of self-worth and identity, close contact with relatives, and, often, a job or career possibilities. All these renunciations result in loneliness, and there is nothing abnormal about that. The impact of uprooting is thus not episodic, idiosyncratic, or singularly pathological, but a general problem that is far more extensive than has been admitted thus far.[11]

Furthermore, if a wife is solely a homemaker and mother, giving up community, friends, and relatives is experienced by her as more of a loss than if she is fortunate enough to be employed in her new locale. The French sociologist Durkheim used the term "anomie" to refer to the condition of the individual that results from such a loss of traditional community supports.[12] A person begins to merely exist rather than live in a rich and purposeful life when deprived of significant community ties. The husband in a family that has just moved may be somewhat affected by a loss of these ties, but he is accepted at work because of his skill and credentials as an executive or professional. On the other hand, his wife must figuratively fight her way into a sometimes hostile community.[13] There is no substitute for the warmth and support derived from putting down roots, and many communities are all but impossible to penetrate. Unlike her husband, the woman married to a corporate employee may find that the part of her identity dependent on the recognition of others is rarely transferable. Since her identity may have been shattered in the family's move, she may have to create another all over again in the new community. In a world where people are recognized only by their credentials, "to lose one's credentials is to cease being a human being."[14]

FURTHER EFFECTS

Growing evidence substantiates the ill effects that moving has on the mental health of corporate wives. For example, a recent study of a group of upper-middle-class women who were depressed found that although the women themselves did not relate their depression to recent household moves, the temporal relationship between the two events was significant.[15] The authors of the study indicate that the women's complaints of increased loneliness, heightened marital friction, difficulties with children, career frustrations, and identity confusion may have been by-products of a "faulty adaptation to the stresses and changes created by moving." They also speculate that the women studied did not associate their symptoms with recent moves because moving itself is an accepted part of American life. Instead, the investigators suggest, the women internalized their stress and blamed themselves for their problems.

In short, the "good" corporate wife does not feel or express anger at being uprooted. In *How to Survive as a Corporate Wive,* she is given the following advice:

> Acceptance and harmony are two basic ingredients a wise woman preserves for her family regardless of the number of physical changes her husband's job may require. Your attitude and sense of "sportsmanship" set the pace for the family.
>
> [When he announces the transfer,] let him know you are happy, able and willing to be his partner in this new step. When you have done this, you have passed the ultimate test of wivesmanship with flying colors.[16]

This exhortation illustrates the kind of self-help books the wife of the corporate employee can find to reinforce her denial of her feelings and her internalization of the anger she feels at being uprooted. Taking advice like the above to heart will result in her continuing to blame herself for her stress, which in turn will cause an increased loss of self-esteem. It is therefore hardly surprising that many corporate wives are seen clinically during their third and fourth decades of life as chronically depressed, lacking in hope or desire, and frequently addicted to alcohol, tranquilizers, and barbituates.[17]

The problems faced by the woman married to the corporate employee are existential as well as psychological and emotional in nature, for her freedom of choice is usually taken away. She is expected to forfeit the human need for individuality and to submerge her destiny in the life of the man on whom she depends. One study considered why a group of husbands of depressed women did not develop the same symptoms of depression even though they were subjected to the same stress of moving.[18] The authors noted that the moves themselves, necessitated by job changes, were usually initiated by the husbands, who therefore viewed them differently from the wives. In general, the husband felt he was the initiator, but his wife felt herself to be helpless and a victim. The inability of a woman to exercise her free will in such a situation contributes to feelings of a loss of power that further disintegrate her concept of self. Until now, the corporate wife has been part of a system that has denied her the requisites for independent growth.

REACTIONS OF CHILDREN

Children have also been the witnesses and victims of the uprooting and alienation that have been the lot of the geographically mobile family. In the process of moving, they have been battered by the loss of friends and those ballasts of community life that are necessary for feelings of security and well-being. To be deeply rooted in a place that has meaning is perhaps the best gift a child can have. Even couples who are themselves willing to substitute the corporation for the community are concerned about the effects of frequent transfers and moves on their children.[10]

Nevertheless, it would be incorrect to say that any move is detrimental to a youngster. Although various traumas may indeed be developmentally injurious to a child, in the author's opinion professionals have tended to exaggerate the overall effect of individual events. More important than when a family relocates is how it does so.[20] During any move it is easy for children to feel pushed aside. They are often ignored by their parents who, understandably, are busy, and the subsequent lack of communication results in a fearful isolation for them. Regardless of the reason for a family's move, it entails a built-in sense of loss for all. Each member of the family will feel this in his or her own way, and periods of depression are unavoidable. It is important for parents to realize this and to convey openly to their children that such feelings are normal under the circumstances.

Studies suggest that children find moves most stressful at ages 3 to 5 and 14 to 16.[21] Those who are 3 to 5 years old often experience emotional difficulties; those who are 14 to 16 years old largely suffer from social frustrations. The small child's fears and sufferings when moving are primarily caused by misinformation and by misinterpretations arising from the fantasy world with which he or she is often occupied. Furthermore, small children frequently interpret a move as punitive and as an act of hostility on the part of powerful parents and often incorporate the move itself into their primitive theories of existence, with at times frightening results.

In regard to older children, adolescence is a period when doubt and uncertainty about the self are already so extreme that any added pressure may exhaust the adaptive energies of the individual. Peer acceptance and confirmation of the individual are necessities for proper emotional and intellectual growth. The issue of a transfer of identity may therefore be crucial for adolescents whose families are planning to move.

In some instances an adolescent may have already been subjected to many moves caused by a parent's job changes, and he or she may elect to remain with friends or relatives when confronted with another family move. Paradoxically, a young person's defiance of the family's decision to move may be far healthier than a passive abandonment of the social supports that he or she has obtained and often desperately needs to sustain the ego. Rejoining the family later can be a reasonable solution for adolescents to the transfer of identity problem and also present an opportunity for a valuable lesson in independence and autonomy.[22] In sum, adolescence, a time of fragile and difficult growth for both child and parents, can often be complicated by a geographic move.

CORPORATE SERVICES

The author has described the implications a geographic move can have for corporate employees and their families. She has also indicated that needed study of a significant problem in this society has finally taken place in the last decade. However, what is actually being done for employees and their families now that some awareness of their problems has come to the fore?

For purposes of this article, six large corporations who frequently move their executives were interviewed by the author regarding the services they provide to employees requested to relocate. None of the companies was found to be dealing adequately or realistically with the problem of relocating personnel. A personnel-communications specialist at one large multinational company stated that since the company had not encountered any reluctance on the part of its employees to relocate, it did not need an orientation program for those transferred within the United States. Instead, employees were expected to consult with their immediate supervisor in the new location if they had any problems.

The relocation policies of the corporation just described were virtually identical to those of other firms contacted. All the companies provide employees with financial help with housing and moving costs but lack any support system to serve as a focal point for the employee with questions or problems. In fact, the personnel director of one large corporation denied that the decision to relocate was of such significance to warrant discussion with a professional counselor.

The most supportive and progressive assistance for employees was found at two companies that use the services of a relocation management firm. Firms of this kind have evolved over the last two decades and provide services to more than five hundred large U.S. corporations. For a fee, they typically provide assistance to employees in selling their homes, managing their property, locating rentals, and, most recently, finding new homes. Although this last service is usually provided free to the corporation, the author learned in an intervew with one relocation firm that only three out of eight companies choose to offer it to their employees.

In helping employees find new homes, the relocation firm provides the person being transferred with a housing counselor. After an initial interview with the family in which their life-style and housing and other needs are discussed, the counselor helps them find an appropriate home and community within the new area. According to the relocation firm interviewed, however, many corporations regard housing counseling as paternalistic and do not offer it as a service to their employees—leaving them instead at the mercy of local realtors.

The relocation firm itself, like all the corporations contacted, did not have a psychological consultant on staff. Unlike the other corporations, however, who deny that any problem exists, it acknowledges that something must be done. On March 7, 1978, the firm sponsored a forum in New York City for its clients, focusing on the reasons why companies must respond to the growing reluctance of employees to relocate and the ways in which they can help make moves easier for all concerned. The blind spot that corporations have revealed in regard to the needs of their employees still exists, but it is to be hoped that progress can be made through efforts such as the forum just described and the services offered by relocation firms.

Finally, the author contacted several moving companies to view from one last perspective the blind spot of corporations toward the problem of relocating employees. One company has been especially active in sponsoring various symposia on the effects of relocating on the wife, the husband, and the children in a family. Although these discussions have been published and are available to the public, the author learned that most corporations show no interest in using the literature for their staff.

NEED FOR INTERVENTION

This article has identified the need within major corporations for progressive and coordinated planning to provide sociocultural and psychological assistance to employees and their families who relocate. Companies should be willing to seek help in structuring effective support systems to assist disgruntled employees and their families. If the dislocated family cannot effectively maintain its life-style and morale, psychological problems are created that lead to personal and family difficulties as well as to low levels of performance on the job.

It would seem that preparing the employee and his or her family before a move would be a worthwhile investment for a corporation. Since the average cost of relocating a family of four is $14,890, how can corporations justify spending virtually nothing on making the move less frustrating or traumatic for those involved?[23] The author is not suggesting that corporations become social welfare agencies. However, the time has come for them to act out of enlightened moral sophistication. If they are interested in long-term growth and development in their employees (and the families of their employees, which, in the author's opinion, should be part of the same commitment), they must radically change the way they treat people. In conducting research for this article, the author found that every company bowed out of the situation after helping the employee with preliminary housing needs, paperwork, and moving costs.

The reaction of each person or family to a move is personal and individual. The problems created by the move therefore require individualized solutions. In this context, each company may choose to respond to its employees' needs with its own individualized program. Nevertheless, a reasonable starting point would in general be to designate a staff person within the major corporate offices to whom transferred employees and their families could go for help with any adjustment problems before and after a move. Having a specific person such as a moderately skilled personnel specialist to go to within their new community would help make a family feel that someone cared, and simple problems could be solved at the outset. If more skilled intervention were required, the personnel specialist could make an appropriate referral to an outside agency.

The author has already described a large multinational corporation that she contacted, which transfers a large number of its employees with regularity and has no personnel specialist to help orient employees who have been newly relocated within this country. (The company does offer some orientation to employees who have been transferred abroad.) Executives with this company are expected to ask their immediate supervisor for help if they encounter a problem after arriving in their new position. However, the flaw in this approach is that employees are often reluctant to speak to their direct manager of the difficulties they are having for fear that any problem may reflect on them negatively. A staff person outside the department of the employee, who is knowledgeable about the problems of a move, has a helping attitude, and knows the community and its resources, could provide effective, supportive intervention before any problems in adjustment arise.

If the number of employees generally transferred by a company does not warrant paying the salary of a full-time or part-time staff person to help with relocation problems, the company could hire a social worker or psychological consultant on a part-time basis. Many companies located in the same geographic area and having a similar need for this part-time specialized service could avail themselves of the staff of a social work agency providing multiple services to corporations and their employees. Such an agency could provide transferred employees with varying degrees of help, depending on their individual needs. Orientation regarding community resources, referral to a housing counselor, and supportive acknowledgement of the feelings experienced in moving may be all that most families need. For those families having greater adjustment problems, short-term group therapy could be instituted. A staff member of a social work agency could select the participants for the group from several corporations in the area. This group experience, whether short-term or long-term in nature, could be extremely effective in helping individuals with any feelings of depression, isolation, or loss. Furthermore, another advantage of having a trained person orient employees who have been relocated is that he or she, while providing initial support for the family, could detect any serious problems and make appropriate referrals at that time.

Finally, other services that social work agencies can provide corporations lie in the area of educating staff about the stresses involved in moving. The studies and symposia of the last five years have increased the information known about these problems, but new insights in this area have not been communicated to the personnel directors, relocation management executives, or general staff members with which transferred employees interact daily.

Human beings think, feel, and act as organisms responding to an environment.[24] Why should their work milieu not be personally satisfying and supportive? An environment conducive to growth and positive personality development would be advantageous for employees and employers alike. Again, the author is not suggesting that major corporations should apply psychological theories to the point of becoming paternalistic or transforming themselves into social service agencies. However, with some appropriate social work intervention, the corporate work environment could become better adapted to the needs of employees and thus ultimately more effective in meeting the goals of the corporation itself.

11

Implication of Women's Employment for Home and Family Life

Kristin A. Moore and Isabel V. Sawhill

Over the last few decades, an unprecedented rise in the employment rate of married women has significantly altered the economic role of women while the emergence of a new feminist movement in the early 1960s has influenced many people's perceptions of women's place in our society. Given women's traditional commitment to home and children—a commitment that now appears to be weakening as new options become available—it would be surprising if these changes had no impact on the American family. There is, in fact, evidence of widespread dislocation in that venerable institution. Demographers have faithfully recorded some of the essential changes. They have found that young women now marry at a later age, a dramatic upsurge has occurred in divorce rates, and birth rates have declined sharply, although the proportion of births occurring outside of marriage has risen (see Table 12.1). While these changes cannot be definitively linked to changes in the social or economic position of women, there is some evidence that the two sets of trends are related, and the shifts of family structure that have occurred to date may well be only minor harbingers of much more fundamental shifts to come.

The increased employment of women means that they have less time to devote to home and family and that they have more economic resources with which to choose a wider variety of life-styles—some of them less family-oriented—than in the past. These possibilities raise questions about the

Reprinted from Kristin A. Moore and Isabel V. Sawhill, "Implications of Women's Employment for Home and Family Life," in *Women Working*, ed. Ann H. Stromberg and Shirley Harkess (Palo Alto, Calif.: Mayfield Publishing Co., 1978), pp. 201–255. Copyright © 1978 by Ann H. Stromberg and Shirley Harkess. Reprinted by permission.

TABLE 12.1
Women's Divorce Rates, Marriage Rates,
Average Age at Marriage, and Childbirth Rates, 1940–73

	1940	1950	1960	1970	1971	1972	1973
Divorces per thousand married females aged fifteen and over	9	10	9	15	16	17	18
Marriages per thousand unmarried females aged fifteen and over	83	90	74	77	76	78	74
Average age of females at marriage	21.5	10.3	20.3	20.8	20.9	20.9	21.0
Births per thousand women aged fifteen to forty-four	79.9	106.2	118.0	87.9	81.8	73.4	69.2

Sources: U.S. Department of Commerce, Bureau of the Census, *Statistical Abstract of the United States, 1974* (Washington, D.C.: Government Printing Office, 1974); U.S. Department of Health, Education, and Welfare, National Center for Health Statistics, *Vital Statistics Report*, various issues (Rockville, Md.: Health Resources Administration, various dates).

welfare of children, the size of families, the stability of marriages, the quality of relationships between men and women, the division of labor within the household, and the distribution of family income. What changes have already occurred in each of these areas, if any, and what kinds of new policy issues are raised by the prospect of further change? Can society adjust to, even plan for, these changes, or will we simply muddle through, as we have so often in the past?

THE FUTURE OF MARRIAGE

ECONOMIC AND SOCIAL BASES OF MARRIAGE

In the past, women have had fewer opportunities to earn a living on an equal basis with men, and as a result marriage has been essential to their economic welfare. Economists—who view the married household as a small unit of production that allocates the time of its various members among different tasks according to each individual's talents—argue that, as long as women are at least as efficient as men in producing household goods and services but have lower market earnings, an efficient allocation of resources requires that women specialize in home production and men in market production. Through marriage each can gain the benefits of this specialization. Thus, the traditional division of labor between husbands and wives is in part economically determined, although social expectations clearly play a major role as well. The consequence of this particular division of labor is that wives are dependent on their husbands for the necessities of life that can only be bought in the market. Although much less has been made of the implicit value of a housewife's services, the important fact is that, in our market-oriented society, homemaking services command a high return in the form of other goods, services, and prestige only within the context of the family. . . .

Even in our present, partially liberated culture, the most important decision a young woman faces is likely to be the choice of whom to marry. Unlike her male counterpart, she must bear in mind that her social and economic standing may depend much more on the outcome of this decision than her own education, family background, or occupational prospects. To be sure, these other factors help determine whom she associates with and eventually marries, but it is the marriage itself that secures her position in the social system. For this reason, a father traditionally worries about a young man's potential ability to support his daughter, a mother teaches her daughters to use female wiles to entice the "right" young man into marriage, and an adolescent girl may give more thought to marriage than to her own education or career.

In the past, women have had very little choice in these matters. Those who did not marry were viewed with pity and often had great difficulty earning a living. Few achieved high incomes or status in their own right. Those who married took on the usual domestic responsibilities of wife and mother happily in response to both social custom and a lack of good economic alternatives. This very specialization, of course, leads to still greater dependence, because over the life cycle a wife's productivity within the home increases relative to her productivity in the market, while her husband's productivity in the market increases relative to his productivity in the home. By the time a woman who has devoted herself to home and family reaches middle-age, she typically has few marketable skills that would enable her to support herself outside of marriage. Thus, she is more dependent than ever on a marital tie. Women's dependence on marriage is further reinforced by a shortage of alternative partners if the marriage is terminated. The ratio of unmarried women to unmarried men increases dramatically with age, partly because of higher mortality rates and partly because men tend to remarry women considerably younger than their first wives. As a result, female prospects for remarriage decline precipitously as women grow older.

Marrying and remaining married, then, are economic as well as social necessities for women deprived of an independent means of support. Men, too, tend to be bound to their marriages by a sense of social responsibility to their wives and children and by the knowledge that the costs of supporting more than one family may be prohibitively high.

One result of this state of affairs is the prevalence of what William Goode has called "empty shell" marriages—marriages in which there is little love or real caring but a reasonably high degree of stability because social and economic constraints inhibit formal dissolution of the marriage relationship.[1]

If this is a reasonable description of the traditional marriages that have characterized Western nations (with some modifications) since the Industrial

Revolution, the next question is how marriages of the future will look (assuming marriage survives). How will they differ from those of the past?

If women move into the labor force in increasing numbers and gain a more favored position in the occupational structure, this will tend to undermine the traditional division of labor within the household and the interdependence this specialization implies. Marriages based on economic considerations alone will give way. The utilitarian basis of marriage will be eroded, and love, companionship, and perhaps children, will become the only reasons for maintaining a particular relationship. These marriages are likely to be less stable than marriages in the past, although those that do endure will probably provide greater satisfaction to the participants than economically motivated and socially constrained alliances.

At the present time, the institution of marriage lies somewhere between the totally egalitarian marriages that could emerge in the future and the highly traditional marriages of the past. Although almost half of American married women are working, their jobs are often viewed as secondary to their family responsibilities and their income as supplementary rather than essential. Partly for this reason, but also because of the strength of ingrained attitudes, men have continued to maintain their authority as household heads, to consider their work as primary, and to share little in the unpaid work of the household. Although most American marriages are based on a democratic commitment to shared decision-making, in fact they tend to be partnerships in which the wife is clearly the junior partner and there are "separate but equal" spheres of influence.

EFFECTS OF WOMEN'S EMPLOYMENT ON MARRIAGE AND DIVORCE

Our discussion above suggests that the future of marriage is linked to changes in the economic and social status of women. There are already indications that when a young married woman has a high income she is less likely to marry (or more likely to postpone marriage) and that when a wife works and contributes to the family income a divorce is more likely to occur. A number of studies have now documented the inverse relationship between, on the one hand, women's high education, high earnings, or strong commitment to the labor force and, on the other, low rates of marriage or high rates of divorce (see Figure 12.1).[2] Some of the data on this question make it impossible to conclude which is cause and which is effect—for example, one possible interpretation is that women who are not very marriageable or who choose not to marry have to work and therefore have a greater need to stay in school and to earn a good income. Another possible interpretation is that men find high-achieving women threatening or less desirable as mates. Some new research on this question, involving a representative national sample of families whose marital behavior was monitored over a period of years, shows that, other things being equal, the likelihood of divorce is greater where wives

FIGURE 12.1
Percentage of Women and Men
Thirty-Five to Forty-Four Never Married and Divorced, by Income

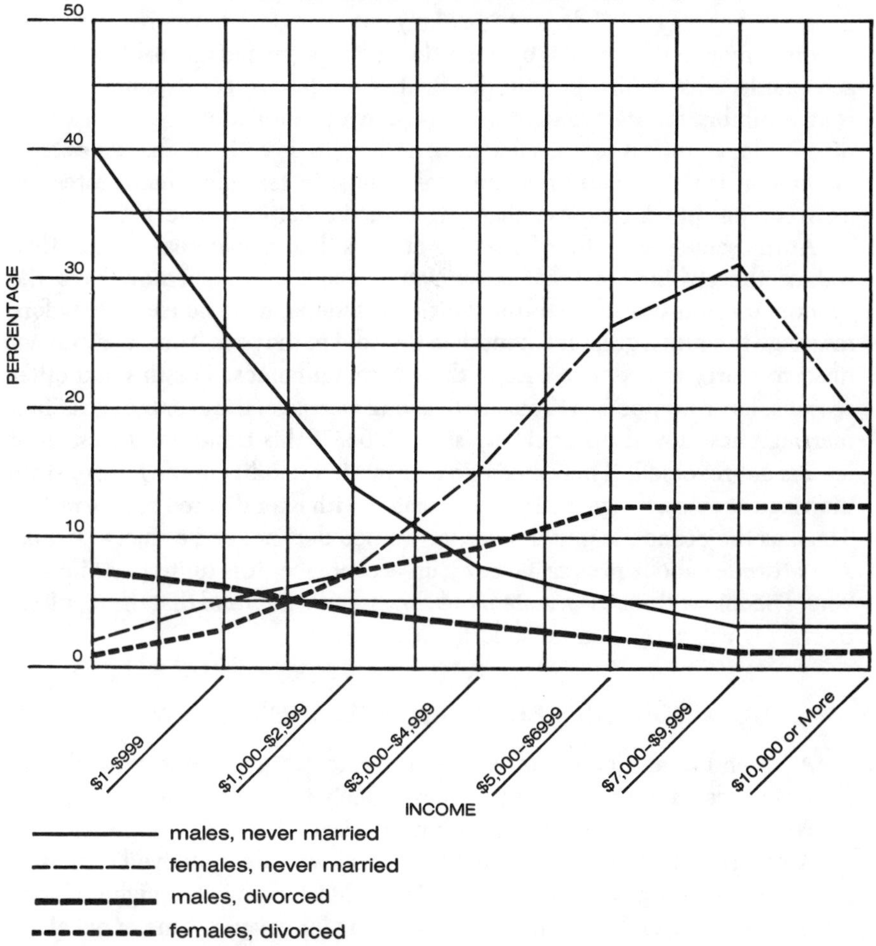

Source: Drawn from Census Bureau data tabulated in E. Havens, "Women, Work and Wedlock: A Note on Female Marital Patterns in the United States," in *Changing Women in a Changing Society*, ed., Joan Huber (Chicago: University of Chicago Press, 1973), p. 217.

have had access to an independent source of income while married.[3] One plausible interpretation of this finding is that, among marriages that are tension-ridden or unsatisfactory for some reason, the costs of divorce are lowest for those in which the wives are capable of self-support. Another possibility is that failure to conform to societal norms about appropriate sex-role behavior is itself tension-producing for one or both spouses. We suspect that both interpretations are true. If we are right, the recent upsurge in divorce rates reflects both greater economic independence among women and the marital strains engendered by changing attitudes about the position of women. Once society has adjusted to more egalitarian norms, the divorce rate might decline somewhat, but if the economic achievements of women continue to undermine the utilitarian character of traditional marriages, a permanently higher rate of divorce is a likely outcome. Furthermore, as divorce becomes more common, it is by definition less deviant and is considered more acceptable; this change in attitudes further erodes the constraints that currently inhibit marital dissolution. Thus, while individual marriages may dissolve for countless reasons that have nothing to do with the changing status of women, it is this more fundamental change in sex roles that creates the environment in which these changing behavior patterns emerge.

At the same time, other forces are at work that may increase rather than reduce the stability of the family. Younger single women now have the economic resources to establish their own independent households before marriage to a much greater extent than they did in the past. Thus many do not need to marry in order to escape their parental homes. For this and other reasons, large numbers of them are delaying marriage: the average age at first marriage has moved up gradually since 1962. If this trend continues, or at least is not reversed, it may mean greater marital stability in the future, since marriage at an early age is highly correlated with later divorce or separation. Thus, as the economic imperatives for women decline, and as more permissive attitudes about premarital sex gain acceptance, it is quite possible that young people will choose a mate more slowly and wisely and that the resulting marriages will rest on more solid foundations.

RELATIONSHIPS BETWEEN HUSBANDS AND WIVES

A second consequence of women's greater commitment to work and increased access to economic resources is likely to be a shift in the relationships between men and women within marriage.

A number of studies have found that wives who are employed exercise a greater degree of power in their marriages. Marital power is higher among women employed full-time than those working for pay part-time or not at all, and it is greatest among women with the most prestigious occupations, women who are most committed to their work, and those whose salaries exceed their husbands'. Working women have more say especially in financial decisions. This tendency for employment to enhance women's power is strongest among lower- and working-class couples.[4]

The resource theory of Robert Blood and Donald Wolfe provides an explanation for these findings:

> The sources of power in so intimate a relationship as marriage must be sought in the comparative resources which the husband and wife bring to the marriage, rather than in brute force. A resource may be defined as anything that one partner may make available to the other, helping the latter satisfy his needs or attain his goals. . . . The partner who may provide or withhold

> resources is in a strategic position. . . . Hence, power accrues spontaneously to the partner who has the greater resources at his disposal.[5]

Thinking along these lines, it does not seem surprising that employed women appear to have more power than nonemployed women: they contribute to family income, and their experiences on the job may provide them with valuable new knowledge and contacts. Of course, factors other than income can act as resources as well—for example, physical attractiveness, skill in cooking or entertaining, and a prestigious family background. Working women may lose power, too, if they have to seek help from their husbands to accomplish household tasks that the husbands consider part of the wives' role and that paid workers would not do or do as well (such as caring for sick relatives or running errands).

The existing literature on marital power has been criticized on the ground that concepts such as "resources" and "power," are difficult to measure and quantify objectively.[6] The basic theory outlined here, however, suggests that, as women move into the labor force and contribute a large fraction of total family income, they will acquire new rights as wives and improve their bargaining position within marriage. The wife who once had to ask her husband's permission to buy a new dress will have a new freedom to decide the matter herself, in addition to the higher prestige that generally accrues to income-earning adults.

THE DIVISION OF HOUSEHOLD WORK

Closely related to the issue of marital power is the question of how the employment of women affects both the division of tasks between husband and wife and the total amount of work done in the household. In general, husbands of working wives engage in slightly more child care and housework than do husbands of women who are not earning income, although it does not appear that the rapid movement of women into the labor force has been matched by a very significant increase in husbands' willingness to help around the house. Data based on household interviews with married couples in Detroit suggest that little change occurred in the distribution of household tasks between 1955 and 1971.[7] Of the tasks considered, three functions were preponderantly the wife's responsibility—doing the dishes, making breakfast, and straightening up the living room. Decisions about the house, the car, life insurance, and the husband's job, as well as responsibility for household repairs, tended to fall into the husband's realm; responsibility for grocery shopping, taking care of money and bills, and decisions about the food budget and the wife's employment were either joint concerns or fell within the wife's domain. Although some changes did occur in the allocation of tasks—for example, a greater proportion of husbands always got their own breakfasts in 1971—the more notable finding was a lack of the kind of change that we might have expected to accompany the movement of women from the home into the labor market. Indeed, in 1971, a *greater* proportion of women than in 1955 always did the grocery shopping and the evening dishes, and a smaller proportion made decisions about life insurance, what house or apartment to take, and whether they themselves should go to work or quit work. Perhaps it takes some time for an adjustment to be worked out, but it does not seem, at least in the short run, that women have traded one kind of work for another. Instead they seem to have taken on a new set of activities without forgoing their traditional responsibilities. Whether this is because men are still the primary breadwinner in most families (that is, they still have substantially higher earnings than their wives), or whether it simply reflects deeply ingrained male attitudes that are resistant to change, is difficult to say.

One sort of accommodation that working women have made is a reduction in the number of hours spent doing household tasks. Joann Vanek has reported that, despite new convenience appliances, nonemployed urban women spent an average of fifty-five hours per week in the 1960s doing household tasks that nonemployed rural women spent fifty-two hours on in 1924. Employed women, on the other hand, spent only half as many hours on housework. This difference holds true after accounting for the fact that full-time housewives have more children, younger children, less household help, a different social class, and a different marital status than employed women.[8] The latter may have lower housekeeping standards, purchase more goods and services in the market (restaurant meals, commercial laundering, etc.), or simply do their work more efficiently. As we have seen, working women get very little extra help from their husbands, so they must be compensating in other ways.

ADJUSTMENTS FOR MEN

Deciding who does the housework is only one area in which the increased employment of married women is likely to affect the lives of men, yet relatively little research has been done on these effects. The traditional male role has been as provider and protector. As women demand more male participation in activities traditionally defined as feminine, and as they begin to share and sometimes usurp men's traditional roles, some response on the part of men is inevitable.

Mirra Komarovsky[9] and more recently Matina Horner[10] have both written on the threat that female competence poses for males. Being married to a woman with a busy schedule, an income of her own, outside friendships and commitments to non-family-members may produce feelings of insecurity and perhaps bewilderment in a husband. The result may be strain or even resentment.

Although this kind of competition is uncommon at present, since so few women approach their husbands' earning abilities, it is likely to be more common as women pursue careers in earnest, without frequent interruptions, and as employers come to honor the slogan "equal pay for equal work." Even now the impact of women's employment is being felt. For example, Kristin Moore reports that white women who make as much or nearly as much money as their husbands are more likely to tell fear of success stories, emphasizing the difficulties and costs attendant on high achievement for a woman.[11] And Larry Long reports . . . that men with working wives are slightly less likely to be involved in long-distance mobility. While the reason for this association is not presently clear, it seems likely that women with job attachments, experience, and seniority are more resistant to moves that may advance their husbands' careers at the expense of their own opportunities. The inability to locate suitable employment for both spouses may create strain.

Traditionally, the woman's job commitment has been viewed as secondary to her domestic responsibilities. A child's illness or a family crisis interrupts the mother's day rather than the father's, a tendency that Joseph Pleck refers to as "the differential permeability of the boundaries between work and family roles for each sex."[12] Serious, steady commitment to a job by a woman will require that her husband share the dislocations and interruptions caused by family needs. A woman's home life has tended to intrude on her work life; a man's work life had tended to intrude on his family life. As the wife's employment comes to require the husband's contribution at home, it may become impossible for him to leave on frequent business trips, work overtime shifts, and bring work home in the evening. The man with a working wife may find himself at a competitive disadvantage compared to a man who can work sixty or seventy hours a week because his wife takes complete charge of the home front.

On the other hand, the man with a working wife may not need to work overtime himself and may find that his wife's income gives him the security to refuse demands from an employer that intrude on his home life. Vital statistics show that, at the present time in the United States, the life expectancy of males is sixty-seven years, whereas for females it is nearly seventy-five. In addition, life expectancy is increasing faster for females than for males. One factor in the relative disadvantage of men is probably the strain of employment. Many men may welcome both the opportunity to share the burden of family support with their wives and the chance to spend more time with their children.

The implications of these changes for male employment and life-styles are unclear. Will men increasingly turn down overtime, refuse travel, and reject transfers because of the work commitments of their wives and the needs of their children? If men are able to share the burden of family support and develop the ability to express their feelings and emotions more openly, will male mortality rates fall? The implications of the rising rate of female employment on the lives of males have yet to be seen and remain largely unexplored. But the reaction of men to greater participation by women in the world outside the home will be an important determinant of how rapidly and how smoothly changes occur and ultimately how society judges this evolution.

To summarize, married couples face new opportunities and new pressures as women's involvement in the world of work increases. These changes are likely to have a destabilizing impact on marriage, to improve the bargaining power and rights of wives, and to unsettle the lives of husbands. As women take on new responsibilities outside the home, they devote less time to housework and child care. To date, there is no evidence that most men have moved toward meaningful sharing of these tasks. A critical issue, then, is what will become of children in a society where almost everyone is committed to activities outside the home.

THE FUTURE OF PARENTHOOD

CHILD-CARE ARRANGEMENTS OF WORKING MOTHERS

Although the total number of children under age eighteen in the United States has been declining because the birth rate is falling, the number of children with working mothers has been increasing rapidly.[13] In 1973, 44 percent of mothers were employed, compared to 34 percent in 1964 and 22 percent in 1950. Mothers of school-age children are even more likely to work—53 percent worked in 1973—although one-third of mothers with preschool children were employed as well. In fact, the number of preschool children with working mothers has increased by over one-third in the last decade.

The arrangements working mothers make for the care of their children vary widely. Although the proportion of children in day-care centers doubled between 1965 and 1970, these centers still provide care for only 10 percent of preschool children of working mothers. The remaining 90 percent are cared for informally—some in their own homes by a father, a sibling, another relative, or a paid worker, and some in the homes of family day-care workers.

Most family day-care workers who take in children are themselves mothers, and they take care of only a few children at a time. They choose this work so that they can stay home with their families while earning some money; sometimes their motivation is to provide company for themselves and their children as well. Parent satisfaction with these informal arrangements has been found to be high, although only 1 or 2 percent of these homes are estimated to be licensed, and the quality of care undoubtedly varies widely.

Since an estimated 6 million children under age six required some sort of child care in 1972, and only about 1 million were cared for in day-care centers or licensed homes, there is pressure for the federal government to provide day-care services on a greatly expanded basis. At least three different groups support an expanded government role in this area. One consists of women who believe that their opportunities or their ability to cope with the dual responsibilities of home and job are limited by the lack of day-care facilities. Another group is concerned about the early environment of children and has argued that quality child care can enhance child development and provide greater equality of opportunity for children from poor families. A third group feels that day-care programs will enable poor women who head families to work and thus reduce welfare costs. Opposition to federal involvement in day-care programs focuses on the cost, concern for the quality of mass child-care services, preference for home-centered family day care, and concern that the availability of low-cost child care might encourage people to have more children and thus aggravate population pressure.

Since quality day care is labor intensive and expensive, especially if it emphasizes child development rather than custodial care, much debate has raged about who should pay and how much. Parents are currently allowed a tax deduction for child-care expenses, and most proposals for an expanded government role include a sliding fee schedule that provides free or very low cost services to poor women.

CONSEQUENCES FOR CHILDREN

Much of the controversy over whether women should work or not centers around the question of whether children are adversely affected if mothers delegate child care to other persons while they are away at work.

One reason for the expectation that maternal employment harms children lies in early research on young children separated from their mothers for long periods or placed in institutions. The severe deprivation of attention and stimulation that these children suffer tends to produce intellectual retardation and social apathy or unresponsiveness. These effects have been extrapolated to suggest that the children of working women will not develop adequately. However, the separation of mother and child for routine, brief, nontraumatic periods does not seem to be harmful if adequate substitute care is provided. Indeed, a number of studies have suggested that the children of employed women compare favorably in intellectual and social development with the children of mothers at home.

A more precise answer than this is impossible without specifying what *type of behavior* on the part of children is likely to be affected by a mother's employment and the total *circumstances* surrounding her employment. A review of several studies on these questions will illustrate the general point.[14]

Early studies explored the presumed association between maternal employment and juvenile delinquency. They found that boys from lower-income families who were inadequately supervised were more likely to be delinquents, and that the sons of employed women were more likely to be inadequately supervised. But it was the quality of supervision, rather than employment per se, that contributed to delinquency. In general, these early reports linking juvenile delinquency to maternal employment have since been qualified, as researchers have taken into account such critical factors as how the children were cared for in the mother's absence, the socioeconomic group studied, and the emotional health of the family.

It is often assumed that children of working women do poorly in school because their mothers have less time and energy to help the children with homework and other intellectual pursuits than mothers at home and because the working mothers may be disinterested in, or even rejecting of, their children. In fact, children of working women do not seem to suffer impaired academic performance. Several studies have even found a positive relationship between I.Q. scores and maternal employment, although one study did find that middle-class sons of working women received lower grades than those with mothers at home. In lower-class families, maternal employment is positively associated with academic performance for children of both sexes.

Children of working women have been found to be higher in achievement motivation and more likely to plan to attend college. Both these effects are slight, however, and researchers have often failed to apply appropriate controls. (For example, college aspirations may be linked to maternal employment because mothers are working to pay for tuition or because children from two-income families perceive college as economically feasible.) It does seem clear, though, that employed mothers provide their children, especially their daughters, with achievement models. (See the next section of this chapter.) . . . Predictably, college-educated daughters of employed mothers have higher career aspirations and achievements than the daughters of nonemployed mothers.

Employed mothers also tend to stress independence in their children. For example, the children of working mothers typically have more household responsibilities than the children of full-time homemakers. This stress on independence appears to be less true among well-educated women and women who enjoy their work, however. The latter seem to compensate for their employment by being especially nurturant toward their young children.

The natural maturation of the child may hold less threat for a woman with alternative satisfactions and commitments than for a mother who has invested all her time in home and family. Betty Friedan decries the softness and passivity of children raised by full-time housewives who are living vicariously through their children.[15] She argues that the child of a woman with a sense of self, with interests and a life of her own, will grow up to be a stronger and more resilient adult. A study by M. R. Yarrow and others illuminates this point.[16] Mothers were divided into four groups: satisfied homemakers, dissatisfied homemakers, satisfied employed women, and dissatisfied employed women. Satisfied homemakers scored highest on a measure of adequacy of mothering. Dissatisfied mothers scored lower, especially the dissatisfied homemaker. Women who stressed duty as the reason for being a full-time homemaker had the lowest scores on mothering. We might speculate that the children of dissatisfied homemakers would be better off if their mothers were employed.

The Yarrow study illustrates the importance of considering labor force participation as more than a simple employed-nonemployed dichotomy. A woman's motivation for working, her satisfaction with her job, the duration of the employment, her husband's opinion of her employment, the adequacy of child care, the amount of help received with housework, and the family's socioeconomic status all seem likely to influence the consequences of maternal employment for children. Further studies should control for these differences. In addition, the date when a study was conducted can affect the results. Research on women who worked during the 1950s, when public opinion generally held that women should be home with their children, may not apply to the 1970s. Finally, little attempt has been made to follow the longer-term achievements and mental health of children, as they are revealed over the life cycle, and their possible association with the mother's employment and other early influences. Until more research is done on this vital and complex question, it is difficult to come to firm conclusions.

SEX-ROLE ATTITUDES

Whatever the effects of a mother's employment on her children's welfare, the transmission of attitudes or values from one generation to the next is likely to be affected by the life-styles of today's parents. In this regard, one set of research findings from several studies shows that the children of employed mothers have a different concept of women's role than those whose mothers do not work.

In a study by Philip Goldberg, college students were presented with short professional articles on topics ranging from city planning and law to art history and dietetics. In some cases, a particular article was attributed to a female author and in other cases to a male author. In every instance, students evaluating the quality of the work rated the manuscripts attributed to male authors higher than the manuscripts attributed to female authors, whatever the topic.[17] These findings were later qualified by a replication of the original study by G. K. Baruch, which showed that the daughters of employed women were significantly less likely to devalue the articles attributed to women than were the daughters of full-time housewives.[18]

Another group of researchers studied sex-role stereotypes in an attempt to learn which traits were seen as masculine and feminine.[19] They developed a list of characteristics, such as "active" and "dependent," and asked samples of men and women to evaluate which traits typified males and which females. Traits categorized as typically male tended to reflect competence (independent, objective, active, competitive, logical, etc.) while those characterized as female tended to form a warmth and expressiveness cluster (gentle, sensitive, tactful, religious, etc.). When describing themselves, women conformed to the female stereotype, even to the point of saying that they were more passive and less rational and competent than men, as well as warmer and more expressive. Daughters of employed women were expected to have a different view of women, however. The researchers reasoned:

> A person's perception of societal sex roles, and of the self in this context, may be influenced by the degree of actual role differentiation that one experiences in one's own family. Maternal employment status appears to be central to the role differentiation that occurs between parents. If the father is

> employed outside the home while the mother remains a full-time homemaker, their roles tend to be clearly polarized for the child. But if both parents are employed outside the home, their roles are more likely to be perceived as similar—not only because the mother is employed, but also because the father is more likely to share child-rearing and other family-related activities.[20]

Daughters of working women did indeed perceive significantly smaller differences between males and females, compared to daughters of nonemployed women. In addition, while they did not differ from daughters of nonemployed women in describing women as warm and expressive, they did differ in describing women as relatively competent. Sons of working women also perceived smaller differences between men and women in warmth and expressiveness.

What these findings imply, of course, is that new experiences of women working tend to generate new attitudes about women that may significantly influence the sex-role behavior of the next generation of adults. This interaction between experiences and attitudes can become a powerful basis for a cumulative movement toward more equality between the sexes in the future. In the past, attitudes and experiences tended to reinforce one another to create a kind of cumulative inertia, but once the system has been disrupted, a return to the previous status is quite unlikely.

Some of the research we have discussed on sex-role attitudes showed that boys as well as girls were influenced by the example of a working mother. This is significant because, as we have seen, one area in which the status quo appears rather firmly entrenched is the amount of household work—including child care—that husbands are willing to undertake. But if young boys are growing up with a different set of attitudes from their fathers', they may behave differently when they become husbands and fathers.

If women continue to move into the labor force and a greater sharing of domestic responsibilities does not come about, then there are two other possible outcomes. One is a much greater delegation of child care and other personal services to public or private institutions outside the family. Another is that families will simply have fewer children. Just as employed women have cut back on the number of hours they devote to housework, they may choose smaller families to accommodate their need to supplement the family income or their interest in careers outside the home.

EMPLOYMENT AND FAMILY SIZE

Raising children and being employed are both extremely demanding in terms of time and energy. Women involved in both activities at the same time may find themselves stretched and drained to the point where they wonder whether they are succeeding at either role. If fact, work overload is such a serious problem for the mothers of preschool children that most of them do not seek paid work. Women with large families are also much less likely to work for pay than those with small families. The association between labor force participation and small families has been consistently documented and is illustrated in 1974 Census Bureau data for women aged thirty-five to forty-four who have ever been married: nonemployed women had an average of 3.3 children; women employed part-time had an average of 3.1 children; and women employed full-time had an average of 2.8 children.[21] Moreover, when asked about how many children they would like to have, or what they consider the ideal family size to be, women who work outside the home mention fewer children than other women.[22] A variety of reasons have been suggested to explain the association between female employment and small families. For one, women who are unable to have children may find compensating satisfactions in a job or career. Alternatively, women who enjoy working may deliberately limit their family size to enable them to work. Working may fulfill needs for self-expression, creativity, accomplishment, and social identity that childbearing has previously satisfied.

In addition, the cost of having a child is substantial, especially if a couple counts the value of the wages that a full-time homemaker could be earning in the paid market place. Ritchie Reed and Susan McIntosh have calculated the cost of rearing a single child through college: they estimated $33,000 for direct costs such as food and medical care, and then added the value of the wife's forgone earnings; the total cost was $84,000 for a woman with an elementary school education, $99,000 for a woman with a high school degree, $122,000 for a woman with some college or a four-year degree, and $143,000 for a woman with five or more years of college.[23] Second children are a bargain by comparison, since they simply lengthen the time the mother spends out of the labor force. The extra cost depends on how closely they are spaced; for example, the cost of a second child born two years after the first, is (depending on the mother's education) $47,000, $49,000, $53,000, or $56,000.

Clearly the cost of not working is highest for well-educated women, and this may be one reason why better-educated women have smaller families. However, there are other reasons why such women may wish to limit their family size. The jobs they hold tend to be more interesting, pleasant, and stimulating than the opportunities available to unskilled women. In addition, they are more likely to use effective contraceptives.

While the association between a woman's education, employment, and family size has been consistently documented, and many reasons have been proposed to explain the relationship, the cause-and-effect pattern is unclear. Do women have small families because they wish to work or need to work? Or do they have small families for other reasons, and then find that they simply have more time to work? If a significant number of women are limiting their families because of the practical difficulties of combining motherhood with work, then increasing the availability of day-care facilities and husbands' participation in housework and child care could reduce the barriers to childbearing and bring about a rise in fertility. On the other hand, if women who work have smaller families because working satisfies needs that they would otherwise meet by having babies, then it is unlikely that changes in day care and in the division of labor between husbands and wives will affect the birth rate much. Linda Waite and Ross Stolzenberg argue that women develop their plans for employment and child bearing jointly and simultaneously—that is, plans for work affect plans for having children and vice versa. They find there is a reciprocal causation, but women's employment plans have somewhat more influence on fertility than fertility has on employment plans.[24] If this is so, it is an important finding.

If women's employment plans are an important determinant of family size, and if women's participation in the labor market continues to increase, the current fertility rate, which is already at an all-time low, may drop still further. Provision of more social supports, such as day care, could modify this by enabling women to combine work and family responsibilities more easily. On the other hand, emerging attitudes about women's roles, about the economy, and about population and environment may diminish people's preferences for having children compared to other possible uses of scarce time and resources.

One distinct possibility is that many families will continue to have strong positive feelings about children but will be forced to curtail childbearing so that wives can contribute to family income. Having a second earner in the family often makes the difference between just getting by and establishing a solid position within the ranks of the middle class. Thus, it may become increasingly difficult for women to *choose* to stay home and to forgo the standard of living that two-career families enjoy. Americans have always judged their economic well-being not by the absolute value of their income but rather by their position relative to other families in the income structure. If most families have two incomes, families with one earner may feel disadvantaged by comparison. This brings us, then, to still another interesting question about the future: What will happen to the distribution of family income if more and more women choose, or feel required, to work?

CHANGES IN THE DISTRIBUTION OF FAMILY INCOME

Although real incomes and standards of living have risen quite dramatically over the past three decades, the distribution of income among families has hardly changed at all. In 1972, for example, the 20 percent of families at the top of the income pyramid received slightly more than 40 percent of aggregate family income while the 20 percent at the bottom received only 5 percent. The total economic pie has been divided about that way ever since the end of World War II.

How does the participation of women in the labor force affect the income distribution of families? If all wives worked and women had the same earning potential as men, then the answer would depend only on who married whom. A tendency for high-income men to marry high-income women would exacerbate the degree of income inequality relative to a world in which only husbands worked.

Of course, at present, less than half of all wives work, and this fact complicates the analysis, because the labor force participation of women tends to be negatively related to their husband's income but positively related to their own income prospects. The net result is that the labor force participation of wives increases as husbands' earnings rise up to the average earnings for all husbands, but then it falls at higher levels. Overall, this causes the current distribution of income to be somewhat more equal than it would be if wives did not work at all. Moreover, according to Lester Thurow and Robert Lucas, the increased participation of women in the labor force over the past twenty-five years has tended to reduce the relative inequality of family income.[25] The stability of the overall income distribution among families, noted above, evidently reflects offsetting influences of other factors; if more and more wives had not gone to work, those factors would have led to greater inequality. So, the desire to keep up with the Joneses and to reduce disparities in income may indeed have been a potent force in bringing more women into paid employment.

An example of how this phenomenon has worked in the past is provided by an analysis of the income differentials between black and white families. Because a greater proportion of black wives than of white wives had traditionally been in the labor force, differences in the income status of black and white families have not been as great as the racial inequality in individual earnings. More recently, however, the labor force participation rate of white wives has surpassed that of black wives for the first time, causing a decline in the relative income position of black families.

This recent development may be a harbinger of greater inequality in family income distribution generally. If there is an influx of relatively well-educated, high-earning women into the labor force—women who in the past married high-earning men and worked less frequently than wives in lower-income families—family incomes will become more unequal in the future. People might then react with demands for more egalitarian tax policies to offset the greater disparity in standards of living.

CONCLUSIONS AND POLICY IMPLICATIONS

In most of the preceding sections, we have not given explicit attention to the policy issues raised by the changes we have reviewed. But policy questions are lurking just below the surface of the discussion.

Clearly, the potentially profound repercussions on home and family life of women's greater work attachment necessitate a rethinking of public policies in such diverse areas as Social Security, divorce, alimony, child support, welfare, and income tax laws. These laws are based on the assumption that the vast majority of women are homemakers financially dependent on their husbands.[26] . . . Such laws need to be retailored to fit a world in which that assumption is false at least as often as it is true. Already working wives are pressing for a revision of Social Security and income tax laws that discriminate against two-earner families; if they succeed, someone else will have to bear the cost. And we may yet see a backlash if highly paid men and women pool income through marriage and exacerbate the disparities in family income.

Women's market participation also has implications for fertility and marital stability that will change the shape of the future. For example, we have seen that improvements in women's economic opportunities appear to be a significant factor increasing divorce rates, currently the highest in the history of this country and the industrialized Western world. This, in turn, has contributed to an unprecedented increase in female-headed families. Indeed, the absolute increase in the number of children living in single-parent homes exceeded the increase in the number living in two-parent homes during the decade of the sixties. In part, this is an indictment of our welfare system, which, according to recent research, may well contribute to the growth of single-parent homes. But given the size of the female-headed family population and the poverty these families often face, we need to reevaluate our present alimony and child support laws. Evidence suggests that these laws are working very poorly.[27] Reform might entail designing a national child support policy, establishing a fund to which all absent parents would contribute and from which all eligible children would draw; or, it might take the form of a system of divorce insurance, an idea that the New York State legislature is already considering.

While these are all interesting questions, the most critical issue is how the essential work of a household, especially child care, can be organized, as women move increasingly into the labor market. The possibilities run the gamut from wholly private, nonmarket arrangements, through increasing market organization, to substantial public involvement in the financing and provision of services. Will husbands and wives work out a new division of labor on a voluntary partnership basis? Certain women are agitating for this, but, as we have suggested, the record on male-female sharing of home tasks is quite thin. Does the lack of sharing result from ingrained attitudes or the absence of appropriate financial incentives? Will either attitudes or incentives shift enough in the future to produce new behavior patterns?

In the event that husbands do not come to share home responsibilities equally with working wives, how will the work of the home sector get done? Will the private market organize ways to carry out these functions, as it already has with capital goods for the home, paid domestic help, household maintenance organizations, and day-care services? Before these private mechanisms can develop, will they be overtaken by plans to socialize household work and to pay some or all household workers out of public funds—for example, a trust fund to which all parents or all adults contribute to pay for individual or group care for all children? Will public involvement go beyond paying people to do household tasks and develop large-scale direct programs to provide household services, with child care as the leading element?

These are some of the policy issues we need to examine. At the present time most individuals or couples are making their decisions and plans alone, with little counseling or social support. The rules are changing, and the final outcome, as well as much about the intervening process, is unclear.

Few social scientists think the family is going to disappear. However, the lower birth rates and increased labor force participation of women will almost certainly continue to change their personal rewards, their power relationships, their role expectations, and ultimately perhaps the definition and prevalence of marriage. More research, discussion, and debate are needed if social scientists and government decision makers are to plan intelligently for the future and if individuals are to embark on that future confidently.

12

Dual–Career Couples Who Live Apart: Two Types

Harriet Engel Gross

Just as was anticipated over a decade ago, the incidence of and interest in dual-career families increased in the period since Rapoport and Rapoport (1971:18) introduced the term to refer to families in which "both heads of household pursue careers and at the same time maintain a family life together." In a recent review article (Rapoport and Rapoport, 1978:3), these same authors distinguish three stages of dual-career research: (1) early studies of the changing roles of women; (2) later delineation of the dual-career family and its functions; and (3) the current stage, elaborating developments affecting such couples. This paper, as an example of this third stage, presents research about a further lifestyle complication confronting dual-career marriages: the decision to live apart; to maintain separate residences as a response to the conflicting mobility demands of each spouse's career.

At the onset of a discussion of marital separation, it is worth noting that the need to live apart is not peculiar to dual-career marriages. Persons in certain occupations have long been associated with marital separation (e.g., politicians, business executives, professional ball players and actors as well as construction workers and merchant marines). Specific circumstances have also caused such separations (e.g., war, immigration, imprisonment, and seasonal work. For discussions of these, see, for example, Hill, 1949; Handlin, 1951; McCubbin et al., 1974; Schneller, 1975; and Abbott, 1976, respectively).

Reprinted from Harriet Engel Gross, "Dual-Career Couples Who Live Apart: Two Types," *Journal of Marriage and the Family*, vol. 42, August 1980, pp. 567–576.

The case of the traveling salesman also comes to mind as an example of an occupation requiring patterned periods of time away from a primary household. But in this case, the associated lifestyle does not usually require a separate residence. Note, too, that, in these examples, it is typically the husband's occupation that occasions the need for family members to live apart. Today, however, the decision to live apart confronts a "new" population as well.[1] Our research (see also Gerstel, 1977; and Kirschner and Walum, 1978) suggests that women's increasing participation in the professions (Ginsburg, 1979) is the basis for the apparent increase in two-residence marriages. This paper concerns this "newer" variant of marital separation which results from an effort to accommodate the career demands of both members of the marital partnership.

A common theme threading through early research with dual-career couples (e.g., Rapoport and Rapoport, 1971, 1976; and Holmstrom, 1972) that later research (e.g., Hopkins and White, 1978; and Hall and Hall, 1979) reaffirms is that these marriages are complex arrangements with unique sources of rewards and strains. Where studies do differ, however, is in their authors' conclusions about these couples' abilities to contend with the complexity of these rewards and strains. Rapoport and Rapoport's work (1971, 1976) left the overall impression that the benefits of such marriages—greater economic and emotional equity between spouses—counter its tensions. Similarly, Epstein (1971) concluded that the potential for better communication and greater mutuality of purpose she found among dual-career couples fortified their efforts to cope with its strains. Larry and Janet Hunt's (1977) work suggests a different view of the lifestyle's manageability. Their analysis points to the inherently depleting effect of withdrawing full-time domestic support from both the career-oriented husband and wife in these marriages, each of whom individually, needs such support.

A limited number of published, research-based analyses focus specifically on dual-career couples who live apart. Such relationships are variously termed commuter marriages (Gerstel, 1977, 1978) or two-location families or married singles (Kirschner and Walum, 1978; see also Farris, 1978). Gerstel (1977) argues that the demands of two-residence living are greatest for couples with dependent children. Because of this she advocates considering both life-cycle and career-sequence analysis. She concludes that the time which best "fits" commuter marriage requirements is in the post-honeymoon and middle ("empty nest") years of married life. In a subsequent paper (1978), she also deals with the notion that differential rewards accrue to each spouse in the two-residence relationship—a finding corroborated by our study. Kirschner's and Walum's (1978) discussion of strains and rewards associated with this variation of dual-career marriages also distinguishes effects for husbands and wives. They suggest that the supports for women in such marriages are greater than those for men. Finally, an article based on an earlier analysis of the data to be reported here (Gross, [1980a]) considers how implicit comparisons with co-residence living frame spouses' reactions to the time/place disjunctions that separate residences entail. That discussion focuses on the strains resulting from such comparisons.

The purpose of this paper is to extend the discussion of specific problems encountered by dual-career couples who live apart and to identify some common ways in which these problems are experienced and defined. Discussion will begin with an elaboration of husbands' and wives' evaluations of their own role in two-residence marriages which seem to flow from implicit comparisons with traditional marital roles. We will attempt to locate configurations among relevant variables suggested by earlier work (e.g., sex, age, length of marriage, career and life-cycle stage) to determine how particular combinations affect the lifestyle's manageability.

THE SAMPLE

The data to be reported here are based on taped, open-ended interviews (averaging an hour and a half) conducted by the author and one research assistant with members of dual-career couples who were legally married and had been living apart (residing separately for at least four days at a time) for at least three months. Interviews were conducted from the spring of 1977 through the spring of 1979.

Since both interviewers were female, it is possible that wives might have been more comfortable since they had an interviewer of the same sex. However, we did not register such an interviewer effect: husbands seemed no more or less comfortable with the interview as a group than did wives. The high educational level of both seemed to predispose them to a willingness to view the interview as "important" and "worthwhile."

At least one of the spouses lived in, or within driving distance (three hours) of the Chicago metropolitan area. A referral procedure generated 43 respondents (26 wives and 17 husbands) representing 28 dual-career marriages (15 couples, 11 wives only and 2 husbands only). The mean age for husbands was 38, for wives it was 36. The couples were relatively affluent, with family income greater than $35,000 for one-third of the men and 45 percent of the women. This high family income reflects the high educational and occupational attainment of these individuals: 94 percent of husbands and 85 percent of wives have completed some graduate work. All but one husband and four wives are either executives or professionals or are currently completing advanced degrees to enable them to become such. High proportions (53 percent husbands; 50 percent wives) are in academia either as graduate students or faculty. This suggests that the frequently noted (Gerstel, 1977; Hall and Hall, 1979) flexibility and autonomy of an academic's schedule may facilitate accommodation to this particular lifestyle's demands.

For the most part, too, these were not newlyweds: husbands were married an average of 13 years; wives 12 years. Typically, they had maintained two residences for a relatively short period: 59 percent of the men and 61 percent of the women had lived apart for less than 18 months. The frequency with which they saw each others seems to be bimodal: about half (husbands and wives) were apart less than one week (i.e., they are together on weekends), about 10 percent from one week to a month, and about two-fifths for longer than a month. Apparently the lifestyle is adopted under two sets of conditions: (1) the spouses expect to see each other often enough (i.e., within a week) to make the separation reasonably tolerable; or (2) the fact of being too far apart to regroup frequently is accepted as a necessary consequence of an unavoidable obstacle (e.g., only one medical school accepted the wife, and it is 1,000 miles from the husband's job location).[2]

ANALYSIS AND DISCUSSION

THE HERITAGE OF TRADITIONAL MARRIAGE

The decision to live apart produces a lifestyle that is difficult at best, endured in the service of career or other goals, but not one endorsed enthusiastically. Those couples who live this way, can, and do, list its advantages, but they do so thoughtfully, without conveying a sense of zest for the lifestyle.

Foremost among the advantages they recognize is the obvious freedom this lifestyle grants to each spouse to continue working at what he/she deems important enough to occasion the decision to live apart in the first place. Closely connected with this benefit is the freedom to devote long and uninterrupted hours to their work. This is a freedom which comes from not needing to dovetail each other's schedules around such constraints as meal times, recreation and sleep patterns.

But the concomitant awareness of the "other side" of this career-enhancing independence is what makes their subjective, overall perception of the marriage so complex. Part of the complexity comes from the fact that, although there are positive aspects to the arrangement, there is mutual realization that some of the advantages specific to each spouse are a source of disadvantages for the other. This manifests itself in resentment over the felt disadvantage, but also in guilt for the resentment. Both these emotions cloud their enjoyment of the advantages they each feel as well. This complex mixture of feelings stems in part from the way in which husbands and wives each view their own roles relative to "other" spouses of their sex.

Each takes traditional marriage as the vantage point from which to assess his/her own nontraditional marriage. Though they both appear to reject traditional marital roles, in which the wife's role is viewed as properly subordinated to the needs and demands of the husband's role, they both use the traditional role relationship as a backdrop, a frame of reference within which to come to terms with their own alterations of this view. They do so because the traditional roles, for all their conscious rejection of them, are still the only model of marital relationship upon which they can draw. They think of traditional relationships as a standard, and they battle with their sense of discord, or discrepancy from this standard. It is what they "know about marriage," even if they want to reject it.

The consciousness of traditional marriage as a reference point came through especially forcefully in one husband's response to the question about what advice he might give to a couple who was embarking on such a relationship. He said:

> The first part would be, make sure you have the husband/wife relationship straight. Know what's going on, why you're separating. Secondly, also get clear why one is staying and the other needs to go, wants to go. I think beyond that there's an underlying assumption about marriage or interpersonal relations that the degree of freedom that one demands must also be freely given to the other. The traditional variety is where the husband has much more freedom than the wife has. I think that is becoming less and less tenable.

The fact that traditional marriage is somehow a backdrop for their innermost feelings is also attested to by their sense of accomplishment at "pulling off" this lifestyle—one of the really positive aspects they talk about enthusiastically.

> We are patting ourselves on the back for being able to do this and pull it off successfully.

The very fact that they take pride in being the kind of people who "care about each other's careers" and who can successfully cope with the inconveniences and hurdles of this arrangement means that they see marriages which cannot do these things as a reference point. Lacking any other model from which to interpret and make sense of their own experience, they use traditional marriage, realizing the lack of the fit, but having little recourse because there is nothing better, in the sense of "more real," for them personally. Properly stated then, it is because this traditional relationship lurks in the background, props up their moral world view, as it were, that they experience some of the discomforts differently.

From the Wife's Perspective. Wives miss the emotional protection that they expect from the concept "husband" and they sense that this is the cost of their gain in independence. More so than husbands in our culture, wives are programmed to think of marriage as an intimacy oasis—an emotionally close relationship that will be "total." Though highly career-oriented, these women still give interpersonal relations, as compared to work-related rewards, a primacy in their lives that their husbands do not.

These career women (both younger and older) are also experiencing the severe throes of the first stages of professional careers in which the pressures and tensions are especially high and they are doing so without an emotional outlet in the form of an interested, sympathetic listener. There is the additional "loss," then, of a partner they had expected to help them work through the strains of professional career preparations. Both husbands and wives recalled conversations in which the husband had said to the wife, "You don't cry as much as you used to." This statement usually came after the wives' initial strains had abated somewhat because they had become accustomed to graduate or professional school or made friends on the new job:

> I think the separation would have been bad, but not nearly as devastating if I had not been under these pressures. Part of the reason I say that, is that, now, a year later, I'm in a part of my training that I'm really finding challenging—equally exhausting, if not more so—still always a feeling of being behind, on a treadmill, working 12 or 15 hours a day and supposed to read when I come home, but I'm too tired. But the separation this fall was not as painful for me at all, not by any means.

Wives also recognize that responsibilities they either expected their husbands would assume, or would at least be shared, become theirs to manage single-handedly. Having to contend with hassles produced by "going it alone"—everyday problems with the car and household repairs and other domestic responsibilities—blemishes the "freedom" they experience. Though wives recognize the value of learning to deal with these experiences, the burdens they create are not unnoticed. They are apt to convey this mixture of feelings as they would talk about necessary medicine:

> I know these things should not be a 'big deal,' but it's hard. Yet I know it's like how you feel when you're sick. You don't want to take the stuff they give you—it tastes bad—but you know it's good for you.

Although in terms of the provision of domestic services, men gain more from marriage than women do (see Bernard, 1972, on "his" and "her" marriage), the presumption that household maintenance and extra household responsibilities (e.g., insurance and loans) will be their responsibility means that wives are more likely to notice these demands as "additional." One older wife even remarked that the necessity to deal with some of the problems for which her husband would normally take responsibility was a way of preparing for widowhood.

From the Husband's Perspective. Husbands also look to marriage for emotional intimacy, but they are less likely to express as much unhappiness about the loss of emotional closeness that living apart can produce. No doubt this reflects in part, their socialization which typically does not encourage examination of and expression of feelings. But, in addition, as a recent psychoanalytically-oriented theorist argues (Chodorow, 1978), they are less likely to feel quite as abandoned if they are not emotionally involved with someone. They are more likely, too, to have learned to view the rewards associated with work as emotional equivalents to the rewards of interpersonal relationships. A typical husband's comments about his wife's reaction to living apart followed by his reflections on his own reaction shows this difference. About her response to living apart, he quoted her as saying, "Oh it's so lonely." Asked how he handled such feelings, he said:

> Well, my reaction is to move harder into starting to teach some classes and developing lesson plans and spending my time working on things like that.

But, though they may not acknowledge as much as their wives do an awareness of missing intimacy in their lives, they do recognize the guilt they feel about not being able to provide the emotional protection they sense their wives need. For instance, a husband says:

> I guess the feeling of being left alone is what was the hardest thing she ever had.
>
> or:
>
> Graduate school has been very tough for her. She cries a lot, not as much now as before. But I do know she could use someone to talk to more often—the tensions are great.

TWO TYPES OF DUAL-CAREER COUPLES WHO LIVE APART: "ADJUSTING" VERSUS "ESTABLISHED"

I have said that the implicit backdrop for the concerns these spouses raise is the discrepancy between expectations associated with spousal roles in traditional marriages and the roles they find themselves playing in this lifestyle. Further understanding of the ways in which implicit comparisons with traditional marriage underlay their responses requires distinguishing two groups. The basis of the distinction rests on age, but there are two other factors that also contribute to the decision to classify a marriage into one or the other type: length of marriage and presence of children. The first group, representing 11 of the 28 marriages, is basically younger. Their ages fall below the mean for husbands (38) and for wives (36); they have been married for less than the mean years married for their sex (13 for husbands, 12 for wives); and none of these spouses have children. The second group (17 of the 28) are older (all but one is in his/her late thirties or older); they have been married more than the mean years for their sexes and they typically have children (13 of the 17 marriages represented).

Resentment and guilt are common to both older and younger couples but it is a theme with different variations. Younger wives and husbands grapple more with career ascendency conflict: whose career commitment should predominate? Compared to the older couples they expend more effort at "adjusting" to the lifestyle. Older couples, because they are more likely to have children, contend more with conflict over increased child-care and domestic responsibilities for the spouse who stays with the family. Though not without difficulties, their response to the lifestyle is less stressful because they are more "established."

Younger Couples: "Adjusting." For the young wife, to have one's professional identity attended to at all, or for it to be a factor in producing the problems separation brings means, from her point of view (and his view of her and his traditional role, too), that she is getting a "benefit" or advantage ordinarily precluded from the definition of a traditional wife's role. She is, thus, "special" and she knows it. Yet, it is not an unalloyed advantage because a certain amount of guilt attaches to the recognition that her "specialness" causes him disadvantages relative to other husbands. Her sense of advantage is mitigated and undermined by the attendant guilt, leaving her with a burdensome, perplexing sense of somehow wronging him.

A wife in medical school expresses these conflicting emotions—satisfaction because she is able to devote herself to her work, unfettered by the usual wifely commitments, and guilt because she feels responsible for hindering her husband's potential.

> I was extremely tired but really enjoying myself and I would come home at night and fall into bed. I was very aware of the fact that if he'd been here, you know—relationships take time. There's a good side and bad side to that—if you don't have time and energy. So I thought, 'Well, while I'm doing surgery, maybe it's better that Dave's not here.'

Later in the interview she says:

> I know he has lots of dreams for what he wants to accomplish in his lifetime. I really have sensed in him this fall a sudden realization that he was getting older—that there's certain things he wants to get done with his life and somehow the way we're living, the separation, is demanding too much. It's too much of a sacrifice.

For the young husband, on the other hand, what contributes to his wife's sense of "having something special" at the same time creates his sense of loss. Although they both take pride in his feminist liberation, this does not compensate enough for the deprivation he feels relative to the perspective of the traditional husband role. After all, he is "giving up" the subordinacy to his needs that is supposed to accrue to the male, the breadwinner, the "necessarily" career-oriented member of the couple. For all his efforts to suppress the resentment, he still feels deprived.[3] It is not the ministrations of a doting wife he misses—neither one of them ever expected to be "picked-up after" or physically catered to. Their sense of equal partnership dismisses such behavior, and, in fact, most of these couples (both younger and older) have a history of a shared domestic division of labor. Rather, what he misses is a wife willing to acknowledge his "inherent" right to first place, to initial consideration. Of course, her career "counts" and is seen as important. It's just not *as* important as his. He both yearns for the subordinacy implied here and castigates himself for wanting it—because he realizes such subordinacy flies in the face of his other standards for their marriage. Yet, at least in this sense, he feels more denied, more "taken from" than she who knows she is being given an option not typically built into the wife's claims on the husband. Furthermore, he cannot acknowledge such feelings openly because, on the face of it, he "wants" full development of her potential as a reasoned, intellectual objective. Emotionally, however, he feels bereft, the loser of a benefit he had learned to anticipate from his concept of a "wife."

In the passage below, a husband tells of the effort it would have cost him to pass up the opportunity his present position affords him. Thinly veiled resentment and irritation with having to wrestle with the decision in the first place permeate his account. He did not want to sound resentful or irritated and seemed upset by the way the words were coming out. It was clear, even to him, that these emotions were there. His struggle also conveyed a sense of diminished, or at least sullied, self-esteem for the ambition and egotism his decision implied. Even more important, he was uncomfortable with the threat of his decision to his view of himself as someone "concerned with his wife's needs":

> We know this professional couple who have made a decision to alternate, giving each one's career a turn in deciding where to go. But that would be very hard for me. I wanted Barb's location to fit in with my plans, but we couldn't work it out. So I felt that it worked out that I had to be away from her; but right now, I needed for her to understand that. I needed for her to see that it had to be this way, for me. I just couldn't have let this go by.

Here the issue is not whether the wife shall have a career—the high educational level and professional orientation of both young people anticipate and even presume her professional life. Yet, each recognizes, at least covertly, that living apart is a response to her need to be somewhere he cannot be. This realization is caught especially well by a phrase used independently by both members of a couple. They each said that they frequently mused privately, as well as confronted each other directly (sometimes playfully, sometimes accusingly), with the question, "Who left whom?" Though she had actually moved out of their apartment in Arizona to attend law school in the midwest, she had done so on the assumption that he was to follow as soon as their affairs were settled. That was what they had agreed to. At the last moment, he decided he could not give up some powerful incentives his company offered him to stay, so now she sometimes feels he left her because he did not follow as planned. He, in turn, nurtures the view that since he stayed where *they* were, the issue is not at all clear. This dialogue, to which they both alluded, framed the tensions created by their mutual awareness of the antagonistic pulls of their respective careers.

The career ascendency struggle, viewed as it is from the perspective of traditional husband prerogatives and wifely responsibilities, is exacerbated by two additional intertwined factors that also reflect on these spouses' relative youth: their marriages have not endured long enough to exist as a solid reality, and the rewards of firmly established professional identities are not yet theirs. They are, thus, more vulnerable on two counts. As marital partners, they are still conscious of themselves in the process of creating a sense of "We-ness" and cannot yet count on a set of shared experiences to act as an emotional reservoir from which to draw. Secondly, as struggling, newly-minted professionals, they do not have the sense of confirmed competence that buttresses the egos of their older counterparts. The concern they share with other dual-career couples, "Is my marriage as important as my career?" is not yet counteracted by a sense of the marriage as one which can, in fact, endure the tensions they see beleaguering it. Because they have not as yet successfully created a marital unit involving two professional careers, they are not at all convinced that they will be able to. Hence, the inner nagging: "What kind of an emotional freak am I? Why is my career as important to me as my marriage is?"

> I think that's how we both saw it. We knew that neither of us was willing to give up the course we were going on so we couldn't ask the other to. Yet implicit in that was the realization that somehow you are making the statement that at least some aspect of your career is more important than being together. I think that's a real issue for today. I get really angry and feel like why do I even have to make these choices, one against the other. It doesn't seem right. There's obviously still a lot of pain.

It is interesting that the strains from the power struggle over whose career commitment should prevail weigh more heavily on them than does the fact of living apart *per se*. For these sophisticated, highly educated young people, a variation from the residence norm for married couples, though troublesome, pales in significance to the variation from the view that the husband is primary breadwinner and, therefore, his career needs should come first. While they neutralize potential pressures on them for living apart as do all such couples (by disengaging from questioning relatives and seeking friendships with singles and other members of commuter marriages), these pressures are not a source of profound discomfort to them. Much more basic to the tone of their own present relationship, and to the marital bond they sense they are still in the process of fashioning, is the struggle between the two of them. True enough, their own career struggles reflect societal views about the role of husband and wife, but they feel this as a power play between them. The power issue is all the more unsettling because these liberated young people *consciously* eschew notions of dominant husbands and submissive wives and because their education has built the expectancy that alternative lifestyles are more appealing than routine ones.

Older Couples: "Established." Career/marriage loyalty clashes of older couples are less violent. The sheer fact of having endured longer as a marital unit in which at least one partner has already contended with such clashes staves off some of the difficulties. They very much realize the importance of this backlog of experiences to their ability to cope with separation's pitfalls:

> We had enough of a base beforehand. I think if we had done this when we were married two or three years, we never would have made it. We have a lot invested emotionally in one another and I think we had a strong enough reserve and had enough smooth times before to make it. I think our bond was strong enough that it overcame all the problems and trauma.

There is another factor related to length of marriage that mutes any career ascendency conflict. For these older couples, there is the sense that the wives are correcting an imbalance in the marital relationship. Since they have been married longer, the past usually includes a time when the husband's career did "come first" while the wife stayed home to raise the children and/or work at a "job" to enable him to succeed.

Now that the wife has decided to plow her own field, they both look forward to the yield. In fact, in these instances, the husbands explicitly say, "It's her turn now!"—a sentiment clearly echoed by the wives. For them, there is at least an equal sense of accomplishment at living a lifestyle that allows them to give the wife "her turn." It is husbands in these marriages who are most likely to say that the "best thing" about living apart is "the opportunity it gives the wife to measure up to her potential," "to fulfill herself," "to be the person she's capable of being," and so forth. These older husbands then seem to react to the obligations imposed on the marriage as a kind of payment for advantages they previously enjoyed. Their sense of being burdened is somewhat softened by the real satisfaction they get from seeing their wives blossom.

Though both these factors, a common backlog of experience and a sense of correcting a previous imbalance, compensate in some ways, these older couples are not without painful sources of resentment/guilt. The very fact that their lives are more interconnected, that they have built up a sense of common identity, makes the separation that much more of a contrast:

> I don't relate intimately to a lot of people, but I do to her, so I've lost a great deal when she's gone.
>
> I really don't handle aloneness well. . . . I really wanted someone to come home to, to be with at night. I still do.

Even more important to the injuries these older mates nurse are those associated with shifts in parental responsibilities, particularly when the children remain with the husband. Husbands who take pride in their wives' accomplishments still resent the increased child-care and household maintenance burdens. Wives, in their turn, miss their children and worry about their lessened input to their children's lives. A quite typical husband says:

> There are chores and running of errands and I felt the anger of the frustration of the needs and demands placed on me by the three kids. More than anything else, the need to be at a piano lesson, to go to the doctor. I'm not sure I was angry at her as much as I was just angry that the need was there, that I couldn't share that.

Understandably the issues connected with childrearing loom large in these accounts. Particularly striking is the painful cost to mothers who leave the family home and relinquish day-to-day responsibilities of child care:

> I don't know how you balance—I'll be 40 when my last child leaves and that means I have from that point a productive 25 years. I don't know how to balance two or three years of wanting to stay and watch your kids against 30 years of your life.

These greater domestic/child-care costs then, are for older couples the counterpart to career ascendancy conflict which troubles younger couples more. On balance, though, the trade-offs each type makes are not equally discomforting because older couples do acknowledge more sources of satisfaction: the solidity of their own relationship; the faith that they can endure the demands of living apart; and the recognition that they are compensating for the wife's past efforts on her husband's behalf. Yet despite compensations, even older couples' accounts suggest that they are coping with the lifestyle more than enjoying it. For each type, then (and for each spouse), a compromise has been fashioned, but it is "no bargain" for either.

CONCLUSIONS

The introduction to this study promised analysis of ways in which selected variables affect a married couple's ability to contend with living in two separate residences. Though the data do allow cautious conclusions, the methodology employed here requires that we underscore the hypothetical nature of such conclusions. Qualitative analysis of responses from nonrandomly selected subjects may generate fruitful insights about the subjective side of a complex lifestyle, but insights they remain until adequately tested.

Given this proviso, a summary of our findings suggests that (1) older couples, (2) those married longer, (3) those among whom at least one spouse has an established career, and (4) those who are freed from childrearing responsibilities may find the lifestyle less stressful. Also, women may be more comfortable with the arrangement (Gerstel, 1978 came to the same conclusion) because of the recognition of their rights (relative to traditional co-resident marriages) that this lifestyle acknowledges.

Beyond this profile, the basically subdued responses of these spouses suggests that the changes propelled by women's increasing labor-force participation necessarily involve difficult transitions for those couples caught between older, traditional, role definitions and newly emerging definitions of marital roles. Two-residence living may be an inevitable outcome of women's currently more realizable professional aspirations. But it may not be an effortless response until our ideas about sex, marital and occupational roles catch up with the changes propelling women into careers.

Certainly the dilemma which generates the two-residence decision in the first place—the need to juggle the divergent demands of two careers—deserves more attention. Although earlier important analyses (Parsons, 1955; Goode, 1963) did raise questions about the interconnections between family and work roles, only recently have the strains produced by attempting to fit changing sex/family role definitions and work goals received the attention such changes demand (see Kanter, 1977; Pleck, 1977; Glazer, 1978).

From the feminist perspective, what seems required to remove the powerful legacy of traditional socialization is a generation accustomed to expect greater equity in marital roles. As the accounts of even these relatively egalitarian spouses indicate, vestiges of traditional socialization erode the most "liberated" resolve. From childhood on, men and women need to experience a non-sexist reality that brings spouses to marriages as equals before egalitarian ideology can become reality.

PART FOUR

Family Coordination of Work and Family Roles

Introduction

In the previous two sections, we have examined the economic roles of men and women and the effects of occupational conditions on families. The next two sections discuss how these linkages are handled on two levels: (1) attempts by men and women to coordinate their work and family roles and (2) institutional policies designed to reduce strains in work/family relationships. Part Four highlights three mechanisms through which men and women attempt to coordinate their work and family roles: (1) role staging, (2) role allocation, and (3) coping strategies. In Part Five, emphasis shifts to policy issues and structural changes associated with the interdependence of work and family roles.

Most individuals at some time perform the roles of worker, parent, and spouse; often all are performed simultaneously. Each involves activities, identities, obligations, and relationships with others. In many cases the obligations of an individual's work and family roles and relationships are too demanding, resulting in work/family overload and work/family interference. Work/family overload exists when demands on time and energy are too great to be met adequately or comfortably. Work-family interference occurs when conflicting demands make it difficult to fulfill the requirements of both work and family roles.

Work/family role staging and work/family role allocation are two major means used by men and women to deal with work/family overload and interference. Within the context of structural constraints, individuals manipulate their work and family roles in order to construct workable patterns of relationships and activities. Individuals juggle competing demands by adjusting the timing of activities over the life course. This adjustment process can be referred to as *work/family role staging*. Work/family role staging may be either simultaneous or sequential. In simultaneous staging, individuals perform both work and family roles across the adult life course. Sequential staging involves eliminating or postponing activities in one domain, either work or family, until a later stage thereby creating a more balanced and manageable mix of activities and relationships.

Individuals also construct relationships by negotiating and bargaining with others involved in role relationships. Families vary in the extent to which husbands and wives participate in work and family responsibilities. Patterns of work/family role allocation may be either traditional or symmetrical. In the most traditional pattern, the husband is the breadwinner and the wife performs the family work. Symmetrical role allocation involves a relatively interchangeable division of labor in which both husband and wife engage in earning outside the home and family work. These varying patterns of work/family role allocation result from negotiation using criteria such as sex-role norms, ability and competence, time and availability, and perceived equity.

The article by Giele, "Changing Sex Roles and Family Structure," sets the stage for this section by formulating several crucial issues regarding work/family role coordination. Giele discusses such familiar topics as increases in female employment and the effects of women's employment on the allocation of housework and child-rearing tasks. She stresses the importance of the timing of work and childbearing over the life course and the need for more symmetrical patterns of work and family roles among men and women. She develops the concept of *crossover* to refer to a more symmetrical pattern of role allocation in which men do more family work and women do more paid work than in the traditional pattern. Her analysis documents the importance of work/family role staging and allocation in meeting the demands of work and family roles.

Sequential staging is the modal type of labor-force participation for women. Most sequencing is oriented toward the accommodation of work-role participation to the responsibilities associated with family career stages. Several types of sequential work/family participation have been documented: *conventional*, in which the woman quits working when she marries or has children and doesn't return; *early interrupted*, in which she stops working for child rearing early in her career development and then returns; *late interrupted*, in which she establishes her career, quits for a period of child rearing, and then returns; and *unstable*, in which she alternates between full-time homemaking and paid employment. These patterns may be contrasted with simultaneous staging in which women pursue work and family activities across work and family career stages with minimal interruptions for child rearing.

The selection by Daniels and Weingarten, "Mothers' Hours: The Timing of Parenthood and Women's Work," reports on a qualitative study of women's timing and staging of parenting and work. They examine tradeoffs associated with early/sequential, late/sequential, early/simultaneous, and late/simultaneous childbearing patterns. The choice between early and late career interruption for childbearing influences the performance of work and family roles over life course. Early parenthood may increase economic pressures on the family and create some difficulties in career establishment with a later entry. However, many women may find advantages in having children at an age more compatible with other women. An earlier period of childbearing also gives women breathing room to formulate goals for a later career effort. Late childbearing allows earlier career establishment with some advantages on return and involves parenting responsibilities when there is less pressure to advance in a career by both the husband and wife. The sequential pattern of role staging involves less overload but may result in slower career progress. Simultaneous staging involves more overload but less career interruption. The article maps out these tradeoffs and provides qualitative examples of women's experiences with them.

Role staging has been used mainly by women to coordinate work and family roles. Women have adjusted the timing of work, marriage, and childbearing to reduce overload and interference and to increase options within the constraints of traditional role allocation. Many employed women perform two full-time jobs—one at work and one at home. This arrangement prompts the perception that the division of work and family roles between men and women is unfair and initiates calls for the husbands of employed women to do more family work.

The development of a symmetrical division of labor is a second basic approach for reducing overload and interference in work and family roles. In a symmetrical pattern of role allocation, husbands perform more family work and women perform more work-role duties than in traditional role allocation. Recent data suggest a slight increase in the amount of time that husbands of employed women spend in family work, although women still spend more time in family work than men. The major contributor to symmetry in family work is the decreased amount of time spent in family work by women. Women's increased labor-force participation also reduces the strain associated with the traditional male provider role. Men whose wives share the provider role have more flexibility to pursue satisfying work and to develop a broader range of interests, relationships, and identities.

In the article, "Men's Family Work: Three Perspectives and Some New Data," Pleck views this changing balance in the context of three value perspectives on men's family work. The "traditional" perspective deems men's relatively limited family work as appropriate. The "exploitation" perspective states that men's traditional family role creates overload for women but implies that change is unlikely. The "changing roles" perspective suggests that men are doing more family work and will continue to do so. Pleck's discussion makes us aware of changing perceptions of what men's family roles are, what they should be, and what they are likely to become.

More detailed analysis of the processes involved in men's changing family role is presented in Lein's article, "Male Participation in Home Life: Impact of Social Supports and Breadwinner Responsibility on the Allocation of Tasks." Lein explores task allocation in two-earner families through intensive interviews with twenty-five lower-middle-class families. She examines sources of ambivalence and resistance to change among men. These men acknowledge the economic contribution made to the family by their employed wives: however, they also see their own paid work as their major contribution to their families. This belief is reinforced by members of their male peer groups. In addition, some wives find it difficult to relinquish family tasks to their husbands. This article complements Pleck's analysis of more general trends by illustrating dilemmas and contradictions in husbands' and wives' perceptions of how work and family roles should be allocated.

These articles on role staging and role allocation map out the beginnings of alternative approaches to work/family role coordination. They indicate the need for changes in attitudes and behavior among men and women to increase flexibility and the range of options available for work/family role coordination under changing conditions.

A more detailed view of how families coordinate work and family roles can be obtained by examining the use of various coping strategies among families. The concept of coping is part of family stress theory, the framework used in Voydanoff's article on unemployment and family stress in Part Two. In this approach, coping is viewed as an active process in which individuals manipulate their role expectations and behaviors to deal with stressful situations. In this context, work/family overload and interference are stressors that families develop coping strategies to handle.

In "Interrole Conflict, Coping Strategies, and Satisfaction Among Black Working Wives," Harrison and Minor examine coping strategies used in different types of interrole conflict. Women with wife/worker conflict are most likely to cope by actively attempting to alter external demands such as problem solving with their husbands. Those with mother/worker conflict are most likely to make private decisions such as setting priorities, changing their own attitudes, or eliminating roles. Those with mother/wife conflict are equally likely to use either strategy. A third strategy—attempting to improve the quality of role performance by working harder or managing time better—is used infrequently. The authors suggest that an approach involving negotiation and changing role demands is more appropriate in the wife role; inflexibility in the mother/child relationship requires more adjustment on the part of the mother to resolve conflicts. The article documents that various strategies are used to resolve different types of conflicts.

Skinner's article, "Dual-Career Family Stress and Coping: A Literature Review," indicates that similar coping strategies are used within the family system of dual-career families, including redefining roles, setting priorities, compartmentalizing roles, and improving performance. In addition, Skinner documents the use of strategies to obtain supports from outside the family; for example, hiring help, developing supportive relationships with friends, and establishing more favorable work arrangements through employment policies such as flextime.

Both articles (Skinner, and Harrison and Minor) suggest that these coping strategies, employed mostly by women, are individual rather than structural approaches to resolving role conflict and strain. In the next section, we explore more institutionalized approaches to coordinating work and family roles.

13

Changing Sex Roles and Family Structure

Janet Zollinger Giele

The revolution in the status of women can most simply be summarized in the fact that 32 million working women won't go home again. . . . The task of the next revolution is to bring about a situation where the work performed at home is a responsibility for human beings instead of a burden for women.

– Carolyn Shaw Bell, "The Next Revolution," *Social Policy* (September–October 1975)

There is a close tie between the change in men's and women's roles and the change in family structure. But the relative status of women in family life is more difficult to measure than their status in public affairs. Political, economic, or educational activities operate in "markets" that assign the individual a formal status and pay a stated income. The family by contrast is "associational" (Weinstein and Platt, 1973: 1–19). The status of each member is enmeshed with facts of birth and death, marriage, or divorce. Participation in the family hinges on the emotional life of others as well as on individual accomplishment. Laws and public policies directed at child care, the elderly, tax rates, or public welfare affect not only one member or one sex but also the whole family unit. Consequently, examination of the relative status of women and men in the family very quickly leads to considering the structure of the family unit and the situational realities that determine its form.

Women's and men's roles will not really change unless family institutions also change, but it is not at all clear in what order and in what direction family life will be transformed. Maybe, as some economists suggest, the next steps to be taken are public measures that will support a new occupation of consumer maintenance, or allow tax deductions for household costs such as heat, light, or child care, much as corporations are allowed tax deductions for their expenses (Bell, 1975; Lekachman, 1975). Or perhaps the next steps must be personal and ideological, through commitment to the idea that the family is the responsibility of both men and women.

No matter what change comes first, it is clear now that the traditional sex-typed division of labor between women's work at home and men's work at a job is under strain in every major industrial nation. Although 40 to 60 percent of women are employed in such countries as the United States, Russia, Poland, and Japan, they pay a penalty of being overburdened by both domestic and paid work (Blake, 1974). Employed American women who have families average a total of 70 hours of work a week (Gauger, 1973: 23). Each week they have a few hours less leisure time than men for sleep or relaxation (Szalai, 1973). Thus more women have entered employment without having secured the needed adjustments in family life.

The balance of work and leisure is only one issue raised by change in sex roles. Other related problems emerge. The poverty of female-headed households is one example. If through divorce, widowhood, or desertion a women is left alone to head a household with children, her children are about six times more likely to grow up in poverty than children living in male-headed families (Bane, 1976: 118).

In relation to changing sex roles, family issues are especially significant as the boundary between public and private life becomes more permeable. On the one hand, demographic shifts caused by the lengthening of life and the changing life cycle of women and families predate current public policy issues such as child care or homemaker allowances. On the other hand, the extension of government supports into various functions of private life such as health care and care of the elderly gives public policy potential power to influence the shape of family life and future sex roles.

THE LIFE CYCLE OF CONTEMPORARY WOMEN

Two major demographic changes have taken place that affect the family life cycle and women's role within it. The child-bearing period has been compressed, and adult women's average length of life has increased. As a result the typical American woman in this century bears fewer children and has her last child at the age of 30; that child leaves home when a woman is in her late 40s, and she can still expect to live 30 more years. As recently as the turn of the century, women were bearing their last child when they were 33, seeing their last child married when they were 56, and themselves living only 10 or 15 years more.

Each major demographic trend affecting women points to the uncertainty of following any single prescribed route over the life course. Marriage may end in divorce; a woman may have to support herself and children; a man may have to work out complicated schedules and relationships with children by a former marriage. Rather than be confined to sex-stereotyped activities or try to meet rigid timetables of accomplishment, men and women may do best to adopt a flexible time perspective that permits them to negotiate twists and turns as they appear. By this perspective the family is not so much a distraction from work as the primary social system for synchronizing the achievement and affiliative needs of both sexes.

Using the life-cycle perspective, Elder (1975) shows that the problems of the dual-career family are frequently ones of timing—handling the decision on when and where to move and whose career should take precedence, or smoothing out the periods when both members are overloaded and neither can relieve the other (Elder and Rockwell, 1976). Early in her life a woman's time at home typically coincides with childbearing and care of young children. Later a woman's employment can help the family meet periods of slowdown or unemployment. Women's work can help raise family status by raising overall income; it frequently evens out income differences of families in the same occupational or social category (Oppenheimer, 1977).

Children are affected by the activities of each parent. A mother's employment appears to provide her daughter with a less restricted view of the female role and may involve the father more in child rearing. However, if the mother is guilt ridden for being employed and has less than adequate household arrangements, or is under emotional stress, her mothering may be less adequate than that of a nonemployed mother (Hoffman and Nye, 1974; Hoffman, 1974). A couple's location in one city rather than another may offer opportunities for a wife's employment and wages that lower fertility by discouraging decisions to have more children (Havens, 1972).

The life-cycle perspective focuses on the family decisions that synchronize events such as marriage, births, education, and employment. The way these decisions are timed has implications for all the family members, not just for the husband or the wife or the children. Timing regulates the interplay of one individual's needs with those of the others. It is too soon to describe all the principles of this "family clockwork." But some evidence is available to suggest that a new set of norms is emerging to govern the interaction of paid employment, parenthood, and household work. The new normative ideal appears to be one that encourages flexibility over the life span in the tasks that one takes up at each age and in the sex-typing of these tasks. In general it appears that greater crossover between age and sex roles may be more widely institutionalized as a result of two relatively new developments. On the one hand, there is wider recognition that work patterns of men and women are becoming more similar over the life span. On the other hand, there is increasing recognition that responsibilities for parenthood and household work fall unequally on the shoulders of men and women, and there are frequent suggestions as to how the tasks might be more evenly divided. These two themes signal an emerging norm of sex equality to be achieved by flexible role allocation over the lifetime of the individual.

PAID EMPLOYMENT

Between 1950 and 1975, the number of families with two workers or more increased from 36 to 49 percent. Most of the increase was due to increased participation by married women in the paid labor force. Slightly less than a quarter (23.8 percent) of all wives participated in the labor force in 1950 as compared with almost half (44.4 percent) in 1975. In 1974, of those women with children aged six to 17, one-half worked at some time during the year, and of those with children under six, one-third were employed. The median income of husband-wife families with a wife in the labor force was $14,885 as compared with $12,360 for the families where a husband only was employed and $8,225 where a wife only was employed (Hayghe, 1976). Gradual acceptance of married women's work and its positive contribution to the family now causes social scientists to examine more closely the internal dynamics of family decision-making that either enable women to work or make such a decision difficult for them.

As household size has diminished, the family enterprise has become a more limited unit requiring less total input of time in its care and maintenance. Yet it is still a demanding unit because there is less help for household work or child care. In 1790 there was an average of 2.8 children under age 16 in each household, and the average size of the private household was 5.7 persons. In 1950 there were likely to be only 1.0 persons under 16, and the average number of people living in the household had dropped to 3.4 (Grabill et al., 1958, 1973: 379; Laslett, 1973). Furthermore, among working-class families who were under economic pressure to support either young or adolescent children, as many as 20 to 35 percent once took in boarders (Modell and Hareven, 1973: 479). The practice of taking in lodgers and boarders declined markedly, however, from the nineteenth century to the present.

More married women entered the work force after 1900 as a result of the decline in the birth rate, the lengthening of women's lives, and the trend to smaller households that took place during the past century. The change is reflected in a steady rise in labor force participation rates of women. Between 1940 and 1974 the proportion of married women in the labor force rose from 14 to 43 percent (Kreps and Clark, 1975: 8). Moreover, the shape of the curve representing their participation at various ages also changed. Whereas the pattern through 1940 showed women entering paid employment, then leaving it at the age of marriage and childbearing, the pattern after 1940 showed a dip in participation around the age of 30, then a rise during the middle years (35 to 54) and then another fall after that as women approached the age of retirement. For men, by contrast, the years between 1953 and 1973 show falling labor-force participation rates, particularly in the later years. For married men between the ages of 55 and 64, the participation rate has fallen ten points in the last twenty years. And since the late 1960s, there has been some decline in the participation rate of married men between the ages of 45 and 54 (Taeuber and Sweet, 1976: 51–52; Kreps and Clark, 1975: 9, 14–15).

The gradual convergence of men's and women's labor-force participation rates and the greater concentration of work in the middle years (caused by longer education in the early years and retirement in the later years) prompts Kreps and Clark (1975: 57–58) to suggest that work should be more evenly distributed over the life span:

> The married woman's earnings have enabled families to finance additional years of schooling for their children. Similarly, the family with two salaries over an extended portion of worklife can afford earlier retirement than the one that must rely on a single worker's income, assuming the same wage scale. Thus, the capacity to purchase an increase in free time for the male is enhanced by woman's market work. Intrafamily support of the young adults still in school and of older men in retirement offers the male greater flexibility in scheduling his work; market activity during the woman's middle years substitutes for the male's labor-force activity at each end of worklife.

But Kreps and Clark (1975: 56, 3) argue that alternative allocations of working and nonworking time could have been made over the last several decades if, instead of accumulating leisure to be used at the beginning and end of adulthood, it had been used in more piecemeal fashion through the middle years as well. "It would have been possible," they say, "to reduce work weeks, add vacation time, or even provide worker sabbaticals for education and job retraining, as productivity improved and the size of the labor force grew." Furthermore, if nonworking time were more evenly apportioned over the work life, "it would greatly enhance the male's availability for home work at critical times in the family's life cycle." Instead, as it is now, much of males' use of time freed of market work cannot easily be applied to daily performance of household chores. Leisure comes in a form that causes it to be applied to other forms of activity or to work-related pressures such as commuting time.

PARENTHOOD

Corresponding to the growing similarity between the labor-force participation rates of men and women, there are important parallel themes in parenting trends. As families grow smaller and women's input of time to parenting diminishes, one possibility is that both parents' time with children declines. There are then smaller families as a result of the relatively higher value of both women's and men's time in the paid labor force. Economists reason that, as the price of our time increases, we substitute services we can buy, such as sending children to a day-care center or sitting them in front of a television set (Sawhill, 1977: 118). Alice Rossi (1977: 14–16, 22) finds alarming the type of similarity between men and women that deemphasizes the child bearing and child rearing functions. Among the *avant garde* advocates of new marriage forms and among the more extreme feminists concerned with women's work achievement, she notes that it is adults' satisfaction rather than the needs of children that is central.

An alternative theme, however, is also finding greater prominence. It emphasizes the role of the father in child rearing and the greater need for more sharing of parenthood responsibilities by mother and father. Beginning in the 1960s, the Scandinavian countries, particularly Sweden, engaged in a great debate over sex roles that resulted in official policies supporting the right of fathers to take leave from work part time during a child's early years. In the United States the Moynihan report focused attention on the positive role of the father in child development and argued for income support systems that would keep the father in the home rather than make him desert so his wife could qualify for welfare.

Now there is a positive interest in showing that fathers can be nurturant parents and adequate to the task if they need be single parents. David Lynn (1974) has marshaled an impressive array of research findings on the positive role of the father in child development and the potentially harmful effects of father absence. James Levine (1976) provides evidence from interviews with contemporary fathers that show child rearing should not be thought of so exclusively in terms of the mother-child relationship. Rather, men are capable of as much role flexibility in moving into the nurturant parent roles as women are of engaging in the paid labor force. Rochelle Wortis (1971: 739), after reviewing the social science literature on mothering, concludes, "The acceptance of the concept of mothering by social scientists reflects their own satisfaction with the status quo. The inability of social scientists to explore and advocate alternatives to current child rearing practices is due to their biased concepts of what should be studied and to their unwillingness to advocate social change."

HOUSEWORK AND VOLUNTEER WORK

It would seem reasonable, if more women are working, that men would be helping women more with the household work. In fact, however, as recently as 1972, men did an average of only about 1.6 hours a day of work in the home, whether their wives worked or not (Hedges and Barnett, 1972). In addition women also use their base in the home to perform many needed volunteer activities in the community. When it comes to taking care of elderly parents or other older members of the community, what evidence there is suggests that these tasks fall overwhelmingly on middle-aged women, usually daughters (Blenkner, 1963: 50–51).

Some historical and sociological studies have furthermore indicated that household work has not shrunk so fast as we might have thought. Survey data show that since the 1920s there has been no homemaker's shortening of the work week, despite improvements in technology and compression of family functions. A study conducted by the Survey Research Center in Michigan in 1965–1966 showed that unemployed women spend 55 hours a week in household work, as compared with an average of 52 hours a week reported by housewives in 1925–1926, before the widespread introduction of the refrigerator or automatic washing machine (Vanek, 1974). And standards were raised: not only were the clothes washed more often and the house kept cleaner, but more time was also spent on child care, because increasing importance was accorded to the maternal function (Cochran and Strasser, 1974; Cowan, 1973; Wortis, 1971). These changes were all particularly salient for the nonemployed housewife.

By contrast employed wives spent only about half as much time on housework—26 hours. The difference could not be accounted for by their having more help either from husbands or from workers in their households (Vanek, 1974). The employed women probably had to "cut corners," accept messier houses, and perhaps eat out more.

Despite the overwhelming concentration of women in the household functions of housework, cooking, and care of clothing, and the tendency for men to take care of yard work and maintenance tasks, there is nevertheless some impressionistic and anecdotal evidence that men's involvement in female-type tasks is becoming more acceptable. Along with the men taking care of children, stories on the family page of the newspaper sometimes feature men doing needlework or cooking. Retired men sometimes become involved in household tasks such as cooking and cleaning. Or they throw their energies into community volunteer activities that were once the preserve of women.

It may be in fact the possibility of experimentation with the allocation of work over the life span that will provide most leverage against the "buffers" that now prevent men from taking on household responsibilities. Joseph Pleck hypothesizes that housework within the family is like the secondary sector of the dual labor market. Men don't engage in it because their energies are reserved for their primary work outside the home. According to Pleck (1977: 420) "the most significant feature of the relation between husband and wife family role performance is the apparent bottleneck in which husbands' family time does not respond to variations in wives' family time resulting from wives' paid employment." In addition the female work role is more vulnerable to family demands. For husbands the work-family boundary is permeable as well, but only in the other direction: to allow demands from work to impinge on family time. As I would also argue using the concept of crossover, Pleck believes that, to balance the new roles of husband and wife, each role must become symmetrically permeable to work and family demands. The question is what will make this permeability or crossover occur?

Some norms have already developed to define how couples can carry dual careers in which both are involved in family and work. For example, there is an increasing belief that a wife should get as much education as possible so that her position in the job market will be advantageous. The more work experience she has before marriage and childbearing, it is believed, the more likely her ability to reenter that world later on. She may be wise to delay marriage or childbearing until her mid- to late twenties. While she has heavy responsibilities at home, she can "keep a hand in" by taking continuing education courses, holding a part-time job, maintaining outside interests, or building up a list of credentials through volunteer work that will lead to a paid job (Loeser, 1974: 117–131).

Implied in the wife's maintenance of flexibility is that the husband will also remain open to his own inner development and perhaps after mid-career choose other directions of activity or choose more involvement in the family in order to develop his emotional side as much as his occupational side. Current interest in the male "mid-life crisis" in large part seems to reflect this emerging set of expressive concerns on the part of middle-aged males (Brim, 1976).

The new flexible life course for husband and wife is not yet fully institutionalized. Not all the public and private supports necessary in industry or education have yet been set in place. Before considering such policy changes as might be needed, we examine some of the major types of family forms that now exist and analyze what elements of each support both flexibility and symmetry in the roles of men and women.

CHANGES IN THE FAMILY STRUCTURE

Given the changing demographic realities for women's lives—they are through raising children sooner, live longer, and are more likely to combine paid work with family life—what will be the shape of family life that will allow them a more equitable share in leisure as well as in work and family? How are family forms even now changing to show us the outlines of a more egalitarian arrangement to come? The answers are important, for they suggest not only how younger generations should be prepared to select from the available alternatives, but also how practical legislation or voluntary efforts may be undertaken that will support the forms that seem most desirable to us now.

If recent books and articles on family life can be taken as any trustworthy guide, there is remarkable convergence on a new, more egalitarian family form, which Young and Willmott (1973) term "the Symmetrical Family." Changes in the industrial and ecological order as well as limited fertility and feminism have brought about this change. The phenomenon is observable not only in the managerial and professional class but also among shift workers in the manufacturing and service trades. Yet at the same time as marriages are becoming less hierarchical, husbands being asked to share more housework, and wives working more outside the home, another development is taking place alongside. Alternative family forms are springing up here and there: communes; female-headed families that result from separation, divorce, or unwed pregnancy; or households made up of unrelated individuals living together. These new forms challenge the assumption on which the traditional nuclear family is based. Alternative styles show, for example, how child-care or cooking arrangements can be modified. But they also illustrate that any social system lives with constraints of one kind or another.

Changing patterns of participation in family life precipitate strains in the established patterns. As we have seen in the case of higher divorce rates, remarriage, and the increase in dual-worker families, new "scripts" for action are being tried out as each family experiments with its internal division of labor and timing of decisions.

There is now a repertoire of several types of family script that may be selected to fit various economic or cultural conditions. There is considerable consensus among historians and sociologists on what these types are, though there may be differences over terminology and more refined categories. Each broad type is associated with a particular rhythm of life and a characteristic ecological niche.

Young and Willmott (1973) used the terms Stage 1, 2, and 3 families to describe the types that they observed in a broad cross-sectional study of 2,600 London families in 1970. Stage 1 roughly corresponds to what others have called the peasant or preindustrial family. The whole family participates in a family-related economic endeavor; family and occupational life are still undifferentiated, and the husband has primary authority. Stage 2 families are similar in form to the Victorian ideal of the early industrial period. In them occupation and family life are no longer joined; husbands are ideally the sole breadwinners, and wives remain at home in charge of children and other domestic responsibilities. Yet the family is not patriarchal in the way it was in the preindustrial form. Instead the two sexes have different and complementary spheres of authority. Stage 3 families have become common only recently. They differ from the Victorian ideal in that both husband and wife typically work outside the home, and ideally both share in family duties. Greater equality emerges between them because their duties are not just complementary but are nearly symmetrical.

Hayghe (1976: 16) estimates that families with both a husband and wife in the labor force now make up 41 percent of all U.S. husband-wife families, a larger single block than any other form; families with husbands only in the labor force account for 34 percent and families with wives only in the labor force account for three percent. Although it has been edged out of first place by the dual-worker form, the Victorian or early industrial type of family still constitutes a major alternative in America today, perhaps especially during that period in the family life cycle when children are young. Variant forms may occur among young adults who have not yet launched their childbearing, or among persons who have experienced marital disruption and are between families. The dual-worker family may be most common among people in the middle years when wives have reentered the labor force.

Although there now appears to be a greater range of family forms available from which people can choose depending on their point in life, the development of these alternatives seems to have been linked to the historical process of modernization. Several historical and sociological reviews of family change have questioned whether any such connection exists. Rosabeth Kanter (1977) notes that the company town, the family store, and the two-person career of the clergyman or doctor have all traditionally blurred the boundary between family and work. Elizabeth Pleck (1976) points out that poor agricultural workers frequently had to hire themselves out as laborers and the work of men and women was separate even in preindustrial times. Tamara Hareven (1975) shows the connection between family time and the actual flow of work in the factory. Nevertheless, in my opinion, the overall process of differentiation between family life and productive work that Smelser (1959) described in the cotton-manufacturing towns of early industrial England still largely describes the main trends in change of family life over the last century. The preindustrial family was both a family unit and a unit of production. The early industrial family separated child rearing and consumption tasks from the productive and instrumental tasks performed in the paid labor force. The modern symmetrical family is open to greater permeability between work and family as a result of further differentiation of tasks, which makes much of the work of males and females potentially interchangeable.

One sign of ferment in the family division of labor comes from American opinion surveys conducted between 1964 and 1974. Over that decade women's attitudes toward the traditional division of labor between husbands and wives showed a consistent trend. In every major segment of the population, the proportion of women supporting the traditional pattern declined. At the same time the proportion supporting women's rights in the labor market and their options for a life without marriage or motherhood increased (Mason et al., 1976: 585).

Symmetrical families are a phenomenon of modern society not just in the United States but in Europe as well. Househusbands are not common in Sweden, but they do exist there and their roles are accepted. Dual-career families in Great Britain are the subject of a major study by Rhona and Robert Rapoport (1976). Other countries of Eastern and Western Europe where high numbers of women are in the labor force have for the time being put women under a heavy overload if they have both families and careers. The way out of this stressful situation has not yet resulted in full institutionalization of the symmetrical family. But a rising divorce rate and growing insistence by women on revising the roles within marriage point in that direction (Fogarty et al., 1971: 96; Sokolowska, 1977; Silver, 1977).

Why is the symmetrical family the likely wave of the future? The answer comes from an analysis of modern society and the kind of capacity for role flexibility that a highly differentiated structure requires. Moreover, when society is changing rapidly and circumstances are uncertain, a high degree of flexibility is more adaptive than rigid adherence to one pattern of activity or another. This is true not only of individuals but of the family itself as well. The family performs its function best when it handles nonuniform tasks that are not easily farmed out to bureaucratic institutions, which can perform them more expertly or more efficiently. But as Litwak (1970: 354–359) has pointed out, what are defined as nonuniform functions change as fast as technology and the social environment change. For the family to perform at its best, it must therefore be able to take on functions that are at the moment defined as nonuniform and to drop them when they become routine.

For example, early in the century laundry was a routine menial task, and there were outside laundry establishments prepared to provide the service; even working-class women sent out their wash. When, however, the home washing machine appeared and new fabrics and automatic washers were introduced, laundry returned to the home. The household could then meet the special requirements of each individual's laundry needs and care for each fabric type better than could the commercial establishment. Litwak (1970: 358–359) concludes analysis of the laundry example with a general rule that gives a clue to the type of family that may be best adapted to our rapidly changing society:

> [The] one key structural need of the family—given a rapidly changing technology—is the capacity to deal with changing functions, the capacity to rapidly change what are legitimate and what are nonlegitimate activities, or most generally the capacity to be flexible.

One of the main sociological consequences of flexibility in the family is role substitutability between husband and wife rather than fixed sex-typed roles. The wife cannot just be an expressive leader in the family and let the husband be the instrumental leader in the world of work outside. She may be the instrumental leader in bringing up the children or managing the household affairs, but she needs the husband's expressive help to handle the tensions that may result, just as he needs her expressive help with anxieties about work. Furthermore, by Litwak's reasoning, the family has major commitments in all areas of life, not just to the care of young children. It is the most effective agent for handling other types of nonuniform problems, such as peculiar circumstances of health or emotional depression, sudden loss of income by some member, some failure in school or work, or some threat to the local neighborhood. To meet such unexpected needs, the "family clockwork" must be able to respond appropriately.

As each family experiments to produce a workable formula of interaction, certain common themes emerge. One is that couples are still more likely to put primary emphasis on the husband's job as a basis for choosing a residential location or timing major family events. The wife's role more often contains the compromises that keep the family flexible. Yet even this pattern may be caught at only one point in time, when the children and couple are relatively young. Later on, the wife's career may in fact take precedence. Families move in and out of different forms, and one must keep remembering that their very flexibility makes it difficult to capture a snapshot of them that is true for more than a moment. It is therefore important to examine some of the forms that families may take over a period of time.

Szalai's survey extended into Belgium, Bulgaria, Czechoslovakia, France, East and West Germany, Hungary, Peru, Poland, the United States, the U.S.S.R. and Yugoslavia, and it collected data from 30,000 respondents. Nowhere had the modern family structure actually been achieved. Husbands helped with household care and important peripheral activities such as maintenance and repair to a degree that almost equaled wives' hours spent in cooking and primary housework. But the two sexes still rarely crossed over to help in each other's domain. Perhaps most telling was the consistent finding that employed men after their contributions to the household still had 50 percent more leisure than the employed women (Szalai, 1973: 28–30).

Where fairness and equity had proceeded farthest, however, was in those societies that were at a high level of socioeconomic development and in those families that had a more comfortable standard of living. Among marriage partners that were better educated and in those couples where the wife was more involved outside the home as a breadwinner or otherwise, the symmetrical ideal was also closer to being realized (Szalai, 1973: 31).

Numerous studies of professional couples where the wife also has a career have shown consistently that even in this type of marriage, the husband's career is accorded somewhat greater priority than that of the wife. Yet Holmstrom (1972: 40), who interviewed 22 career couples, notes:

> The wives accommodated to their husbands' careers more than vice-versa, when deciding where to live. But the more surprising finding is how much the husbands' decisions were affected by the career interests of their wives. In quite a departure from middle-class norms, many husbands went out of their way to live in places where their wives could also obtain desirable employment.

It would be a mistake to suppose that the ideal patterns of role symmetry and sharing that are occasionally realized in a few dual-career families are yet in fact a reality for the great majority of two-worker families. With respect to sharing of household work, data reported in 1969 and 1970 by Kathryn Walker are sobering: Women at that time still performed considerably more housework than men—4.8 hours a day for the married women employed 30 hours a week or more as compared with 1.6 hours for the employed men who were married to working wives. Child-care routines still assume that the mother is the parent primarily responsible for coming to school conferences, delivering the child to weekday extracurricular activities, and being at home when the child is sick. Joseph Pleck (1977) perceives the differential permeability of men's and women's careers to the demands of family as patterned in such a way as to reinforce the priority of husband's commitment to work and wife's commitment to family.

WORKING-CLASS FAMILIES

New efforts to understand working-class families in the United States closely parallel the findings of Young and Willmott in London. Working-class people in some ways give more devotion to family than middle-class people, presumably because their work lives are less stimulating and all-consuming. The 1974 Virginia Slims Poll found for example that, when women were asked what they wanted most for a son, a happy marriage or an interesting career, far more of the less-educated women gave priority to family than to work.

Of course, it is also true that the older respondents gave more priority to family than to work, and, to the extent that age and lower education are associated, differential responses by education may not be related just to social class but to age as well. Yet such results seem to make sense out of what some have found to be the puzzling rejection by working-class women of women's liberation. College women and their husbands have the education that would open interesting careers to them. Educated women thus feel frustrated when doing housework, because they compare it with the work that they might do for pay. But working-class women, whose alternatives are repetitive factory work or menial service occupations, find their liberation through independence in home life, cooking, and household work. To them being a good wife and mother is one of the few routes to significant satisfaction, and the middle-class women's liberation rhetoric seems to them to be devaluing a world they consider to be of primary importance (Seifer, 1975; Levison, 1974; Meade, 1975; Coles, 1973: 106).

Nevertheless, there may soon perhaps be a convergence between the working class and the middle class in their attitudes toward family life and the roles of husbands and wives. In reviewing what is known about blue-collar women, Victoria Samuels (1975) finds signs that there has been some change since Rainwater and Komarovsky surveyed working men's wives in 1959. At that time working-class women lived a routine life segregated from much companionship with men. One day was pretty much the same as another. Husbands resisted wives' working, and wives seemed to lack self-confidence (Rainwater et al., 1959; Komarovsky, 1964). In the 1970s more working-class women view themselves as being competent in the role of housewife than the number reporting such competency in 1959. They show more interest in work and freedom to work. And they seem to feel that they can be more assertive in the home (Samuels, 1975). Even in the drabness and frustration that Rubin finds in the lives of working-class women, there is an underlying theme that more egalitarian relationships within the family are desired. The implicit ideal is more talking, more understanding, and more sharing of emotional life between wives and husbands. Ann Oakley (1975) contends that housework is also boring to working-class women. And among the working class Lein et al. (1974) finds that a significant number of husbands share in housework and child care when their wives are working.

In her studies of working-class women, Nancy Seifer (1975) got to know a few women in various parts of the United States—for example, the wife of a coal miner in Alabama and a secretary in a steel mill in Gary, Indiana. Each of these women became an activist for women's rights through some catalyzing experience that touched her own job or her family's interests. They all had been turned off by middle-class feminist rhetoric that devalued the wife and mother role, but when they perceived their common interests with other women over issues such as equal pay, opportunities for promotion, or the family health insurance plans of their unions, they became involved.

Just why such changes have occurred is still hidden. Many have speculated that a wife's working actually changes the power relationship in any couple. The husband has less opportunity to dominate when the wife also brings in a paycheck (Bahr, 1974: 184–185). In the past a wife's employment might have threatened a husband's self-esteem. But rising participation of women in the work force is now apparently changing that norm. Short-term unemployment or a cutback in working hours or overtime is such a common threat to the working class that a wife's work is unquestionably an asset for tiding the family over lean times. Seifer (1975: 14) has recently estimated that the majority of women in working-class families are now employed for at least some part of the year. Dougherty et al. (1977) found in a study of fourteen Boston area dual-worker blue-collar families that every family had experienced at least one layoff of either husband or wife in the recession period since 1972–1973. Husbands tremendously valued a wife's contribution when her wages helped keep the family income up to the standard they desired.

EMERGING FAMILY FORMS

High rates of marital breakdown have put large numbers of women "at risk" of forming single-parent households. Divorce has also given rise to remarriage and reconstituted nuclear families. In addition, communal experiments and individuals in transition between single or married states have created intimate networks and other variant forms. Of these we shall give most attention to the single-parent households, reconstituted marriages, and experiments with communal and modified extended families because they have the most far-reaching implications for women's status. Each of these variant forms can provide information on the structural conditions that are conducive to equality in household and work roles, legal provisions, child-care arrangements, and leisure.

From the point of view of women, the significant feature of single-parent families, particularly where a woman is head of the household, is that resources may be less than in the nuclear or extended form, and as a result the female head may be unusually burdened with responsibility. Much effort has been devoted to lowering the number of such women on the welfare rolls by means tests or by getting them into the labor force. But not even the majority of single heads of family are on welfare. Those not on welfare also have needs that should be met for the sake of the family and the children.

The proportion of white families headed by women has not changed in 40 years, although it has doubled for blacks. What has changed markedly is the proportion of these families in younger age groups with children. It is the presence of children that makes the difference between poverty and an adequate standard of living for the families with a single head. In 1972 the Michigan Panel Study of Income Dynamics studied 5,000 families over a period of several years and found that 65 percent of all families with mother heads had no income from welfare and no more than a fifth of all mother heads received as much as half of their income from welfare. Only 47 percent received any alimony or child support from fathers, and the median amount of such support was only $1,350 (Heclo et al., 1973: 12–13). But a relatively high percentage of even college-educated female heads of families are poor, 18 percent as compared with 3 percent of college-educated male heads. Lack of male support coupled with women's frequent lack of marketable skills and much lower earning power, even if they are fully employed, makes it more likely that a female-headed family will be poorer than either the male-supported nuclear family or the reconstituted family.

How do these women and their families survive? More than half (56 percent) derive at least $500 or more from their own earnings and receive no welfare income. Furthermore, many of these female-headed families (10.2 percent of all families with children) reconstitute themselves into nuclear families with a husband and wife within five years. The single-parent state thus seems definitely transitional.

But the possibility that a single-parent family is a transitional state should not make us forget that, in the difficult years, parents without partners need emotional support, help with household chores, flexible working hours so that they can meet their dual-family and work responsibilities, and publicly available provision for child care so that they can meet emergencies, get away on occasion, and see that their children get proper attention while the parent attends to other responsibilities. Cogswell and Sussman (1972) note the prevailing assumption that a mother will be available to come to school during the day for a parent-child conference, take time off to get children to the doctor or dentist, chauffeur children to recreational areas, or be available to fix lunch and supper. For some working women, heading a household and meeting these expectations can prove a loss to working hours and needed income. Rather than impose on such persons the system designed for the nonemployed wife in the husband-wife family, Cogswell and Sussman suggest that mobile health-care units come to school yards, recreational facilities be in walking distance for young children, round-the-clock child care be available for emergencies, and eating facilities be present in the neighborhood where children can take morning and evening meals either accompanied or unaccompanied by parents. While there might not be sufficient demand for such services in suburban middle-class areas to be feasible, one can easily imagine what a boon such facilities would offer to poor working-class or middle-class single-parent families in large urban areas.

While the income outlook for reconstitued families is definitely better than for single-parent families, other problems remain in legal impediments and psychological drain. Established legal routines have generally given custody to the mother, thereby causing fathers a sense of loss of their children. If custody is not awarded to the mother, there is a common tendency to assume that something must be wrong with her. Visitation rights for either parent may provoke inconvenience and further conflict.

Division of property between the former spouses is likely to be a further bone of contention, particularly where a couple entered the marriage arrangement unprepared for any possible termination and merged their assets in a way that makes an equitable reckoning at the end difficult.

Finally, continuing provision for support of children or a dependent wife of a former marriage may constitute an almost intolerable burden for the husband who has also to contribute support to a second marriage. Undoubtedly in a few cases fathers do not support their legitimate offspring by a former marriage because of such a dual burden. However, this reason should not be exaggerated. One study done in 1970 in five California counties found that nonsupporting fathers were similar in their occupational distribution to the entire male population, neither predominant in low-income occupations nor more heavily represented among the unemployed: 10 percent were professional or managerial and 8 percent were craftsmen or foremen. Usually these fathers were living in the same county as their children. And they were not supporting any other children; 92 percent of the nonsupporting fathers had a total of three or fewer children, and only 13 percent were married to other women. Furthermore, the amount of child support awarded was not unreasonable, typically on the order of $50 a month (Winston and Forsher, 1971: 15–16). Heclo (1973: 33–36), however, explains nonsupport largely as the inability of fathers to pay. He notes that four-fifths of the fathers involved receive less than $10,000 a year. Many administrative and legal factors also contribute to nonsupport—the attitudes of the judges who make the awards, the lack of incentive for officials to enforce the order, and the lack of legal interest in the problem.

Aside from these economic complexities, which may underlie reconstituted marriages, there are also knotty interpersonal issues that may arise. The kinship terms are lacking for referring to one's spouse's children by another marriage or to the second wife whom one's father married. Household avoidance patterns and the incest taboos have to be redefined (Bohannan, 1970). As with the communes and extended family experiments that we consider next, the structural problems have just begun to be identified. Satisfactory solutions still have to be found.

In the last decade a number of variant family forms have arisen. Their sheer variety and the amount of popular attention they have aroused suggest that their significance is larger than the mere curiosity factor. Some students of the phenomenon in fact contend that these experiments are a sign of strains in the traditional nuclear family and a clue to the mutations that it must undergo if it is to be adapted to contemporary society (Cogswell, 1975: 391).

A great deal of interest has centered upon the conventional sexual arrangements that are found in the new family forms. Some people have tried "swinging," intimate networks, and multilateral marriage as alternatives to the sexual exclusivity of the nuclear family. However, it turns out that sexual activities have lower priority than obligations of work, child care, and home duties even in the new intimate networks (Ramey, 1975). It is with respect to these daily household obligations that the new family experiments offer the most innovative alternatives for the changing domestic roles of women and men.

Betty Cogswell (1975: 401) makes the insightful observation that traditional family forms emphasize constraints, while the participants in the experimental forms speak primarily of freedom and opportunity. Yet any viable social system sets constraints as well as offers opportunities. Both age-old limits and new possibilities have been discovered by experimentation. The main innovations revolve around (1) flexible work opportunities for female and male alike, (2) ways of sharing cooking, cleaning, shopping, and other household duties, and (3) new approaches to maternity, pregnancy, and child care.

Shared living arrangements among a group of adults or couples can result, for example, in rotation of responsibility for meal preparation and home maintenance, thus particularly freeing women for job responsibilities. Such experiments have been tried most notably in the kibbutzim, the Chinese collective enterprises, and the contemporary urban communes in the United States.

There is a tendency, however, toward a more traditional assignment of women to the home and kitchen tasks when children arrive. This happened when the Israeli kibbutzim were transformed from revolutionary frontier communities to more settled establishments that began to have families with young children. Women were more and more assigned to the kitchens and nurseries as part of their communal work (Talmon, 1972). Contemporary rural communes in the United States have generally had a more traditional division of labor from the beginning (Schlesinger, 1972; Berger et al., 1972). When the contemporary urban communal households begin to have children, there is some tendency for men to desert, leaving women to handle the responsibility (Bernard, 1974: 309–310). Or people do not choose to have children and are ambivalent about their care. Kanter found that there were remarkably few—only ten "full-time children" in 58 Boston area communes that she studied (Kanter, 1972: 27). It may also be that, viewed in terms of the life cycle, the experimental marriage or commune is primarily a transitional state and that people will leave when they decide to set up their own households or marry and have children (Giele, 1976). Nevertheless, recent feminist interest in public child-care facilities has drawn considerable impetus from foreign communal experiments in child care, particularly in China, Israel, and the U.S.S.R. (Sidel, 1972; Bettelheim, 1969: Bronfenbrenner, 1970).

Curiously, the idea of communal eating facilities has never caught on to the same degree among the noncommunal family population. One of the leading theorists of feminism, Charlotte Perkins Gilman (1898, 1966), in the last century, visualized a day when there would be neighborhood kitchens that would save each family's making its meals separately. Perhaps the hamburger chains, the frozen dinner, prepared mixes, and other convenience foods, together with advanced household appliances such as the gas or electric stove and the refrigerator, have obviated this alternative. By contrast, no such comparable shortcut for child care has yet appeared or, for that matter, is likely to.

Although communes have received considerable attention, there is one family form to which perhaps more examination is due than it has yet received, what Litwak (1970) has called "modified extended families." If we picture that many of the needs families are called to fill are personal, emotional, and physical, and that the individuals who fulfill them are at best in a trusting and intimate relationship to those receiving help, it is usually a relative or group of relatives who turn out to have the deepest and longest-lasting loyalties that will sustain these demands. One possibility for modifying the nuclear family, therefore, is to extend it in ways that activate and maintain these ties with a larger group of relatives. This would not be the traditional extended family of patriarchal legend, but a more flexible and egalitarian group, able to help its kin with crises of child care, illness, or financial distress. It would probably be maintained by geographical proximity, impromptu visiting, and perhaps even common economic or ethnic ties that prevail in certain farming, mining, manufacturing, or professional milieux. The nineteenth-century pattern of taking in roomers and boarders may have helped to sustain such an extended network in a tight economy. Communes in the Canadian West (which are similar to those in the United States) apparently even now take in former members on a temporary basis, much as a kinship group would operate in the past (Gagné, 1975). There may be other networks sustained through church, lodge, or colleague relationships that operate in similar fashion and of which social scientists as yet have little formal knowledge.

Affluence may allow people to buy services and support separate living arrangements in a way that diminishes the human ties based on noneconomic exchange. Or geographical mobility may be so great that even relatives who wish to maintain helping ties are prevented from doing so by their distance from each other. If this is so, we will have to decide whether such a trend is to be allowed or encouraged or whether it in the end promotes an antifamilial policy.

14

Mothers' Hours: The Timing of Parenthood and Women's Work

Pamela Daniels and Kathy Weingarten

Motherhood gave me a chance to think about things. I never felt that I was ready after college to move into something earth shattering. I wanted time to think. Having a child around the house is hardly time to think. But it was, actually. As a mother I had a job, and a reason for being. I also had space and time to think about what to do next.

— A 42-YEAR OLD JOB CAPTAIN IN AN ARCHITECTURAL FIRM
WHO HAD HER FIRST CHILD AT 21

I would have had a hell of a time if I'd had children earlier. It would have been almost impossible to come where I've come professionally.

— A 52-YEAR OLD PSYCHIATRIST
WHO HAD HER FIRST CHILD AT 31

Whatever the timing of parenthood, its occupational consequences are played out primarily in women's lives. By and large, mothers take on the work of parenting; caring for children is essentially *their* occupation. Whatever else they do, whether they choose to be full-time mothers or to combine parenting with other work, it is women who see to the dailiness of family life. This is especially true in the early years of parenthood, but it remains true throughout our children's lives.

One of the ways women express and enact developmental change in adulthood is to shift and vary the balance between parenthood and work in the world. A mother's resolutions and compromises in the two spheres of generativity reflect her adaptation to the fact that the impact of parenthood in the sphere of work is dramatically different for women and men.

Among the couples in our study, the women's experience was much more like each other's than it was like the men's. For all but 6* of the 72 women—whether they became mothers early or late—the birth of their first child, or the pregnancy itself, perceptibly changed their activity and their emotional involvement in the sphere of work beyond the home. Whatever work they were doing was modified or interrupted. For some women the effect was dramatic, for others slight, but in every case some accommodation was made, almost always drawing the mother back into her home, toward her child.

We need to make clear what we mean by work, and by women's work in particular. Broadly defined, work is physical or mental effort or activity directed toward the production or accomplishment of something. At its best, when it is generative, work is creating, producing, organizing, taking care. Work is doing. For women, as for men, the "doing" may take place away from home and family: work means earning a living, holding a job, going to school, pursuing a career. (More than 50 percent of American women are now in the paid labor force; and women account for more than 50 percent of all college enrollment.) Work also means involvement in politics, community effort, and volunteer activity. And it includes "work of one's own"—autonomous, creative, often very private work such as writing or sculpting, which may not be paid and which is not necessarily justified by its contribution to family livelihood.[1] Throughout this chapter, when we refer to women's "work beyond the home," to their "nonfamily work," we define it in this comprehensive way, as the women we interviewed described it to us.

Unlike most men, women also work at home, especially women with families. The orchestration and supervision of the minutiae of family life—what Adrienne Rich calls "the million tiny stitches, the friction of the scrubbing brush, the scouring cloth . . . the invisible weaving of a frayed and threadbare family life"[2]—commands our physical and mental effort and activity. Women acknowledge the labor of love; they know that love is work. As Amy Anderson said to us, "I'm 32 and my children are behind me. That is, what's behind me are the years of *giving lots of labor to them*."

Women feel (as men seldom do) that the work they do at home, their "family work," is not only hard work but also a job: "You have to have food in the house, meals on the table. You change another set of sheets, wash another load of laundry. All the little things. Buying clothes, attending to needs, getting toys. Thinking ahead." In the words of Elise Everhart, a 52-year-old mother of five, "It was our decision to start our family young. I put in 25 years of hard work, 24 hours a day. And I feel I did a good job of it. That may be an arrogant thing to say, but I really and truly think it was a job."

In order to emphasize the value of the work women traditionally have done and do at home and to acknowledge systematically (as the slogan has it) that "every mother is a working mother," we have modified the word "work" in phrases such as "nonfamily work," "work beyond the home," or "work in the world" when we mean the work women do for whatever reason—to earn income, to satisfy ambition and desire, to express themselves—in their nonfamily time.

For the present and in the foreseeable future, then, women (but usually not men) who want to have a family *and* work of their own beyond the family must deal with the dilemma of how to integrate the responsibilities of their two occupations, their two "primary roles,"[3] from day to day and in the long run. This need to juggle and compromise, this living out of the occupational consequences of motherhood, creates the common denominator in mothers' lives. It is the unspoken work history hidden within every formal résumé.

What do the stories of the women we interviewed tell us about the ways in which women accommodate their two works over time? And how does the timing of parenthood influence their accommodation? Current feminist belief, shared by many of the programmatic postponers in our study, suggests that a woman would do well to establish herself in the work world before starting a family; it is easier to return to the world of paid work, with a shorter time out for parenthood, than it is to start from scratch after years spent exclusively at home. While this is good advice, especially for young women with well-defined career goals, the full picture is more complex.

In all three generations, the women we met pulled back from their outside work when they became mothers, regardless of when their first child was born. Sixty-five of the 72 women were in the paid labor force or in college or graduate school before their first children were born, but only one out of four worked outside the home during the first year of parenthood. By contrast, at the time of our interviews, 42 of the 72 women were employed (in our sense) half-time or more, and 13 were enrolled in a college or graduate-degree program to complete or advance their education.

Looking beyond the first year of parenthood, we found two distinct patterns of combining motherhood and work in the world for both early- and late-timing mothers: a *sequential pattern,* in which a woman staggers or alternates her two occupations; and a *simultaneous pattern,* in which the intensive years of mothering may combine or overlap with employment and commitment outside the home. Each pattern has characteristic features that are recognizable in spite of a wide range of individual variation.

In the *sequential pattern* of staggering the two commitments, some period of parenthood is cordoned off, as it were, insulated and protected from the competing demands of other work. There are three versions of the sequential pattern. (1) In the motherhood-follows-employment sequence, a woman goes to work or embarks on a career before she has her first child, at which time she puts her original work aside altogether with no intention of resuming it. (2) In the employment-brackets-motherhood sequence, she interrupts her education or employment to devote herself exclusively to motherhood, and at some subsequent time she reenters the work force or returns to her own work, adding this commitment to her family responsibilities. (3) In the employ-

TABLE 15.1
Sequential Pattern of Accommodating Parenthood and Other Work

		MOTHER'S AVERAGE CURRENT AGE			
		33 1/2 years	*44 years*	*53 1/2 years*	
Family-Timing Pattern	*Early*	(A):9	(C):12	(E):11	32
	Late	(B):5	(D):7	(F):8	20
		14	19	19	N=52

ment-follows-motherhood sequence, a woman begins adult life with motherhood as her first career, and after a period of full-time parenting takes up a second, "extraparental" occupation.

Fifty-two of the 72 mothers in our study adopted some version of the sequential pattern of accommodating parenthood and nonfamily work. That is, more than 70 percent took time out for parenthood—some for the preschool years only, others for as long as it took to see the last child launched. They represent all three generations and both college and noncollege backgrounds. Thirty-two are early-timing mothers, and 20 are late-timing mothers. (See Table 15.1.)

In the *simultaneous pattern* of overlapping parenthood and nonfamily work, the mother juggles the two sets of responsibilities. Logistically, she must coordinate child care and family work with the demands of her job or career; emotionally, she stretches herself to incorporate and integrate both commitments. Although the balance, in time and in emotional involvement, varies from woman to woman as well as from year to year in any one woman's life, for the woman who adopts the simultaneous pattern, both kinds of work occupy and preoccupy her at the same time. Respecting the variation in the balance of work in these mothers' lives, we have included in the simultaneous category any arrangement in which a mother works away from home (earning a living, doing meaningful work of her own, or preparing to do so) at a rate of half-time (20 hours a week) or more for more than half of the first six years of her first child's life.

Twenty of the 72 women in our study followed a simultaneous pattern, less than half as many as those who mothered full-time for an extended period of their children's early lives. (The numbers attest to the strain imposed by the simultaneous solution, given the structural arrangements that sanction and perpetuate the traditional division of labor between women and men.) Four of the 20 are early-timing mothers, 16 are late-timing mothers. By a margin of

TABLE 15.2
Simultaneous Pattern of Accommodating Parenthood and Other Work

		MOTHER'S AVERAGE CURRENT AGE			
		33 1/2 years	*44 years*	*53 1/2 years*	
Family-Timing Pattern	*Early*	(A):3	(C):0	(E):1	4
	Late	(B):7	(D):5	(F):4	16
		10	5	5	N=20

four to one, the simultaneous, "double duty" mothers in our study are late-timing parents, women who postponed childbearing until their late 20s or early 30s. . . . They postponed in order to enhance their ability to combine family and career successfully. (See Table 15.2.)

In the beginning, the mere fact of becoming a parent affects women's work lives similarly, pulling them back from other commitments in order to make room for parenthood. When we look at the work experience of early and late mothers beyond the first year, timing makes a difference in whether women follow a sequential or a simultaneous pattern of accommodating family and other work. Whereas the late-timing mothers divide fairly evenly between the sequential (20) and the simultaneous (16) patterns, among the early-timing mothers eight times as many women opted for a sequential arrangement (32) as for a simultaneous one (4).

THE EARLY-TIMING SEQUENTIAL PATTERN

"What do you do after you've hung your last drape?"

The sequential pattern in which a woman is employed in the paid work force before the mothering years but not afterward is becoming increasingly rare. Few families can afford to have only one income earner, and fewer women are satisfied and nourished by family work alone as their children get older and their families' needs diminish. Women in all generations no longer view motherhood as their final career. In one 42-year-old housewife's metaphor, "What do you do after you've hung your last drape?"

Most women do take up nonfamily work at some point in their adult lives. As with the other critical life decisions women make, the timing of the decision to enter or reenter the paid work force varies. Many "reentering" women use education—going to college, finishing college,† getting special training or an advanced degree—as a path out of the home and into paid employment. Some chart their reentry through volunteer work. Others move directly into the labor force to paid work in a familiar field or in a new one. Some women gradually increase their hours at work away from home; an adult-education course flows into a volunteer activity, to casual paid work, and finally there is a full-time job. So careful are they to calibrate the steps of their return with changes in their families' needs that their husbands and children hardly notice the shift in commitment. Other women make a more dramatic transition. At home one day, they are in the paid work force the next.

Eleanor Egan, a 51-year-old mother of five grown children, waited 21 years until she "went back to work." After high school, Ellie, as she is called by all who know her, trained as a nurse and worked as an L.P.N. for eighteen months. She was planning to go back to school when she met Ed. Their whirlwind courtship and quick marriage changed her plans: "I didn't have any intention of getting married at that point, but when you meet a man who makes the bells ring for you, you don't wait."

In retrospect, Ellie Egan feels that she made a momentous transition not once but twice: first, leaving the work world for family life; and then, when her fifth and last child was 13, moving outside her family and back into the world of paid work. Of the first transition, she says, "I gave up a service career to have my children, and 99 percent of me has never regretted it. When the kids were growing up, they and Ed were my whole life. I didn't care that I wasn't doing anything else. But when they grew up, and Ed too started to do other things—expanding the business, getting into local politics—there wasn't that much to do any more.

"I had always planned to go back to the working world. I wasn't going to be a housewife, homemaker— call it what you want—for the rest of my life. . . . When I was young I was a very good student, a super student, and that remained dormant. That's perhaps the one thing I regretted as my children were growing up. Ed always said what a super-smart wife he had. He meant it, and I believed him. But I had no opportunity to show anybody. At the age of 40 I had to prove—to myself—that I had some of that intelligence left. I wanted to rejuvenate my gray cells. I had to prove that I was still worth something *in that way*.

"I remember thinking, years ago, that when my youngest child was in school all day, I would get a part-time job. Medicine had always interested me. I thought that I would probably take a refresher course and go back into nursing. But I decided I really didn't feel like going back to school, and I thought nursing hours would be too restrictive, even though the pay is good. I like hospital life and I had office background, so I thought maybe I could put the two together. There was an ad in the paper for someone with office skills and knowledge of medical terminology, and it just sounded like me. Ed said, 'How do you think you're going to get a job after all these years? You haven't been working.' "

Like many people ten years ago, Ellie subscribed to the prevailing definition of "work" as paid-labor-force work; what women do at home was something else. Apparently accepting Ed's remark without noting the irony, she went on, "I *hadn't* worked for 20 years. I'd been a housewife and mother, and was very happy doing it. But he got my Irish up and I said, 'What do you mean, I can't?' So I marched down to that hospital and got that job. And it was my salvation—with the kids moving off, and Ed leaving the nest too, in his way. I thought it would be just a trial thing, but I find I like it very much. I like the *people* I work with."

Ellie Egan explained the timing of her decision to "get back out into the working world" in terms of a developmental shift. She felt ready to return to work when her children no longer needed her at home full-time. "More of me was free, more of me was not *bound*, doing for my children. So I had time to reevaluate my own self." In this, Ellie is like most of the women who added paid work to their family work: They described the transition as a reflection of their readiness *in relation to their feelings about their children's needs* to shift the focus of the generativity. Women experienced this readiness differently, and family financial circumstances frequently influenced the decision and its timing. Nevertheless, the women framed the transition in terms of a feeling that they and their families were ready.

The early-timing mothers who returned to schooling or paid employment in mid life did not meet with objections from their teenage children. "Go to it, Mom," was the typical response. Adolescents might grumble when asked to do a larger share of household chores, but they agreed to take responsibility for dishes, laundry, a certain number of meals per week, arranging their own transportation to athletic events—knowing that the family's lifestyle, vacations, and their chance at college depended on their mother's as well as their father's job and income.

Children hailed their mothers' decision, but husbands often had mixed feelings. For most of these early-timing mothers, readiness to "go back to work" also meant readiness to renegotiate their marriage, disengaging their husbands from traditional assumptions and expectations, or coming to terms with their husbands' feelings and incorporating them into their decision. Ellie Egan, for example, expressed a cautious wifely tact with regard to her husband's role as the primary provider in the family. "I went back to work mostly for my own reasons and to give us extra money for some of the pleasures of life. We don't really need the money. If I stopped work, we'd still live as we do. And it's important, psychologically, to Ed that my job is part-time. I don't think he'd let me have a full-time job. This way, it doesn't really count. It doesn't take away from him being the provider. It's extra."

Ellie clearly feels that in order to continue her work, she must do it in a way that will not threaten her husband or jeopardize their marriage. She has limited the hours she works, and therefore the money she makes, to ensure that she does not surpass the limit of Ed's tolerance—a limit she feels as concretely as if it were a physical restraint. She sees him struggling, as it is, to accept the seriousness of her commitment to her "job." A career would be "too much."

Clare Cooper is 10 years younger than Ellie. She felt ready to turn seriously to work of her own 10 years sooner than Ellie did. For different reasons, she too does not think of paid work in career terms. Clare is a special-education consultant who works 30 hours a week 9 months of the year in a large suburban school. She was 31, and her third and last child was in kindergarten, when she went back to school, part-time, to get a master's degree in special education.

Education has always been important to Clare Cooper, but the nature and substance of its importance shifted during the ten years between completing her B.A. (while pregnant with her second child) in 1960 and returning to school in 1970. Like other women who attended college in the late 1950s and early 1960s, she did not view her education from a career perspective. "On the surface, you were preparing for one thing in college," she reflected, "but underneath, everybody knew something else was much more likely. The degree was important not for what I could *do* with it, but because I couldn't hold my head up in society without it. I had no idea of having a career, or even of working. It never entered my mind. Women stayed home. When the children were grown you were expected to do community work as a volunteer, but home came first. The idea wasn't that you would use your education to actually go out and work; but you had to be qualified, in case."

What precipitated the shift? "I was ready for more, I guess. I was ready to get out. But I had to have flexibility. Actually, I was *always* out quite a bit, even when the kids were very young. Anything that came equipped with a baby-sitting service I would do. I'd do any volunteer job, so long as it didn't have to do with children. After all, if I was going to leave the children with a sitter, I wanted to be involved with something different. I took a course at the Y on reading problems—that's how I discovered our son had a learning disability—and I became very interested in the field of learning disabilities and special ed."

Like many other gifted and successful women of her generation, Clare feels that she drifted[4] into the work she now does. Twenty years ago, she wouldn't have predicted it. "My generation wasn't trained consciously to plan their lives. We fell into things that were available to us. I didn't reach out for it, it reached in for me, and I was involved before I knew it." Clare had amassed 55 hours toward her master's degree when her husband's job transfer located them in a new community. Clare found herself blocked, her credits nontransferable.

"I sat here and did nothing, for a year. Oh, PTA and the League of Women Voters, but that's not what I mean. I felt stuck. While I was sitting around wondering what to do, one of the kids' teachers suggested I call the head of the learning-disabilities program and volunteer as a tutor. I was hired, 14 hours a week. The next year I became the program coordinator in one of the schools. I was simply ready to move ahead."

The motherhood years themselves provided the ground out of which Clare's subsequent occupation evolved. Not having been employed before,‡ nor having thought she ever would be, she had no idea what kind of work might satisfy her. Even now, having found satisfying work, she disclaims a career identity. Like other college-educated women of her generation who were mothers first and who retain a traditional stake in parental and householding roles, she says: "I think I'm intelligent, and I'm well educated; I work hard at what I'm doing, and I have been able to be successful, increasingly so. But although I am an active person, I'm not a career-oriented person. My family comes first. Charlie supports me all the way, but I'm the one who knits it all together.

"And I want time for myself. A 30-hour week gives me the flexibility I need to do all the little things that never quite get done otherwise. To me, a career connotes more than an 8-hour day, or even a 10-hour day. It's full-time—not just 40 hours a week, but nights and weekends. And I think it takes that. Regardless of your skill, I think it takes that kind of devotion.

"I see how Charlie works. If you marry somebody like him, extremely ambitious, extremely preoccupied with his work, aiming for the top of his field, I don't see how a family is going to stay together and have any cohesion as a family if the mother is doing the same thing."

Times change. Early first-time mothers in the generation 10 years younger than Clare Cooper and 20 years younger than Eleanor Egan view their work lives differently. They spend fewer years in exclusive full-time mothering,§ they ask more of their husbands at home as they assume income-earning responsibility away from home, and they no longer hesitate to call their nonfamily work a "career."

These younger early-timing "family women," like their counterparts in the two older generations, perceive their readiness to extend themselves beyond the mothering role in terms of a shift in the balance between their own and their children's needs. The fact that they are experiencing this shift sooner in their lives than women once did is an expression of *psychohistorical change*.[6] By psychohistorical change, we mean that as "outer" social and economic realities change, so too do people's private, "inner" individual and family arrangements. Thus, for example, in the 35 years since the oldest woman we interviewed gave birth to her first child, more and more people are acknowledging the value of the second paycheck, the legitimacy of women's desire to have careers as well as children, the appeal of smaller families, and the alternatives to mother care for school-age children.[7]

As social change permeates individual consciousness, lives and psyches change. And vice versa: as individual changes in our private lives begin to inform social and cultural constructions of reality, creating "themes, forms and images that are in significant ways shared,"[8] cultural norms and values change too. Social change is not only played out in the inner reality of individual experience, it is prefigured there. The psychohistorical shift in the timing of women's sense of readiness to turn to work beyond the home is nowhere clearer than in the contrast between the 50-year-old early-timing mother who told us that when she applied for readmission to college at the age of 44 she felt herself "holding onto the rim of the nest with white knuckles," and her counterpart 20 years younger who sent the youngest of her three children to his first day of kindergarten a day early.

THE LATE-TIMING SEQUENTIAL PATTERN

"I had had a career for many years. I had had a previous life. Now I was totally devoted to being a mother, and I didn't want to do anything else, absolutely nothing."

Motherhood in the 20s can serve as a useful career moratorium in women's lives. For the late-timing mothers in our study who set aside established jobs and careers in order to devote themselves totally to family life in their 30s, motherhood, far from being a moratorium, for a while became the chosen career. There was nothing provisional about it.

Of the 20 mothers who adopted the late-timing sequential pattern, 13 are high-school-educated women who did not view their preparental work as a "career." Rather, they had jobs at which they worked with varying degrees of enthusiasm, some women devoted to their work, others merely tolerating it.

Bettina Boyd was a secretary for a supermarket chain for 13 years before her daughter was born in 1976, when she was 31. Under "current occupation" on our identifying data questionnaire, Bettina signed herself "domestic engineer." An intense, intelligent, thoughtful woman, she was one of three in the study who had prepared in writing for our interview. As we talked, she referred to her notes on the coffee table in front of us. She spoke of her preparental life and work as might a historian who has been assigned the task of giving a chronicle of another time: "There were five children in my family and I'm the third-oldest. My father worked for the transit authority. My mother never worked. She was always there, always available. Both my parents lived for their children. They did very, very well raising the five of us.

"After high school I went to secretarial school, then to my first job, and I never left the company. I loved the people so much. They were like family to me. I worked there for 13 years."

Bettina and Barney met in high school in the early 1960s, but started dating only when Barney got out of the service. They were married in their mid 20s. "I had a wild youth," said Barney with a quiet smile. "I settled down as a person when I married Bettina. I had a good job in a bottle company; I was moving up.

"Bettina came from a strict family. Her mother wouldn't let the kids do anything around the house—make a bed, dry a dish. Bettina thought love and marriage were going to be like a fairy tale, and that kind of sobered me up. I had to show her things. I had to be very gentle with her."

In one sense, Barney has been for Bettina what some early-timing mothers were for their emotionally young husbands—a consistently caring presence. Barney's steadiness provided Bettina with a safe mooring, enabling her to care for their daughter with confidence and delight.

Bettina and Barney are devoted parents. "When Lisa was born, everything was her," Bettina said. "The two of us took great pride in her, teaching her to talk. You can teach her anything. She could say the Pledge of Allegiance at 18 months, which was quite an accomplishment.

"When she came, it changed my life in every respect. I enjoyed it immensely. I enjoyed taking care of her. I was happy just watching her all day. First of all, I had worked those 13 years, so it wasn't something I had missed out on. It's not like getting married right after high school, just starting a job, and then all of a sudden having a baby. I think I would be raring to get out there at that point.

"My job was not all that spectacular; I sat behind a desk and it was fairly boring—typing letters, answering phones. It was only the people I missed when I left. When and if I go back to work I want something more interesting.

"But for now, I believe in taking care of Lisa. She needs me. Children do. I think a mother should be home when they come home from school; it's just something I believe in. I want to be here to greet her and listen to her problems. When she's old enough, I will go back to work, and maybe to school. I've always been interested in law; I wanted to be a legal secretary. There are things I never did. Now I just might, as time goes on. But I will be home when she's home. I will work, but only mother's hours."

Bettina is not in a hurry to return to outside work, but she is confident she will do so when the time is right. Many factors contribute to her decision and her desire to be at home for now: her readiness to leave the paid work force after 13 years in a routine job; her perspective on motherhood as a change of pace, years to be savored; Barney's solid job and income (they could afford to let that second paycheck go); her mother's example of staying home; her own experience of having been nurtured and protected by such a mother; and, in Lisa, a gratifying child. Bettina's work history is unfinished; the last word is not in. As another woman in her early 30s said to us when we asked about her plans and prospects, "I've accepted the fact that mothering is what I'm going to do during these years. Who knows what the future will bring? Come back in ten years."

Beryl Bellamy was 29 when she had the first of her two children. A programmatic postponer with a master's degree in public health, she delayed childbearing partly in order to get career-building work under way first. Her decision to devote full time to child care during her early 30s and her daughter's early childhood meant giving up work that she loved as a health-services management consultant. It also meant withstanding peer pressure in a careerist academic community: "Well, yes, you have a kid, but what else do you do?" Beryl differs from Bettina in that she had launched a career to which she intends to return. She maintains contact with her colleagues, accepts an occasional free-lance assignment, and keeps up with activities and developments in her field. She is like Bettina in knowing that full-time motherhood is right for her now: "I'm more and more convinced of the rightness of my own decision for my own situation."

Beryl has temporarily set aside her career for parenthood; she is flexible about the timing and pacing of her reentry into career work: "Of course I get antsy once in a while, but not antsy enough. The way I'm raising her seems right. I don't feel obligated to do this until she is 12, but I feel it *is* important during the young years. Brad could have been the one at home. I don't feel it *has* to be the mother. But given our personalities, we both agreed that this was the best plan.

"I'm doing a few things now. A project with a friend that has nothing to do with health care, but it's intriguing to me. I work on it around my hours with Julie. I imagine I will continue doing casual things like this until I'm ready to plunge in again. I'm open. I'll work when I'm ready."

In some respects, the late-timing sequential pattern may offer the best of both worlds. The preparental work years are free of competing responsibilities and tasks. When parenthood comes, the experience can be savored in "purer" form. Unlike early-timing mothers who are drawn into the dependencies of family and home before venturing out on their own, late-timing mothers like Bettina and Beryl have lived on their own, supported themselves, and explored the scope and the limits of their autonomy and ambition. Usually, but not always, they retain a faith in themselves that early-timing mothers sometimes lose. They know what they are missing when they stay home for a few years; and they know what they are *not* missing.

The disadvantage of this version of the sequential pattern lies in the area of career development, not in the sphere of family life. Developmental continuity and a sense of cumulative accomplishment are of course interrupted when women take time out for mothering. Income is forfeited when women leave jobs to stay home full-time. They may also lose benefits and the other "perks" of accruing seniority. In terms of career advancement, if women are not promoted "on schedule," if they do not move up at the same pace as their peers, their superiors may lose track of them. These costs do not count equally to all women. Women who construe their work as a career, with a developmental trajectory to it, may care more about the loss of momentum and on-time advancement than women who view their work as a job.

Women who leave paid jobs and careers to mother in their 30s are different when they reenter the work force in mid life. They are ripe, generative, and eager in a new way. As a 50-year-old full-time Department of Labor administrator, who became a mother in her late 20s and took time out to do so, said, "I thought of myself as a social worker in my 20s, but I did not project my work into the future. I did not have a long-range professional goal, I did not consider the work a career. When the kids were little I did casework for the extra income, and we enjoyed the money my work brought in. But I was conscious of working very part-time. As the kids grew up, I progressively took on more work. There is an advantage to building up your work incrementally. When your children come of age and you're free to increase your work to a full-time load, you're not tired of working. You're ready for new challenges."

THE EARLY-TIMING SIMULTANEOUS PATTERN

"I tried to explain to him that I couldn't work full time, take care of the baby, meet all of his needs, help out with my family, and stay sane. His 'unsinkable' wife was about to go under."

The great majority (32 out of 36) of our early-timing mothers combined family and other work sequentially. Of the 20 women who mothered and pursued outside work at the same time only four are early-timing mothers. Three had finished high school; one had an undergraduate degree. Only the college-educated woman, Alison Adler, can be said to have "chosen" the simultaneous pattern of accommodation. For the other three women, economic realities in effect forced the "choice."

Alison Adler, is a division head in a high-technology firm. Just 30 when we met her, she had had the first of her two closely spaced children at 22. Married to a young business-school graduate who had just set up his own consulting firm, pregnant her senior year in college, she graduated without a vocational objective, gave birth to her son that summer, and found herself feeling "dependent and desperate," "beginning to go bananas," by the end of the year.

"I suddenly didn't like myself," she said, "because I found I was so dependent on Arnold. He was traveling a great deal, and having a child tied me to the house. I didn't have any friends with small children, and I desperately needed him to be with, to talk to. I sometimes wonder, if Arnold had been a civil-service type who'd come home and we'd gone out dancing every night, whether we would have had less tension those first few months. Because I was so tired, I expected so much.

"The tension was tremendous, building up in me. And I was *bored*—bored with myself and with my situation. It was this feeling bored and confined and at loose ends that gave me the guts to go out initially and find a job.

"I knew that philosophy, which is what I majored in, was worth nothing on the job market. Computer science sounded intriguing, so I bought a book or two and read them. IBM has a self-instruction manual and I read that. It seems laughable now, but it wasn't bad as a start. Then I put an ad in the paper for a sitter, interviewed women, found one who suited me, and started out the door one day to look for a job. Mrs. Thomas began the first Monday in March, and I wanted her to come from then on, until I found a job, and forever after.

"I would go out to the industrial parks, and go in and out and in and out. The 19th place I hit hired me, as a programmer. I had had other offers, but they wanted me to be a secretary and work up—that old story—and I'd been warned that 'no secretary becomes a programmer.'

"It took about two weeks of interviewing to land a job, and it was gruelling. It made me realize now how unbelievably unhappy I was, that I did that. And it was youth, too; the gall of me to think that I had anything to offer anybody! If I had to do that now I don't think I'd have the guts. I'd *know* that I don't know anything; then, I thought I did. I hadn't had time to lose my nerve.

"Another thing—I decided right then that I would work school hours, even though school was years away. I demanded the hours I wanted, and they started me at three-fourths time, from eight to two."

When we met Alison, seven years later and one more child later, she was moving up the management ladder in the same company and going to school part-time to get a master's degree in business administration. Defying parental expectation that she become a lawyer, Alison married and had a baby right out of college; resisting parental prescription that women who are mothers center their lives on their children, Alison insisted on pursuing a business career as well.

For Aggie Ahearn and her husband, Andy, the situation was very different. Aggie and Andy were married in 1968, a year to the day earlier than they had planned, after they discovered Aggie was pregnant. Aggie was 19, Andy, 20. Looking back on more than a decade of incredible strain and hardship, they both feel that they gained something special, if not unique, from the experience.

"Aggie and I were a million-to-one long shot and we made it," Andy said. "I wouldn't recommend it, because of what we went through, but we did make it and I wouldn't change it for the world. We've become so damn close, what with the traumatic experiences we've lived through. We've grown up together. We're like one person, almost, and it comes from going from nothing to something—together."

Aggie was working in a bank as a credit-card verifier and Andy had just squeaked through his first year of college when they met in 1967. "He was the man of my dreams," Aggie said. "Only I wasn't supposed to meet him until I was 24, by which time I was going to be finished with college and working a few years. I had it all figured out. Then there he was, in my life, much sooner than I'd planned on."

The eldest of several children, Aggie had worked all through high school. Her mother, widowed very young, the head of her household, worked at a low-paying service job. Aggie was the mainstay of her family. They counted on her income and on her nurturing vitality. "She's unsinkable," Andy said. By contrast, he was the only son in a large Irish family that doted on him. He had been supported by his parents all his life.

"I had no idea what the hell marriage meant, or anything about responsibility," Andy admitted. "Where we were going to live, what we were going to do for money—I had no idea. I simply knew that marrying Aggie was the right thing to do, and I left everything else to her. We got married, and basically nothing changed for me. I went to school, I played ball. Aggie worked overtime at the bank until the baby came. We lived at her house; she had to help her mother and look after the other kids. Aggie never said anything, she never complained, she really babied me. Only when I saw the baby and thought, 'Holy mackeral, can you believe this? This is my kid,' only then did I smarten up. I got a job the next week driving a cab."

Andy also began to settle down in school. In some ways, he grew up overnight. In other ways, he did not. Like so many early-timing mothers, Aggie found herself ministering to two "dependent others." Six months after their baby was born, Aggie cried out for help. "Andy was on semester break, and he hurt himself playing ball and came home with his ankle taped up. That evening he and the baby woke up at the same time. He began to howl, 'My God, Aggie, help me. My leg is going to fall off.' The baby was screeching for something to eat, and I spent about 30 minutes running back and forth between the two of them, 'I'll be with *you* in a minute,' 'I'll be with *you* in a minute.' And that night I had to go to work.

"I was always so tired. I thought I was a terrible person because I wasn't smiling and happy. I was sick, I wasn't getting any sleep. I finally had to write Andy a letter to explain that I couldn't work full-time, take care of the baby, meet all of his needs, help out with my mother and my brothers and sisters, and stay sane. His 'unsinkable' wife was about to go under."

The letter worked. They agreed to save money toward their own apartment so that Aggie would have less responsibility for her mother and siblings. Andy agreed to take care of the baby while Aggie worked nights. No longer were Aggie and her mother the primary caretakers; Aggie and Andy were. By the end of the first year, they had worked out a pattern that carried them through the next two years. Andy went to school days and drove a cab during the early evenings. He came home at around nine, and Aggie went to work. She slept whenever the baby did, and whenever Andy was home from classes. They had no car, but used public transportation. All their funds went for survival and for Andy's tuition. They became "split-shift" parents[9] and split-shift workers. They rarely saw each other awake for more than 15 minutes at a time.

When Andy graduated from college they agreed it was now Aggie's turn. Andy supplied the moral support, for in spite of her fervent desire to go to college Aggie doubted herself and her ability to "make it": "I had been home too long and felt like I didn't know anything. My job hadn't demanded any thought. I had a terrible inferiority complex. Andy wanted me to go to school full-time. 'I can't go full-time. I can't hack it,' I wailed. 'Yes, you can. You hack full-time. You get yourself into a school.' "

Aggie did. Andy got a job teaching and coached hockey at night while Aggie went to school during the day. Like other couples of limited means who must both generate income and yet who believe that children should be cared for by their parents, Aggie and Andy again chose to work in shifts so that one of them would always be home when the children were. When both had to be away at the same time they relied on their brothers and sisters and older nieces and nephews to help them out. In the entire nine years before their children were in school full-time, Aggie and Andy never paid for child care.

The Ahearns' version of coordinating work and family life has to be understood in historical context. Had they married a decade earlier, in 1958, they might very well both have worked full-time to enable Andy to finish college. What is historically bound, we feel, is that Andy and Aggie decided to continue in overdrive so that Aggie could attend college when she was young too. Their commitment in 1972 to Aggie's education is an expression of the psychohistorical change wrought by the feminist movement—change that gives coherence to Aggie's desire to "make something of myself" and support for Andy's accommodation to her academic aspirations. The sacrifices that the Ahearns have made for each other make sense to them and to their peers in a way they would not have 20 or even 10 years earlier.

But their sacrifices have been great. Aggie, like the other early-timing mothers who adopted a simultaneous pattern, missed the classic "moratorium" experience of testing one's wings and being carefree. The vocational moratorium of the 20s is compromised by having the responsibility of dependent children; the parenthood moratorium is compromised by having to focus energy and attention on one's paid job. There is no "time-out," only time in, and all that time is overloaded. Often, financial necessity means that the simultaneous pattern is not a choice but a must. Everything is compressed. What might be pleasurable if experienced singly becomes fraught with tension. There is not time to enjoy life, each other, the children, or the work.

The leverage within this pattern comes from the energy of youth, the innocence of inexperience, and the sense of accomplishment in managing it all against the odds. The advantage is that at thirty both career and parenthood are under way. As Alison Adler put it, "I'd hate to be where I am now professionally, wanting to have children, and trying to figure out when to make the break."

THE LATE-TIMING SIMULTANEOUS PATTERN

"For the first time in my life I was having to make trade-offs. To work, to have a child, to be a wife, to take care of a home, and to try to do all of these things well meant that something had to get cheated a little bit in each area. Not enough so that anybody else would notice, maybe, but I did. I noticed it."

The 16 late-timing mothers who chose to work and raise their children simultaneously are predominantly (69 percent) college-educated women and overwhelmingly (80 percent) programmatic postponers. For these women, the combination of motherhood and nonfamily work in the 30s is, in part, a logical outcome of the preceding "moratorium decade." All 16 women (in the older as well as the younger generations) had deferred childbearing in their 20s in order to pursue their own agendas, to build their commitments gradually, and to keep their options open—work options, play options, and partner options. As they neared the end of their 20s, they began to transform provisional choices into commitments: choosing husbands, deciding to have children, confirming career direction.

Florence Faison, a successful artist and illustrator now in her 50s, postponed motherhood until her early 30s in order to let her imagination play, her ideas and images take shape, her work "come together." She referred to this time, to her *use* of this time, as the "knowing, necessary drift."

"If I had had children when I was younger," she said, "my work never would have formed itself. In my life, the 20s were the years when I was putting everything together, without even knowing what I was doing, and evolving a style and getting my work going. When I was 20 I didn't know what I was going to do with my life; I would have been very surprised if I had known then. But I knew I wanted to paint. The closest I can come to understanding what makes creative work happen is *time*—to have as much free time as possible to bring it forth. Having children in those years would have been an enormous disruption of the creative process."

Daniel Levinson and his colleagues at Yale have identified and spelled out the developmental importance of "the Dream" in men's construction of their adult lives. "More formed than a pure fantasy, yet less articulated than a fully thought-out plan," the Dream, they write, has the quality of an anticipatory "vision of a life," of what a man might accomplish in his adult years, how he will use them. It is "an imagined possibility that generates excitement and vitality."[10] In the experience of the men Levinson interviewed, forming a Dream frequently hinged upon occupational decisions. The life Dream was often indistinguishable from the occupational Dream.

What of the Dream in women's lives? It is at least as important for women as for men, and much more complicated, for the life Dream and the "occupational piece" of it are not necessarily one and the same. Women must integrate imagery of self-in-family with self-in-the-world, self-in-relation-to-others with self-in-work-of-one's-own.[11] And this is what Florence Faison did in her 20s and early 30s.

As her work took definite shape, so too did her intimate life. Florence disengaged herself from an unhappy early marriage and met and married a more compatible mate, with whom she decided, at 32, to have a child. In her 30s she continued to work at her art and care for her son—the two simultaneous generative passions that had emerged from her moratorium years.

For a woman who graduates from high school or college without a strong sense of vocation or a defined Dream of adult accomplishment, motherhood in the 20s can provide a time for "creative drift."[12] Domestic time-in may prove to be a useful time-out from public, worldly work. It can be time in which to ponder latent career dreams and to envision a life and a work beyond motherhood.

On the other hand, if a woman *has* an occupational Dream, the 20s are the critical years of giving it form. When women devote full time in their 20s to the work of mothering, an inchoate Dream may remain unformed, unactivated, "untranslated" into reality. The postponement of children, while affording no guarantee, leaves the decade of the 20s open for the activation of the Dream. This strategy seems critical for women who want to fashion a lifework in traditionally male professions, such as medicine.

Faith Fromm, a 52-year-old psychiatrist who gave birth to the first of her two children at 31, consciously put family thoughts "on hold" during her 20s in order to pursue her Dream of a career in medicine. The daughter of a physician and of a "mother who did not work," Faith "always wanted to be a physician and always wanted to have kids." For her to have both, the late-motherhood timetable was crucial, because it enabled her not only to complete her medical training, but subsequently to integrate her two careers, to make them "all of a piece."

"I wanted to be finished with at least something before I became pregnant," she said. "I didn't want to take time out, or reduce my work hours, until I was through with my residency. Then I wanted to have my family quickly, because I wanted to get back to work. I planned it quite carefully in my head.

. . . I would have had a hell of a time if I had had children earlier. It would have been almost impossible to come where I've come professionally."

For Faith, the simultaneous pattern was an obvious and natural means of "acting on the Dream." From adolescence on, her identity, and her expectation of adult accomplishment, included an active sense of herself as a physician and as a mother. Practicing her profession along with taking care of her children was the option that best fit her image of herself and her life.

"I chose to work part-time when my children were small, and I had a wonderful time, not being on a tight schedule and being able to give myself to my kids. . . If you are a maternal person, when you have little babies you concentrate a lot of emotional energy on them, and your external involvements fade for a while. But when the youngest child is six or seven, somewhere in there, it comes back, the outside interests. The passion for the work you'd set aside. The *passion* for it, not just the doing of it. From then on, for me, it was a steady progression of involvement and ambition."

From the point of view of career continuity, the simultaneous pattern had numerous advantages for Faith. She never lost touch with her field; nor was she "lost" to the network of colleagues, contacts, and referrals upon which so much career advancement is based.

Deborah Diamond's version of combining motherhood with a medical career is somewhat different. A late-timing mother ten years younger than Faith Fromm, Deborah shared the dilemma of many programmatic postponers whose career commitments ripen coincidentally with family responsibilities. And she believed she had worked out the perfect solution to the problem. Like Faith, she moved briskly through medical training, married, completed her residency in neurology, and had her first child when she was 31. At that point she stepped back and deferred the customary next move into private practice or full-scale research, for she had always planned a full time-out during the children's early years.

After her first child was born, she agreed to write a textbook on neurology, which she thought would be "a good interim solution" calling for about 20 hours a week on her own time at home. "Writing a book seemed like a terrific plan," Deborah recalled. It was a way of turning resolutely toward motherhood while at the same time nourishing a piece of her career, of "keeping her oar in." Still, she construed the time as a career lull, a step off the established track; she knew it might jeopardize her professionally.

With book and baby she was actually working more than full-time, as hard as she ever had. The life Dream of medicine and motherhood was a crucial baseline during these years. It was something to come back to whenever she was besieged by doubts, her own and those of others. For all her eventual success as evidenced by her royalties, while she was writing she worked in virtual isolation, out of phase with the traditional timetable for medical careers and out of contact with peers and colleagues, mentors, and supervisors. While she was writing she often found herself wondering whether the book "counted"—in the view of the medical establishment, in the eyes of her husband, in her own estimation.

So long as the rules of the workplace and of professional success are defined by the "clockwork" of male career sequences[13] and so long as the psychological and structural boundaries of men's (but not women's) careers remain impermeable to the competing responsibilities of parenthood,[14] anything less than a man's work schedule compromises a woman's chances of having men's career opportunities and options. The irony, then, for late-timing mothers who choose to pursue careers simultaneously with caring for small children is that if they do it any less than full-time, if they cut back their hours, even temporarily, to fashion for themselves a tolerable total workload, they may still be penalized in the long run.

Faith Fromm, older than Deborah and now many years past the period in her life when she worked "mother's hours," feels that those mothers' hours *have* cost her in terms of position and status, and probably authority, within her chosen profession: "I'm not the chief here. And I might have been if I'd never cut back."

In the short run as well, the price of holding down two demanding occupations, one at home and the other away, is high: constant fatigue and overloaded circuits. "The tiredest I've ever been," Faith Fromm said, "was when I was pregnant, carrying a nine-to-two job, and a 20-month-old baby. Then I was really tired. It was worse than interning." But she never lost her desire or doubted her capacity to "do both." She knew she was a maverick, and the knowledge sustained her conviction and her courage.

Barbara Brodie also wanted to maintain the double occupation once she had children. Teaching for her was a matter of politics as well as an occupational Dream. However, by 1973, when her daughter was born, the psychohistorical context in which a woman did both had changed. Among her peers, Barbara was no maverick; her decision was not exceptional. Rather, hers was the "liberated woman's life plan" of the 1970s: personal quests and career development in one's 20s, hence programmatic postponement of child-bearing until the 30s, with an early resumption of the worldly career. All but two of the 14 programmatic postponers in our study continued to work, usually cutting back to part-time for a while, at careers and enterprises other than child care after their first children were born.

Barbara Brodie, however, as a new mother, found herself that first year with a full-time job she had not planned for. When she became pregnant at 29, she was teaching in a small country school. She had arranged with her school board a half-time teaching position for the following academic year. This arrangement fell through when the school found itself short-handed, and Barbara, an experienced, familiar, and respected teacher, was prevailed upon to teach full-time. . . . This change in plans precipitated a crisis at home: "Something had to give."

In one way or another, all of the simultaneous double-duty mothers (regardless of whether their first child was born early or late) experienced the "something has to give" feeling. In no other situation was so much conflict so consistently reported. At the most obvious level, conflict was generated by the competition between the spheres of "work" and "love," job and child, by the tension inherent in caring about both. "The whole issue of career versus parenthood had been a raging one for me for years," Barbara said: "whether I could stay with my work and be a mother too, whether I could have both."

Women who postponed childbearing, in part, to get careers under way expected parenthood to interfere with their careers; they did a great deal of advance thinking about ways to minimize that interference and mitigate its effects. They were startled to find that their perspective changed with parenthood itself and that they experienced their jobs, not their infants, as the source of interference. Bev Bajian, for instance, with a master's degree and an impressive résumé, was in a position to design for herself, in advance, a flexible post-partum job with a consulting firm of city planners. The job allowed her to schedule her work around her baby's needs. She was surprised to find that despite her careful planning, the simultaneous responsibilities at work and at home put her under great strain: "The first few months were really difficult—going back to work, and the arrangements and the responsibility . . . all of a sudden all my circuits seemed overloaded.

"New motherhood brought out the conflict between motherhood and work. It brought everything closer to the surface. If my job was causing me more frustration than it was giving me pleasure, why should I leave this adorable little kid? Things I would have taken at work a year or two ago, I was simply not willing to put up with any more. I guess I required a lot more satisfaction from what I was leaving the house to go do than I had before."

For Barbara and for Bev, as for the other programmatic postponers who continued with careers while they cared for their children, the centrality of those careers as their major life focus was challenged by the arrival of their children and their enjoyment of parenthood. These women found that although they still wanted both family and career, the meaning of each was different from what they had expected. They had not counted on being enthralled by their children.

These mothers did not talk about feeling guilty when they left their children to go to work. Rather, they described a sense of loss, of missing out on key moments (and mundane ones) in their children's lives. Barbara Brodie said, "You know the line about 'it's the quality of the time you spend with your children that counts'? Well, that's only part of it for me." She found that to spend a sustained quantity of time with Laura also "counts." "Finding myself on 'Laura time,' as we used to say, while it could be very boring, gave me pleasure too." Logistically, it was as demanding as she had known it would be to combine old and new occupations, but emotionally it was a struggle too—a struggle to combine old and new loves.

Like Bev Bajiah, Barbara talked about "cutting corners in everything," to avoid the sense of overload.[15] She spoke for many of her peers when she said, "For the first time in my life I was having to make trade-offs. To work, to have a child, to be a wife, to take care of a home, to have friends, to be a part of our new community, and to try to do all of these things well meant that something had to get cheated a little bit in each area. Not enough so that anybody else would notice, maybe, but I did. I noticed it. Sometimes I feel like my life is one long skid. Every moment I don't careen into something, I'm grateful."

However difficult it was to integrate motherhood with work beyond the home, these women did not see this as a reason to stop what they were doing. How did they cope? First, some women were successful "mentors" to their husbands in the dailiness of child care and family work. All of these women could and did turn to their husbands, not only for moral support when the going was rough, but as partners in the daily tasks of parenting. Second, they relied heavily on baby-sitters or family day-care arrangements, painstakingly recruited and financed from their salaries, to care for their children during the day. Finally, in dealing with stress in their lives, some women turned to the informal networks within which women have always sought counsel and support. They sought out neighboring women with older children for the wisdom of their experience, and like-minded friends and peers for empathy and reassurance. A few women relied on psychotherapy.

We are struck by the fact that these women sought personal solutions to their dilemmas. Feminist values in the early to mid 1970s provided a climate of confirmation for their aspirations, but these young women still found little or no societal or institutional support for resolving the tensions and accomplishing the tasks implicit in those aspirations.

For these late-timing "double duty" mothers, the task of orchestrating family and career proved feasible but tough. Like the tip of the iceberg, programmatic postponement is but one aspect of an underlying style of perfectionism and high aspiration. Many of these women were compelled to cut corners in everything for the first time in their lives. This necessary, continuous compromise, while it enabled them to extend their generativity to several spheres at once, at a deeper level threatened the very identity of omnicompetence upon which their multiple commitments were based.

In their experience of overload and compromise, the late-timing mothers now in their 30s differ in an important respect from the late-timing programmatic postponers in the two older generations and also from their early-timing peers. In our study, no other group so consistently defined themselves in terms of the double generativity of parenthood and the pursuit of "work in the world," or judged themselves by this dual standard. As new mothers, these women must continuously meet a double test of their resilience—both in the sphere of being, stretching the boundaries of the self "to make room for an absolutely dependent someone else in my life," and in the sphere of doing, expanding one's caring capacity and coping energy to meet and manage the double demands of a double occupation.

Twenty years ago, women were not expected to combine career with family (nor men, family with career). It took a maverick disposition to consider both, and tremendous capacity and energy to accomplish the goal. Women who wanted both knew it would be a struggle. Success in maintaining one's career while mothering was a personal triumph, an enhancement of self-esteem, as it was for Faith Fromm.

In the last ten years, societal and personal expectations of women have escalated dramatically. To have children while holding one's own in a career is no longer considered exceptional but par for the course. In this context, a woman may interpret the problems she encounters as personal shortcomings, as if somehow she hasn't measured up.

In idealizing the all-competent, "multidimensional" woman, the popular media and professional commentators have jointly fostered the idea that it is easy to take care of family and career simultaneously. Economic necessity and feminist career orientation seem to rule out anything less. Yet the struggle will be formidable unless we create the institutional supports that are as necessary as the right of women to pursue both meaningful work and family life. So long as women bear the sole, or even primary, responsibility for the care of preschool children—whatever their family-timing strategy, wherever in their adult life they locate their parenthood—they are likely to experience conflict and overload. If Superwoman supersedes Supermom as the persona women believe they must strive for, we will only have replaced one set of obligatory myths with another—imposing on individual lives a confining cycle of unrealistic expectation and inevitable disappointment.

At this moment in history, women may need a life Dream as developmental fuel even more than men do. We need it to overcome the inner conflicts that are the residue of female childhoods in a patriarchal world; and we need it to improvise our way through the circumstantial conflicts of lives increasingly defined by not one but two spheres of generativity.

Women will work. At the time of our interviews with them, 42 of the women in our study were working outside the home 20 hours a week or more. Twenty-one of these women were late-timing mothers and 21 were early-timing mothers. For the most part, their jobs or careers gave them satisfaction as well as income. In terms of eventual and ultimate labor-force participation, family timing has made no difference. However, when we look at the timing of their turn to nonfamily work, and their feelings about the work they do, family-timing differences do emerge. On the average, early-timing mothers took up nonfamily work 10.5 years after the birth of their first child, whereas late-timing mothers began combining motherhood with work in the world 4.2 years afterward. Fourteen women are doing work that represents the enactment of an occupational Dream, and 11 of these women are late-timing mothers.

For women who bring an occupational Dream into adulthood with them, late family timing seems to offer the best solution for integrating the two generative enterprises of parenthood and work in the world. A late-timing mother who chooses the simultaneous generativity pattern can continue to pursue the Dream in her 30s. For late-timing mothers who choose the sequential generativity pattern, the activated Dream can be sustained in private and actualized later once more. For women who do not have an occupational Dream, the question becomes whether motherhood or worldly work during the 20s will provide the most constructive drift out of which such a Dream may be claimed.

Women's generativity experience is fraught with complexity and compromise. Our careers unfold slowly. Interruptions are the rule, daily, and over time. Increasing numbers of women have no intention of forfeiting career for motherhood, or vice versa. A good life Dream is a groundplan for negotiating the conflicts that emerge along the way. A good Dream can see us through an unpredictable life sequence of "times-in" and "times-out." A good Dream can center a life.

The postponement of parenthood during the 20s seems to facilitate acting on the Dream, but it cannot guarantee it, just as early family timing does not foreclose it. The work histories of the women in our study make plain the indelible importance of individual personality and the historical moment. A woman's identity and ideology as well as the social and economic realities of her time combine with age and family timing to affect the ways in which she integrates parenthood into her life.

15

Men's Family Work: Three Perspectives and Some New Data

Joseph H. Pleck

Observers of the family and of men's roles within it are beginning to renew attention to men's performance of housework and childcare, or of "family work."[1] Many clinicians have reported that husbands' relatively low participation in family work is more often a bone of contention in marital relationships than it used to be. At the same time, researchers are investigating the division of family work with increasingly sophisticated interview methodologies and statistical analyses.

Yet, at the same time that there is increasing agreement that men's performance of family work is an important topic, there is still considerable disagreement about what the data on men's family work show. There is also little agreement about what men's level of family work should or can be expected to be. This paper offers a perspective on these disagreements by analyzing the different ways that men's family work has been conceptualized and studied in past research and also presents some new data about it.

THREE PERSPECTIVES ON MEN'S FAMILY WORK

In past and current literature, there appear to be three different perspectives concerning men's family work. We call these the traditional perspective, the exploitation perspective, and the changing roles perspective. These three

Reprinted from Joseph H. Pleck, "Men's Family Work: Three Perspectives and Some New Data," *The Family Coordinator*, vol. 28, October 1979, pp. 481-488.

perspectives form an historical sequence in that the later viewpoints successively reject the conclusions of the earlier ones. In brief, from the traditional perspective it is acknowledged that men do little family work, but this is viewed as appropriate. From the exploitation perspective, by contrast, men's low level of family work is viewed as having profound negative consequences for women and is viewed as unlikely to increase. Finally, from the changing roles perspective men are perceived as doing relatively little in the family at present, but it is believed that men's family role is changing in a positive direction.

It is beyond the scope of this paper to review each perspective comprehensively.[2] Nonetheless, the most important theories and data which contribute to each of these perspectives will be briefly presented. These perspectives are not theoretical orientations on the order of Hill and Hansen's (1960) "five conceptual frameworks" for family research as a whole. Rather, the three perspectives analyzed here are ultimately *value* perspectives about what men's work roles in the family should be. As such, they are not necessarily perspectives held by the individual theorists or researchers to be discussed below. Instead, it is more useful to view them as perspectives held by the society as a whole which simultaneously help shape the questions researchers ask (and the methodologies used to ask them) and provide a social context in which the results of research become intellectually meaningful and widely (often uncritically) accepted.

Understanding the different value perspectives underlying research and theory about men's family work is useful not only for researchers but for family educators and practitioners as well. All research is conducted and theories are constructed within the context of values researchers hold about what they are studying. The three perspectives considered here lead to different conclusions about what men actually do and what they can be expected to do in the family precisely because they are rooted in different values. By understanding these values, educators and practitioners can more easily grasp the meaning of research and theory in a particular area such as men's family roles. By doing so, they can use research and theory to help students and clients make more informed value decisions.

THE TRADITIONAL PERSPECTIVE

The traditional perspective on men's family roles is so named because it is the one which emerged earliest in the family field. Until recently, it has been the dominant perspective as well. It is also traditional in the sense that it provides a value context in which a limited role for men in family work is viewed as justifiable and appropriate. In simplest terms, this traditional perspective holds that husbands are not responsible for any substantial amount of housework and childcare in the family. Rather, husbands are responsible only for providing the family's economic support through their paid employment outside the family. Three well-known ideas or theories in the family field have played an important part in this traditional perspective: role differentiation, exchange theory, and resource theory.

The first important notion contributing to the traditional perspective is Parsons and Bales' (1955) formulation that the family exhibits "role differentiation." In this role differentiation, the male responsible is for the family's relationships with the outside world while the female is responsible for the family's internal needs. Parsons and Bales believed role differentiation on this dimension to be a universal feature of all social groups, including the family. Thus, men do little family work as part of a larger family division of labor in which men specialize in the external family breadwinner role while wives monopolize the internal family work role.

Another important idea prominently employed by the traditional perspective is the concept of "exchange" between husband and wife. Scanzoni's (1970) particularly influential statement, applying social-psychological "exchange theory" to the family, indicates that husbands are, in effect, exchanging their successful performance of the family breadwinner role for their wives' provision of love, companionship, and household services. In this view, each partner's contribution to the mutual exchange places an obligation on the other partner to provide his or her complementary contribution. Scanzoni's application of exchange theory to the family does not in principle imply that marital exchange always does or should take the particular form it does in traditional marriage. Nonetheless, exchange theory has been widely used as though it did.

A third idea important to the traditional perspective is what has come to be known as "resource theory." Blood and Wolfe (1960) introduced resource theory to the family field in their analysis of the division of household tasks between husband and wife. The basic idea is that roles vary among people in families because people vary in the "resources" needed to perform these roles. Blood and Wolfe developed and applied resource theory to answer three questions about the division of domestic labor: why husbands and wives perform different tasks; why wives perform more tasks than husbands; and how the marital division of labor changes in response to variations in wives' and husbands' employment status.

Blood and Wolfe could not really answer the first two questions with their data. However, they did perform a detailed analysis which supported resource theory and answered the third question. We will describe their conclusion here, but will defer criticizing it until we consider the exploitation perspective in the next section.

Blood and Wolfe showed that employed wives reported that their husbands performed a higher proportion of the family's household tasks than non-employed wives reported about their husbands. This result supports resource theory because it shows that when wives have less of the principal resource needed for family work—less time, as a result of being employed—they do proportionately less family work, and their husbands do more. Blood and Wolfe also showed that husbands' proportion of household task performance varied inversely with their own paid work hours: the more time the husband spent at his job, the smaller proportion of the houshold tasks he performed. This result likewise confirms resource theory.

To further support resource theory, Blood and Wolfe also performed a limited test of an alternative hypothesis that the division of household labor is determined by traditional family ideology. They tested this alternative hypothesis by comparing rural with urban families, as well as Catholic with non-Catholic families. Blood and Wolfe argued that rural and Catholic families were likely to have more traditional ideology than urban and non-Catholic ones. The researchers found hardly any differences between these groups on the division of household work. Combining this with their earlier results, Blood and Wolfe concluded that husbands' relatively low contribution to household work did not derive from traditional ideology about family roles. Rather, they argued, husbands' low contribution is a rational response to the fact that husbands have fewer resources, particularly time, with which to perform these tasks.

Altogether, through the use of role differentiation, exchange, and resource theories, the traditional viewpoint about men's family roles is a value perspective from which the traditional division of marital roles, with its limited male family work, is viewed as legitimate, desirable, and not in need of change. This traditional perspective sees husbands' limited role within the family as logically following from their predominance as family breadwinners. But from this perspective, the latter is viewed as something which can be taken for granted and which does not need to be further analyzed. A particularly important corollary of this perspective is the belief that husbands increase their family work role appropriately when their wives are employed.

THE EXPLOITATION PERSPECTIVE

Starting in the early 1970s, a quite different view about men's family work began to be expressed, and its underlying theoretical basis was feminism. The feminist movement, from its very outset, identified the unequal burden of housework and childcare carried by women as an important aspect of women's inferior status in society. Mainardi's (1971) widely-circulated and pointedly-titled essay, "The Politics of Housework," underlined the importance of housework inequality as a form of exploitation experienced daily and in a direct way by almost all women in relationships with men. Farrell's (1974) *The Liberated Man*, probably the most widely-read book on men's liberation, likewise argued that men did very little family work. Farrell noted that in his observation, housework was the issue "liberated"men most avoided dealing with. Perhaps the strongest critical indictment of the traditional male family role was Polatnick's (1973–74) argument that men burdened women with housework and especially childcare responsibility as part of a deliberate strategy to maintain power over women (see also Berheide, Berk, & Berk, 1976; Pleck, Note 1, 1977; Vanek, Note 2).

At around this time, new data, collected with a newly rediscovered methodology, provided a research basis for the exploitation perspective on men's family roles. Several large-scale studies conducted in the mid-1960's and early 1970's (Meissner, Humphreys, Meis, & Scheu, 1975; Robinson, 1977; Walker & Woods, 1976) examined family participation with a time budget (or time diary) methodology, a technique first introduced by home economists in the 1920's but not widely adopted in social scientific research until the 1960's. In this methodology, respondents are given diary forms dividing the day into hours or even smaller blocks of time, and are asked to describe their activities during each block of time for a particular recent day (e.g., yesterday). These activities are then coded, making possible summary figures for time spent in categories such as housework and childcare. These studies revealed three extremely important facts about men's family participation.

First, husbands' performance of family work (i.e., housework and childcare) is quite small in absolute magnitude. In Walker and Woods' (1976) investigation of 1296 upper New York State families, men's family work occupied about 1.6 hours per day, compared to 8.1 hours per day for housewives and 4.8 hours per day for employed wives. It had always been known that husbands performed less family work than wives, but exactly how much less had never before been described so clearly.

Time budget research revealed a second, and more important, fact about men's family work. These studies consistently showed that husbands of employed wives did *not* spend more time in family work than did husbands of non-employed wives. According to Walker and Woods' data, for example, in families in which the wife was not employed, wives spent an average of 8.1 hours per day in family work, and husbands spent 1.6 hours per day. In families in which the wife was employed 30 or more hours per week, wives reduced their family work to 4.8 hours per day, but husbands maintained theirs at precisely the same average level of 1.6 hours per day. The other time budget studies showed exactly the same pattern of results. This result was quite startling, and was not widely accepted for some time. (As a personal note, I remember having many exchanges about this matter with colleagues who insisted that this simply could not be the case, often citing Blood and Wolfe (1966) in their support.)

Actually, the contradiction between the time budget results and those of Blood and Wolfe is only apparent, for Blood and Wolfe's measure assesses only the *proportional* or *relative* contribution of each spouse to family work. The husband's proportion of total family work did increase when the wife was employed, but his absolute contribution did not. That is, his proportion increased not because he was actually doing any more but only because his wife was doing less. To illustrate with Walker and Woods' (1976) data, husbands of non-employed wives performed 1.6 of 9.7 hours of family work (1.6 for the husband and 8.1 for the wife), or 16%. When the wife was employed, husbands performed 1.6 of 6.4 hours (1.6 for the husband and 4.8 for the wife), or 25%—a higher proportion, but the same absolute amount.

Third, this time budget research permits a further analysis concerning the total work performed by husbands and wives (i.e., the sum of family work and paid work). The total amount of work performed by employed wives has been shown to be considerably greater than that performed by their employed husbands. In Walker and Woods' (1976) data, for example, employed wives spent an average of 10.1 hours per day in total work (4.8 hours of family work plus 5.3 hours of paid work) while husbands performed an average of only 7.9 hours per day (1.6 plus 6.3 hours)[3]—about 2.2 hours less per day. Robinson's (1977) and Meissner et al.'s (1975) studies yielded similar figures. By contrast, in families in which the wife was a full-time homemaker, wives' and husbands' total work hours were more nearly equal in the various studies. Thus, employed wives can be described as experiencing a substantial "overload" in their combination of work and family roles as compared to their husbands. Employed wives' role overload has negative consequences for them. As one concrete example, employed wives have less free time and sleep less than their husbands. Employed wives' role overload is also associated with an increased sense of time pressure and diminished well-being (Robinson, 1977).

These three findings from the time budget research of the 1960's and early 1970's dramatically undermine the traditional perspective on men's family roles. Today, in the near-majority of husband-wife couples, both husband and wife are employed—47% in March, 1977 (Hayghe, 1978). Since the employed wife works 2.2 more hours *in toto* per day than her husband in these couples, it is simply not intellectually tenable to view men's limited family roles as the result of an equitable "exchange" between husband and wife resulting from their different resources. The traditional perspective may fit the data for the declining minority of husband-sole-breadwinner families, but it breaks down when applied to the emerging majority of two-earner families.

THE CHANGING ROLES PERSPECTIVE

Most recently, a third perspective on men's family work has emerged. From the changing roles perspective the basic data on men's family participation reviewed above is acknowledged but it is interpreted in a different light. In particular, the changing roles perspective rejects the pessimism of the exploitation perspective. The exploitation perspective is often used in a way that makes change in men's family roles seem impossible and gives little or no attention to concrete strategies that might bring change about. The exploitation perspective may provide an adequate basis for indicting men, but by itself it does not provide a basis for helping them change.

The underlying theoretical basis for the changing roles perspective is a macrosocial and historical view of the evolution of paid work and family roles. Myrdal and Klein (1956) introduced the phrase "women's two roles" to describe how contemporary women have added a second role—in paid employment—to their traditional role in the family. As Myrdal (1967) herself was perhaps the first to observe, women holding two roles ultimately requires that men need to have "two roles" as well—adding a greatly enlarged family role to their traditional role in paid employment. Young and Willmott (1973) expressed a similar view in their concept of the "symmetrical family" in which women and men each combine family and work responsibilities. From this point of view, an increased family role is the single most important manifestation of change in the male role in contemporary society, just as increased labor force participation is probably the most important change in the female role.

As Rapoport and Rapoport (Note 3) put it, the problem today is a "psychosocial lag" between the slower rate of change in men's roles in the family compared to the relatively more rapid rate of change in women's roles in paid employment. Rather than view this discrepancy as a permanent feature of our society, it is more useful to view it as reflecting a transitional problem of adjustment. It is not intended that this perspective imply the pollyannish optimism that we need only wait for men to transform themselves. Rather, it is implied that men can and will change if appropriate educational and social policies are implemented, requiring effort and commitment on the part of the family field.

The differences between the changing roles perspective and the two perspectives mentioned earlier can be summarized easily. From the traditional perspective, men in the family are seen as doing relatively little in the family, but no reason is seen for change. From the exploitation perspective, men are seen as doing relatively little in the family, but little hope for change is seen. From the changing roles perspective, men are seen as doing relatively little in the family at the present time, but increasing men's family roles is seen as possible and as one of the major challenges facing the family field today. Although the changing roles perspective is by no means the dominant viewpoint at present, it is likely to become an increasingly important viewpoint in family studies in the future.

Five kinds of research that have contributed to the changing roles perspective on men's family work can be described:

1. *Monitoring of change*. Because many phenomena concerning family roles and sex roles are in a state of flux today, it is important to monitor change in men's family roles in the society as a whole. Although we should not expect change to be rapid, we must nonetheless carefully look for, note, and give due attention to any change that is occurring in men's family roles.
2. *Examination of subgroups and innovative patterns*. It is important to recognize the diversity of men's family roles. Men's family roles may change more or less or in different ways in some segments of society than others. Innovative patterns of male family experience may be emerging (e.g., single fatherhood) which, though not involving large numbers of men, nonetheless are important in demonstrating that men can take a much larger family role than previously thought possible. Examining special subgroups of innovative patterns should not re-

duce our attention to the family roles of more typical men. Nonetheless, these patterns may provide useful models for change. Levine's (1976) analysis of four non-traditional and innovative types of fatherhood—single-parent fathers, fathers deliberately holding part-time jobs, single adoptive fathers, and househusbands—is an exemplary study of this sort.

3. *Analysis of the sources of variation in men's family roles*. If we recognize that there is diversity in men's family experiences, a logical next step is to explore what factors appear to lead to a greater or lesser male family role. Of particular interest are attitudinal factors as well as demands from the work role, which are at least potentially changeable through intervention programs or social policy innovations. By identifying such factors associated with variations in men's family roles, it becomes possible to design effective change strategies. A good example of such a study is Lein's (1979) analysis of differences in the nature of husbands' and wives' social networks, and differences in the ways that families interpret husbands' and wives' employment make it difficult for men to increase their family role when their wives are employed. Such analyses do not mean that it is fine for men's family roles to stay as they are; employed wives really are overworked. But studies such as Lein's give us new insight into the dynamics through which men's low level of family work occurs. By understanding its dynamics better, we can know better how to change it.
4. *Analysis of consequences of increased family roles for men*. It is also important to examine the consequences of increased male family roles. Two general kinds of consequences are particularly important. First, increased male family roles hopefully would be associated with positive outcomes for husbands themselves, their wives, their children, and for family life generally. Data validating this expectation would lend support to those advocating an increased male family role as well as to men struggling to increase their own family role. Research is needed to determine to what extent and in what ways this expectation is confirmed or disconfirmed. Second, increasing men's family roles may have negative consequences for men in certain areas, in terms of conflicting with men's work role demands or with the expectations and attitudes of peers. It is valuable to assess to what extent these negative consequences occur and what strategies are useful to men in dealing with them.
5. *Evaluation of programs and policies increasing men's family roles*. Levine (Note 4) has observed that a variety of programs and policies are in operation today which have as either an explicit or implicit goal increasing men's family roles. Such programs can be classified as either educational or institutional in nature. Educational programs include parenthood education curricula emphasizing men's roles, many childbirth preparation programs, and new family planning curricula directed at males. Examples of institutional practices include new

hospital policies permitting men to be present during delivery and to have greater contact with the newborn during the hospital stay after delivery, the paternity leave policies which have been adopted in certain firms and union contracts, and reforms in child custody legislation. Levine's planned policy analysis of these programs and their effectiveness will be a major contribution.

This set of five topics constitutes a rather formidable agenda for future researchers working within the changing roles perspective.

MEN'S FAMILY WORK AND WIVES' EMPLOYMENT: A NEW STUDY

The final part of this paper presents some results from a recent study rooted in the changing roles perspective. These results bear on the first of the topics above: monitoring of change. The Men's Two Roles Study (MTRS) (see Pleck & Lang, Note 5; Pleck, Staines & Lang, Note 6) was designed to investigate a variety of questions concerning men's family work and men's family roles more generally. It put particular emphasis on analyzing the nature, sources, and consequences of men's family roles, in comparison to men's paid work roles. It also devoted considerable attention to the conflicts men experience between their family roles and work roles. Reported here are results concerning men's time in family work and the relation of men's time in family work to wives' employment.

Data for the part of the MTRS described here came from the 1977 Quality of Employment Survey (Quinn & Staines, 1978), a national representative sample survey sponsored by the U.S. Department of Labor and conducted by the Institute for Social Research, University of Michigan. This survey's national sample of 1575 persons who were employed 20 or more hours per week included 757 married men and 270 married women (not from the same couples). Data in the survey were collected through a 70-minute personal interview. Full technical discussions of the methods and results of the study appear in the references cited earlier.

Respondents were asked to estimate how much time they spent on "home chores—things like working, cleaning, repairs, shopping, yardwork, and keeping track of money and bills," both for the average working day and average non-working day. They also estimated the time they spent "taking care of or doing things with your child(ren)." These estimates were then converted into hours per week, taking into account the exact number of working and non-working days per week. Employed husbands estimated they spent an average of about 14.5 hours per week in housework. Husbands with children under 18 spent about 20 hours per week in childcare. The former is about half of employed wives' average estimate of their own housework (about 31 hours per week), and the latter is about two-thirds of employed wives' childcare estimate (33 hours per week). These findings cannot be directly compared with the earlier time budget studies discussed above to determine possible trends over time because the present study employed respondents' own summary estimates of their time use, not actual time diaries.

Another important finding in the present research, however, can be compared with earlier studies. In this 1977 representative national sample, employed husbands with employed wives reported spending 1.8 hours per week more in housework ($p < .073$) and 2.7 more hours per week in childcare ($p < .05$) than did employed husbands with non-employed wives. When converted to minutes per day, these increments are obviously not large. Nonetheless, they appear to be the first finding of non-trivial increments in husbands' family work associated with wives' employment in a study assessing family work in terms of time in a large, representative sample.

Thus, in contrast to earlier time use studies, it is indicated from this study that men are beginning at last to increase their family work when their wives are employed. There is no question, of course, that wives continue to hold the primary responsibility for family work. But even as this reality is acknowledged, it is important to recognize that men's behavior is changing on an important social indicator. The pace of change may seem slow. Yet, it should not be dismissed or taken for granted. Change of this magnitude in a national sample actually represents a substantial phenomenon. Those working to facilitate future growth in men's family roles—researchers, educators, and clinicians—should take heart from it and build upon it.

16

Male Participation in Home Life: Impact of Social Supports and Breadwinner Responsibility on the Allocation of Tasks

Laura Lein

As a result of women's increased participation in the paid labor force, men today feel pressure to increase their contribution to the nurturing and homemaking aspects of family life. Figures from the United States Census illustrate the dramatic change in labor force participation of married women with children under six. In 1950, 11.9% of such women were employed in the paid labor force; by 1976 this figure had tripled (U.S. Bureau of the Census, 1978). Most men and women do perceive that the entry of women into the labor force, particularly during the family's child-rearing years, requires some changes in the day-to-day organization of family life. However, time budget studies (Pleck, 1979; Robinson, 1977; Walker & Woods, 1976) indicate that husband's contribution to the household did not increase when wives entered the paid labor force in the 1960's and began showing small increases only in the late 1970's.

It has been argued that men do not increase their family participation because they perceive the work of the home as demeaning and that they enjoy their privileged position in the family, resenting and resisting any attempt to change. Data from the Working Family Project (Note 2), to be described in this article, suggest that men's response is not so much reluctance as ambivalence, created by a number of factors.

Men's ambivalence to changes in the structure of home life reflects the multiple pressures on them as citizens, workers, and concerned family

Reprinted from Laura Lein, "Male Participation in Home Life: Impact of Social Supports and Breadwinner Responsibility on the Allocation of Tasks," *The Family Coordinator*, vol. 28, October 1979, pp. 489–495.

members. The informal social support systems in which men tend to participate differ in certain respects from those of women—leaving men relatively unsupported to meet heavier demands for involvement in family life. Men's values concerning paid work and their sex-specific relationship in the paid labor force conflict with increased involvement in the day-to-day functioning of the home. Effort expended in home life is often perceived as energy diverted from the primary effort of breadwinning.

This article draws on "intensive" data from the Working Family Project to explore men's ambivalent response to pressure for change in their role. Regardless of the attitude of husbands towards a wife's initial participation in the labor force, the change in her economic and work status is reflected in changes and new tensions in the home. Men, like women, are caught in the grip of family and societal forces which exert considerable pressure on them to maintain traditional standards for the organization of family life. Some of the tensions and ambivalence which this article seeks to explain are illustrated in the example below:

> *Husband:* Yeah, like now she feels I should help her more around the house when she's working. Of course, I don't agree one hundred percent with her there. This is something we've never agreed on, and I don't think we ever will. How can she compare her work with me laying brick all day? I broke my hump today. So after supper, I just wanted to go downstairs and watch the news. "Well, what about the house," (imitating wife). She didn't actually come out and say it but she kind of hinted. So I said, "Well, okay, I'll take the kids with me." But I guess she feels I should do more. Most of the nights I don't mind, but once in a while. . . . I figure she should let me go when I've had a tough day, 'cause I do more than my share.
>
> *Wife:* Well, he probably wouldn't admit this, but he is real old-fashioned in the way that a man should work and woman should be at home. And I think it comes out of the fact that to a certain extent he would never say that a woman is equal to a man. We were just arguing tonight about who was going to do the dishes, and I think he feels that if I am working, I am going to expect him to do certain things that in his mind a man shouldn't do. A woman should do, like any type of housework, dishes, and things like that. I mean, he'll take the kids out and take them for a ride and get lost rather than help me make a bed or something like that, and I think this—call it an identity situation—I don't know exactly how to word it, but he really, as much as he says he doesn't mind my working, I know he does.

Although reluctant to share the breadwinner responsibilities and undertake new tasks at home, many men are aware of and respect the importance of the home maintenance role and crave a more active participation:

> It would be nice if I could be the one to be available to share the problems they may have in school, for instance, during the school day . . . be there when a child was sick. . . . I'll come home and my wife will say, well, this happened today or that happened. I'll sort of wish that I was there to experience it. You feel like you're missing something.

These quotes pulled from the Working Family Project material illustrate the dilemma of many men as they mediate home and work responsibilities.

THE WORKING FAMILY PROJECT

Material for this paper was drawn from the Working Family Project, an "intensive" interview and observation study of twenty-five middle American families in the Boston area. Intensive small-sample research is particularly valuable for understanding how societal pressures and counter-pressures related to family roles impact on family life. Across many disciplines and problem areas, policy analysts, service personnel, and scholars are calling for intensive research work to explore family process and the complex motivations underlying the behavior of family members (Ryder, 1973). Work such as that of Howell (1973), Rubin (1976), and Stack (1974) exemplify the richness and strength of intensive studies of family life. Their work elicits the complexity of detail that forms family life and analyzes the meaning of daily experiences to its participants. Although such research does not have high generalizability in the manner of large-scale survey work, it has a compelling validity. Only through such intensive work can we understand the meaning of large-scale social trends for the family and its members.

The Working Family Project began in 1973 as a result of two concerns. First, there was little intensive research available on nonproblem families. Most work on families and family life had concentrated on families with preidentified problems: poverty, alcoholism, drug abuse, family violence, and so forth. In addition, there was little intensive study of the effect of women's increased entry into the labor force on the psychosocial interior of the family. In this project we investigated the variety of ways in which ordinary two-worker American families manage the planning, problem-solving, and decision-making involved in raising a family.

Our sample included 25 Boston area families with both parents present in the home and employed in the paid labor force. This represents an increasingly common family structure, although one different from traditional expectations. We selected only families with preschool children, since this is a time of particular stress on families.

Because we were interested in studying a variety of families, we selected families solely on a fairly broad income criterion. Therefore, the families in the Working Families Project came from many walks of life. We restricted the sample to families with incomes between $6,000 and $20,000. The median income for families in the United States at the time the study began was about $13,000. We were particularly interested in including families in the study who, on the one hand, could not afford such options as a full-time housekeeper but who, on the other hand, were not eligible for government subsidy. Because of our interest in locating a diverse group of families, we included families from different racial and ethnic groups that, to some extent, represented the variation among families living in the Boston area. All parents were native-born Americans.

Data collection from each of the 25 families included one or two interviews with the wife alone, one or two interviews with the husband alone, one interview with the couple together, and at least observations of the parents with their children. Where preschool children were regularly cared for in other settings in addition to the home, researchers observed there as well. If grandparents were an active part of family life, researchers requested an interview with them.

Material from interviews and observations created a body of 100–200 pages of transcript and notes on each family. This material was coded into fourteen content areas (Working Family Project, Note 2). The analysis presented in this paper is based on data from three of the content areas—"Women's Employment," "Tasks and Roles in Family Life," and "Social Networks."

MEN'S SOCIAL SUPPORTS

A man who engages in behavior deviant from traditional expectations can expect comment—not only from family, friends, and acquaintances—but from anyone observing it. One father, for example, reported on the response of neighborhood women to his frequent presence on the community playground as the afternoon caretaker for his son: "I heard one woman whisper to another, 'That poor little boy. His mother must be dead—it's always his father who brings him here.' "

The possibility of such commentary inhibits many men from public expression of the traditionally feminine role of caring for and nurturing young children. Members of the Working Family Project staff discovered that observations of father-child interaction were frequently hindered by the father's reluctance to display loving behavior (hugging, holding, kissing his child) before an observer. For example, when children made what appeared to be routine overtures for their father's affection during an observation period, the fathers often responded with an embarrassed shrug, an attempt to distract the child, or a limited response. Only through the child's clear expectation of a demonstrative response did we learn that such interaction was usually forthcoming.

The amorphous pressures of the larger society are powerfully represented specifically by men's peer groups. Analysis of the Working Family Project materials indicated that men's social networks were substantially different from women's. Although men were acquainted with as many or more people than women, they knew fewer people as close friends. Second, men's networks tended to include co-workers for friends rather than neighbors or relatives. For instance, men may know people at work and through an organization they belong to but not know neighbors or keep in close contact with their family. As a result, their peer groups provide little practical household help. Men in the Working Family Project never reported drawing on their own social network to help with child care and housework. Women tended to call on people from the neighborhood, their families, and a variety of formal and informal groups.

The membership of men's and women's social networks is due in part to the different demands placed on men and women in their traditional roles. A man's traditional family responsibility is to act as the interface between the family and the larger, more complex, and scarier outside world, and the prime function of his network is the provision of information on how the system works (Granovetter, 1974). For women, social networks tend to act in a more concrete way, substituting for the individual when she cannot undertake her entire responsibility to the household as it is traditionally defined. For men it is more useful to know people who know other people. For women it is more helpful to have personal contact with people who can pitch in.

In addition, men's peer groups often explicitly ridicule or ostracize their members for what they perceive as effeminate or weak behavior, including male involvement in what have been traditionally women's responsibilities. Men may down-grade the efforts of other men to contribute to homemaking and pressure them to spend more time and effort on the job or in the peer group. Here speaks one father who had begun to help out more at home as his wife entered the labor force:

> I know I do more than most of the guys I know as far as helping their wives. Ninety percent of them I know don't ever do shopping for their wives. There might be a few of them that wash the floor for their wives. . . . We talk about it at work. We talk about it when we have a get-together with a half dozen couples, and they say, "What, are you crazy?" We get very personal, you know. The guys want to kill me. "You son of a bitch! You are getting us in trouble," and the wives say, "Does he really?" The men get really mad.

MEN'S BREADWINNER RESPONSIBILITY

Men's responses to their wives' employment in the paid labor force is related to men's and women's different experiences as paid workers. All but two or three of the fathers in the Working Family Project families felt personally responsible for their family's financial support, even though their wives participated in breadwinning activities (Dougherty, Note 1; Working Family Project, Note 2). Most Working Family Project fathers saw paid work as the primary male contribution to family life, rather than as an activity removed from the family.

This sense of responsibility explains some of the differences between men's and women's work histories in Working Family Project families. Before marriage, labor force participation patterns for men and women were similar. Men and women both have worked several jobs before marriage, not staying in any job for more than a year or two. This pattern did not change dramatically at the time of marriage. However, at the birth of the first child, there was a significant shift in male work patterns. The majority of the men in the Working Family Project families remained at the time of their interview (from 3 to 20 years after the birth of their first child) in either the company where they had been employed at the time of the child's birth or in one to which they had changed during the first year of the child's life. Most fathers indicated that this was a direct reflection of their family's increased need for stable income and for the additional benefits (e.g., unemployment insurance, health insurance, pension) that almost always adhered to the husband's job.

One husband commented:

> My wife would like me to change jobs, but I promised myself I would stay with this job. It's secure—it has good benefits. I used to be flighty about my work, but now I know I will stay in this job.

A second husband:

> I changed jobs twelve years ago because there's more job security in teaching, and there was very little security in my other job. Besides, teaching salaries improved.

Women, on the other hand, became more sporadic in their labor force participation. If hours were difficult, if they disliked the job, they left the labor force temporarily or changed jobs. Thus, one mother described her job history:

> I worked part-time after our first child and then I worked full-time. If you wanted a job, you put your name on a list, and they got you a job. I worked there a year and then left for the E____ Corporation. . . . That was really wonderful . . . but then my boss left, and the guy that took his place wasn't so hot . . . so I figured it's time to leave.

The reasons for women's participation in the paid labor force vary widely, but, nonetheless, differ from men's more powerful orientation toward family support. Some work out of family necessity; some work to give their family additional benefits; some work regardless of financial constraints, either to have a break from household responsibilities or to further their own personal development and build a career. Most women work, in part, for all of these reasons. In any case, in the two-worker families of the Working Family Project, women's paid work was seen as "helping out" the wage-earner rather than as a change in the primary responsibilities of husband and wife.

One husband said:

> Really, in all sincerity, I count my blessings with my wife, because I know I got a gem. . . . I didn't ask her to go to work, I didn't push her at all. She

asked me how I felt about it, and I said, "If you want to—I don't particularly go for it, but if you feel you want to, okay." She felt she was helping, 'cause I hadn't been working for a while. . . . I'll never forget that; she did it to help take some of the pressure off me. And I can't say enough for the girl, really . . . when I look at some of these guys—*their* wives wouldn't do it—I mean, they wouldn't go out of their way, you know. . . . Even a couple of guys down to the station have said to me, "Geez, your wife's working, what do you think of that?" And I say, "What do you mean what do I think—if she wants to, if she wants to help out, you know." . . . She's a pretty good girl.

Thus, although women are spending more time in the paid labor force, in most two-parent families they are not undertaking the primary breadwinning function in either their own eyes or their husbands'.

Men's primary responsibility for wage-earning in most two-earner families was clearly related to the higher wages and better benefits earned by men in the Working Family Project. This was due partly to women's patterns of part-time work and partly to the lower hourly rates women were paid. Men's higher earnings reinforced their sense of financial responsibility. One husband described his feelings about work and its relationship to family responsibility:

It's at the point now where I have to spend a great deal of time on office matters. And, that coupled with the fact that the pressures get greater as the years go by, consumerism what-have-you . . . makes it more and more difficult. It's at the point now where I go to work in the morning and I come home at night, and I don't feel that I've accomplished anything. I used to, at one point, have that feeling—well, we solved a problem here—but I don't have that feeling anymore. And that sort of changes things. . . . I've even thought of changing jobs for a period of time, but . . . I've not thought seriously enough to do anything about it. My job pays, you know, decent wages . . . and you know . . . it probably does affect my family . . . when I come home depressed, and I do bring my work home with me at times . . . you know, I get very moody at times. . . . They only have to look at me at times and they don't say anything. . . . I feel that I have an obligation to provide the security my family deserves. I certainly wouldn't take a chance on something that would leave us short. . . . Plus, if something did crop up and I wanted to try it, it would have to be moderately close to what I'm doing now as far as financial. . . . I wouldn't make a drastic change in income, since that would affect my family. They are uppermost, foremost, in my mind.

Men do not see their wage-earning activities apart from family life. As they see it, working in the paid labor force is their primary contribution to the well-being of their families.

There are several factors which reinforce male adherence to the breadwinning role. In many families husbands perceive both wife's employment and increased male participation in the work of the house as the relinquishing of primary responsibility for wage-earning, leading to consequent changes in the husband-wife relationship.

> She was working at the S____ Market . . . and when she was working there, I sort of, I guess, felt inadequate. I did not like this thing of having to have my wife work to allow us adequate income to survive on. . . . I wanted to know that I could support my family myself, and that they could be dependent on me. I didn't want to go through life feeling that she had to work—that did bother me. There were occasional times when she gave me the impression that she felt a little independent, because of this, and I didn't care for that. She was working and I was working, and if I came home and my supper wasn't ready, I might get a little stern about it. And she would say, "Well, I was working too." I felt that if she couldn't handle the work at home, then she shouldn't be working outside. But, of course, we both knew that it was necessary for her to work, and I was resentful of the fact that she had to work and that she couldn't do the things that are expected of her at home.

For many such husbands it appeared crucial to adopt a stance that the wife's employment did not represent real participation in the family support function; therefore, it should not change the family balance of power and decision-making. One husband, for instance, explained that his wife worked only because of a special financial commitment she had undertaken:

> I used to think about her not working. But now the way conditions are, you need two. I said, "You don't have to work if you don't want to; that's up to you," but we just bought a summer place up in New Hampshire that's being built, so now she'll have to work, because that's her project. And if anything goes wrong, it's her project. She made the decision; I didn't want to go (with the New Hampshire purchase), but she did.

Reluctance to give up roles may be a problem for wives too. One husband and wife agreed that as they tried to work out an arrangement for sharing responsibility for household tasks, the wife "took on this incredible ability to see dirt." She was at least as reluctant to relinquish her primary responsibility for the household as her husband was to relinquish responsibility for making the family living. In fact, in some Working Family Project families husbands and wives distinguished responsibility from help with tasks in a way that allowed them to maintain traditional role expectations, while husband and wife helped each other out a great deal in fulfilling their respective role-assigned responsibilities.

CONCLUSIONS

The difficulties men in families face in meeting new obligations and demands are not simply the result of personal weaknesses or lack of commitment to family life. Rather, they stem from inconsistencies between family expectations and the expectations of the wider society; from the structure of men's and women's participation in the paid labor force; and from deficiencies in men's social support systems.

In dealing with families that are negotiating new roles and responsibilities, it is important for family educators and practitioners to deal with the following facts that impinge on the husband and father's ability to participate in family life:

1. Husbands perceive their paid work as their primary contribution to the family.
2. Both husbands and wives may have difficulty relinquishing responsibility for their primary roles in the family, respectively bread-winner and homemaker.
3. Men and women tend to experience community reaction and the reaction of the larger society as a pressure against change in the allocation of responsibility and tasks among family members.
4. Men experience very different social support networks than do women, and these networks tend to preserve traditional roles.
5. The allocation of tasks in the household reflects other aspects of the relationships among family members: the relative importance of earnings in the paid labor force, the balance of decision-making power in the family, and the sense of self-image as a participating family member. It is impossible to change task allocation without affecting these and other facets of family life.

17

Interrole Conflict, Coping Strategies, and Satisfaction Among Black Working Wives

Algea Othella Harrison and Joanne Holbert Minor

This study focused on interrole conflicts experienced by black employed wives with children, strategies used to cope with interrole conflict, and the degree of self-satisfaction with role performance. Using Levinson's (1959) definition of role as a process, Hall (1972) has developed a model of coping strategies used by persons to handle interrole conflicts. Levinson (1959) described three components of the role process related to a person in a given social position. The three components (Levinson, 1959) of the role process described were: (1) structurally given demands (i.e., norms and expectations that guide, impede or support the functioning of a person in a specific position); (2) personal role conception (i.e., the person's inner definition of what he is supposed to think and do); (3) role behavior (i.e., the way in which persons act in accordance with or in violation of a given set of organizational norms). Given these three components of the role process, Hall (1972) defined the type of coping mechanism that would intervene at each.

Type I was defined as the coping strategy used for structurally imposed demands, that is, structural role redefinition. In this case, one would attempt to alter or change the expectations of others regarding one's performance in the specific role. In other words, one would reduce role conflict by changing external demands on one's behavior from others. This type of coping behavior requires communication between the person in a social role and role senders for the purpose of redefining the role. According to Hall (1972:474), the

Reprinted from Algea Othella Harrison and Joanne Holbert Minor, "Interrole Conflict, Coping Strategies, and Satisfaction Among Black Working Wives," *Journal of Marriage and the Family*, vol. 40, November 1978, pp. 799–805.

critical features of behaviors that would be classified at Type I coping "all involve dealing directly with environmental transmitters of the structurally imposed demands, actively attempting to alter (reduce, reallocate, reschedule, and so forth) these demands and coming to agreement with the role senders on a new set of expectations."

The specific behaviors of Type I coping are: the elimination of role activities, but not entire roles; role support from outside the role set, role support from inside the role set (usually the family), problem solving with role senders, role integration; and the change of the societal definition of one's roles (Hall, 1972). An example of behavior categorized by Hall (1972) as Type I coping was that of a woman who stated that she and her husband openly discussed conflicts and he helped her decide how to deal with them; i.e., problem solving with role senders.

As noted by Hall (1972), this type of coping represents a more stable, permanent resolution of conflict. Hall also described the coping mechanism for the personal role conception. He called it personal role redefinition or Type II coping. In this case, the person attempts to make internal changes in attitude and perceptions to reduce role conflicts. In contrast, Type I coping involves attempting to change the external environment as well as the internal. According to Hall (1972:477), in Type II coping the actual behavior of role senders may remain unchanged, "but by seeing one's own behavior or the external expectations in a different light, one attempts to reduce the amount of conflict actually experienced." Specific behaviors included in Type II coping are: establishing priorities; partitioning and separating roles; overlooking role demands; changing attitudes toward roles; eliminating roles, etc. (Hall, 1972). For example, when a subject responded that she stopped working because she felt that her child was deprived and she was exhausted, Hall (1972) categorized her behavior as Type II coping (i.e., eliminating roles). Furthermore, in Type II coping, the individual makes private decisions and does not seek consensus from the role senders. Finally, relief from interrole conflicts using Type II coping is less permanent since the expectations and perceptions of the role senders may remain unchanged.

The last type of coping defined by Hall (1972) was Type III, reactive role behavior. In Type III coping one attempts to satisfy the demands of role senders by improving the quality of one's role performance. Hall (1972:474) noted that an implicit assumption in using Type III coping was "one's role demands are unchangeable and that the person's main task is to find ways to meet them; this also involves a passive or reactive orientation toward one's roles." The type of behaviors included in Type III coping are: planning, scheduling, and organizing better; no conscious strategy; and working harder (Hall, 1972). Moreover, Hall (1972) viewed Type III behavior more as defensive than as coping behavior. Type III coping involves considerable personal strain and, contrary to Type I and Type II coping, there is no attempt to change internal or external perceptions of one's role.

Hall (1972) explored the relationship between the three coping strategies (i.e., Type I, Type II, and Type III) and personal satisfaction with data from two samples. The subjects in both a pilot sample and a systematic survey were white, predominantly college educated women. In the pilot sample (Hall, 1972), satisfaction was related positively to Type I coping ($p < .01$). On the other hand, the relationship between satisfaction and Type I coping for the main sample (Hall, 1972) of women only approached significance ($p < .07$). However, Type III coping was related negatively to satisfaction ($p < .01$) with the main sample as compared to no significant relationship with the pilot sample. Hall (1972) surmised that his explorations indicated that Type I and Type III coping are related to satisfaction of married women with their roles. After this development, Hall (1972) cautioned that it was not possible to generalize these results to other role conflict situations without considering the type of role conflict. Accordingly, the present study was designed to investigate the relationship among three types of interrole conflicts (i.e., wife and worker, mother and worker, and mother and wife), choice of coping strategy (Type I, II, or III) and satisfaction.

THE STUDY

The present analysis was not a replication of Hall's (1972) study but used data from another sample, that of black working wives. A large percentage of the black female population combines the roles of worker, wife, and mother. Fifty-nine percent of black married women with children under the age of 16 living in the home are employed (U.S. Bureau of the Census, 1970). Indeed, black wives often work when, by white standards, they would not be expected to (Beckett, 1976). In families in which the male worker earned more than $15,000, more black wives (53.5 percent) than white wives (28.6 percent) were in the labor force (U.S. Bureau of the Census, 1970). Therefore, data on how a selected sample of black working women are coping with interrole conflicts should be useful for the discussion of coping strategies.

In coping with interrole conflicts, the sample, it was hypothesized, would vary their choice of coping strategy with the type of conflict. Hall (1972) noted that the major role problem faced by women was interrole conflict (conflict from multiple roles) rather than intrarole conflict (conflicting expectations with a given role). Employed married women with children living in the home are performing three major roles: wife, worker, and mother. Thus, it is inevitable that conflict will arise between these roles because of time and personal energy limitations. For instance, a woman whose job requires a lot of physical exertion may experience such conflict when her husband demands that they entertain frequently to further his career. It was expected that, for wife and worker interrole conflicts, the choice of coping strategy for the sample would be Type I; i.e., structural role redefinition. Black males are generally supportive of working wives and black females believe that their husbands expect them to work (Axelson, 1970; Entwisle and Greenberger,

1970). In addition, black males tend to be less stereotypic in their view of the female sex role than white males (O'Leary and Harrison, 1975). Also, black women with high career expectations thought that most men they knew preferred more work involvement for their wives (Turner and McCaffrey, 1974). Moreover, black wives are rated higher than white wives by their husbands on having the knowledge and experience to hold a job (Scanzoni, 1975). Since black husbands are receptive to the idea of their wives working, it was hypothesized that their wives could easily communicate and negotiate with them when conflict arose; i.e., Type I coping.

Although it was predicted that Type I coping was used to handle wife and worker conflicts, it was assumed that mother and worker conflicts were resolved with Type II; i.e., personal role redefinition. A possible conflict between mother and worker roles exists, for instance, in the case of a mother who is required frequently to work over-time on her job. The person must decide whether to continue working at her present job or to get another job if she wants to spend as much time as possible with her children. Most black females want to work outside the home after marriage and the arrival of children (Kuvlesky and Obordo, 1972) and this decision is strongly influenced by the economic conditions of their lives. Being a "good provider" is viewed as an essential part of being a successful mother (Myers, 1975). Also, more black than white women thought a working mother could establish as strong a relationship with her children as a nonworking mother (Mosley, 1976). Interestingly, black more than white children perceived both parents as effectively able to fulfill both instrumental functions (i.e., ability to obtain food, clothing, shelter, etc.) and expressive functions (i.e., ability to provide emotional support, warmth, patience, etc.) (Beckett, 1976). Therefore, it was expected that women in this sample would use Type II coping to handle mother and worker conflicts. That is to say, the subjects would cope with mother and worker conflicts by altering their own perceptions and attitudes to reduce conflict between these two salient roles.

The coping strategies developed for handling conflicts in the worker and wife role are (Type I) and the worker and mother role (Type II) were expected to prevail in handling mother and wife conflicts. Bell (1971) found that for lower-class black women the mother role was valued more highly than the wife role. Indeed, working-class black wives found the role of wife less satisfying than did white wives of the same category (Blood and Wolfe, 1971). Since motherhood is valued highly by black women (Ladner, 1972), it was expected that they would priorize the mother role over the wife role or negotiate with husbands concerning their expectations. Therefore, it was assumed that the subjects with children would use a non-Type III (either Type I or Type II) strategy in coping with mother and wife conflicts.

This study also investigated whether or not satisfaction with the role of worker was influenced by husband's approval of working. It has been reported that black wives were more likely to work in spite of negative attitudes on the part of their husbands (Beckett, 1976). Although black wives may enter the labor force without their husbands' approval, their husbands' attitude would influence their satisfaction with the worker role. It was reasonable to expect that if a woman has prepared herself for a career, her husband would not object to her working. If she was working to supplement family income, however, this would impinge upon his male image and increase conflict over the worker role. Therefore, it was predicted that there would be an interaction between the subject's job status and husband's approval of working on satisfaction with the worker role.

The experimental hypotheses thus investigated were:

1. There is a relationship between type of interrole conflict (i.e., wife and worker, mother and worker, mother and wife) and choice of coping strategy (Type I, Type II, Type III).
2. There is a relationship between the use of Type I coping strategy in wife and worker conflicts and overall satisfaction.
3. There is a relationship between the use of Type II coping strategy in mother and worker conflicts and overall satisfaction.
4. There is a relationship between the use of Type III coping strategy in mother and wife conflicts and overall satisfaction.
5. There is an interaction between professional and nonprofessional job status and husbands' approval of working on career satisfaction.

METHODS

INSTRUMENT

A 34-item questionnaire was used to collect the data. The first 14 questions requested demographic information. Of the remaining 20 questions, 10 were relevant to this study. Interspersed in the questionnaire were three questions that assessed whether or not the respondent experienced conflict between two specific roles; e.g., "Do you see conflicts between your role as a mother and as a wife?" Respondents were given a choice of answers on the following 5-point scale: never, every now and then, occasionally, often, or always. In the same manner, subjects were questioned on mother and worker and wife and worker interrole conflicts. Immediately after each question on a specific type of interrole conflict the subject was asked, "How do you handle the problem?" The response format for these questions was open-ended. These responses were categorized following Hall's (1972) model of three types of coping strategies. The open-ended responses were coded independently by two social psychologists that were not a part of the research team. Intercode reliabilities on coping strategies were .79, .75, and .75 for the open-ended responses. Following Hall's (1972) procedure, satisfaction was measured with a broad question, "How satisfied do you feel with the way you deal with your roles in life?" Responses were categorized on a 3-point scale with scores ranging from 1 = strongly dissatisfied, mildly dissatisfied, neutral; 2 = mildly satisfied; and 3 = very satisfied.

There was also a specific question related to career satisfaction: "How satisfied do you feel with your career?" The responses to this question were scored in the same manner as the question relating to general satisfaction. Finally, a question relating to husband's approval of working was included: "Does your husband approve of your working?" The responses were categorized into 1 = strongly disapprove, mildly disapprove, neutral; 2 = mildly approve; and 3 = strongly approve.

SAMPLING

A small city approximately 20 miles from a large urban center was chosen for sampling. The membership lists of two black professional and civic women's organizations were used as a source for the sample. One of the researchers met with both groups and asked permission to speak to the groups about the research and use of the membership lists. A short presentation of the research was given at a general meeting. The questionnaire was then distributed among those members present with a return envelope for mailing. The members of the groups not present were mailed the questionnaire with an explanatory cover letter. A total of 170 questionnaires were distributed; 82 (48 percent) were returned.

In addition, an effort was made to include nonprofessional black women in the sample to increase the generalizability of the study among black working wives. The size of the black community in the target city lent itself to the use of the random intercept method (Word, 1977). This technique has been successfully used in low-income black communities where there is a reluctance on the part of blacks of this economic status to complete and return questionnaires. Furthermore, blacks in this economic group are reluctant to participate in surveys when they are approached in their homes (Word, 1977). Therefore, the decision was made to approach black nonprofessional women in work locations. A black female student distributed one hundred questionnaires to nonprofessional workers at a local elementary school, two beauty parlors, three fast food eating establishments and the main gate of an automobile plant. She approached the women and explained the purpose of the research, and gave them a questionnaire with a return envelope. Forty-seven (47 percent) were returned. Of the nonprofessional questionnaires, 43 were appropriate for this analysis, in addition to 61 of the professional questionnaires.

SUBJECTS

All the subjects in the study ($N = 104$) were full-time employed, black married women with husbands present in the home. The median age of the subjects was 34. All of the subjects had children under the age of 18 living in the home. The average number of children for the sample was 2.4, with a range of 1 to 6. The median number of years employed was 10 and the median number of years married was 11.

In response to the queston, "Did you stay home more than one year when any of your children were born?" 59 percent said "No." Family income in the sample was separated into three categories: two families earned under $10,000, 28 between $10,000 and $25,000, and 74 over $25,000.

Occupational data provided by the subjects were used to divide the sample into professional and nonprofessional groups. The job titles were categorized as professional or nonprofessional based on information from the *Dictionary of Occupational Titles* (U.S. Department of Labor, 1977). The women in the professional group were employed in the following positions: 11 administrators, two psychologists, 42 educators, and six social workers. The women in the nonprofessional sample were employed in the following positions: seven sales workers, 14 service workers, seven assembly line workers, and 15 clerical workers. A preliminary analysis of the data indicated no significant differences between the professional and nonprofessional members of the sample on responses to questions pertaining to interrole conflict and coping strategies.

RESULTS

The first hypothesis predicted a relationship between the type of interrole conflict and the choice of coping strategy. The subjects had described separately for each type of role conflict (i.e., wife and worker, mother and worker, and mother and wife) how they handled the problems. The responses to each role conflict were categorized as either Type I, Type II, or Type III. The results of a *Chi*-square for independence are presented in Table 18.1.

There is a significant association ($X^2 = 22.752$, $p < .001$) between type of interrole conflict and choice of coping strategy. In wife and worker role conflicts 64 percent of the sample chose Type I, 15 percent used Type II, and 21 percent used Type III. In mother and worker role conflicts, the majority of the subjects (46 percent) were using Type II and the remainder of the sample were evenly split between Type I (27 percent) and Type III (27 percent). For

TABLE 18.1
Type of Interrole Conflict and Choice of Coping Strategy (in Percents)

	Type I	Type II	Type III
Wife and worker	64	15	21
Mother and worker	27	46	27
Mother and wife	44	41	15

Note: $X^2 = 22.752$; $p < .001$

mother and wife role conflicts, only 15 percent of the sample used Type III coping strategy; the others used either Type I (44 percent) or Type II (41 percent).

It was also hypothesized that there were relationships between the choice of coping strategy for a specific interrole conflict and overall satisfaction with role performance. The choice of coping strategy was coded as 1 (for the least effective, Type III) to 3 (for the most effective, Type I). There is no significant relationship between overall satisfaction and choice of coping strategy for wife and worker roles ($r = -.07$); mother and worker roles ($r = -.06$); or mother and wife roles ($r = -.14$). Finally, in terms of overall satisfaction with role performance, 46 percent of the sample were very satisfied, 42 percent were mildly satisfied, and 12 percent were dissatisfied.

Finally, it was hypothesized that there was an interaction between job status of the subjects and husbands' approval of working on career satisfaction. Results of analysis of variance (2 × 3) are shown in Table 18.2.

There is a significant difference between the professional and nonprofessional categories on satisfaction with career ($F\,[1, 94] = 12.99, p <.001$). The data indicate that husbands' approval of working had no effect on career satisfaction. There is a significant interaction between husbands' approval of working, career satisfaction, and professional and nonprofessional categories ($F\,[2, 94] = 3.50, p < .034$). However, the significant interaction is mainly due to the job status of the subjects.

DISCUSSION

The present experiment provides support for the hypothesized relationship between type of interrole conflict and choice of coping strategy among black wives. Whenever there was a conflict between wife and worker roles, the subjects chose Type I coping strategy to handle the conflict. In mother and worker role conflict, the most frequently used coping strategy was Type II. In other words, this sample of black working women varied their choice of coping strategy as the identity of the role sender changed. In addition, the choice of coping strategy for mother and wife role conflicts was evenly split between Type I and Type II. It appears that in mother and wife role conflicts, Type I is used with the husband in explaining the priorizing of the mother role and renegotiating the husband's expectation. One respondent reported: "I meet

TABLE 18.2

Analysis of Variance Comparing Professional and Nonprofessional Wives and Husbands' Approval of Working on Career Satisfaction

Source		SS	*df*	MS	F	p
Professional-Nonprofessional	(A)	6.87	1	6.87	12.99	<.001
Husbands' approval	(B)	.22	2	.11	2.0	.812
A × B		3.71	2	1.85	3.50	<.034

the needs of my children unless great conflict arises, then I try to compromise." Type II is also used in mother and wife role conflicts to meet the role expectations of children. For example, one subject reported, "Since we are adults our needs are usually held up while I deal with the children."

While subjects are varying their choice of coping strategy depending on the roles in conflict, this behavior does not relate to overall satisfaction. One possible explanation for this finding is that the use of a less effective technique (Type II) in handling other role conflicts negates the positive effects of using Type I for wife and worker role conflicts. In other words, the high use of Type II coping strategy in mother and worker and mother and wife role conflicts negates the positive effects that may be expected from using Type I coping.

The change in coping strategy; i.e., use of Type II in mother and worker and mother and wife role conflicts, may relate to the importance of motherhood. Historically, the role of mother has been of primary importance. This perspective has not changed significantly for today's working mothers. In addition, the sample included a large number of professional women who work for more than economic reasons. These women reported feeling guilty (76 percent) about the amount of time spent away from their children. For these reasons, when the mother role is involved in conflicts, whether with the worker or wife roles, the subject gives priority to the mother role. Priorizing roles does not eliminate the role demands of the role sender but requires the working mother to choose her mother role while giving lower priority to other roles. Thus, none of the children's demands are discussed or negotiated. Instead, the mother tries to meet all the role demands of the children and put other roles on a secondary level.

Paradoxically, almost half (44 percent) of the sample indicated satisfaction with the way they handled their roles in life. This could mean that the women in the sample have accepted the need to use varying coping models when dealing with role conflict. The socialization process for women supports their giving priority to some roles and negotiating role demands for others. Consequently, the subjects perceive themselves as having adjusted to their role demands in the best possible way. Therefore, they do not attempt to cope to maximize satisfaction. They have accepted the reality of their lives and see no options for change through varying coping strategies to maximize satisfaction. These subjects are coping with the traditional way and they are satisfied.

This study also investigated whether or not husbands' approval had any effect on worker satisfaction, since black wives work whether or not their husbands approve. It was found that husbands' approval did not affect the subjects' satisfaction with worker roles. The greatest influence on career satisfaction was whether or not the subject was a professional worker.

SUMMARY

The purpose of this study was to investigate the relationship between three types of interrole conflicts (i.e., wife and worker, mother and worker, and mother and wife) and choice of coping strategy (Type I, II, or III). In addition, the relationship between the selective choice of coping strategy and overall satisfaction with role performance was examined. Furthermore, the difference between professional and nonprofessional wives in worker satisfaction was also considered. The subjects ($N = 104$) were employed black wives with husbands present in the home. It was hypothesized that the type of interrole conflict would influence the choice of coping strategy. It also was hypothesized that there was a relationship between choice of coping strategy and overall satisfaction with role performance. Finally, the third hypothesis stated that there is a difference between professional and nonprofessional wives in worker satisfaction.

Results of the analysis of data revealed a significant association between type of interrole conflict and choice of coping strategy. There was no significant relationship between choice of coping strategy and overall satisfaction. There was a significant interaction between job status of wife, husband's approval of working, and worker satisfaction. The main reason for the interaction was job status of the worker.

18

Dual–Career Family Stress and Coping: A Literature Review

Denise A. Skinner

A significant influence on contemporary family living is the increasing rate of female participation in the labor force. Examination of Department of Labor statistics reveals that the married woman is the key source of this growth and helps explain the growing interest in dual-career families reflected in both the professional and popular literature. Although it is difficult to assess the number of married *career* women in the work force, it seems reasonable to assume that the percentage for this group is positively related to the general increase in labor force participation rates of women (Hopkins & White, 1978). As more and more women seek increased education and training, along with an increased demand for skilled labor and a greater awareness of sex-role equality, the dual-career lifestyle is likely to increase in prevalence and acceptability (Rapoport & Rapoport, 1976).

A significant feature of the dual-career lifestyle is that it produces considerable stress and strain. The often competing demands of the occupational structure and those of a rich family life present a number of challenges for dual-career family members. Much of the literature implies that the stress is inherent in a dual-career lifestyle. However, some of the constraints of the lifestyle might be explained by the fact that it is a relatively new and minority pattern. In coping with the pressures of this variant pattern, dual-career couples have been forced to come up with individual solutions as no institutionalized supports exist (Holmstrom, 1972).

Reprinted from Denise A. Skinner, "Dual-Career Family Stress and Coping: A Literature Review," ***Family Relations***, vol. 29, October 1980, pp. 473–481.

The research on dual-career families has been primarily descriptive in nature and has focused on women. Rapoport and Rapoport, who coined the term "dual-career family" in 1969, were pioneers in the study of the impact of career and family on each other. Their research was followed shortly thereafter by other definitive studies on the dual-career lifestyle (Epstein, 1971; Holmstrom, 1973; Garland, 1972; Poloma, 1972). More recent dual-career research has focused heavily on the stresses of the lifestyle and on the management of the strains by the participants (Rapoport & Rapoport, 1978).

The purpose of this literature review is to delineate the sources of dual-career strain and summarize the coping patterns employed by dual-career couples in managing stress. Hopefully, this summary will benefit family practitioners as they assist individuals in making adaptive lifestyle choices as well as aid dual-career participants in effective stress-reduction and in developing coping strategies.

THE ETIOLOGY OF DUAL-CAREER STRESS

Rapoport and Rapoport (1978) in reviewing the 1960's studies of dual-career families have noted that the stresses of this pattern have been differently conceptualized by various researchers. "The concepts include *dilemmas* (such as) overload, . . . network, identity; *conflicts* between earlier and later norms . . . , *barriers* of domestic isolation, sex-role prejudices . . . , and *problems* such as the wife finding an appropriate job" (p. 5).

Although there is a considerable degree of variation in dual-career stress, there are also common patterns. In the review that follows, an adaptation of the Rapoports' (1971) delineation of strains confronting dual-career families will be used as an organizing framework in highlighting these common patterns reported in the literature. Although interactive and cyclical in nature, strains have been classified as primarily (a) internal: arising within the family; or (b) external: the result of conflict of the dual-career family and other societal structures (Bebbington, 1973).

INTERNAL STRAIN

Overload Issues. The problem of work and role overload is a common source of strain for dual-career families (Epstein, 1971; Garland, 1972; Heckman, Bryson, & Bryson, 1977; Holmstrom, 1973; Poloma, 1972; Rapoport & Rapoport, 1976; St. John-Parsons, 1978). When each individual is engaged in an active work role and active family roles, the total volume of activities is considerably increased over what a conventional family experiences (Portner, Note 1). In dual-career families this can result in overload, with household tasks generally handled as overtime.

The feelings of overload and the degree of strain experienced varied for couples in the Rapoport's study (1976). The Rapoports suggested that overload was affected by four conditions, which were, in part, self-imposed:

> (a) the degree to which having children and a family life (as distinct from simply being married) was salient; (b) the degree to which the couple aspired to a high standard of domestic living; (c) the degree to which there was satisfactory reapportionment of tasks; and (d) the degree to which the social-psychological overload compounded the physical overloads (pp. 302–305).

There was a positive relationship between the conditions in items (a), (b), and (d) above, and the degree of strain experienced. Satisfactory reapportionment of tasks was a coping strategy that helped alleviate strain.

Identity Issues. The identity dilemma for dual-career participants is the result of discontinuity between early gender-role socialization and current wishes or practices (Rapoport & Rapoport, 1976). The essence of masculinity in our culture is still centered on successful experiences in the work role, and femininity is still centered on the domestic scene (Heckman, Bryson, & Bryson, 1977; Holmstrom, 1973). The internalized "shoulds" regarding these traditional male and female roles conflict with the more androgynous roles attempted by many dual-career couples, resulting in tension and strain.

Bernard (1974), focusing on professional women, observed that intra-personal integration of work and domestic roles and the personality characteristics associated with each, does *not* constitute the "psychological work" of the career mother. Rather, the major difficulty, according to Bernard, is that the woman *alone* is the one who must achieve this identity integration.

Role-Cycling Issues. The dilemma of role-cycling, identified by Rapoport and Rapoport (1976), refers to attempts by the dual-career couple to mesh their different individual career cycles with the cycle of their family. Bebbington (1973) noted that role-cycling, unlike other sources of strain, has a developmental pattern. Both employment and family careers have transition points at which there is a restructuring of roles which become sources of "normative" stress.

Dual-career couples attempt to avoid additional strain by staggering the career and family cycles such that transition points are not occurring at the same time. Many couples establish themselves occupationally before having children for this reason (Bebbington, 1973; Holmstrom, 1972; Rapoport & Rapoport, 1976). Stress may also result when the developmental sequence of one spouse's career conflicts with that of the other (Bebbington, 1973). The structural and attitudinal barriers of the occupational world, yet to be discussed, further contribute to the difficulty in role-cycling for many dual-career couples.

Family Characteristics. Holmstrom (1972) identified the isolation of the modern nuclear family as a barrier to having two careers in one family. The difficulty of childrearing apart from relatives or other such extended support systems is a source of strain.

The presence or absence of children as well as the stage of the family cycle seems to affect the complexity of the dual career lifestyle (Holmstrom, 1972; Rapoport & Rapoport, 1976). Heckman et al. (1977) found that it was the older professional couples and those who had not had children who saw the lifestyle as advantageous. The demands of childrearing, *particularly the problems associated with finding satisfactory childcare arrangements,* are a source of strain for younger dual-career couples, especially for the women (Bryson, Bryson, & Johnson, 1978; Gove & Geerken, 1977; Holmstrom, 1972; Orden & Bradburn, 1969; Rapoport & Rapoport, 1971; St. John-Parsons, 1978). In relation to this, a child-free lifestyle has been noted by Movius (1976) as a career-facilitating strategy for women.

EXTERNAL STRAINS

Normative Issues. Despite changing social norms, the dual-career life-style still runs counter to traditional family norms of our culture. Rapoport and Rapoport (1976) have explained that although intellectually the dual-career pattern is approved, internalized values from early socialization are still strong and produce tension, anxiety, and guilt. Pivotal points such as career transitions or the birth of a child can activate these normative dilemmas.

One of the more frequently cited problems by dual-career professionals is the expectation on the part of others that the dual-career husband and wife behave in traditional male/female roles (Heckman et al., 1977). This is consistent with the earlier findings of Epstein (1971) who indicated that dual-career individuals experienced guilt because they were not conforming to the socially approved work-family structure. Furthermore, the women often had to deal with the implied or overt social controls placed on them by their children according to Epstein's study.

Occupational Structure. Holmstrom (1972, p. 517) has commented on the inflexibility of professions noting that "pressures for geographic mobility, the status inconsistencies of professional women because the professions are dominated by men, and the pressure for fulltime and continuous careers" are a source of strain for dual-career couples.

The demand for geographical mobility and its effect on dual-career couples noted earlier by Holmstrom (1972) was also examined by Duncan and Perrucci (1976). They found that the egalitarian orientation toward decision-making promoted in dual-career living was not carried out in job moves with the wives experiencing more of the stress. However, Wallston, Foster, and Berger (1978) using simulated job-seeking situations, found many professional couples attempting egalitarian or nontraditional job-seeking patterns. These authors have suggested that institutional constraints are in part responsible for highly traditional actual job decisions.

Finally, the demands of particular professions for single-minded continuous commitment, for other family members' needs to be subordinated to the job, and for a "support person" (typically the wife) to be available for entertaining, etc., are a source of stress for dual-career couples. The "two-person career" (Papanek, 1973) which depends heavily on an auxiliary support partner is incompatible with the dual-career orientation, accordinng to Hunt and Hunt (1977). Handy (1978) in a study of executive men found that the dual-career relationship was infrequent and difficult when the husband was in such a "greedy occupation."

Social Network Dilemmas. Maintaining relationships outside the immediate family is a problem for dual-career members for a variety of reasons. The general dilemma exists because of the overload strain discussed earlier, which creates limitations on the availability of time to interact with friends and relatives (Portner, Note 1).

Rapoport and Rapoport (1976) found that the dual-career couples whom they studied reported problems in sustaining the kinds of interaction that their more conventional relatives and friends wanted. Not only was there less time for socializing, but, also, kin were at times asked by the dual-career couples to help which sometimes produced tension. St. John-Parsons (1978) reported that kin relationships deteriorated when dual-career couples could not meet some of the expected social obligations. The husbands in his study experienced the greater loss as ties to their families of orientation lessened.

The study by St. John-Parsons (1978) revealed that none of the dual-career families maintained extensive social relationships. According to the author, "a salient reason for their social dilemma was their sense of responsibility for and devotion to their children" (p. 40).

IMPACT OF STRAIN

The sources of strain delineated above suggest that dual-career families are vulnerable to a high degree of stress. However, family stress literature has indicated that the family's definition of the situation is an important component influencing the impact of various strains on the family (Burr, 1973). Bebbington (1973) has differentiated between the following two kinds of stress which can co-exist or operate separately in a given lifestyle: "(a) that deriving from an unsatisfactory resolution of conflict as between ideals and behavior; and (b) that deriving from intrinsic properties of the lifestyle, though ideals and behaviors may be consistent" (p. 535). Bebbington has suggested that dual-career participants do not seem to find the principle of "stress minimization" operative with regard to the second type of stress, but rather, accept an orientation of "stress-optimization" in interpreting inherent lifestyle stresses. Dual-career couples have accepted a high degree of the second type of stress as their solution to the dilemma of avoiding the discontinuity stress of the first type, according to Bebbington. They come to view their problems as having both positive as well as negative components and of a more routine than unusual nature.

The cumulative effect of various strains arising from occupational and familial role transitions can be estimated as "transitional density" (Bain, 1978). Bain has hypothesized that the stress experienced and the coping ability of a family in a particular transition is proportional to the stress generated by the transitional density. Applied to dual-career families this idea is specifically related to the particular family characteristics and the multiple role-cycling strains previously discussed. The degree of stress experienced from other sources of strain (e.g., overload) may be compounded for a given family by the strain of their family life cycle stage or the newness of the dual-career pattern for them.

MARITAL RELATIONSHIP

A considerable portion of the dual career literature focuses on the marital adjustment, happiness, or satisfaction of dual-career couples implying that the stress inherent in the lifestyle has an impact on the marital relationship. In Orden and Bradburn's (1969) study of working wives and marital happiness, they found that a women's choice of employment (vs. full-time homemaking) strained the marriage only when there were preschool children in the family. They concluded that the woman's decision to work is associated with a high balance between satisfactions and strains for both partners.

Bailyn (1970) found that an all-consuming attitude toward career was associated with lowered marital satisfaction. Overinvolvement in one's career can result in strain on the marriage, according to Ridley (1973) who found marital adjustment highest when the husband was "medium" and the wife was "low" on job involvement. He concluded that tension in the marital relationship may occur when either partner becomes so highly involved in a job that family obligations are excluded. Occupational practices such as discriminatory sex-role attitudes can also heighten the stress in the dual-career marital relationship (Holmstrom, 1972; Rosen, Jerdee, & Prestwich, 1975). Finally, Richardson (1979) examined the hypothesis that marital stress would be attendant if working wives had higher occupational prestige than their husbands. He found no support for this hypothesis and suggested that its "mythic content" may be sustained, in part, because it is congruent with conventional sex-role orientations.

Rice (1979), focusing on personality patterns, noted the following psychological characteristics as typical of dual-career individuals:

> A strong need for achievement, reliance on an extrinsic reward system (promotion, spouse recognition of efforts), hesitancy in making sustained interpersonal commitments, and vûlnerability to self-esteem injury through dependency frustrations and fear of failure (p. 47).

The adaptive aspects of, for instance, high achievement may facilitate career advancement for both partners and contribute positively to marital adjustment, or high achievement needs may contribute to competitiveness in the pair.

SEX DIFFERENCES

An overwhelming proportion of the literature reports that the impact of dual-career stress is felt most by women. Bernard (1974) has noted that a man can combine a professional career and parenting more easily than a woman can because less is expected of the man with regard to familial responsibilities.

Overload strain is a significant issue for dual-career women. Heckman et al. (1977), in assessing problem areas for dual-career couples, found that the women reported more problems in more areas than did men, and that many of the comments about problem areas by husbands were issues that had indirectly affected them because the issue had directly affected their wives. These researchers reported that several women in their study made significant concessions with regard to their careers because of family demands. They concluded that the continued existence of role conflict and overload strain are often at the expense of the woman's personal identity and career aspirations.

Occupationally, it has been the woman more often who takes the risks, sacrifices more, and compromises career ambitions in attempting to make the dual-career pattern operative (Epstein, 1971; Holmstrom, 1972; Poloma, 1972). Interestingly, however, some studies have reported that dual-career wives are more productive than other females in their respective professions (Bryson, Bryson, Licht, & Licht, 1976; Martin, Berry, & Jacobsen, 1975). One might conclude, as the Rapoports (1978) have done, that the wives were simultaneously exploited and facilitated.

Life for the dual-career male is not without its periods of stress, although the impact of various strains does not appear to be as significant as that reported for women. Garland (1972) reported that dual-career males felt strain in attempting to find free time, but overall, noted the advantages of the lifestyle. The findings of Burke and Weir (1976) do not provide as positive a report for dual-career men, however. While working wives were found to be more satisfied with life, marriage, and job than nonworking wives, husbands of working wives were less satisfied and performed less effectively than husbands of nonworking wives. Burke and Weir indicated that the greater stress experienced by the dual-career husband may be due, in part, to him losing part of his "active support system" when the wife commits herself to a career outside the home, and also to his assuming roles (e.g. housekeeping) which have not been valued as highly in our culture.

Using more sophisticated methodology, Booth (1977) replicated the Burke and Weir study and reported different conclusions. He found very little difference between working and nonworking wives, and reported that the wife's employment had little effect on the stress experienced by the husband.

Furthermore, Booth concluded that the dual-career husband may be experiencing less stress than his conventional counterpart as the added income and personal fulfillment of the wife outweigh temporary problems in adjusting to the lifestyle.

CHILDREN

Dual-career couples may increase the degree of strain they themselves experience in an attempt to prevent the lifestyle from creating strain for their children. As was noted earlier in the study of St. John-Parsons (1978), some of the social strains the couples experienced was due to their sense of responsibility to their children. There is no evidence to suggest that the dual-career lifestyle, in and of itself, is stressful for children. What may be more significant for the children is the degree of stress experienced by the parents which may indirectly affect the children. In her study of maternal employment Hoffman (1974) concluded that

> . . . the working mother who obtains satisfaction from her work, who has adequate arrangements so that her dual role does not involve undue strain, and who does not feel so guilty that she overcompensates is likely to do quite well and, under certain conditions, better than the nonworking mother (p. 142).

COPING STRATEGIES

Just as the type and degree of strain experienced varies for dual-career families, so do the strategies employed for managing the stress. As was mentioned earlier in this paper, Bebbington (1973) suggested that "stress optimization," the acknowledging of dual-career stress as inevitable and preferable to the stress of alternative lifestyles available, is an orientation of many dual-career couples. Defining their situation as such may serve as a resource in successful adaptation to the stress. Dual-career couples also employ stress-mitigating strategies. These coping behaviors are aimed at maintaining or strengthening the family system and at securing support from sources external to the family.

COPING BEHAVIOR WITHIN THE FAMILY SYSTEM

Poloma (1972) outlined four tension-management techniques used by the dual-career women in her study. They reduced dissonance by defining their dual-career patterns as favorable or advantageous to them and their families when compared to other alternatives available. For instance, the career mother noted that she was a happier mother and wife because she worked outside the home than she would be if she were a fulltime homemaker. Secondly, they established priorities among and within their roles.

The salient roles are familial ones and if a conflict situation occurs between family and career demands, the family needs come first. A third strategy employed was that of compartmentalizing work and family roles as much as possible. Leaving actual work and work-related problems at the office would be one way to segregate one's work and family roles. Finally, the women in Poloma's study managed strain by compromising career aspirations to meet other role demands.

Compromise is a common coping strategy noted in much of the dual-career literature as a way of reducing stress and making the lifestyle manageable. Women, in particular, compromise career goals if there are competing role demands (Bernard, 1974; Epstein, 1971; Heckman et al., 1977; Holmstrom, 1973). However, men in dual-careers make career sacrifices also; e.g., compromising advancement opportunities in an attempt to reduce role-conflict.

Prioritizing and compromising are coping strategies employed not only to deal with conflicts between roles but also in resolving competing demands within roles. Domestic overload, for instance, may be managed by deliberately lowering standards. One compromises ideal household standards because of constraints on time and energy in achieving them. Structurally, the domestic overload dilemma can also be managed within the family system by reorganizing who does what, with the husband and children taking on more of what traditionally has been the woman's responsibility. In these instances dual-career families are *actively* employing coping behaviors within the family aimed at strengthening its functioning and, thus, reducing the family's vulnerability to stress (McCubbin, 1979).

Some dual-career individuals take a more reactive orientation toward stress, and cope by attempting to manage and improve their behavior to better satisfy all of the lifestyle's demands. Homstrom (1971) reported that the couples in her study adhered to organized schedules and that the women, in particular, were very conscious of how they allocated their time and effort. Flexibility and control over one's schedule are highly valued by career persons in attempting to meet overload and time pressures.

Finally, the presence of what Burke and Weir (1976) have labelled a helping component in the marital relationship can serve a stress-mitigating function within the dual-career family. Qualities such as open communication, empathy, emotional reassurance, support and sensitivity to the other's feelings, characterize this therapeutic role; the presence of these qualities would serve to strengthen the relationship. Related to this, Rapoport and Rapoport (1978) reported that couples established "tension lines," "points beyond which individuals feel they cannot be pushed except at risk to themselves or the relationship" (p. 6). Couples organized their family lives with sensitivity to these tension lines.

COPING BEHAVIOR INVOLVING EXTERNAL SUPPORT SYSTEMS

Dual-career couples also employ coping strategies aimed at securing support outside the family to help reduce stress. Holmstrom (1973) reported that couples were quite willing to use money to help resolve overload strain. Hiring help, especially for childcare, is a common expense in this lifestyle. Couples also buy time in various other ways such as hiring outside help to do domestic work and purchasing labor- and time-saving devices.

Outside support in terms of friendships were also important to the couples in the Rapoports' study (1976). The dual-career couples formed friendships on a couple basis, associating with other career couples. "Friendships, while gratifying, are also demanding, and in many of the couples there was a relatively explicit emphasis on the mutual service aspects of the relationship as well as the recreational aspect" (Rapoport, p. 316). Thus, establishing friendships with couples like themselves helped to validate the lifestyle for these dual-career couples and provided a reciprocal support structure.

The literature suggests that dual-career couples are increasingly interested in negotiating work arrangements which will reduce or remove some of this lifestyle's stress. Flexible scheduling, job sharing, and split-location employment are used by some dual-career couples as coping mechanisms to reduce the family's vulnerability to overload stress.

Finally, most of the researchers noted that achieving a balance between the disadvantages and advantages of the lifestyle was the overriding concern of dual-career couples. Although noting the numerous strains associated with the lifestyle, dual-career couples were equally aware of the gains—things like personal fulfillment, increased standard of living, pride in each other's accomplishments, etc. The goal for most dual-career couples, then, is to "plan how to manage the meshing of their two lives so as to achieve an equitable balance of strains and gains" (Rapoport and Rapoport, 1976, p. 298).

IMPLICATIONS FOR PRACTITIONERS

Increasingly, people are choosing dual-career living, a trend that will, no doubt, continue in the future. This has several implications for family life practitioners, particularly given the stress associated with the lifestyle. Certain changes seem necessary in facilitating dual-career living but these changes must occur by concerted efforts at many levels (Rapoport & Rapoport, 1976).

Individuals opting for the dual-career lifestyle, or any other family form for that matter, would benefit from knowledge of the issues central to that lifestyle's functioning. As Rapoport and Rapoport (1976) suggested, "the dissemination of a detailed knowledge of a range of lifestyles like the dual-career families will increase the potential for satisfactory choice of options in future" (p. 21). Such an education would enlarge traditional conceptions about men's and women's occupational and familial roles recognizing that different individuals would then have greater opportunities for making adaptive lifestyle choices.

Practitioners in marriage and family therapy may increasingly work with dual-career couples as their numbers increase and as the strains of the lifestyle remain. Rice (1979) has reported that competition, issues of power, and difficulty with the support structure are three common problem areas in dual-career marriages. He has suggested that "the guiding principle in therapy with dual-career couples is to help the partners achieve or restore a sense of equity in the marital relationship" (p. 103). Group-support sessions are suggested by Hopkins and White (1978) as a helpful therapeutic strategy with dual-career couples. Common-problem groups and groups of couples at differing life-cycle stages can provide a supportive structure for mutual sharing of concerns and coping skills. The goal of both preventive and remedial approaches should be to help couples assess their needs, increase interpersonal competencies, and deal constructively with the stress they experience (Rapoport & Rapoport, 1976).

Each family life professional has the opportunity to serve as a spokesperson for societal and institutional changes which would positively affect the functioning of dual-career families. Societal changes which would increase the quantity and quality of all kinds of services (educational, domestic, childcare, etc.) would strengthen the dual-career lifestyle. Institutional changes which would increase the flexibility of the occupational structure would also aid significantly in reducing or eliminating some of the stress associated with the lifestyle. Flexible scheduling, increased availability of part-time employment, on-site day care facilities and maternity and paternity leaves are some of the occupational changes advocated to enable individuals to combine work and family roles with less strain. Assuming an advocacy role on behalf of the dual-career lifestyle involves initiating and supporting social policies which promote equity and pluralism (Rapoport & Rapoport, 1976). A society where these values prevail would enhance not only the dual-career lifestyle, but would serve to strengthen family life in general.

PART FIVE

Social Policy to Accommodate Changing Work and Family Roles

Introduction

In Parts Two and Three we documented the interdependence of work and family by examining the economic roles of men and women in relation to family life and the impact of several occupational conditions on families. We now analyze the policy needs of families deriving from these two types of interdependence. Economic policies—that is, income support and employment policy—address issues regarding the economic roles of men and women. The impacts of occupational conditions on family life are tempered by family-oriented personnel policies.

The White House Conference on Families held in 1980, with delegates from all walks of life and all parts of the country, developed a diverse set of policy recommendations to meet the needs of families. The top-ranked recommendation, approved by 92.7 percent of the delegates, advocates family-oriented personnel policies including flextime, leave policies, shared and part-time jobs with benefits, transfer policies, and child care. Large majorities of delegates also approved recommendations to ease economic pressures on families by promoting full employment, reducing inflation, and enforcing legislation against discrimination in employment (White House Conference on Families, 1980). The strong support for these policies indicates the importance of these two major work/family issues to a broad segment of the population.

The selections by Keniston and by Schorr and Moen address policy implications of economic roles in families. These policies are generally of two types: income support and employment. Income-support policies are designed to provide income to families in need. Major programs include Aid to Families with Dependent Children, unemployment insurance, general welfare assistance, Social Security for survivors and the disabled, and experimental income maintenance and negative income-tax programs. The criteria for need and the amount of support provided vary considerably across programs. The United States has no comprehensive income-support policy that provides a basic minimum income level for all families. It also has no comprehensive policy to ensure full employment, a stated national goal. Public and private job-creation and job-training programs are instituted at various times, especially during periods of high unemployment. As with income support, the approaches used by these programs are dissimilar. Many families in economic need have no able-bodied adults available to work; many of those employed in low-paying jobs do not earn enough to support a family. To meet the economic needs of all families, income-support and employment policy need to be integrated with each other. Since previous research indicates that income-support programs do not inhibit the incentive to work to a significant extent, the two approaches could complement each other in providing economic security to families.

In "The Myth of the Self-Sufficient Family," Keniston discusses the assumption that families unable to take care of themselves economically are deficient and responsible for their problems. This assumption has created severe economic and social problems for children, who are the main victims of low income, unemployment, and inadequate services for families. Keniston presents an extensive agenda of economic policies to assist families and children in contemporary society, including (1) full and fair employment backed up by income supports and services for those in need and (2) work practices enabling parents to better combine work and parenting responsibilities.

Schorr and Moen's selection, "The Single Parent and Public Policy," complements Keniston's analysis by applying a similar approach to single-parent families. Single-parent families are mistakenly considered to be marginal and deviant although statistics on family patterns indicate large increases in this family type among a broad spectrum of the population. Many economic difficulties and work/family strains are more acute among single-parent families because there is one less adult to grapple with problems of income, employment, and work practices. Single-parent families are diverse in their origins and needs and would benefit from the types of policies recommended by Keniston and by Schorr and Moen.

In Part One we suggested that the myth of separate worlds prevents a recognition of the interdependence of work and family. In this context, policy to deal with work/family linkages is very unlikely to develop. The Keniston and the Schorr and Moen articles argue that myths associated with family life hinder the development of effective economic policies to strengthen the economic roles of men and women. These analyses reveal the role of beliefs and values in the development of social policy.

The remaining selections deal with several workplace practices that provide a better mesh between work and family life. These practices address the occupational conditions discussed in Part Three; for example, (1) time scheduling and (2) job transfers and geographic mobility. However, the most developed and frequently used programs are those that meet the goals of employers regarding productivity, recruitment, turnover, absenteeism, and profitability. The most extensive program, flextime, was originally designed to reduce commuting time and expense and to maximize the use of expensive equipment. The fact that family-oriented personnel practices meet the needs of both employer and employee is a reflection of the interdependence of work and family.

Child care has developed into a critical need as more mothers of young children join the work force. As Feinstein points out in "Directions for Day Care," most children are cared for in a home—either the child's home, the home of a relative, or a family day-care home. These arrangements meet the needs of many families; however, they also reflect a lack of day-care centers in the neighborhood and place of employment. Because of differing economic conditions influencing the demand for workers, the United States lags behind European countries in the development of a national day-care policy. U.S. policy is limited to tax benefits for parents and businesses. The issue of child care will remain high on the policy agenda for the foreseeable future.

In "Family Support Systems Paychecks Can't Buy," Sullivan examines corporate responses to the family needs of employees. She describes the current "state of the art" of several policies being given attention by American businesses, including employer-supported child care, employee assistance programs to deal with employees' personal and work-related problems, flexible work schedules, and transfer policies that assess the costs and benefits of transfers and help the spouses of transferred workers find employment. She acknowledges that dealing with the interdependence of work and family serves both realms, and specifies the advantages to corporations of sensitivity to the family needs of employees.

In "Balancing Jobs and Family Life," Bohen and Viveros-Long report on a study of one type of family-oriented policy, flextime, in which workers are able to adjust the times at which they begin and end work each day. They present data showing that flextime is most helpful in reducing work/family stress among men and women who do not have primary responsibilities for child care, women without children, and men. They conclude that working mothers need more than a slight change in working hours to significantly reduce their work/family stress. They argue that flextime is an important first step in helping workers balance work and family responsibilities but is not sufficient to induce equal participation in work and family roles by men and women. More extensive changes are required to meet this objective, including policies such as parental leaves for men and women; more varied flextime programs; flexible workplaces; part-time employment; child care; and parental insurance as an income support for parents. Underlying value issues regarding the appropriate work and family roles of men and women also must be resolved if more role sharing is to occur and if work/family strain is to be reduced among workers with primary responsibilities for child rearing, namely, working mothers.

Family-oriented policies are dealt with from a cross-cultural perspective by Kamerman and Kahn in "Societal Learning." This selection summarizes a study of income benefits and child-care service policies for working parents in five European countries and the United States. They link the increasing development of benefits and services to a recognition that women will continue to work and that the problems associated with work/family linkages are generic to two-earner families. Their study indicates a wide range of interest and policy initiatives among six countries with the United States having the least advanced approach. Kamerman and Kahn describe a relationship between the mix of benefits and services in each country's policy package and the perceptions within the country of the needs of children, of the necessity for women to participate in the labor force, and of the desirability for men to participate more fully in family life. They strongly endorse a policy package that enables all adults to be productive both at home and at work.

The first three sections of the book document the interdependence of work and family and analyze two aspects of this interdependence: (1) the economic roles of men and women and (2) the impact of occupational conditions on family life. The articles in Part Four and Part Five provide a wide range of approaches, both individual and institutionalized, to improve the ability of individuals and institutions to better mesh the demands and rewards of work and family life.

Currently, individual approaches to work/family issues are more developed than institutionalized approaches. When families have difficulty with economic roles, they tend to develop strategies to cope with limited resources, to increase the number of earners in the family, and to have earners that moonlight or work overtime if possible. Families also are relatively adept at managing occupational conditions by using various coping strategies, by adjusting the division of labor in the family, and by staging work and family roles over the life course. The use of income supports, employment programs, and family-oriented personnel practices are secondary to the strategies developed and used within individual families.

A major reason for this imbalance is the normative milieu in which the institutional policies are developed and used. Income-support and employment programs operate in a context in which individuals and families are perceived as ultimately responsible for their own economic well-being. Although recognition of the structural constraints on family economic security exists, belief in individual responsibility and high levels of self-blame for difficulties are pervasive and influence the perceived need for the programs and the willingness of those in need to use them.

The development of family-oriented personnel policies and practices is also hindered by normative constraints, but of a slightly different nature. Several of these practices have been developed from the perspective of women's desire to combine work and family with higher priority for family responsibilities. These practices include part-time employment, job sharing, maternity leaves, and flextime. However, using these programs is often associated with low-paying jobs, limited opportunity for advancement, and few fringe benefits.

In order to reduce the burden on the family of accommodating occupational conditions, it is necessary for these family-oriented workplace policies to be extended to and used by men. This change will require (1) increased recognition of the legitimacy of family responsibilities for men and (2) an understanding of the implicit career penalties involved. For example, flexibility regarding the refusal of job transfers is increasing. However, after an individual has refused a certain number of transfers, there is still a tendency to question the individual's commitment to work and to limit career advancement accordingly.

The balance between individual and structural accommodations to the changing nature of work and family responsibilities and their interdependence will be a major issue in the next decade. The material presented in this book provides background and understanding in this area of great importance to men, women, employers, and families.

19

The Myth of the Self-Sufficient Family

Kenneth Keniston

The Carnegie Council on Children began as a group concerned with the needs of children in coming decades. Our concerns soon widened to include the well-being and integrity of families, in which most children grow up today, and in which we believe most children will grow up in the foreseeable future. We define families broadly: to include not only the isolated nuclear family that is the ideal middle-class model, but single-parent families, chosen families, adoptive families, and so on. The welfare of most children depends in large part on the well-being of these families; therefore, those who are concerned with children must seek to support the vitality of American families.

In considering the needs of families, we were inevitably led to consider the family's economic position and the role of jobs and work practices in the lives of parents. One flaw in our traditional approach toward families and children has been to concentrate too exclusively on the provision of services, some of which are a way of undoing the damage done by an economic system that fails to provide millions of families with jobs, a decent income, and work that can be combined, without undue conflict, with parenting. In the end, we believe that no proposal to extend services can be adequate unless it is accompanied by economic supports for families.

Were there space, I would like to examine some of the outdated assumptions we as Americans bring to most discussions about children and families. I would like to explore the myth of self-sufficiency, and how, even in today's

Reprinted from Kenneth Keniston, "The Myth of the Self-Sufficient Family," *National Elementary Principal*, vol. 55, May/June 1976, pp. 42-47.

interdependent world, it leads us to define families that admit to needing help as inadequate families. Today, all families need help raising children. The chief difference is between those families who can afford to pay for necessary services and those who cannot.

I would also like to discuss the myth of equal opportunity through schooling. That myth still leads us to defer our dream of a more just, more equal society, which places on schools and on children the burden of correcting—sometime in the future—the inequities of our society today. And I would also like to talk about how the power of these highly individualistic myths blinds us to the role in our lives, and the lives of our children, of the economic and social forces that lead us to blame individual parents and children for the effects these impersonal forces have on them. I would like to talk about the myth that we live in an essentially open, classless society. In fact, ours is a two-track society, in which the lives of the poor and the nonwhite differ qualitatively from those of the nonpoor and the white, and where most of those born into the bottom track are socially condemned to remain in it.

Most important, I would like to argue that many (perhaps most) of our social programs affecting children and families—from the welfare system to the health system to the school system—have the perverse effect of consolidating this two-track system, providing inferior and stigmatizing sources of income and services for those in the bottom track, and convincing many children in that track that they deserve to remain there because of their inadequacy, inferiority, or stupidity. But I will have to stop with only these hints of what I believe to be the false myths that underlie some of our traditional thinking about children and families.

One point I must address, however, is that of our operational neglect of the powerful role that economic forces play in the lives of children and their families. I call it "operational neglect" because we all pay lip service to the role of jobs, work, and income in family life. But when push comes to shove, what we do—how we operate—has little to do with this lip service. Instead, we fall back on a long American tradition of trying to solve social problems by reforming, educating, and uplifting individuals. In practice, we forget what Urie Bronfenbrenner calls the ecology of family life and child development, and we devote our greatest energies to changing people. The fate of the war on poverty is a case in point: it produced admirable programs like Head Start, aimed at improving children, along with good job training programs, aimed at improving their parents. But in the end, it did not produce jobs and it did not produce income, and it did not make a significant dent in the restrictive practices that bar women and minority group members from a fair chance in our economic system. The war on poverty is the rule, not the exception. Most efforts to help children and families have tried to reform the victims, not change the forces that victimize.

The hard fact is that of all age groups in America today, children are most likely to live in poverty—whatever tool we use to measure poverty. And the equally painful fact is that every index of distress in childen and families is strongly correlated with poverty—from infant mortality to school failure, from family breakdown to child abuse, from malnutrition to mental retardation. No one would rush to claim that poverty is the sole, simple cause of all problems of families and children. The children of the rich and superrich have their problems, too. But not so oddly, they seem to have fewer problems, and, also not so oddly, they seem to be able to find more effective help in solving them. Even if poverty is not the only cause of the problems of children and families, it is a major cause.

But what causes poverty, or near poverty, or the inability to find the sources to sustain family life and the healthy development of children? There are many theories, all with some grain of truth. But the strange thing is that these theories, however profound, often overlook the obvious fact that the only thing all poor and near poor children have in common is lack of parental income. In our society, income is both a requirement for buying the goods and services necessary for a minimally livable standard of living, and a powerful symbol of personal worth, merit, and virtue.

There is no need to belabor the obvious. I suggest, however, that each of us try living for a year or so on the poverty line income, or even the Department of Labor's "minimum budget" for a family of four. Experience what it does not only to the material conditions of your family, but to your mood, to your feelings about yourself, and to your responsiveness to your children. And especially watch what happens during those crises that inevitably beset most families, such as parental or child illness, unemployment or job frustration, parental discord. We all know the consequences: both children and parents suffer. Or try to get good health care when you can't pay for it; try to find decent child care when you can't afford it. And finally, recall that family poverty is a relative concept, related to family need. Ninety-five percent of American families are poor if they have a severely handicapped child who requires special education over a period of years. Only a handful of families have enough savings or insurance to tide them over a year of parental unemployment.

My point is really a simple one. Children need many things in the course of their development: love, responsiveness, guidance, continuity of care, physical vitality, adequate nutrition, health care, parents with self-respect, and so on. Parental income cannot guarantee any of these. But low income makes every one of them more difficult to deal with, more problematic.

The social causes of poverty are not too hard to discern. First, millions of American parents who want to work cannot find jobs. Second, millions of others who do work cannot earn enough to provide even a minimal standard of living for their families. Third, there are millions of parents who cannot work and should not be forced to work (about 50 percent of welfare recipients, for example). And finally, there are millions of parents for whom the inflexibility of existing work practices requires an impossible choice between neglecting their children and earning a decent living. These are the problems that the economic component of a policy for children and families must explore.

In discussing these economic issues, I must disqualify myself from any special expertise. By force of circumstances, my colleagues and I have become amateur economists because our analysis has led us to conclude that changes in the economic status of families are essential if services are to do their job properly. But for all of our efforts to inform ourselves in the area of economic policy, we are well aware of the gaps in our own knowledge and, in some cases, of the deep controversies that divide economists and politicians on these issues.

Very briefly, let me suggest some of the lines of our present thinking about long-term goals that seem to us vital components of any national policy to support children and their families.*

First, we would emphasize both *full and fair employment*. Imagine American society if there were jobs enough for all those who were willing and able to work; if these jobs paid a decent income; and if access to jobs and promotion were without any discrimination based on race or sex. Parents who wanted to work could then find jobs, minority group members and women would not face the job ceilings and promotion barriers that they now encounter in virtually every occupation and profession, and a family could live at a minimally decent standard of living on the wages it earned from work. Tens of millions of American children would benefit. But as a nation, we have never truly committed ourselves to full employment, tolerating instead unemployment levels 200 and 300 percent higher than those found in other industrial democracies. Even today, in a period of extraordinarily high employment, we have yet to muster the political will to commit ourselves to a job for every American who is willing and able to work.

What might the outlines of a full and fair employment policy be? For one, we must go beyond the traditional emphasis on job creation and job training programs as emergency or crisis measures. Unemployment has been high, relative to comparable nations, for more than twenty years in this country. We believe that our long-term goal should be an economy that tolerates only "frictional" unemployment; that is, inevitable unemployment caused by changing jobs, seasons, or locations.

Second, jobs held by Americans who are responsible for the upbringing and care of children should provide a decent wage, one that approximates the Department of Labor's minimum budget for a family of four. This amounts to approximately 50 percent of the median family income; that is, about 50 percent of $14,000 a year, or $7,000. Seven thousand dollars a year is hardly a princely wage for a family of four. What is shocking and intolerable is that there are so many millions of children today, with parents working full time, who fall so far below even that modest figure.

Third, we believe that a full employment policy must include at least three strategies: (1) fiscal stimulation of national growth of the economy as an overall measure to promote the economic well-being of the country; (2) public stimulation of the private sector through public action to create socially useful jobs; and (3) direct public employment as necessary, especially in providing human services as a means both of creating jobs and of providing Americans with the services that so many now find it impossible to obtain. To rely on economic growth alone, on stimulation of the private sector alone, or on public job creation alone would be a mistake; all three strategies are complementary and necessary.

Fourth, any employment policy must attack head-on the problem of racial and sexual discrimination in work; that is, the problem of fair employment. Obviously, vigorous enforcement of existing laws and more adequate funding of state and federal fair employment practice commissions is called for. But beyond that, stronger affirmative action, with vigorous searches for qualified minority and women candidates for all positions and promotions, must be insisted on. Equally important, given the historic patterns of discrimination against nonwhites and women, are efforts to enlarge the pool of eligible nonwhite and female applicants for higher level jobs. Without such steps we could well be left with a society that offered jobs to all American families but that still relegated nonwhites and women to the economic bottom of our society.

The second main component of any program of economic supports for children and families must be a back-up program of living standard supplementation or income supports. Parents who cannot work or who should not be required to work must have a standard of living that enables them to raise their children with some dignity. Economists and politicians have been discussing such supports for many years; dozens of plans exist for supporting the incomes of those at the bottom of the economic hierarchy. Our long-term national goal should be to supplement full and fair employment by income supports not significantly below one-half of the median income.

Both politics and justice require that any income support program have a number of features: income supports should aid, to some degree, all families whose incomes fall below the median income, avoiding the sharp cutoffs, high marginal tax rates on earnings, and work disincentives present in the existing welfare system. It is ridiculous to claim that those whose incomes fall one hundred or a thousand dollars above the poverty level do not need income supplementation because they fall above an admittedly arbitrary cutoff line. Moreover, it is politically essential that income supports benefit a majority of the population, providing diminishing but nonetheless tangible benefits to families up to and including those of median income. The costs of such a program—which would be considerable—should be borne largely by people whose incomes fall in the top 10 or 20 percent of the population. Again, economists and politicians differ as to the best way to provide the funds; increased progressive taxation with closing of tax loopholes that currently benefit the very rich seems indicated.

The third component of a policy of economic reform must be an alteration of work practices to enable parents to combine meaningful work and effective parenting. The most important ingredient of altered work practices involves the scheduling and timing of work, both on a daily or weekly basis, and in terms of each adult's life cycle. On a daily and weekly basis, we need increased opportunties for part-time and flexible employment, especially for parents to take sick leave when their children are sick. We need work schedules that take into account the desire of parents of school-age children to be at home when their children are home. In short, we need work policies that are deliberately planned so that workers can combine work with parenting, rather than having to choose between the two. Benefits currently available to full-time workers must be extended on a prorated basis to part-time workers as well, including sick leave, health insurance, Social Security benefits, and paid vacations. Other nations have shown that flexible work scheduling, part-time work, and so forth, are not only possible but economically feasible and, indeed, productive. We need to begin to experiment and act on this front.

In addition, many parents withdraw from the labor force when their children are young to devote full time to the care of their children. At present, economic pressures conspire to make them pay an excessively high price for leaving the labor force. We need much more conscious public policies that facilitate the reentry into the labor force of parents who have withdrawn from it. Long-term parenting leaves, job retraining, skill renewal programs, and reemployment without penalization for withdrawal from the labor force are all obvious steps in this direction.

The goal of both private and public policy in this area can be simply stated: to enable parents to better combine parenting and work and to place the role of the parent in national economic policy where it stands in our national rhetoric—as an honorable, valid, and socially useful role. The goal is, in short, to broaden the range of significant parental choices, minimizing the pressures that require parents to work at the expense of their children or to care for their children at the expense of working.

At another time, I should like to discuss the relationships between these three facets of a policy of economic support for American families: full and fair employment, income supports, and flexible work practices. These relationships are complementary rather than opposed. To cite an example: the existence of adequate income supports for all American families would make it less necessary for single parents who wished to devote themselves entirely to their young children to work solely out of economic pressure. Income supports would also create political pressures toward full employment, since the alternative to full employment would be heavy public expenditures in the form of income support for the unemployed. There are also important budgetary relationships between the several components of an economic policy for families and children. For instance, a society in which there was decently paid work for all those who needed it would be a society in which the costs to the public for income supports would be greatly diminished. The higher the level of employment, the less the need for—and the cost of—a supplementary program of income support. The best way to reduce the costs of any income support scheme would be to provide work for the overwhelming majority who wish to work.

I have deliberately chosen to imagine a society much better than our own. And in so doing, I have temporarily put aside my awareness of the political and economic obstacles that lie between today's reality and that better society—obstacles such as lack of political will and, according to some, lack of money necessary to institute such programs.

We are well aware of these constraints, but we believe that in each area, it is possible to set in motion a process that makes the attainment of the ultimate goal of providing economic support to families more likely. For example, among the many employment bills currently before Congress, there are some that embody the basic principles I have discussed. Both major parties have, in recent years, put forward income support schemes, such as Nixon's family assistance program and McGovern's income redistribution scheme. Many private industries are experimenting with part-time and flexible work practices, finding them not only pleasing to their employees, but productive to the firm. No sane person expects that Congress will enact into law this year all of the proposals I have advanced. But in every area it is possible to begin now, modestly perhaps in terms of funding levels, but on a sound basis that would permit more adequate funding as political support grows and larger funds become available. In practical politics, uncompromising insistence on all-or-nothing usually means nothing. The short-term goal for child advocates should not be "all," but to make a beginning in the right direction now, and to push for more extensive economic supports as time passes.

In each of the three areas I have discussed—employment, income, and work practices—there are important political and economic questions that deserve greater attention than space allows. For example, full employment includes controlling the inflationary potential of full employment and developing effective means of creating useful jobs; income supports include, above all, how best to revise the tax system to fund income supplements for those in the bottom half of the income distribution; flexible work practices include an analysis of the costs, in terms of overall efficiency and labor productivity, of flexible work scheduling. The problems are complicated, but they are not in principle without solution. We should be working on these problems directly when we talk about supporting children and families.

Child care and health care are two of the most essential services for American children and families. I wish only to emphasize that a policy of expanding services and a policy of increasing economic supports to American families are not only consistent with each other, but they are mutually necessary. Consider, for example, the issue of child care. Let us imagine, for a moment, that all the long-term targets I have mentioned in the economic area have been achieved: full and fair employment, a back-up system of income supports, and altered work practices. For children and families, these policies would be ineffective unless they were accompanied by the expansion and upgrading of child care facilities. Without child care facilities, either children will be neglected or at least one parent—the only parent in a single-parent family—must stay at home. The extension and support of child care is a complement to economic support for American families.

The connection between economic change and change in the service system is budgetary as well as operational. Full employment at decent wages would enable more American families to pay more of the costs of child care from their earned income; the need for public subsidies for child care would diminish. Similarly, adequate income supports might well permit larger numbers of parents—especially single parents—to choose not to work when their children are young, reducing the need for child care outside the family. More flexible work scheduling would obviously reduce the need for and the costs of full-time child care.

Advocates for children sometimes view each proposal for supporting children and family life as somehow competing with other proposals; for example, those who favor increased support for child care sometimes oppose those who favor income supports. In the short term, these oppositions are easy to understand, for advocates of publicly supported child care and advocates of income redistribution are both competing for the same limited budgetary pie. But these are short-term conflicts. They are arguments over strategy and timing rather than arguments over principle. In the end, we need both more adequate income supports and universal access to the services that all children and families need; economic change and change in services require each other.

Earlier in this article, I noted that public policies that affect families and children have evolved from the myth that there are two quite different kinds of families and children—adequate families that do not need help, and inadequate families that do need help. Starting from that myth, we have evolved a two-track system, one track involving inadequate public assistance, the other involving essentially private or nongovernmental means of gaining income and reliance on the market for services. Public policies perversely act to perpetuate the tracks, condemning a significant majority of those born into the bottom track to a permanent place there. A prime goal of public policy for families and children—and, indeed, in other areas as well—must be to create a single track for all families and children, one that combines the strengths of both of the existing streams. All Americans should have approximately the same range of significant choices.

In moving toward change in our present two-track society, both economic change and more adequate provision of essential services are needed. At present, social services are too often a way of applying Band-Aids to those who lack adequate economic support. The result is a perversion of services. Child care becomes a way of relieving poverty and racism by pushing poor and nonwhite women into the labor market; publicly supported health care becomes a way of undoing the harms caused by bad housing, inadequate income, and malnutrition.

Those who devote their lives to the improvement of services should not be deflected from their efforts. But they should, whether as professionals or private citizens, also reflect on the economic conditions that create many of the problems they are called on to solve. They should work toward the long-term goal of a society in which all American families and children have available to them, as a matter of right, both a decent standard of living and those services that are essential in modern America for bringing up a family. To squabble about alleged conflicts between economic and service supports for children and families is a waste of energies that are urgently needed for other causes.

20

The Single Parent and Public Policy

Alvin L. Schorr and Phyllis Moen

The divorce rate in the United States is at an all time high; we are commonly said to have the highest divorce rate in the world. One result of this has been a striking increase in female-headed families; the number of divorced women heading families nearly tripled between 1960 and 1975 alone.[1] As a result, the number of children living in one-parent families increased by 60 percent in the last decade.[2] A number of quite different forces have contributed to these changes—the increased propensity of mothers without husbands to form separate families, women's increased labor force participation, and the spread of no-fault divorce.

Despite these changes, somewhere in their minds Americans still tend to hold a conventional view of the family as having two parents and two or three children. This conventional version of the family is so powerful that scholars, like citizens, label other family forms pejoratively—as "deviant," "broken," or "unstable."[3] Indeed, single parents label themselves as unique and "abnormal."[4] Nor are conventional views quite repudiated by minorities and the poor. On the contrary, while in some neighborhoods or subcultures half or more of all children live in single-parent families, their parents regard their single status as demonstrably normal on one hand and as evidence of failure and delinquency on the other.

Meanwhile, the traditional family—husband, wife, and children from the first marriage of the spouses—accounts for only 45 percent of American

Reprinted from Alvin L. Schorr and Phyllis Moen, "The Single Parent and Public Policy," *Social Policy*, vol. 10, no. 5, March/April 1979, pp. 15-21, published by Social Policy Corporation, New York.

families.[5] The next most frequent types are the single-parent family (15 percent) and the nuclear-dyad—husband and wife alone without children (15 percent).

By the age of eighteen, nearly one out of two children will have lived a period of time with a single parent.[6] Meanwhile, the number of husband-wife families has begun to decline. At any moment in time, 25 to 30 percent of all children are in one-parent families.[7] The gap between the public image of the single-parent family and reality cannot be laid to a new situation we have not had time to recognize. It may be stipulated that conditions are changing, but they have been changing for a long time, and there was extensive foreshadowing of current patterns. There have, for hundreds of years, been single-parent families and considerable variation in family form, including the three-generation family, the commune, and the nuclear family. Early death of the father combined with an extended span of child-bearing has made the single-parent family fairly common in the twentieth century.[8]

The view that the single-parent family is unique and deviant has other elements bound up in it. Single parenthood is seen as a transitional state. For example, four out of five divorced and widowed persons remarry. Nevertheless, past the age of 30, a greater proportion remain single[9] and the tendency to remarry appears now to be declining.[10] A recent longitudinal study of unmarried women who headed households found that fewer than one-fifth had married in a five-year period.[11] Single-parent families may live "as if" in a permanent state, whatever their futures may hold, though policy-makers may see their status as transitional.

Pathology is a prominent element of the public view of single parenthood. Although the term has come to be associated with the "Moynihan controversy" of 1965, in truth professionals and social agencies have long regarded single parenthood as pathological for reasons arising from their own backgrounds.[12] "Trained in the clinical model, [they] are conditioned to recognize pathology. While some attention in professional education may be given to preventive care and normal growth and development, the overriding emphasis is on the successful treatment and reversal of problems."[13] Against the background of this public image of single parenthood, policy has been couched in terms of improving the stability of existing intact families and services have been designed to facilitate the reconstitution of families.

Public discussion of the single-parent family in the last decade or two has come to overlap considerably with a discussion of black family life and welfare. Consequently, the mainstream of single-parent families is hidden. A larger proportion of black families than white families have single parents, 35 percent compared with 11 percent. For reasons that are all but obvious—single-parent families are usually headed by one wage-earner who is usually a woman and likely to earn less than a man—single-parent families are likely to rely on welfare. Still, a third of the women-headed, single-parent families never receive welfare.[14] The stereotype that recipients have simply resigned themselves to welfare has no relation to fact. Of seven million mothers who received welfare over a ten-year period, the typical woman was assisted for two years, left welfare, and eventually received it for two years more. Only 770,000 received welfare for nine or ten years.[15]

Generalizing inevitably leaves an impression of uniformity but the situation of single-parent families varies considerably. For example, single fathers may be in a markedly different position from single mothers. Though still a small minority, single fatherhood is increasing at a faster rate than families headed by women.[16] In part, this reflects changes in courtroom attitude toward custody, but also changing conceptions of the roles of men and women. As women have sought to define identities apart from that of wife and mother, so too have more men seen themselves in roles other than wage-earner.[17]

The most prominent difference is that single fathers command higher incomes. The average income of single mothers in 1973 was $6,000, compared to $12,000 for single fathers.[18] Though a single father's income may more easily permit him to buy housekeeping services, recent studies show that he too usually performs housekeeping duties—helped by his children.[19] Still, many of the stereotypes that constrain women also confine men. Since child care is not seen as their role, it is difficult for fathers to adjust their working hours to meet the needs of their children.[20] Although they report a need for services—child care in the evening, transportation to day care, and so forth, single fathers express feelings of success and satisfaction about parenting; in this they are like single mothers.[21]

Widows with children are a significantly different group from the divorced and separated. Less than a fifth are under 35 (compared with 55 percent of divorced and separated women with children). Possibly for that reason and because they usually receive Social Security benefits, their total income is substantially higher.[22] On the average, black single-parent families are different from white. Black single mothers are twice as likely to have three children or more—30 out of 100 compared with 15 out of 100 for white single mothers. Black single parents are less likely than white to be working; they have higher unemployment rates, lower educational levels, and higher rates of poverty.[23]

One may attempt to classify single parents logically—as widowed, divorced, separated, and unmarried.[24] Such a distinction directs attention to the rather different causes and feelings that may be at play for the families. For example, death may be a more sudden and final blow. Separation may be a stage on the road to divorce. The unmarried mother faces more stigma, though possibly this is changing a little. She is likely to be younger than the others, and her financial difficulties even more serious. Unmarried mothers are becoming increasingly consequential, as one birth in seven in the United States is now illegitimate.[25]

In whatever ways they differ, however, all single parents suffer from public images of the ideal family.

PARENTHOOD, WORK, AND INCOME

Closely linked to the image of the traditional two-parent family is an ideological stance concerning the proper division of labor within the family. Specifically, the male is thought of as the head of the household—the "breadwinner" of the family. Weitzman speaks of the "hidden contract" of marriage: (1) that the husband is the head of the household and responsible for economic support and (2) that the wife is responsible for child care.[26] Consequences of this role differentiation by sex are profound for women in general and especially painful for single mothers. Because women are viewed as marginal workers, they are given marginal jobs—low paying, low status, and insecure.[27]

Most of the wage differentials between men and women arise either from the smaller amount of labor market experience attained by women or from discrimination against women. The former arises directly from the hidden contract of the sexist assignment of roles. Discrimination arises indirectly and directly from the image of the male as provider.[28]

Because women earn 40 percent less than men, on the average, in every occupational category,[29] it is not surprising that in general the most important single determinant of a change in family economic well-being appears to be a change in family composition.[30] With divorce, the economic status of women relative to need goes down while that of men apparently goes up.[31] Three out of five poor children are in single-parent families.

One cannot explore single parenthood and work for women without becoming aware that work affects marital status and vice versa. More divorced than married women work and more work full time at every educational level.[32] Most divorced and separated mothers work a full year; others work less than a full year only because they have been laid off.[33] Conversely, the better a husband provides, the less likely is divorce.[34] Separation rates are twice as high among families where the husband experiences serious unemployment, suggesting that it is not the amount of income alone but its stability that is part of a decision to remain married or separate.[35] Studies of women's earnings produce quite consistent findings. As more women work, some postpone marriage and fewer get married in total.[36] Other things being equal, the higher a wife's earnings, the more likely that a couple will separate.[37] In short, a man's income tends to cement a marriage and a woman's tends to make dissolution possible.

It is important to remember that the amount of income alone does not equal financial security. For example, a study of women who had been divorced for up to two years found every woman saying that despite reduced income the family was better off financially. The researcher suggests that stability and control may have been more important than amount. Respondents said such things as, "I don't have much money to spend, but at least it's regular," and "Now I can buy things for the children."[38]

In any event, the problems concerning work for women are general and rooted in social arrangements broader than single parenthood. They have special impact for single parents but cannot be dealt with within that framework, nor avoided simply if single parenthood could be avoided.

Structured for time and commitment, jobs leave no more time for domestic activities to the mother than to the father. Hours are inflexible and long; few part-time jobs pay enough to support a family. Unless informal care is at hand, adequate, reliable, and inexpensive child care is rarely available. And institutions and businesses operate on the assumption that there are two parents, one of them free to carry on transactions during the day. As we noted the combined effect of working and mothering at once upon the income of single mothers, we now note the strain working creates for housekeeping and parenting. (The problem is felt by married mothers as well; half of them are employed.) If the parenting of single parents may suffer, part of the reason is that, like many mothers with husbands, they work outside the home.

A critical aspect for single parent and dual-worker families is that children are likely to be cared for by persons other than the parents. Implicit in the public image of poor parenting is the belief that small children spend their time in over-crowded institutional settings.[39] The fact is otherwise: Nine out of ten preschool children with working mothers spend their time in informal settings—with relatives, neighbors, or friends. Nor is that because congregate care is scarce, though to be sure it is. Single parents, poor parents, and welfare parents, like middle-class parents who live together, prefer informal care both because it appears to be better and is more practical.[40] As to congregate care, research reveals no effect on intellectual development but possible difficulty in emotional and social development. Studies have generally failed to distinguish between good and poor congregate care though and it is possible that studies of good care would produce different findings.[41] There is no body of research on the effects of informal care.

A modern view regards substitute care as a supplement to maternal care rather than as a substitute for it.[42] A considerable argument can be made for such a development as moderating the "hothouse" aspect of the mother and child bond and "shifting back towards a more natural [i.e., less confined and intense] way of life for both women and children."[43] Seen in this light, conflict is no longer so sharply drawn between maternal and substitute care. The questions about substitute care are no longer categorical: Is substitute care intrinsically a good or bad idea? What qualities are required in substitute care? What duration optimum? And so forth.

Single parents do, of course, face special circumstances. An asset in the two-parent home is the presence of another adult to provide consultation and support with respect to children.[44] "Parents . . . need to have other voices joined with theirs in transmitting values and maturity demands to their children."[45] Single parents may have no one to provide emotional support. The sense of failure which separation may have provoked may readily lead—without adult company and support—to feelings of isolation.[46] A British study reports these feelings as the main personal problem of single parents.[47] Conversely, children with single parents have access to fewer adults and tend to emphasize peer relationships.[48]

The presence or absence of both parents *per se* makes little difference in the adequacy of child-rearing[49] or the socialization of children.[50] There is no evidence that the absence of a father from the home has an effect on the child's sense of sex identity.[51] Single mothers hold the same values for their children as mothers with husbands.[52] A series of studies over the years has found more delinquency in unhappy intact homes than in single-parent ones.[53] In their famous study, Glueck and Glueck found the quality of maternal supervision more important for delinquency than the presence or absence of a man.[54] "What scientific evidence there is suggests that divorce is often better (or at least less harmful) for children than an unhappy conflict-ridden marriage."[55]

What can one make of all this? Do strain and the absence of one parent or another not alter child-rearing noticeably and adversely? Perhaps the key point with respect to parenting is that the choice of the parents and children does not lie between a sound marriage and single parenthood. Happy couples rarely separate. The choice for many children lies between an unhappy home and a single parent. Parents themselves—though they commonly worry about the effects of a divorce on their children[56]—with experience come to think they have done well by them.[57]

To be sure, some children from single-parent homes pay a penalty, and curiously they may suffer more from maternal than paternal absence, since a single mother without a family, friends or the money to purchase help often must deprive a child of her company and attention; that is the deprivation the child feels most keenly.[58] This is consistent with the British finding that damage to school attainment and social adjustment, when they are observed, result from poverty rather than single parenthood itself.[59]

One final effect of single parenthood is relevant. Today, a higher proportion of children under five are living with only their mothers than ever before.[60] The number of children in institutions and in substitute families is declining. One reason is that children are remaining with single parents.[61] For children, single parenthood is an alternative not only to a two-parent family but to no family at all.

Of a sample of single mothers with preschool children, 72 percent had "a moderate or severe distress problem compared to 46 percent of 'married' mothers."[62] While this study shows the disadvantage of single-parent families, it is surely more important that half of the intact families has the same problem. If one starts with that as the basic issue, one can understand the reason why young mothers may feel exhaustion and depression and how single parenthood may add to the problem.[63] But the problem becomes general and not solely one of single parenthood. It is within that context that one must ask how society is to help single-parent families.

PUBLIC IMAGE AND PUBLIC POLICY

The core of the argument here is that single-parent families are misrepresented to the public and to themselves. They have special problems and they may benefit from special institutional supports, but that is true of any number of groups otherwise regarded as normal and acceptable. The unemployed, veterans, and widows are examples at one end of the alphabet while single-parent families are statistically and historically in the American mainstream.

Yet the image is itself a powerful policy. The most moving effect of misrepresentation is that many single parents believe what is said of them and add that belief to the problems they face. Separation and divorce are a troubled if not stormy period and so the people involved are vulnerable. While separation is part of every married person's at least occasional speculation, and the actual event a crystal around which fantasies cling, the people involved usually blame themselves, adding normality to their worries about financial responsibility, judgment, concern about children, sexual responsibility, and self-worth. The stereotypes involved are about as legitimate as most that are involved in discriminatory behavior—and as destructive.

It is apparent that changing the image would imply broad changes in government, employment, and other policies. Conversely, such policies are potent in maintaining or altering the image. Each set of policy issues requires extensive exploration not possible here. An examination of these issues indicates the powerful and pervasive influence of the current image in our social arrangements.

If one sees women as normal and regular wage earners, issues of sex discrimination in wages and occupational opportunity must be faced. Both work at home with children and at outside occupations must permit more flexibility. On one hand are questions of aids for child care and homemaking, and also the operating assumption that shopping and transactions with physicians and utilities can be carried on in the middle of the day. The spread of single parenthood creates a demand that has moved some businesses to expanded hours, but professions and public utilities seem less sensitive. On the other hand are questions of the structuring of work and careers, the scheduling of employment, the feasibility of shared work, and the growth of part-time work.

Issues in income maintenance policy are similarly complex. The financial problem of the working poor, much debated in the last few years, is from another perspective an issue of single parenthood and minimum wages. That is, a single year-round minimum wage does not provide enough income to keep four people (a couple and two children, a single parent and three children, a grandmother, her daughter, and two children) out of poverty. Most industrial countries have tried to meet this problem by relatively small payments for all children. Americans have preferred to regard the issue as a welfare policy problem, seeing low-paid working people pitted against separated or unmarried women—though often enough they are the same people.

If we see these two groups as sharing a problem rather than competing, the solution of a small subsidy for children to which other Western countries have come may seem appealing. The Earned Income Credit, recently introduced into the federal income tax, would, if improved in level and expanded to all children, serve quite well.

In implementation, policies that favor two-parent families are likely to operate to the disadvantage of single-parent families. For example, a woman with children might receive a higher payment from welfare compared with the family's entitlement if the husband were present. Obviously, the family needs more if the husband is not there. On the other hand, making equivalent payments to two-parent families would present costs that are impossible in the real world of limited resources. The result is commonly a smaller payment to the single-parent family than even the amount thought minimally necessary. Regarding this issue, Isabel Sawhill has proposed an attempt to "define a neutral policy—that is one which would neither encourage [nor] discourage various kinds of family behavior such as marriage or childbearing." She concludes that considerations such as equity and need make a quite neutral system unlikely.[64] Nevertheless, seeking a system that neither rewards nor penalizes family structure would open negotiation about program design in a way that might portend progress.* But it would be difficult to work at designing neutral programs while talking the language of a policy partisan to intact families.

Another direction to go in income maintenance, more special to single parenthood, is to recognize separation and divorce as social risks similar to the risk of being widowed. There have been proposals to establish a program of "fatherless child insurance"—or "single parent insurance"—along lines well understood in Social Security. As single parenthood is voluntary, when compared with being widowed, careful design is required but appears to be feasible.[65] In one conception, such programs may be taken as supplementing income that would otherwise be inadequate. In another conception, one may argue that it is sound and constructive for one of the single parents to remain in the traditional role of homemaker, and not to work. The same programs providing "income by right," with possibly larger payments, would enable them to do this.[66] More conservatively and more limited, it has been argued that even if income is not provided, at least the government should provide credit toward Social Security for the work implicit in homemaking.[67]

The issue of parental support of children when there is marital separation is not, by any means, simply a welfare issue. "The primary purpose of child support laws is the protection of the public purse,"[68] but with respect to non-welfare families, the primary issue is one of family law. Courts and administrative agencies are likely to be more lenient in securing support than the law might seem to require. Each estate has a welfare standard, a non-welfare standard or understanding, the understanding that will really be enforced, and the agreements that result from the pressures and evasive tactics that husband and wife can bring to bear. There is no general social contract to which courts, agencies, or couples (if they wish to avoid dispute or exploitation of one another) can refer. In this absence of public agreement, as always, the weakest and poorest suffer most.

A CHANGE IN OUTLOOK

In this field, the development of a reasonable set of ideas that might lead to consensus would be a giant step for single "mankind." It is a difficult problem, for it involves reconciling concepts as old as common law with twentieth century reality; and balancing the rights and needs of a wage earner and, chances are, the wage earner's new family against those of the family that is being left; all in a context in which everyone's standard of living is at risk of declining.

The delivery of social services contains its own complex set of issues. Counsellors, for example, need to approach giving help in terms of managing the transition from a marital to a post-marital way of life.[69] Underlying this is professional acceptance that marital separation is a normal transition, a statement that may sound disarmingly simple but requires a profound change in professional point of view. Similarly, if single parenthood is regarded as a normal way of life, practical aids and supports must assume a degree of importance they have possibly not been accorded by social agencies. Day care for children has received a good deal of public attention; we have noted that the single-parent family seems to prefer and have good practical reason for using informal and neighborhood arrangements rather than the congregate care that has been extensively discussed. Beyond this, service organizations attentive to their clients should help them to secure reasonable aid or arrangements from employers, public schools, hospitals, and other institutions. Once again, a more profound change in posture is implied than may have been indicated at first.

With or without the aid of established organizations, it would be constructive to see self-generated groups of single parents organize. In the nature of single parenthood, individuals tend to move in and out of such groups. Nevertheless, they provide a means for sharing experience, moderating the sense of loneliness from which single parents may suffer, and reinforcing their sense of self-esteem. Under certain circumstances such groups can exercise broad influence in securing the social changes that may be important.[70]

Employment, income maintenance, child support, and social services present relatively self-evident issues, but when we grasp the broad changes that have swept over us, other issues will also appear. For example, it seems possible that single parents are living in housing designed for other times. That is, the basic design of apartments and houses was long since established for large families and other two-parent families. While the basic design has been modified to suit smaller families and new construction methods and to meet exigencies of cost and financing, those modifications have been mechanical, not functional—that is, fewer bedrooms, room sizes scaled down, and rooms devoted to certain functions (the dining room, the kitchen) in some cases made rudimentary. However, housing is not designed for one-parent family living. Preparing food and dining may be a unitary activity and more significant for single parents than for others; it may be that a single larger room would serve them better than the conventional kitchen and dining room. Again, it may be that two combination bedroom-work (or play) rooms would serve a parent and child better than the conventional two bedrooms and a living room.[71] Such issues will not be raised until we think of single parenthood as normal rather than marginal. Then designs may be worked out, money ventured, and the judgment of the market cast.

A good deal more thought is required about the issues related to single parents. This discussion is simply intended to indicate how issues change focus if one views single parenthood as a normal and permanent feature of our social landscape.

21

Directions for Day Care

Karen Wolk Feinstein

A book that examines the impact of female employment on family life would be incomplete without special consideration of the needs of children. In 1975, 44 percent of all children under the age of 18 and 36 percent of all children under six had working mothers. As a result, there are many children in this country who have no parent at home during the workday and no parent for whom the care of children and household affairs is a full-time responsibility. Feminists have argued that this is not, in itself, undesirable; children of any age do not require the full-time attendance by a mother to develop into happy, healthy adults. They cite the many advantages of jobs and careers for women and suggest that other societal institutions and new family arrangements can provide for the care of our nation's children (Safilios-Rothschild, 1973). National employment trends over the past decade indicate an increasing involvement of mothers in the labor force. . . . Women's motivations for employment are complex among all ages, races, and social classes; family economic considerations are wedded to desires for independence, occupational challenge, and adult companionship. Women of means work for economic independence as well as career satisfactions; poor and working-class women derive personal satisfaction as well as financial gain from employment.

Internationally, the increasing preference of women for paid employment and the reliance of families on external sources of child care is an almost universal phenomenon (Giele and Smock, 1977). Nations that have attempted

Reprinted from Karen Wolk Feinstein, "Directions for Day Care," in *Working Women and Families*, pp. 177–193, copyright © 1979 by Sage Publications, Inc., with permission.

to reverse the trend toward women's labor force participation, either to reduce unemployment or increase population growth, have found it difficult (Kahn and Kamerman, 1977). As Chafe states in reference to the experience of the United States:

> There appears to have been a simple cultural logic at work in the employment of women since World War II. Those who first broke the barriers against married women's employment were middle aged. With no children in the home, they posed the least threat to traditional ideas of women's 'place' as homemakers and mothers. Later, a major increase in employment occurred among mothers with children six to seventeen years of age. By the late sixties, in turn, the major change took place among mothers of younger children. It was almost as though each step in the process was necessary to prepare the way for the next one, until by the mid-1970s there was consistent departure from the traditional norm of mothers staying at home full-time to care for children [1976:25].

Working mothers with young children need substitute care for infants, preschoolers, and primary school-aged children. In nations with institutionalized day care systems (state, locality, or employer-based), this procedure involves choosing among options: center-based care, family care, or in-home care. For instance, mothers in Sweden, Norway, Hungary, and the Soviet Union can participate in publicly sponsored or supervised full-day programs for infants and preschoolers in neighborhood creches, in licensed municipal family day care homes, in extended-day programs and sick-care services for school aged children, or they can make private arrangements with individuals and programs outside the national system. In nations where no day care system exists, where child care is a private, not public, responsibility and day care options vary considerably from city to city and neighborhood to neighborhood, families encounter more difficulties in providing for their children during working hours.

Extensive support systems have been legislated by governments in almost every European country to provide for the children of working mothers. These systems are often inadequate to care for all the children in need of service and to provide the high quality of care many parents prefer. Many parents will choose private, in-home arrangements even where an extensive national system of group care exists. However, what is important is that the governments of these countries *have assumed responsibility* for the welfare of children of working parents. In most of these nations, parents share similar concerns about day care. There are complaints about the quality and quantity of care, and real ambivalence about the value of group centers for children under three. Yet, the prevailing attitude is that such care is a national necessity; mothers of young children are entering the workforce and the national disposition is to minimize the harm such work preferences may have on women, children, and families.

In this chapter I will examine the national policy response to the day care needs of children with working mothers in America. Particular consideration will be given to the selective nature of this response. I will also identify the major providers of day care in America—both public and private, emphasizing the present potential for, or limitations to, growth in each sector. I use the term "day care" here to denote the custodial care of children (from birth to adolescence) while mothers work. Although a day care program may include special education or social services, day care is primarily regarded as a "parent substitute" service and not as a cultural enrichment, preschool, or parent education vehicle. It may take place individually or in groups, in homes or in formal centers. Programs such as nursery schools which may, incidentally, provide day care for part of the day while addressing a major objective of preschool education, are not considered as day care providers *unless* they offer full-day care adjusted to the work schedules of employed mothers (e.g. 8:30 a.m.–5:30 p.m.).

In a final section, I suggest future directions for day care in America, which evolve from my exploration of the national day care terrain. These suggestions are predictive and descriptive rather than normative, and I offer no ideal model of a national day care system. However, I suspect that in spite of the unique economic and political factors which shape American day care policy and which have led us down a distinctive policy path, our final destination will be suprisingly similar to that of other industralized nations. In communities throughout the world, authorities, service providers, and parents are searching for programs to provide care for children of working parents within the constraints of inadequate resources, inadequate consensus on child development principles, and limited models of group care.

In this chapter, I question whether our system will evolve "from the bottom up" or "from the top down"; will much of the day care programming occur at the local community level or emanate from national legislation? An important issue is who will pay for services and who will receive federal subsidies. Sometime in the future, will our "nonsystem" of care involve a far wider range of options for all families at the local community level, and by addressing universal child care needs, will it come to resemble the more deliberate and coherent day care systems already intact in other nations?

NATIONAL DAY CARE POLICY

Why do nations invest in social parenthood? I suggest that child welfare considerations are not sufficient motivation and that day care policy considerations are intimately linked with economic conditions. The more aggressive national response to day care needs in European countries, for instance, can be partially explained by the shortage of workers in economies that require more manpower. National day care efforts are directed at attracting new workers to the labor force as much as promoting family interests. In France, for instance, concern about underpopulation has resulted in the development of children's support services in an attempt to make childrearing more palatable and alter parental preferences for small families.

In the United States, there is no worker shortage at present; in fact, we are facing problems of unemployment. National policymakers are concerned about measures which might increase the existing pool of workers. Among the many Americans who have no children in need of day care, this costly service is not high priority.

Other authors have adequately chronicled the forces of resistance to a national day care program in the United States (Greenblatt, 1978; Kamerman and Kahn, 1976; and Steinfels, 1973). Primary among the forces working against any national system of care are:

- Philosophical disputes over the purpose, sponsorship, program, and scope of such a system
- Financial resistance to subsidizing a costly service in the absence of a documented critical need
- Economic fears about stimulating maternal employment in an economy with high unemployment
- Political disagreements over who should administer such a program and control the day care dollar
- Organizational uncertainty over how to best administer and deliver a national day care system

To overcome these obstacles, a concerted day care coalition must convince policy makers and their constituents that day care will address a critical national need. In the past, national leaders have been successful only in establishing a federal day care system during times of national emergency: the Great Depression and World War II. Extensive day care networks were set up to meet generally acknowledged national needs: jobs for the unemployed, social welfare services for children of the unemployed, and manpower for the war industries. In both instances, executive directive rather than legislative fiat created the day care programs, first under the Works Projects Administration in 1933, and then extended under the Community Facilities Act of 1941. Both acts were passed to meet critical manpower problems in depression- and later war-impacted areas, and were not aimed at establishing a new national social service. Housed within and administered by local school systems, these temporary day care programs did constitute a public day care system. Although extensive evaluations of the programs are not available, they were filled to capacity and seem to have provided adequate care. After the war, when such centers were believed to accentuate rather than relieve manpower problems by prolonging maternal employment, they were disbanded. No serious federal day care initiatives were proposed until the 1960s.

During the 1960s, the federal government again became involved in preschool education and day care; the intent was not to provide relief for working mothers, but to (1) compensate for the emotional, physical, and intellectual deprivations of poverty, hence interrupting the "cycle of poverty," or to (2) enable and encourage mothers on welfare to enter the work force. Programs such as Head Start exemplify the first approach; day care funding through Titles IVa, IVb, and IVc and Title XX of the Social Security Act represent the second.

Both Head Start and Social Security policies addressed another national purpose of current concern: the need to reduce economic dependency and the welfare roll. They are targeted at small groups of children from low-income families. The popular Head Start program was instituted under the Economic Opportunity Act of 1964 to offer comprehensive child development services (educational experiences, medical and dental care, psychological counseling, nutritional support and social services) to children in poor families on a demonstration basis. It is essentially a compensatory educational program; except in those few centers operating for a full day, it is not a day care program. This program has received broad national acceptance. However, researchers have been unable to prove that it has long-term effects on school achievement. Furthermore, it has established a national standard for preschool care that is very costly. For these and other reasons, efforts to expand this project have been unsuccessful.

Most of the federal funds for day care in the 1960s were directed at welfare reform and came under the Social Security Act of 1962. The objective was to enable and encourage welfare mothers to undertake employment or training. Other federal manpower and antipoverty initiatives also involved the establishment of day care centers, so that by 1970 there were more than 200 programs allocating funds for child care (Grubb, 1977:8). The Title XX amendments to the Social Security Act, effective in 1975, consolidated many of these funding sources by providing block grants in the form of matching funds to states for social services. Each state can decide which services to offer and can serve a broader range of clientele. Although federal guidelines permit individuals and families with incomes up to 115% of a state's median income to participate, funding limitations have tended to restrict eligibility to the poor (Grubb, 1977:10). It is uncertain whether the states will continue to allocate a high percentage of these monies to day care services. When the funding was categorical, day care services accounted for 30%–40% of the federal social service funds.

Other federal legislation, such as the Elementary and Secondary Education Act of 1965 (Titles I and III) and federal legislation for the handicapped (PL94-142), provided funding for preschool programs for children in deprived areas and with special needs. These are educational programs targeted at special populations and are not intended to meet the needs of working mothers. As I will discuss later, however, these acts are significant because they involve the federal government in financing preschool programs through the sponsorship of local school districts.

In 1971, a child development coalition of labor groups, day care proponents, liberal congressmen, and child welfare leaders did secure passage in both Houses of Congress of a comprehensive child development bill which would have established a national system of compensatory preschool education and day care for children in low-income families. The Nixon administration balked at issues of community control, the range of services proposed, and the number of children to be served. President Nixon vetoed the bill with the excuse that:

> For the Federal Government to plunge headlong financially into supporting child development would commit the vast moral authority of the National Government to the side of communal approaches to child rearing over (and) against the family-centered approach [Steiner, 1976:113].

It is unlikely that Nixon and other prominent administration decision makers actually feared the "Sovietization" of American children through center-based day care. Sensing that support for the bill was not sufficient to damage him politically, Nixon had no reason to pass the measure other than to provide day care. No evidence has come forth to indicate that preschool programs are adequate to break the cycle of poverty. To accomplish a more important purpose—bringing welfare mothers into the labor force—a more direct, less comprehensive program would suffice (Steiner, 1976).

The government now provides general assistance for day care through its fiscal relief measures. The 1976 Tax Reform Act permits a tax credit for child care and household services for working parents. The Act extends to all taxpayers and allows a credit of up to $400 per year per child. Tax credits help pay for day care; they do not create programs. However, a provision of the Revenue Act of 1971, viable until 1982, permits businesses to deduct, at an accelerated capital-investment rate, the expenses of "acquiring, constructing, reconstructing or rehabilitating property" for use as child-care facilities (Canon, 1978:85). In addition, a 1973 ruling by the IRS (73-348) permits companies to take expense deductions under Section 162 of the Internal Revenue Code for the cost of child care for preschoolers if such expense (1) enables an employee to obtain proper care for children, or (2) reduces the company's costs of training, job replacement, and absenteeism. A bill (H.R. 3340) was submitted in 1977 to amend the Code to allow deductions for the incremental costs involved in using any portion of a dwelling unit to provide licensed day care services, even if not used exclusively for such service.

On paper, the government has tried a more aggressive approach to stimulating work organizations to establish day care. Executive Order 11478, the affirmative-action mandate to federal executive agencies, designates responsibility for enforcing the Equal Employment Opportunity Act among federal departments to the U.S. Civil Service Commission. In 1973, the Civil Service Commission issued Chapter 713 of the Federal Personnel Manual to comply with this responsibility. It called for agency programs to improve "employment opportunities and community conditions that affect employability"; and urged "cooperation with community groups in the establishment and support of child day care centers needed by employees or applicants" (Douglas, 1976:25). These national policies for equal employment and affirmative action also affect all private businesses and service contractors doing business with the federal government. The Office of Federal Contract Compliance in its Revised Order #4 of 1974 states that

> in order for government contractors to meet their affirmative action obligations to the Government regarding all employees—especially minorities and women, they are to encourage child care, housing, and transportation of employees and applicants with their firms [as quoted in Douglas, 1976:26].

The wording of these guidelines is vague and it is not surprising that compliance with this mandate, within government, industry, and higher educational institutions, has been weak and no organization has been penalized for noncompliance. There is no reason to anticipate more aggressive enforcement of these guidelines in the near future.

THE PUBLIC DAY CARE TERRAIN: STATES AND LOCALITIES

State governments serve primarily as conduits for federal day care funding, reimbursing public and private organizations for rendering care. As Kamerman and Kahn describe:

> Since most federal legislation offers options for states in relation to administrative arrangements and services, and since states and local governments in turn are organized in diverse ways and relate to different voluntary agency patterns, the resulting administrative and operational arrangements defy simple description. If the term system implies uniformity and coherence, there is no general child care system in the United States [1976:62].

Several state agencies, for example the welfare, education, and public health departments, may all share responsibility for day care programs.

Only one state, California, has subsidized what could be described as a statewide day care system. After World War II, California decided to maintain its Lanham Act day care centers through state subsidies to individual school districts on a matching funds basis. Today, many of California's school districts offer full-day preschool and school-age care for children of working mothers, often from infancy to 14 years of age. The introduction of federal funds in the 1960s which are earmarked for the disadvantaged, however, has limited participation to children of the poor.

In considering the role of localities in day care, primary attention will be paid to the local school systems—the most obvious source of child care services.

THE RESPONSE OF THE PUBLIC SCHOOLS

On the whole, the response of the public schools to new needs of children has been slow and tentative. Public school systems operate on limited budgets and, until recently, in limited space. Educators have been reluctant to undertake new responsibilities outside their areas of expertise. Efforts to propose new projects for the schools have met with resistance from parents of children who would not participate, faculty, taxpayers, and other providers of services to children.

Recently, however, some schools have expanded their services to include preschool education, extended-day care of school-age children, and even day care for infants and toddlers. James Levine, in his book *Day Care and the Public Schools* (1978), has described some representative programs. These include programs operated by a school district, programs operated through parent-sponsored independent corporations, a partnership between a school district and a large nonprofit day care agency. These programs were aimed at very different populations: one project was a school-affiliated, family day care program; another provided infant care of children of teen-aged parents as well as a laboratory for high school preparenthood education. All of these examples covered district-wide programs; many individual schools also offer day care services, such as full-day Head Start, outside of a school-system approach. Levine offers some reasons suggestive of greater public school involvement:

- Schools represent the major normalizing institution for children in our society; they are available to all families regardless of income, geographical location, race or religion.
- Passage of federal legislation for the handicapped in 1976 (PL 94-142) requires schools to provide preschool and other services for handicapped children. Public schools are becoming involved with preschool programming.
- With declining enrollments, public schools have the space and the staff to cover new projects.
- The political strength of the "school lobby" is very significant. It includes such groups as the American Federation of Teachers, the National School Boards Association, the National Congress of Parents and Teachers, the National Association of State Boards of Education. Its ability to secure program funds from Washington is not to be underestimated.

THE PRIVATE DAY-CARE TERRAIN

The vast majority of children in America, about 75 percent, are cared for by individuals (either relatives or nonrelatives) in their own or another home. These arrangements include individual and small-group care. Only 10–12 percent are cared for in center-based arrangements (Woolsey, 1977:131). Other than Head Start programs and public school day care, most day care centers are private facilities. Many are run by philanthropic organizations, (churches, settlement houses, social agencies), parent cooperatives, or nonprofit institutions (hospitals and universities). Most of these centers were developed to meet a specific need—substitute care for children of working mothers. However, the high cost of satisfactory center-based care restricts the use of licensed centers to the poor (who receive federal reimbursement) and the more affluent. Also, these centers are not evenly distributed around the country; some areas have very few nonprofit day care centers. These facilities do not, in any sense, constitute a national system of care and it is unlikely that the number of private nonprofit day care centers will expand significantly in the near future. Stringent federal licensing standards require costly programs to entitle operators to federal reimbursement. Few parents can afford to pay for such care on their own, particularly in single-parent families.

Proprietary day care centers operate to make a profit. During the 1950s, such centers represented the majority of day care providers (Greenblatt, 1978:105), but very little has been written about them. Some of these programs are simply nursery schools that offer full-day care or small programs in the homes of proprietors. Such centers are independent, widely scattered, and have a tendency to be financially unstable (Greenblatt, 1978). During the 1960s, in line with the current boom of other business franchises, much attention was paid to the potential of day-care franchises as a source of profit. When day care franchises proved unprofitable, many chains were discontinued, although several still remain on the scene. Susan Stein refutes criticisms about the inherent low quality of profit-making programs involving child care:

> The general bias against profit-making child care does not seem to be founded on a comparison of quality but rather on the ideological notion that business doesn't belong in child care at all [1973:260].

Proprietary centers must struggle to balance competing priorities; that is, to make a profit, to keep costs low enough to attract participants, and to keep program quality sufficiently high to meet licensing standards and satisfy users; often the first two objectives supercede the last. Extensive expansion in the proprietary sector through public funding is not forecast, unless licensing standards are relaxed or federal subsidies increased.

DAY CARE IN INDUSTRY

Industrial day care, once widely available in European nations, has never been a factor on the American scene. During the heyday of welfare capitalism (1880–1930), a number of businesses offered day care to employees' children. During the Civil War and the two world wars, some employers opened temporary day care centers to meet worker shortages. Greenblatt (1978) refers to industrial day care in the United States as a "miniature curiosity" because of its failure to become established. Federal day care initiatives during the 1940s and '50s bypassed the corporation almost completely.

Some of the reasons given for government's unwillingness to fund corporate efforts were: the noise and pollution of factory settings, the dangers of bombings, the inconvenience of bringing children to work, and parental preferences. Possibly, the government feared losing control over these centers after the war. The government's overall objective was to sponsor temporary services which would terminate at the end of the war, when all mothers would return to the home and the job vacancies would be filled by returning servicemen. If the industrial-based centers remained open, this goal might be impeded (Rothman, 1973:21).

After the war, a number of employers sponsored their own day care centers, particularly in work settings where large numbers of women were employed (textile plants, hospitals, and telephone companies). However, the vast majority of the 150–200 employer-sponsored centers were in health, university, or other nonprofit institutions. Relatively few private companies set up programs. A 1970 survey by the Women's Bureau discovered only eleven companies providing day care. Nevertheless, when the concept of day care gained great popularity in the early 1970s as many mothers of preschoolers entered the labor force, various persons heralded industrial day care as an answer to the critical shortage of services. A significant number of journal articles, pamphlets, and books were written on industrial day care during the period 1971 to 1973, testifying to the growing interest in the issue. Actually, in spite of all the attention and enthusiasm over the potential of industrial day care, relatively few industrial projects were initiated. Most companies which did become involved with day care did not actually open centers themselves, but offered advice and start-up costs to independent sponsors. Of the handful of programs that were initiated during the late 1960s and early 1970s, many of the notable experiments (such as Whirlpool, Abt Associates, AT&T, Levi Strauss, KLH) have been terminated or transferred to different sponsors. Employers discovered that day care did not meet its intended goals; it did not reduce turnover, absenteeism, and tardiness; it did not seem to increase worker satisfaction; and many employees were either unwilling to pay the standard fee or preferred other arrangements (Levitan and Alderman, 1975:30–32). It is doubtful that industrial day care will ever become a significant factor in American day care landscape.

CONCLUSION

In the previous pages, I have briefly mapped the national day care terrain, showing that we have no national system of care providing a spectrum of alternative day care arrangements available to persons of different incomes in all local communities. What we do have has been well summarized elsewhere.

> This city, in the meantime, typifies the situation—a pluralistic, decentralized, categorical system, varied in quality and philosophy, not adequately

> serving the very young and the school-age children of working mothers . . . and running the risk of pricing out of the market the working-class users above welfare eligibility scales [Kammerman and Kahn, 1976:117].

The day care picture in America consists of fragments of service scattered over the national landscape. Significant populations such as infants and school-age children go largely ignored by national programming and other institutional day care providers. At present, I forecast limited expansion for profit-making, philanthropic, and industrial centers unless significant new sources of funding for service reimbursement appear.

It is unlikely that a national system of care will be legislated in the near future. In the first place, we lack a national purpose for day care sufficiently compelling to overcome philosophical and economic resistance to a national day care program. As yet, there is no widespread evidence that large numbers of children are unable to obtain care or are receiving poor care. That does not mean that this is not, in fact, the situation, but that it has not been well documented to date. The lack of a coherent and effective political lobby also has hurt the "children's cause" in the last few years. As Gilbert Steiner concluded after the defeat of the comprehensive child development legislation of 1971:

> Both the appearance and the apparent disappearance of comprehensive child development from the congressional agenda came abruptly. Unlike national health insurance, medical care for the aged, federal aid to education, and other compelling social issues—in which determined congressional sponsors and interest group supporters assumed that success might ultimately take a decade and that interim failures were not final—child development had a quick fling and was gone. Its legislative success in 1971 resulted, in part, from the interaction of congressional initiative and HEW bungling. Comparable opportunities for the effective use of congressional initiative in child development are not readily foreseeable, one reason that future legislative success will be harder to accomplish [1976:91].

Disputes among child development professionals and advocates over what constitutes "adequate" day care programming, sponsorship, and parent involvement has served to further confuse and diffuse persons supportive of child welfare legislation in general. A refusal to eliminate compensatory education and comprehensive child development goals from day care programming has led some advocates to insist that day care homes and centers offer *more* than substitute parental care, thus making the service extremely costly and alienating potential supporters. Suzanne Woolsey (1977) suggests that parents are, at present, receiving the type of child care they prefer; that is, informal, in-home care by relatives and nonrelatives. This type of care is not easily addressed by federal day care policy, which thus deserves its position as a secondary political issue. Other writers (Grubb, 1977; Kamerman and Kahn, 1976; and Steinfels, 1973) acknowledge a serious need for more day care options, noting the imperfections of the private day care market and the selectivity of federal subsidies. They agree, however, that one national system of care is less desirable than federal support for a variety of public and private alternatives.

My prediction is that incremental increases in federal financial subsidies (through Title XX, tax reform, and other special needs legislation) and local programming will result in substantially more formal day care options in communities throughout the United States. Many of these programs will be developed by local school districts and individual schools to serve children 3–12 years of age in response to parental demands for such services.

The public school is the one institution in our society equipped to coordinate a broad range of services to families of all incomes and in all parts of the country at the local level. There is reason to anticipate support for an expanded role for the schools from teachers and administrators, parents, and local communities who do not want to lose their schools or their jobs because of declining school enrollments. As extended day programs in existence have demonstrated, new services do not need to be a part of the standard school program. They will be contracted with other agencies; some will be parent-controlled and financed by a combination of user's fees and federal reimbursements for those with lower incomes. No national program of child care is necessary; different communities will initiate their own service package according to local need.

Depending on the vagaries of state welfare department purchase of service preferences, some expansion in the private voluntary and proprietary sector is also predicted. Ideally, agencies and schools will begin to address as yet unmet needs for (1) good infant care; (2) summer holiday and vacation care; and (3) care for sick children. In the meantime, these services will continue to be provided by private individuals through in-home and family day care, and by private summer camps.

An important issue is the future of day care under Title XX. Will the states continue to allocate a significant portion of their federal social services funds to day care? Will subsidies be extended to low and lower-middle income families so that these parents also have sufficient options of alternative service arrangements? In the long run, many parents will continue to prefer informal in-home arrangements, just as they do in countries with extensive national day care systems. However, more and more options will become available in our local communities as mothers with young children participate in the labor force in ever greater numbers, and eventually our nonsystem of care will resemble a system.

22

Family Support Systems Paychecks Can't Buy

Joyce Sullivan

The productivity crisis in the United States has focused needed attention on the interrelationship between work and home life. The family's need for more sensitivity in the workplace is not a unique concern to supporters of family life. What happens between eight and five does, indeed, influence the family, and, by the same measure, what happens at home does affect productivity at work. Work and family are fully integrated. When difficulties occur in either job or marriage, performance correspondingly deteriorates in the other. The emergence of increased dual income families and single parent families tends to magnify this relationship. As roles change and values are more clearly defined, adjustments in both family and corporate structures will become increasingly apparent.

There is growing evidence to suggest work patterns, family lifestyles and corporate policy may simultaneously formulate models designed for more optimal integration of the demands and rewards of family and the workplace for both men and women. The ultimate goal of this emerging phenomenon needs to be of mutual benefit to individuals, families and corporations. Higher levels of integration of work and family life will provide men and women greater personal and family security which should in turn provide a basis for increased levels of productivity in the job.

This paper will focus on contemporary examples of corporate and family responses to shifting roles and changing work/life values. Work in this context

Reprinted from Joyce Sullivan, "Family Support Systems Paychecks Can't Buy," *Family Relations*, vol. 30, October 1981, pp. 607-613.

will be defined as occupational employment, business or professional pursuits, financially compensated.

Until recently the American family has allowed work to shape the family lifestyle (Velle, 1973). Family residential patterns, family mobility and child-rearing responsibilities have traditionally been assigned in conjunction with the demands placed upon the family wage-earner by his/her employer. Workplace demands frequently determined where families lived, when they moved, when they ate and which members assumed the roles associated with child-rearing.

WORK/LIFE VALUE CHANGES

The rapidity of value change, coupled with the increased demand for economic security has given rise to a wide array of experimental lifestyles. The oncoming generation is less willing than their parents to pay the high cost of "total commitment" to their jobs thus risking stress disease in exchange for high wages. This value change is reinforced by the acceptance of women in the work force and by the concept of equal pay for equal work. The choice to become a two-paycheck family has been selected by approximately 25 million couples. Every year an increasing number of women join the labor market regardless of the level of their husbands' income. For the first time in history the number of two-income families outnumbers single-income families.

New yardsticks, often far removed from the size of the paycheck, are being applied to measure the validity of career decisions, such as job potential, job satisfaction, geographical location and feasibility of combining full-time work and home life. The two-paycheck family has advantages and disadvantages unlike those of the single-paycheck family. Mobility, once only a male occupational necessity, has become a major family issue of conflict for many two-career couples. Frustrations mount as more and more dually employed couples attempt to combine the multifaceted demands of family and work. Hall and Hall (1978) claim that the dual-career couple represents a "corporate time bomb" which will exert its greatest impact as these employees advance to responsible, critical positions in management.

For millions of other Americans, many of whom clearly identify with Johnny Paycheck's song, "You Can Take This Job and Shove It," satisfaction and involvement in the company are real issues. For those who find the grind of work a necessary exchange of boredom and drudgery for a weekly paycheck, negative attitudes toward work can readily spill over into family relationships.

For many young families, inflation has made staying at home to rear the family a luxury rather than a necessity based on value judgment. Dual-career couples, single parents, working women and unsatisfied workers are exerting influences on the institutional structures of family, community and the corporation. Innovative suport systems are being developed in all of these sectors.

THE CORPORATE RESPONSE

Through sheer numbers, women have become one of the most vocal influences on American business. Seventy percent of women work, not necessarily because they want to but because they must. For the first time in U.S. history, married, employed females outnumber full-time homemakers. Five and a half million working mothers of preschool children, the fastest growing segment of the labor market, have become keenly aware of the nation's need for higher quality and more affordable day care facilities. Surprisingly there are fewer licensed day care facilities available today than there were in 1945. Approximately 20% of preschool children are currently enrolled in day care programs; the remainder are cared for by relatives, friends, or private or home-care programs.

CORPORATE DAY CARE INVOLVEMENT

During the 1960's over 200 employers offered day care programs using government funds. But as these funds ran dry in the 1970's, many were forced to close the doors. Although the costs of these programs were amortized over five years, corporations often found their operation too costly and troublesome.

Large corporations such as Polaroid have recently ventured into corporate day care by providing child-care discounts for employees who utilize the Cambridge, Massachusetts Community Child Care Center. The Ford Foundation has instituted a plan where moderately paid staff members are provided vouchers for day care provisions of their choice ("Leading Two Lives," 1980). PAC International in North Carolina, recently featured on television news, operates and subsidizes a child center for employees which is open until midnight. The staff is highly qualified, highly paid and includes a company nurse. Company officials claim increased employee satisfaction, decreased absenteeism and tardiness are only a few of the benefits realized since the inception of the program. Increasing concern for productivity along with increasing demand for quality day care will most likely increase lobby activities for more company-operated child care centers at work sites.

The commitment to equal opportunity and equal pay for equal employment brings into sharp focus the complex relationship between employment practice, public intent, and family well-being. Prenatal concerns as well as support systems for child care is an issue of consideration for business as well as for families. The Pregnancy Discrimination Act of 1978 and the Extended Pregnancy Law of 1979 prevent discrimination on the basis of pregnancy and require health insurance plans to reimburse pregnancy and delivery expenses, and disability benefits on a comparable basis with other medical coverage. Some corporations have taken a further step. AT&T, for example, provides both parents with unpaid pregnancy leaves of up to six months (Pifer, Note 1).

The government offers tax credits for child care expenses and has proposed a "cafeteria benefit plan." The proposed "cafeteria benefit plan" allows the employee to have input into how fringe benefits will be allocated. A set dollar value of benefits is given to each employee, some of which is marked for fringe benefits. The remainder may be earmarked for other benefits as determined by the employee. Younger workers may choose to contribute a portion of their benefits to child care programs; older employees may choose to allocate more to a retirement program (Skalka, 1979).

EMPLOYEE ASSISTANCE PROGRAMS

Alcoholism treatment programs were originally instituted in some large corporations to help corporate officials and/or members of their families overcome this often job-related problem. The programs were cost feasible when the total cost of losing a top executive and retraining another were considered. The programs met with such a high degree of success for both employees and employers that they have now been expanded in many major corporations to include drug dependency and emotional problems. United California Bank employs human resource counselors to help employees identify personal, financial, or health-related problems, discuss alternatives and assist the employee in seeking outside counseling services ("Human Resources," 1980). United Airlines has recently instituted an Employees Assistance Program. Although difficult to assess, United conservatively estimates that alcoholism alone once cost the airline company over $27 million per year. Since the program has been launched, absenteeism and sick leave have been reduced by 70% (*Friendly Times*, Note 2).

Other corporations are attempting to organize preventive programs for employees in addition to or in lieu of rehabilitation-type programs. Corporate exercise rooms, exercise programs, diet workshops, seminars dealing with reduction of stress and anxiety are frequently offered. Annual paid health examinations, once provided only for top-level management, are now often available to many workers, especially those in stress-related occupations (Skalka, 1979). In addition to corporation concern for employees' health and physical condition, there have also been noted increases in corporate training programs for employees in the area of self-esteem, personal development and career pathing.

EXECUTIVE GYPSIES: CORPORATE ENDANGERED SPECIES

Perhaps the most devastating corporate practice imposed on executive or mid-level management personnel is the need for family relocation resulting from the "move-up-or-move-over syndrome." This practice was no doubt based upon the assumption that the corporate wife was an extension of her husband's identity. Her social role was often indirectly assigned in a set of unwritten expectations ranging from social hostess to a community witness of her husband's success and prestige. If the corporation deemed it advisable to transfer the executive, family movement was expected.

Traditional career mobility has, for men, implied the possibility of residential mobility for the family (Van Dusen & Sheldon, 1977). Numerous legal and social sanctions have arisen to reinforce this expectation. The assumption was so widely accepted as a necessary fact of life for executives and their families that, ironically, the phenomenon received very little attention in research until the 1970's.

Several researchers have traced male occupational mobility and have noted that wives have had virtually little or no impact on movement decisions. Duncan and Perrucci (1976) concluded a husband's occupational mobility has an overall deleterious effect on career-minded wives, but the employment concerns of the wife were not influential in a male's geographical mobility decision.

The shifting priorities of dual-career couples have caused a reevaluation of "executive transfer." Widening occupational horizons for women have also contributed to the "acceptability of employment" of upper middle-class women. Executive wives are no exception. Approximately one-third of the wives of corporate executives are currently employed full-time and another one-third are employed on a part-time basis. Many of these women are involved in their own businesses or in management of large corporations. It is increasingly apparent to more and more corporations that a wife with a career can drastically reduce the male executive's geographical mobility or vice versa. In the past few years many executives have chosen to limit options for geographical mobility because of the careers of their wives. Several major corporations are exercising caution about transferring employees with employed spouses, although they continue to recognize the two-career family can "create a problem in upward mobility." One representative of an international executive recruiting firm claims, "Our clients are learning that to attract many of today's brightest young executives, they've got to find career opportunities for the spouse as well" ("The New Corporate Wife," 1979, p. 94).

Other illustrations of changing corporate practices are surfacing. One oil company is currently utilizing six-months offshore assignments rather than permanent transfers in an effort to reduce the necessity of family relocation. The company flies the scientist back to the family every couple of weeks. Another company offers child care or live-in expenses incurred in managerial out-of-town business trips.

Several companies have launched the practice of job hunting or paid placement search services for the spouses of transferred executives (Hall & Hall, 1979). Rosabeth Moss Kanter, in her critical review of work and family in the United States, claimed corporations will change social aspects of their functions to a more businesslike approach in the future. For example, she predicts that out-of-town business meetings will be shorter and will not include the executive's spouse (Kanter, 1979).

FLEXITIME: ALTERNATIVE TO THE EIGHT-TO-FIVE MODEL

The topic of changing hours of work has received widespread interest. Currently 17% of the U.S. companies and 237 government agencies offer flexitime options to employees ("Leading Two Lives," 1980).

Flexitime has been incorporated into more and more of the nation's businesses and is considered to be highly successful. It is defined as a work schedule which offers, within certain boundaries, the opportunities to start and finish work at one's own time discretion, provided a fixed number of work hours per week are completed. Many corporations have discovered flexitime has increased worker productivity, increased work satisfaction and decreased tardiness. Several patterns of flexible scheduling are currently available in the United States. Some companies are experimenting with a compressed three or four day work week of 30 or more hours. For some organizations, this option is viewed as an alternative to layoffs during slow periods of production as well as an opportunity to provide employees with larger blocks of free time. Other companies have experimented with compressed work months similar to the schedules to which riverboat pilots have been accustomed. This results in 30 days of work and 30 days off work. A six-months-on, six-months-off work schedule has also been proposed for some positions and organizations.

An extension of flexitime, referred to as debit-and-credit flexitime, offers the possibility of banking hours during one period to be carried over to another period. This system reduces overtime and provides employees with flexible scheduling for family responsibilities (Glueck, 1979; Swart, 1979).

Some companies have instituted permanent part-time employment. This concept permits employees to work fewer than 40 hours per week without a set minimum number of hours. These positions offer fringe benefit packages similar to full-time work. For business, it provides a previously untapped resource of committed workers who wish to work part-time out of necessity or desire. Permanent part-time employment is becoming more attractive to two-income families as well as single heads of households. Further, it offers the older worker new career opportunities during advancing years.

Permanent part-time options can be expanded into job-sharing positions. Two persons hold one full-time job, arranging work schedules most suitable to each other. Flexibility in production demands can thus be easily covered without addition of overtime compensation. Job-sharing also provides permanent part-time workers with a potential for upward mobility, more time to devote to family responsibilities, education or personal fulfillment ("One Job," 1981).

CHANGES IN WORK SPACE AND PLACE

As the cost of transportation increases, it may be more advantageous to work out of the home or at locations other than the traditional office. Home offices would save time and energy without decreasing productivity for certain types of positions, at least on a limited basis.

A fuel-tight future may demand and produce many changes in work scheduling. Analysts predict a heavy increase in the utilization of home telephones as fuel shortages and increased fuel costs affect business and industry. The necessity of many business trips could be drastically reduced as new technology enables us to make face-to-face visitations with clients in distant cities without leaving home. According to experts of AT&T, new technology will soon enable us to connect home telephone lines with home computers and television screens ("Analysts See Americans," 1979).

THE FAMILY RESPONSE

Women who work because they have to and women who work because they want to are both seeking new avenues to provide the best of marriage and the best of job or career. Increased inflation, tighter job markets and rapidly changing roles among both groups of women continue to demand new support systems in both family and corporate structures. Women in dual income professional families, who can better afford to take financial risks than lower income groups, may well be establishing future options. Relocation is no longer a factor for males only. The highly qualified, mature woman is in top demand. Frequently it may be the woman who has the greatest career potential if she is mobile. The president of a large Dallas bank recently stated, "So great is the demand for bright career women that there is hazard in losing them after they are trained" (Kronholz, 1978).

LONG-DISTANCE MARRIAGES— A VIABLE ALTERNATIVE FOR SOME

In response to marital/career conflicts and pressures for career mobility, some contemporary marrieds have elected a lifestyle termed commuter marriage, weekend marriage, two-location marriage, married singles, dual-career variant, or long-distance marriage. Whatever the term used, this lifestyle connotes a relationship in which the spouses voluntarily live apart, maintaining separate residences in distant cities for the purpose of pursuing individual careers, while at the same time maintaining their marital relationship and family responsibilities.

Career advancement and commitment to work were viewed as major advantages by long-distance marrieds studied by Orton and Sullivan. Loneliness was the most frequently mentioned disadvantage of those engaged in the lifestyle. Although the majority of couples would overwhelmingly favor living together again if the opportunity arose, the self-gains and career advantages were seen as beneficial enough to offset the disadvantages encountered in the two-location arrangement. Some women said they actually preferred it to a one-residence lifestyle since they felt they had more time for their careers and for themselves (Orton & Sullivan, Note 3). Holmstrom (1970) suggests that as long as geographical mobility is a critical issue of employment, it would be to each spouse's advantage to choose a geographic residence independently.

ANOTHER ALTERNATIVE: ALTERNATIVE PATHS IN CAREER MODELS

During the past few years corporations have become more aware of the impact of occupational mobility on contemporary family lifestyles and have decreased the incidence of transfers among young executives. However, changes in occupational mobility patterns alone will not be a sufficient remedy to cure the problematic symptoms which modern marrieds face. Greater flexibility and wider alternatives will be demanded within the corporate and family structures to allow both women and men to combine personal family priorities within the realm of occupational responsibilities. One alternative might be a drastic change in the traditional career path.

The work ethic avenue to career success has typically been college degree entrance into a position and then on to the proving grounds. This necessitates working through many phases of the organizational structure while under constant and stringent evaluation from superiors. Achievement- and result-oriented persons recognized the constant demand for productivity and commitment if they were to "get ahead." The harder one worked, the greater the dedication to the job, the more likely one would be recognized and rewarded with advancements and promotions. These advancements, in turn, demand more responsibility, more time and energy devoted to the job and greater job pressure. The climb to the top leaves little time for family togetherness or consideration of the development of the spouse's career.

Bailyn (1979) suggests other models which may be more viable for combinations of career and family development. The apprenticeship model, for example, involves fairly long periods of continued learning and training during the early phase of career development and operates at a slower pace than the traditional career success mode. Commitment to job and involvement in the corporation increases with time on the job and age of employee. This model would have many advantages for young men and women concerned about career pathing as well as family planning.

New concerns pertaining to the role of fathering in today's society bring attention to the multifaceted demands on both wage-earners and parents with more and more couples considering the implications of having a family as well as a career. Two parents and two wage-earners do, indeed, impact on roles, values and priorities.

A culture which measures male success by the size of the paycheck leaves little room for occupational experimentation. Launching of women into higher-paying positions will ultimately reduce pressure on the male and allow for more flexible models leading to career success and fulfillment for women and men. It will provide possibilities of rotational models which permit one person in the coupleship to further career training and development while the other places concern on earning the family income. It will virtually double the opportunities for couples to accept promotions, transfers, career shifts, job changes, sabbaticals, and so forth. Corporations have already begun to change some of the traditional criteria for career success. What was once a sign of personal instability and referred to as job-hopping may now be evaluated by some business concerns as an indication of personal drive and breadth of experience (Bailyn, 1979).

THE ROLE OF THE FAMILY EDUCATOR IN THE WORKPLACE

The American society is in the process of accepting full employment of women, not only in the workplace, but in a philosophical, pragmatic and legal mind set as well. The rapid increase of married women and single parents in the labor force will continue to affect family need for sensitivity in the corporate structure. Increased employee autonomy and greater flexibility have proven to be beneficial in terms of increased productivity and job satisfaction in hundreds of companies, regardless of size or type of business, including Lincoln Electric Company, Western Electric, Metropolitan Life Insurance, TWA and McDonald's Fast-Food Restaurants (O'Toole, 1980). The need to more fully integrate work and family should become an integral part of family life education.

Professionals with backgrounds in family life education can help to bring about positive and productive change in business and industry by helping to develop sensitivity to family needs. This awareness needs to be incorporated into the policies and practices of corporations, and can best be realized through training and development programs designed to help both the individuals and organizations become the best they can be. The concepts and principles which operate to develop potential within the individual are the same as those which underlie the potential for organizational development. Family educators have the knowledge, skills and abilities to assist both individuals and organizations in the process of actualization. A recent study at Harvard University claimed that 85% of success in business is dependent upon interpersonal and communicative skills. The business environment can serve to help develop the skills which will enhance not only the work climate but the conditions needed for total living.

Humanization of the corporation will be realized when employers recognize "What is Good for General Motors is Good for the Family" (Skalka, 1979) and when employees begin to think in terms of "Thank God It's Monday" (O'Toole, 1980) rather than singing "You Can Take This Job and Shove It" (Johnny Paycheck). It is high time for employees to march to a different drum.

23

Balancing Jobs and Family Life

Halcyone H. Bohen and Anamaria Viveros-Long

For 95 percent of employed Americans, the places where they live and the places where they work are two separate worlds. Typically half-hour's travel time lies between job and home. Yet people have daily responsibilities in both settings, especially if they have children who depend upon their care.

Most of the daylight hours, most days of the week and year, the children are one place and their parents are somewhere else. Both parents of a majority of American children are employed, including almost all the fathers and half of the mothers. Depending upon their ages, children are at school, at home, in child care facilities—or in a variety of other places doing things with or without adults other than their parents.

These characteristic circumstances of work and family life in the United States in the late 1970s led to interest in the topic investigated in this study. Would giving employed adults some flexibility in scheduling their hours of work help them to function successfully in both their job and family worlds, for their own sakes and those of their children?

FEDERAL GOVERNMENT FLEXITIME

Flexitime means essentially that workers have some choice about when to begin and end work each day. Each workplace sets up its own system, but

Reprinted from Halcyone H. Bohen and Anamaria Viveros-Long, *Balancing Jobs and Family Life: Do Flexible Work Schedules Help?*, pp. 3, 16–19, 191–203.

usually there are both flexible bands—in the morning, mid-day, and afternoon—and "core" times—usually during mid-morning and mid-afternoon—when everyone must be present.

Flexitime was officially introduced in the federal government in 1974, when a manager in the Social Security Administration headquarters in Baltimore requested that the Civil Service Commission grant a waiver from Title 5 of the United States Code, which reads, "working hours must be the same each day." At that point the Civil Service Commission determined that because the law was intended to protect employees from arbitrary designation of work hours by employers, "working hours" could be interpreted to include all the hours during the day when an employee is permitted to work. Thus, the Baltimore experiment proceeded in accordance with the law; when initial evaluations showed improved morale and reduction in the use of sick time and overtime, the program was systematically expanded throughout the Social Security Administration. It was learned subsequently that as early as 1972 the Bureau of Indian Affairs (BIA) had developed essentially the same system on its own; thus, the BIA probably had the first federal flexitime program, but unofficially. By the fall of 1978, about two hundred thousand federal employees were on flexitime, that is, about 10 percent of the federal government civilian workforce.

In 1977, when we began the study, all federal flexitime programs required employees to work eight hours a day—no less and no more (except at the employer's request and at overtime pay). Thus, the version of flexitime being considered in this study allowed people simply to start or end work a couple of hours earlier or later each day. At that time most federal flexitime arrangements were *modified*, that is, employees could pick their daily starting and ending times, but had to keep to those times, with a fifteen- to thirty-minute leeway period, unless they arranged in advance for exceptions. Thus, flexitime in the federal civil service meant that people worked from whenever they started in the morning until they reached eight and a half hours a day—unless they flexed" at mid-day for longer than the thirty-minute lunch break.

Evaluations of government flexitime, like those in the private sector, reported high levels of satisfaction from employers and employees. In 1977, the General Accounting Office (GAO) surveyed thirty government organizations on flexible schedules (representing 133,000 of the 200,000 employees on flexitime). Favorable effects most often mentioned included: less tardiness (83 percent); less absenteeism, less short-term leave taken (71 percent); longer service hours for the public; and higher employee morale (86 percent) due to more job satisfaction, easier commuting, easier child care arrangements, and control of one's own time. "Improving employee morale" was the most common objective in introducing flexitime. According to the GAO, the organizations it surveyed felt that morale improved when people were "allowed more freedom to control the work situation and to assume responsibility for their own actions" (U.S. Comptroller General 1977, p. 11; Cowley, 1976).

While the Seminar was considering which work policy to select for family impact analysis, legislation was pending that would expand flexitime and part-time options to approximately five hundred thousand more federal workers in the course of three-year experiments. These new federal experimental programs also significantly expanded the concept of flexitime. The law authorized agencies to let workers choose to work either more or less than eight hours each day, as long as they averaged eighty hours each fortnight (an arrangement called *banking and borrowing of hours*). The law also authorized experiments with compressed schedules (e.g., four-day weeks). The Office of Personnel Management (formerly the Civil Service Commission) was to monitor and evaluate the impact of the experiments on (1) the efficiency of government operations; (2) mass transit facilities; (3) levels of energy consumption; (4) service to the public; (5) increased opportunities for full-time and part-time employment; and (6) families and individuals generally (U.S. Congress, HR 7814; Causey 1976,1978).

The legislation passed and was signed by President Carter in September 1978. The mandate to evaluate the effects of families of increased use of flexible work schedules resulted from an amendment to the House of Representatives bill proposed by the Family Impact Seminar, in response to a request from the Committee on Post Office and Civil Service that the Seminar comment on the pending legislation.

STUDY CONCLUSIONS AND POLICY IMPLICATIONS

Given the increasing use of flexible work schedules and the claims for their value to families, this study of federal employees on flexitime aimed: first, to contribute empirical data to policy and research on the topic; and second, to experiment with the process of conducting family impact analysis on public policies.

As stated above, the project appeared simple. A particular workplace innovation of recent years had caught the popular imagination. It seemed to please both employers and employees—and to be of benefit to people's lives beyond the workplace. Observers from many quarters enthusiastically proclaimed that flexible work schedules are good for family life.

Investigating these claims for flexitime required looking behind the cheerful consensus to find out, first, what improvements in family life people expected from flexitime—and for which family members; and second, what differences in family life, if any, there were between a group of workers on flexitime and a group on standard time. Finally, the outcomes of these two inquiries suggested questions about what additional social policies might be useful in helping people balance job and family responsibilities.

The results of this investigation challenge the predominant optimism about flexitime in five important ways:

- Analysis of the testimony in the congressional hearings on alternate work schedules revealed that various spokespersons had virtually contradictory expectations for how flexitime might help families.
- The survey data in this study revealed that the families most helped by a modest flexitime program are those with the fewest work-family conflicts, namely, those without children.
- More flexibility in work schedules, as well as other programs and policies, probably are required to help families with the most pressing work-family conflicts.
- The supplementary interviews suggest that complicated and unresolved value questions both about men's and women's roles, and about the relative importance of work and a family, underlie the ambiguous expectations for, and effects of, flexitime.
- Minor changes in the formal conditions of work (like scheduling) will not significantly affect the family variables measured in this study (like sharing of family work). More substantial structural changes, as well as shifts in values and expectations about people's participation both in work and a family must occur first.

CONTRADICTORY EXPECTATIONS FOR FLEXITIME

With respect to the hopes of how flexitime may help families, the contradictory expectations appear to have emerged in the following way. At first glance flexitime seems a logical way out of the most frequently mentioned work-family conflict, namely, between children's need for parental time and parents' need for work time. Flexitime seems to respond directly to the incongruence between children's school schedules and adult work schedules. In addition to the traditional conflicts between work and school schedules, other work conflicts—for people with or without school children—include those between the demands of the job and the needs or desires of workers for time alone; time with children, friends, spouses, and other relatives; or time in community activities, recreation, or other interests.

By age three, most American children are away from home part of the day, but usually not as long as their employed parents. If school and work schedules were better synchronized, the logistical conflicts between jobs and schools might be reduced for employed parents. Allowing parents choice in scheduling their work might allow them to coordinate their work-family responsibilities more easily—and permit them to spend more time at home.

But a few pieces of the logistical puzzle are left over. Most workdays are still several hours longer than school days. What should be done with children under age three for whom out-of-home care is not universally available? What should be done when older children are sick and cannot go to school? Or when elderly and infirm family members need attention? How can job demands and schedules accommodate all the activities related to sustaining family life that take place outside job and school hours?

As soon as these questions about family care become concrete, the notions about how flexitime will help families become elusive. Who (meaning men and women), will do what (meaning take care of dependents and household chores), and when (meaning parts of the days or years)? Where will the care take place (at home or elsewhere)? Or what will be gained (meaning satisfactions in time with children, grandparents, and domestic activities) by those who take time from employment (or leisure) to give to family work? Also, who will pay for the time spent in child rearing? Individual families or general taxation? Private or public systems? When both men and women are employed in comparable ways, in terms of hours and responsibilities, can flexible work scheduling affect how and by whom these functions are managed?

Conflicting answers to these questions emerge from the congressional hearings on alternate work schedules. In this sense, the focus on flexitime may be seen as a benign battleground for an historically novel work-family debate: should males and females have equal roles in both? Within the comfortable coalition supporting flexible work arrangements are two competing points of view about male and female roles in work and family.

The first view assumes that flexitime, and other alternate work arrangements, are useful in order to allow women to continue to bear primary responsibility for family work—with less stress. This outlook essentially expects contemporary women to embody both the female-family ideals of one era, and the male-employment ideals of another; that is, women are expected to perform both at-home family functions and at-work job functions as if neither of the other responsibilities existed. At the same time, reverse expectations do not prevail for males. They are not expected to take primary, or even equal shares of domestic responsibilities. Thus, imbalances between males and females are the expected norms.

The second view of male and female work and family roles holds that men and women should have equal employment and family opportunities and responsibilities; flexitime and other alternative work arrangements should be used by men, as well as by women, for this purpose.

What seems unique in this view, in contrast to earlier historical periods, . . . is the expectation that the labor of men and women should be interchangeable; that is, either a man or a woman should be able, and should be eligible, to do any job and any family activity (except giving birth to and nursing babies). In other words, the division of labor based on sex should fall away both at home and at work.[1] Thus, the contradictory expectations for flexitime flow directly from the competing contemporary views of appropriate male and female roles in work and family.

EMPLOYED PARENTS NEED MORE THAN FLEXITIME

The survey findings suggest that the families most helped by flexitime are those with the fewest work-family conflicts, on the basis of the following reasoning. Employed women in the sample continue to bear primary responsibility for family work, as measured by hours spent on home chores and child rearing, whether they or their husbands are on flexitime or not. Women without children have less stress if they are on flexitime; but mothers (i.e., those workers with the most job-family conflicts), with or without spouses, are equally stressed on either work schedule. Thus, the first point of view above—that women should still bear primary responsibility for family work —is sustained. But those women presumed to have the most to do—i.e., mothers—have no less stress when they have this modest flexitime option.

With respect to the second view above, men on flexitime with employed wives do not spend significantly more time on family work than those on standard time whose wives are also employed. But flexitime men whose wives are not employed do spend more time on family work than their standard time counterparts—and they feel less stress.

What can be made of these somewhat confusing trends in stress and the division of domestic responsibilities in the survey data? To those who hoped that employed parents will have less stress, will spend more time with their children, and will share family work more equally, the flexitime program examined in this study seems to have little to offer. Yet recognizing that such social changes are not likely to occur overnight (e.g., within a year of the initiation of the MarAd flexitime program), some encouragement may be found in the fact that fathers on flexitime whose wives are not employed are spending more time on home chores and with their children than their standard time counterparts (but not more time than the two-earner fathers on both schedules whose wives are employed). This trend prevails even when controlling for the fact that the standard time men work an average of two hours a week more than the flexitime group.

Thus, for three groups—fathers with unemployed wives, employed married women without children, and all single people—the MarAd flexitime program makes a measurable difference in the ease with which workers can take care of personal and family chores and activities. In short, for people without primary childcare responsibilities, a slightly greater degree of control over their time helps a lot.[2]

For those employed adults with the most family-related obligations, however (namely, single mothers and employed parents with employed spouses), the small degree of schedule latitude permitted in the MarAd program does not make a measurable difference in job-family stress, or in the amount of time workers spend on family activities—suggesting, therefore, the necessity to look further than flexitime for ways to help such families.[3]

SEX-ROLE EXPECTATIONS CREATE CONFUSION

The interviews with a small group of survey respondents and their spouses enrich and enliven the information from the survey in several important ways. Above all, they suggest that as desirable as flexible work schedules are for most people, other factors are far more influential in determining how people distribute their time and energy between jobs and family life. The most powerful influences are sex-role expectations and work expectations—both internalized and institutionalized.

Like the survey respondents at large, the interviewees had different expectations for the work and family roles of men and women. Even when career training was the same, career performance was different: women expected less of themselves in quantity and sustained quality. In turn, they were more absorbed in their family lives than their husbands. Even men who wished to be more engaged in child rearing found it difficult because of their work pressures and commitments. And men who were less work absorbed simply felt less responsibility for day-to-day home and child care—and in turn their wives did not expect it from them.

In short, cultural values about work and family roles for men and women dictated who did what, as well as what stresses were felt by whom—more than the formal work structures like flexible scheduling. For professional men and women, in particular, the current asymmetry between male and female roles in work and family, plus the heavy time requirements of each, leave enormous uncertainties about where their energies and emphases should be. Flexitime helps them to juggle the choices around the margins, but it does not help decide how to make the choices. For less work-absorbed women with family responsibilities, a little schedule leeway is a great boon in managing the logistics of daily work and family life—but these women are still left with the primary responsibility for most of the home demands.

NEW WORK POLICIES NEEDED FOR FAMILY WELL-BEING

Perhaps the major importance of the present study for policy-makers and employers is to dramatize the fact that families with the most work-family conflicts may need more accommodations to their dual sets of responsibilities than are currently available. In other words, in light of changing employment, fertility, and life expectancy patterns, even stable, middle-class, civil servant parents—like those in the study—may require more substantial changes in the structure of work than minor schedule flexibility if they are to better balance their lives both as employees and family members.

Eli Ginsberg, chairman of the National Commission for Employment Policy, has stated his sense of the changes sweepingly: "A revolution that alters the relation of one sex to the world of work will inevitably impinge on a great many social institutions and mechanisms. . . . No aspect of life will be untouched by the revolution in womanpower, and there is reason to believe that the changes will improve the lives of both sexes" (Ginzberg 1975, p. 154). Similarly, in Kamerman's stark view, failure to respond to these changes will have negative and predictable consequences for families:

> Clearly unless women are supported in their efforts at fulfilling work and family roles, one of these domains will suffer; they will perform inadquately

> at work and remain (if at all) in low wage, low status positions; they will have fewer children, or none; they will have children but be inadequate as mothers; family crises will occur with frequency.
>
> Kamerman 1978, p. 35

The popularity of flexitime results, in part, from the fact that it seems to be an easy structural solution to the strains produced by rapid social changes. But its very simplicity obfuscates the competing hopes for what it can accomplish. On the one hand, flexitime is agreeable because it costs very little and changes very little about what employers can expect by way of a day's work from employees—while apparently making people more cheerful about what they get paid to do.

On the other hand, for those who want to alter the traditions which make it difficult to combine "paid work" and "family work," the concept of self-determined working hours seems a step towards a multitude of far-reaching changes in the structure of work. But on the basis of the findings in this survey, modest versions of flexitime alone—like that in the Maritime Administration—cannot be considered significant changes in the existing organization of work, that is, in terms of their impact on work-family conflicts. The complexities of the social, economic, and demographic changes that now encourage men and women to have comparable work roles throughout their child-rearing years require policy responses far beyond flexitime—if the goals for families with children are, in part, those held out for flexitime, namely, to reduce parental job-family stress, to enable parents to spend more time with their children, and to increase equity between males and females in paid work and family work. What other policies might help? At least two levels of change can be discussed: expansion of existing programs and large-scale economic and land-use changes.

Expansion of Existing Programs. Those which are already in use and could be used more widely in the United States include:

- Parental work-leave policies. In Sweden parents may divide nine months of leave after the birth of a baby. Either parent may stay home with the infant. France and Norway also have national parental leave policies.
- More flexible work schedules and flexiplace. New United States federal flexitime legislation allows people to average eighty hours every two weeks, with more or less than eight hours daily, as they wish (within strictures of agencies who have made use of the new law). Some businesses now allow mothers on maternity leave to work at home, as far as possible in terms of their assignments (Kronholz 1978). Sabbatical leaves are being conceived in terms of redistributing time to education, leisure, family work and paid work over the life cycle (e.g., Best and Stern 1977; Strober 1976).

- Shorter work days for parents (i.e., variations on part-time). Parents may now work six-hour days in Sweden until their youngest child is eight years old, with less pay than for eight-hour days but without jeopardy to their jobs (Ministry of Health and Social Affairs 1977).
- Increased pre-primary school programs and more after school programs. More programs for children from age two to three through age five are desired and in use in some places, for example, in Belgium and France. Expansion of such programs will gradually do away with the artificial historical dichotomy between day care programs and pre-primary care, and will acknowledge the interest of most parents in having their children have some group experience from ages three to five (Kamerman 1980; Kamerman and Kahn 1979, 1980).
- Parental insurance (instead of maternity benefits). Swedish parents may divide between them an entitlement to stay home from work for child rearing, either as an absence of two to four hours per day, or for a period corresponding to three months of full-time absence from work at any time up until the child is eight years of age. They will be paid at 90 percent their actual income for two of the three months (Ministry of Health and Social Affairs 1977).

Economic and Land-Use Changes. More utopian and costly efforts to respond to work-family conflicts might include attempts to reduce the major physical separations between work areas and living areas that now characterize American city and suburban life. Energy shortages may already be encouraging families to try to live closer to their workplaces. But without larger upheavals in existing job, housing, and school patterns, the physical and temporal distances between family life and work life cannot be substantially reduced for many Americans. But perhaps, as suggested by Myrdal and Klein (1956), policymakers should increase their efforts to reverse the trends that have functionally divided huge metropolitan areas.

VALUE CHANGES NEEDED FOR BETTER WORK-FAMILY BALANCE

Even if policies and programs like those suggested above are legislated, they will not alleviate work-family conflicts unless they are accompanied by shifts in values about the appropriate connections between work and family life, as well. Kanter's list of the five dimensions of work experience that have bearing on family relations . . . suggest areas in which prevailing values may have to change in order to mitigate work-family conflicts.

For example, flexibility in job schedules will increase time in family work only if people have jobs in which they can earn enough to support their families without excessive overtime; if the jobs are challenging and fulfilling; and if they choose to spend some of the non-work time in family life. Excessive work hours will be reduced for committed professionals only if their criteria and rewards for successful lives are non synonymous with long work hours.

More equal sharing of family work between spouses will occur only if expectations about sex role divisions of paid labor and home labor are altered.

Demographic and economic factors are also likely to influence each of the above. For example, as people have fewer children and longer work lives, more time with the children may seem more desirable. As women share more of the economic support of families, and men are encouraged to value their family time more, men may feel less compelled to be absorbed in work. And as women's lives are challenged and diversified by participation in the labor force, they may have greater pleasure and success in their parenting.

To conclude, as this study does, that flexible work schedules of the sort examined in this research cannot alone make significant differences in the work-family conflicts of employed parents is not to discount the potential importance of an innovation like flexible schedules. On the contrary, unlike the more economically and politically difficult programs and policies suggested above, flexitime is being used—and being expanded conceptually—as in the new experiments for federal workers authorized by the September 1978 legislation. Flexitime may be an important first step towards altering the traditions in which work roles and work organizations have been defined and structured as if the family did not exist, as the Rapoports and their co-authors put it,

> except in the background, after hours and compliant to the primacy of the work role . . . What is needed is a more open-minded, innovative approach to the problem of the structure of work. . . . It is difficult for individuals or families to change a work situation. Though many . . . may wish to accommodate family interests, they may also feel uncomfortable or insecure about being the one to be pushing for change. . . . At present, a frequent situation is one in which husbands indicate a readiness to be "fair" about taking domestic responsibilities but feel reluctant to ask employers for latitude to do so for fear of losing ground in the competitive situation of the job. . . . The idea that workers should be primarily responsive to the job is so ingrained that it is impossible for many employers to envision change. There may, therefore, be an actual collusion between employers and employees to see any alteration of the status quo as out of the question.
>
> Rapoport et al. 1976, p. 178

Pleck also sees the problems of contemporary families as extending beyond individuals and requiring institutional and value changes:

> It does not seem possible for large numbers of families to function with *both* partners following the traditional male work model. Such a pattern could become wide-spread only if fertility dropped significantly further or if household work and child care services became inexpensive, widely available, and socially acceptable on a scale hitherto unknown. In the absence of such developments, greater equality in the sharing of work and family roles by women and men will ultimately require the development of a new model of the work role and new model for the boundary between work and the family which gives higher priority to family needs.
>
> Pleck 1977, p. 425

24

Societal Learning

Sheila B. Kamerman and Alfred J. Kahn

The question of how adults are going to manage work and family responsibilities emerged as an increasingly important issue in the 1970s, as more industrialized countries experienced a rapid growth in the number and proportion of women—especially young married women with children—entering the labor force. Those countries in which such behavior characterizes more than half the mothers of young children (and far more than half the women of childbearing age) have already selected some form of policy—or policies—in response to this development. Other countries which have yet to reach such a high level of female labor force participation may not have made a deliberate policy choice yet; however, it would appear that given the nature of current trends, pressure to make some explicit decisions will increase over the next five years.

This growth in labor force participation rates of married women with young children has served to highlight the tension between work and family life as a fundamental problem for industrialized countries. The conflict between work and family could be masked, and the tension between the two domains managed, as long as one parent was prepared to devote full time to unpaid work at home. But that situation has changed.

The rapid growth of sole-parent, female-headed families in several countries during the late 1960s and 1970s brought with it indications of work-family tensions as a problem for at least this kind of family. However, this could be

Reprinted from Sheila B. Kamerman and Alfred J. Kahn, "Societal Learning," Chapter 6 in *Child Care, Family Benefits and Working Parents*, pp. 244–263.

interpreted as merely one more problem for single mothers, who clearly were a minority in the population in all countries and who were often viewed as a deviant group that should perhaps be expected to carry an extra burden. Moreover, the problem could be viewed as possibly containable (at least in those societies committed to a basic minimum living standard) by provision of a relatively low-level cash benefit to such families. Women, at best, could not be expected to earn as much as men in the marketplace and it would be cheaper to support them at home than to pay for a high-quality child care service. This view could be sustained especially for the many single mothers who were poorly educated and unskilled.

Once the work-family relationship became an issue for most two-parent families, however, a very different picture emerged. The two-paycheck family is already dominant in five of the six countries we have discussed. Today, women work for the same reasons that men work: for economic reasons primarily, but also for nonpecuniary reasons. Even though in most countries median female wages are still only 60 to 65 percent of median male wages (for full-time work, all year round) and the average working woman contributes only about 26 percent of family income (one-third of all working women work part time and thus earn a low wage), the percentage of women making this contribution to family income has expanded phenomenally during the past decade. Furthermore the percentage making a far higher contribution to family income has increased significantly also.[1] Nor is the pattern likely to be reversed. Indeed, the contrary is likely to be true. Temporary economic dislocation and rising unemployment may only serve to confirm families in their conviction of the necessity for two earners in a family.

Regardless of the reasons why specific, individual married women have entered and remain in the labor force, an immediate consequence is that the tension and potential conflict between work and family life has become more visible and more universal.

Thus far, we have described and analyzed the policies and programs through which each of our countries addresses or fails to address this new situation. We turn now, in our final chapter, to the question of *what can be learned* from the country experiences: Can we identify the components of an optimum policy? Is there a policy choice that, in the context of current realities, would appear to be good for children, women, men, families, and the society at large? What, if anything, can be recommended?

What follows seeks to be immediately relevant to all those countries that have yet to make a commitment but that, clearly, will soon have to deal with this issue, such as the FRG, the United Kingdom, and the United States. The review may also have meaning for still other countries, whether or not covered by this study, that may wish to make some mid-course corrections.

As noted, we launched our study with the assumption that the problem we were dealing with was a problem for women and children, primarily, and only individually a problem for men. Moreover, we assumed that the policy choices were relatively clear-cut. Thus, countries either wanted women in the labor force or wanted them home. Countries that wanted to facilitate female labor force participation would provide extensive out-of-home child care services, while countries that wanted women out of the labor force (and at home bearing and rearing children) would provide equally extensive cash benefits.

We discovered, as the study progressed, two things of significance: First, the fundamental problem goes well beyond the concerns of women or of women and children. It is more than a problem of changing sex roles, even when broadly defined. Instead, the most appropriate definition of the problem is that of the tension between work and family life for all adults who expect to—or want to—bear and rear children and for societies which, if they are to survive, need children.

The policy response cannot be simplistic, even if societies begin with concern only for working mothers. Whether or not women should be in the labor force is not a subject for a simple, clear-cut, unidimensional policy strategy. Actually, countries have multiple goals, and these goals may be inconsistent at the same time or over time. The ultimate policy choice a country makes represents a compromise—an amalgam of responses to complex and diverse factors within the context of distinctive historical and ideological elements. For example, a country may need women in the labor force but also want to be sure that they have children; a country may want to make it easier to rear children, but not be prepared to provide an alternative to earned income to more than a relatively small group; a country may have changing needs for an expanding labor force and therefore changing incentives for attracting women who have previously not been in the labor force; a country may recognize that highly educated, high wage-earning women will not remain out of the labor force for long, regardless of the policy system's preferences; a country may want to attract women into the labor force but not be able to expand child care services rapidly enough to meet the demand and, therefore, may be concerned about the consequences of inadequate provisions for children. And a country may value flexibility and diversity whatever its labor market or population trends.

Clearly, labor market and population concerns have been and continue to be paramount in the choice of responses. Influencing how these concerns become implemented in a specific explicit or implicit policy choice are the economic resources of the country; the need and degree of conscious desire to protect the quantity of future generations; the value placed on male and female equality; what child care already exists within the country; the relative emphasis on options and choices; the comfort with government action; and the time and authority it takes to initiate and implement major policy changes.

Thus, policy choice seems to balance labor market against population objectives, in a context of history, ideology, and existing resources. The issue for the future will be: What combination of which benefits and which services can best fulfill a country's objectives?

So far, the result, in each case, has been the visible emergence of what we have called a benefit-service policy package—a package that includes both cash and in-kind benefits to provide income, on the one hand, and out-of-home child care services, on the other. In other words, although the balance may vary, the policy choice is not cash *or* services but rather some combination of both. The issue is not whether to establish more services and provide less in the way of benefits, or vice versa, but rather, what should the particular mix be, and what is the best selection of benefits *and* services to assure the optimum mix. Such a combination or package may represent alternative options for *different groups within the same country* or, perhaps of equal importance, may represent a decision regarding the optimal policy choice for most women—or adults—*at different stages* in their own life cycles or at different points in historical time. The ultimate question then becomes: How much cash, for whom, for how long a period of time, under what circumstances, and how much child care services, of what types, for which children, under what circumstances, and how financed?

In reviewing current trends in all our countries, we would note in brief:

- The GDR is expanding benefits steadily, and expanding services—the former priority—somewhat slowly now, but steadily.
- Hungary is expanding services, albeit at a moderate pace.
- France is expanding benefits for low-income women and services for all.
- Sweden is expanding services as rapidly as it can, and discussing new benefits.
- The FRG is debating expansion of benefits still further, and experimenting with services.
- The United States is beginning to notice the issue.

Four of the countries studied have already made more or less major commitments and are now making some modifications or filling in gaps. The FRG has not shaped a definitive policy yet. Other countries, like the United States, have made no explicit policy choice either, and still assume the equitable functioning of the "invisible hand" of the economic and political marketplace. Under the latter circumstances, some women who want to have children and who have income which permits them to remain at home, do so. Others work and pay whatever the market price may be for care of varying—and often unknown—quality. Still others either work and do not have children, or they attempt both and "manage," often at serious cost to themselves—and their children, husbands, families. The choice is up to the individual. The consequences are borne by all the individuals involved as well as by the society at large. The consequences for society, thus far, are too rarely noted.

It is difficult to believe that the United States, which ranks low or last on much child care provision and in all family social benefits, can continue to ignore the consequences. The social and labor force trends we identified initially have continued. As of March, 1979, over 62 percent of the mothers of school-aged children, over 52 percent of the mothers of children aged three to five, and 41 percent of the mothers of children under the age of three, were in the labor force, and most worked full time. The labor force participation rate for U.S. women with children under the age of three increased more than 11 percent between 1977 and 1978, continuing the trend for these women to enter the labor force at a more rapid rate than any other group. Thus, these U.S. women, like women in many other countries, are increasingly trying to "manage" both having children and working. The policy-making system is challenged to respond in some way to the strain created for working mothers, their families, and their children.

RELEVANT TO CHOICES

What, then, have we learned from this study? Is there any clear societal learning as to an appropriate response to the work and family problem in a modern industrial society?

First, a summary of some of the specifics we have noted thus far, some of it assembled in this research, some reported by other researchers:

- Adult women—married or single, with or without children—are increasingly entering the labor force, with the greatest increase among married women with young children.
- Adult males—married, with young children—have for some time had the highest rate of labor force participation of all adults.
- There is some correlation between the extensiveness of out-of-home child care service and the rate of female labor force participation, but it is unclear which comes first.
- There is some correlation between low birth rates and high female labor force participation, but here, too, causality may run both ways.
- Although there may be some correlation between the growth in female labor force participation and the increase in divorce rates, the latter trend seems to be leveling off.[2]
- There is no evidence that children develop inadequately as a consequence of their mother's working or as a consequence of their experience in group care.
- There is some evidence that children develop *better* when their mothers work.[3]
- There is some evidence that women who are at home alone, with very young children, may become depressed.[4]
- There is clear evidence that women's wages and occupational progress —and male-female equality—are impeded by encouraging women to leave the labor force for an extended period of time.
- There is clear evidence that in-home child care will be less and less available over time—and indeed, this decrease in availability has been noticeable for some years.

- There is some evidence that family day care, long-term, is not a "cheap" child care option. As more women enter the labor force, while those who remain at home view care for others' children as a job, the latter come to expect equivalent wages and benefits.
- There is no evidence to suggest that women who try to manage both work and child rearing suffer negative consequences (or that their children or families do). But the history of this behavior is quite recent, and common sense suggests that as child care by relatives and informal child care becomes more difficult to obtain, the strain for those who cannot afford market care will increase—as will the strain for those who select care which they view as unsatisfactory but choose because they have no other option.
- There is some evidence to indicate that the husbands of working mothers contribute more in the way of time and labor to household, family, and child-related tasks than do men with full-time "at-home" wives.[5]
- There is general consensus (among more than just the countries included in this study) that it is better for the physical and emotional well-being of mother and child if women are able to remain at home for a brief time before childbirth and for a more extended period of time following childbirth, without the family suffering an income loss as a consequence.
- There is growing consensus that fathers can and should play a significant role in their children's development, even when children are very young.
- There is no evidence to suggest that most countries are prepared to provide a substitute for earned income to an adult who is healthy and employable for more than a relatively brief period of time—except when there are no jobs.
- There is growing consensus that any policy that provides income as a replacement for earnings while mothers remain at home to care for children should be designed in such a way as to avoid undue penalties for women in their work and family lives.
- There is general consensus that it is better for the overall development of children if there is available to them, after a certain age (the age is debated), a group experience with other children, for at least some portion of the day, if their parents wish it, regardless of whether their mothers work. (The consensus is that children are certainly deprived if such experiences are not available by the time a child is three. The debate focuses on which younger age is the most appropriate and beneficial for beginning a group experience for children). There is a growing trend in several countries to begin such care at age two or two-and-one-half.

SHAPING A FRAMEWORK

How does one put all this together? What are appropriate assumptions, basic values, which may be shaped into a policy framework?

Our first premise in choosing among the possible policy components is that the debate regarding whether or not women *should* work is over. Women are working, in growing numbers. The time when women remained at home, first for childbearing and rearing, and then in full-time leisure, has ended—or will end soon—for most women. This pattern, never complete, and concentrated among the more affluent, had a relatively brief history—about 100 to 125 years or so. Nineteenth- and early twentieth-century women had shorter life spans, longer periods of childbearing and rearing, and larger numbers of children. The present-day life cycle, in which women have a first child while in their mid-twenties and a second and last child by the age of thirty, means that the period of intensive child care demands is limited to a relatively few years. There is now a very long time between a woman's child rearing years and her death—even between the departure of all her children from the home and her own social insurance entitlement.

Women thus work for personal as well as financial reasons. Moreover, in several countries, women with one child are even more likely to work than women with no children. Only the presence of three or more children is likely to inhibit labor force participation of mothers, and this family size is increasingly rare in all industrialized countries.

In the predictable future, work is likely to continue to be a central part of the personal identity and life experiences of all adults. The prime labor force in all these countries is increasingly comprised of married adults with children. Although some adults will continue to choose traditional role models—one "at home" and one "at work" (and they should be able to do so)—it is likely that the number of people who choose this will become smaller and smaller. In any case, the society does not owe an equal standard of living to the families that prefer to trade the home contributions of one partner against income from work. Thus, any policy choice must be premised on the likelihood of labor force participation for most adults, regardless of sex.

For industrialized countries generally, the range of choice is certainly restricted. Women represent about 40 percent or more of the labor force among the Western European countries, and the only potential source of additional labor unless foreign workers are imported. In contrast to the 1960s, when young entrants—in addition to married women—flooded the labor market (and an astonishingly large number were absorbed despite the high rates of young unemployment), the 1980s (because of demographic trends) will see a significant decline in the numbers of young people entering the labor market. The likelihood is that many countries will experience a labor shortage by the mid-1980s, and female labor will be an increasingly important resource. Thus policy choice can be premised on the need for female labor by the society unless the unlikely choice is made of a slowdown in economic growth (beyond what may occur in the energy crisis).

A third and fundamental assumption is that whatever choice is made must ensure the well-being of children as well as their parents, men as well as women, the society as a whole as well as individual families. Indeed, much of the discussion of the need for a new policy perspective is predicated on the belief that what now exists in many countries is either "bad," or "not good enough," for children, parents, and society.

Clearly, any concern with adequate family income, and thus an adequate standard of living for children, highlights the significance of female earnings and points to the need for more equality of opportunity for women in the labor market. Inevitably, such an objective leads to more attention to provision of child care services. We are convinced, however, that providing child care merely to facilitate reentry of women into the labor force (for whatever reason) would be an error. In other words, neither labor market policy nor policy for women's interests should be the sole determinant of family policy.

We would argue rather that the well-being of children, parents, and society is not a "zero sum" game in which improving the situation of one always results in worsening the conditions of the other. What is "good" for women may not always be good for children, but certainly what is "bad" for children cannot be good for their mothers or fathers, and vice versa.

What assumptions, therefore, regarding what is good for children must underlie any ultimate policy choice?

With the decline in family size in recent years, children have much less opportunity for sibling relationships, peer group experiences, and the essential socializing activities with other children, such as existed earlier. The opportunity to be with other children in a group becomes an important developmental experience for children who are increasingly likely to be isolated at home, regardless of whether a parent works or not. Similarly, in homes in neighborhoods in which fewer and fewer adults are present during the day, preschool programs offer an important exposure to a variety of adults in a consistent and supportive manner, while providing relief from the intensity of a restrictive, all-encompassing relationship which previously did not characterize the family, but now often does.

The world as once known (let alone imagined) has changed, as have neighborhoods and families. Even for families with a parent at home the experience is very different for children growing up today. Increasingly, the young child kept at home may be a deprived child in relation to his fellows, just as the eight- or nine-year-old would be if he or she were kept at home instead of attending school.

Thus, we are convinced that it is appropriate for policy (1) to attempt to ensure good care for children when they are cared for outside the home (and not to undertake as a societal obligation the responsibility to maintain a parent at home for an extended period of time); and (2) to search for ways to maintain an appropriate balance between family and home, on the one hand, and child care services, for part of the day, on the other. It is also our belief that children can benefit far more from having the care and attention of both parents (when two parents are available) for some portion of the day than from living their days with one parent primarily.

Although the precise best age for benefiting from a group experience may still be debated, there is a high degree of consensus that such experiences are valuable even for the very young child.

The argument with regard to men seems clear-cut. We begin with the assumption that more gender equality is better than less and that many men believe this, too. Most married men are sufficiently rational to appreciate the economic contribution of their working wives—and the intrafamily "unemployment insurance" that results from having a second paycheck to fall back on in emergencies. We also are convinced that many men would enjoy the opportunity to be more active fathers, not just financial contributors, and would respond in particular to changes in the society that would make a more active family role possible, especially if the explicit values of the society supported such a role.

Thus, our ultimate policy choice must be one that (1) enhances opportunities for children to develop well; (2) expands opportunities for men to be more active at home, in the family, as fathers; and (3) increases opportunities for women to participate more fully in the labor force and the society at large, while attenuating the stress of having to carry full responsibility for home and family at the same time.

Underlying all this, of course, is an assumption regarding the need for children in all industrialized countries. Almost all of Europe is experiencing the consequences of declining birth rate. Any further decline would serve only to generate a still greater demographic panic. Some countries already show evidence of such anxiety, and it is highly likely that others will too, whether for labor market, consumer market, tax base, or nationalist reasons. Thus policy choice must be premised, also, on the need for children to be born (and well cared for) even as adults are increasingly likely to be in the labor force.

We turn now to the question of how to select among the benefits and services, not only the appropriate mix, but the preferred components within the cluster of benefits and services that make up our package. We have already described and analyzed the existing array of benefits and services in each country, and indicated something of the advantages and disadvantages—the costs and benefits—of choosing among these. We do not intend to repeat here what has already been said earlier. Instead, to summarize, a desirable child care benefit-service package would:

- Make it possible for all adults to participate in the labor market, not only in a search for a lifestyle pattern that could ensure an improved standard of living for families without concomitant negative consequences for children, but as part of a lifestyle in which children and adults would be provided with greater opportunities for individual and family development and satisfaction
- Expand the possibilities for men to participate in home and family life, for women to participate in the labor market, and for all family mem-

bers—adults and children—to participate in the community and society in which they live
- Increase the value placed on children, childbearing, and child care in the society at large
- Ensure some equity in the treatment accorded different types of families

We may now present our suggested model of a child care benefit-service package . . .

THE CHILD CARE POLICY BENEFIT-SERVICE PACKAGE

THE BENEFIT COMPONENTS

If we have described the realities accurately and if the goals outlined are shared, they argue for a policy approach whose core component would involve: (1) entitlement to a leave from work at the time of childbirth or adoption; (2) a cash benefit providing short-term temporary replacement for earned income during that leave; and (3) eligibility for the benefit to cover either parent. More specifically, our recommended benefit component would be something akin to the Swedish Parent Insurance benefit. Such a benefit should:

- Guarantee the right to a leave from work covering a period of not less than six months at the time of childbirth or adoption, including the right to take up to six weeks before expected parturition, and not more than one year at such time
- Assure job protection, seniority, and the continuity of pension and social insurance entitlements, as well as other employee benefits, throughout this period
- Provide a cash benefit for the period of entitlement at the level of full wage replacement, for the equivalent of any wage up to and including the wage covered under social insurance
- Be defined as the equivalent of earned income and, therefore, taxable at whatever the rate is in a country for personal earned income
- Include an option to prorate the childbirth-related portion over a longer period of time to cover a shorter work day (half- or three-quarter time for those who would prefer this pattern)
- Guarantee the right of employees to a specified number of days each year to permit a parent to remain at home if a child is ill, without loss of income
- Be financed in a manner consistent with the way in which health and unemployment insurance financing are carried out in the given countries

Such a benefit would protect maternal and child health as well as family income; encourage fathers to play a more active role in parenting while assuring mothers of sufficient time to do so even when in the labor force; usually provide an incentive for women to enter the labor force early while providing a disincentive for extended labor force withdrawal by either parent; minimize the possibility of concomitant labor market stigma falling on women exclusively or especially; avoid contributing to increased income disparity among families while protecting against excessive horizontal inequities among different family types; and, finally, be within the realm of economic and political feasibility in all industrialized countries.

Virtually all major industrial countries have maternity benefit programs, some generous and some modest.[6] The United States has no statutory entitlement. An updated program along these lines becomes the cornerstone of any response to the question of child rearing and child care. It assures a good start for parenting and for child growth, with both parents able to participate, and in a financially viable way. It represents social endorsement of parenting, yet it is not so extensive as to create negative consequences for women who want to continue work, and it does not create financial incentives to stay away so long as to lose the continuity of the workplace attachment. It treats women and men equally and equitably.

THE CHILD CARE SERVICE COMPONENTS

The central component here would be the establishment of publicly subsidized child care services for all children under compulsory school age whose parents wish them to participate:

- Provided as a separate program or under the aegis of the public education authorities, or perhaps (for children under two or two-and-one-half and for family day care) social service authorities
- With priorities set (until there is sufficient provision) so as to favor the children of working parents (one-parent or two-parent families) and children with other special needs
- Free as in elementary school, or with subsidized but income-related fees, varying with country practice
- Covering the normal work day, but with some children staying shorter periods of time as needed and preferred
- With some options among sibling and age-segregated groups and with whatever are the prevailing options for group size and staffing patterns and qualifications
- Including support of licensed, trained, and supervised family day care programs, in which the family day care mothers receive wages and fringe benefits comparable to similar staff in center or group programs, to serve some children from about the age of six months to two to

two-and-one-half years, and older children with special needs. Here, parental preferences still vary. Moreover, time and resource constraints may require the use of family day care until sufficient space is available in group facilities. Thus, the principle would be to ensure good quality family day care for those who use it out of preference or because of temporary expediency. Or, if the costs can be met and it is preferred, it could remain within the programming repertoire, better integrated with group programs. Indeed, it is quite likely that some family day care will always be needed, whatever the cost, not so much for the parents who prefer the informality, flexibility, intimacy, and intensity of a one to one relationship (since if the quality is high it would be an extremely expensive form of care) but for children with special needs.

To the extent that there continues to be separation between preschool (from ages two-and-one-half or three to age five), on the one hand, and day care (ages six to nine months to two-and-one-half or three), the respective programs may be based in different systems, such as education (a *separate* department) and personal social services. Of course, there are models for one integrated free-standing system, as in Sweden, and other patterns may be invented to meet special country circumstances. What is needed is a child development orientation and a programming pattern attuned to the degree of age integration or age segregation which is preferred.

A CONCLUDING NOTE

SOME QUESTIONS

The kind of policy package we are recommending and the premises on which it is based inevitably raise questions. We have already commented on the most obvious of these insofar as our study sheds light on them:

- The trend for women to work and the value of their working
- The consequences of women working
- The effects—the costs and benefits—of out-of-home care for children
- The impact of various cash benefits on family income
- The consequences of any of these policies for fertility or for labor market behavior
- The factors influencing differential policy choice

Data are limited and knowledge is incomplete. Clearly, many questions remain unanswered, including exactly why countries did more in different directions initially (although it is easier to explain why policy choice seems to be converging in many ways today). Precise cost estimates of specific policy options cannot yet be made, although it seems clear that monetary costs alone have not been determining factors in the policy choice of individual countries.

Inevitably, however, in reviewing our conclusions and recommendations, other questions emerge. Some were raised by individuals who had an early opportunity to learn of our study and to review study findings.

1. *Why should society substitute paid work in a new "female" industry, child care, for unpaid work in another female "industry," at home?*

We would doubt that an expanded program of child care services would create a *new* female industry. However, it might be a substitute for a declining, but much lower status, lower skilled and lower paid female industry, namely, domestic service. Indeed, we would guess that jobs in an expanded child care service program would represent a higher status position for many women. Those who took on such work would be assured of some economic rewards and related status, but could also be provided opportunities for training and upgrading. Such a development might also serve to upgrade the existing nursery or day care center or child care service worker, too, who continues to be paid at a much lower level (with much less regard) than a preschool teacher (who in turn is of lower status than primary school teachers and so on up the ladder).

Despite this, we would urge continued attention to societal values about child care and child rearing, and encourage the entry of young men as well as women to this work. From the point of view of child development, increased participation of men in child care services would be almost as important as increased participation of fathers in the at-home care of their children. Certainly, any child care expansion plans must include attention to this matter. Some progress has been made in recruiting young men to work in elementary schools in some countries, and there are beginnings in child care.

2. *By making it easier for two-earner families to manage home and work responsibilities, are we not encouraging women with high earnings potential to work? Would not this add further to income inequities between educated/skilled and uneducated/unskilled women—and between one- and two-parent families?*

We recognize the potential problem here. Our concern is to protect the adequacy of family income where there is only one wage-earner, without offering an incentive for labor force withdrawal, on the one hand, and without creating undue stress for a sole parent who is coping with work and family on the other. Ultimately this issue must lead to further study of alternative policies for providing income to families with children. (Indeed such a study, codirected by us, funded by the Social Security Administration, DHHS, is a natural outgrowth of the work reported here. The study is expected to be completed in 1981.) It is our assumption here that all adults will probably be in the labor force. Where there is a sole parent, the need may be to supplement earnings as well as to attenuate the work-family conflict. Where two-parent families are concerned, some may choose a lower income and a lower standard of living for a period of time in order to permit one or the other to withdraw from the labor force. Such withdrawal might be for reasons of child care, but it might also be because of a desire to continue formal education, to return for retraining or a different kind of education, or for some other reason. Some assurance of adequate income for families with children is essential regardless, but the assumption is that except for relatively brief periods, most adults will work.

3. *Why develop a policy package premised on having more women in the labor force when, clearly, unemployment is on the increase—both because the economy is contracting and because technological advances will eliminate jobs?*

The technological "bogey man" has been announced before, yet despite the enormous advances in automation during the 1960s, more women entered the labor force, and the labor force grew everywhere. Although technology may eliminate some jobs, it may also create new jobs. Moreover, most of the jobs which have been eliminated are in the production of goods, not in the industries involved in the delivery of services, where most women work. Women were affected far less than men in the 1973–74 recession in the United States. Assuming that we may face a much more severe recession, we might hypothesize that even if women are affected, the existence of a wife's wages in the face of a husband's unemployment may make female contributions to family income even more important to some families. Regardless, the likelihood is that service jobs will continue to grow in availability for women. Long term, the question will be whether more women can move into the male-dominated occupations, not whether women will be in the labor force.

4. *Given the existing resource limitations, how can such a policy package be paid for?*

Here our assumption is that countries are constantly making choices with regard to policies and programs. If the demand is large enough, a constituency for such a policy package will emerge and press for a response. Given the demographic pattern of the coming decade in the United States, with the "baby boom" at the peak of its childbearing, child rearing, and employment responsibilities, such demand could reach significant proportions. Even if economic constraints persist, the choice could be to move toward a shorter work day and week rather than to press for higher wages or to accept higher unemployment. This is a generation that for some time now has shown a preference for an improved quality of life. U.S. taxes do not yet approach those of most major industrial societies in Europe. But all countries can and will decide what is important enough to afford and what is not, and whether the obviously necessary constraints on spending should affect one domain or another.

5. *If the ultimate objective of the proposed benefit-services package is to facilitate the management of work and family life simultaneously, without undue stress for adults or children, while assuring adequate family income for*

families in which there is only one wage-earner—how will the society support the decline in productivity of the work force?

This is really a different aspect of the earlier question, just answered. If there are advances in technology, there may be a concomitant offset in raised productivity. If, on the other hand, this does not occur, the cost of a decline in productivity may be viewed as being offset by an improved quality of life. The productivity argument is not new. It has been posed every time proposals have been made to shorten the work day or week. One could argue either the compensatory increased benefits, or the likelihood of technological advances, as offsetting this. Here, as in other areas, value choices must be made. Our basic view is that the contributions here discussed to child socialization, family life, and gender equality justify a claim on resources but will not necessarily decrease productivity overall: they will or could be offset by more work by mothers, more productivity by working mothers in the labor force more continuously, and even an end to the birth rate decline!

THE LARGER VIEW

We end by noting that the evidence provided by the countries themselves underscores the need for a larger perspective than we have proposed thus far—a perspective that goes beyond the research here reported. We began by identifying a child care and working woman issue and suggested at the outset that what was really being discussed was a family policy issue in which the policy choice must be directed at the question of how all adults—men and women—can achieve fully equal status in society. In other words, how can all adults be productive both at work and at home? How can they be in the labor force and be able to marry and have children, too? Thus, our first finding of significance was that this problem we addressed went beyond the care of the very young child, under age three, to the larger question of how work and family life are to be related to one another and what the role of government should be in facilitating a closer relationship between the two domains, and in assuring broader support for family life as it is increasingly experienced in industrialized societies.

We noted subsequently that all countries other than the United States already provide income supplementation to families regardless of family type, labor force status, and, in some instances, regardless of income. For example, family or child allowances (cash benefits or tax credits) are available to parents regardless of income, as are health and medical services. Some income supplements may be targeted at low-income families only, but these are not restricted to certain family types (even if single parents may be entitled to higher benefits), and they are not reduced or withdrawn when parents work (unless wages are too high).

In contrast to such support for child rearing which already exists in many countries, attention to the interface of work and family life is only now emerging. Most countries provide a paid childbirth-related leave from employment, even if only three, thus far, have extended this entitlement to both parents. (Several countries provide an entitlement to an unpaid leave from work to either parent, with full job and pension protection for one or two years.) Some countries have statutory benefits that provide for a paid leave to care for an ill child at home; sometimes this benefit, too, is available to either parent. Clearly, this is an essential entitlement as women move increasingly into the labor force, and not just for parents with children under age three but for those with older children, too.

It is in this context that we would conclude by noting that we have concentrated here on the role of government in facilitating a closer yet less conflict-ridden relationship between work and family life. Our premise was that individuals—families and family members—had already made adjustments in managing the two domains, and that society had an obligation and responsibility to support these dual roles and to attenuate the stress. Clearly it was a matter of societal self-interest for government to respond in some way.

Now we conclude by underscoring that other kinds of adaptation are needed too, in particular within the domain of employment. Included here are such things as flexible working hours, part-time employment with proportionate entitlement to fringe benefits, seniority and so forth, longer vacations, and, the most fundamental adaptation of all, a shorter workday for all.

Moreover, until the standard workday becomes shorter, supplementary child care programs will also be needed for school-aged children, as well as preschool and day care attendees, when school hours and days do not coincide with parents' work schedules.

It is possible for adults to work and still build strong families. It is possible for mothers and fathers to share work and home responsibilities. It is possible for them to draw upon extensive child care services to help them in this, without sacrificing any of their rights and duties as parents. All this is possible, but only if the work world, along with government and communities, adapts and cooperates.

Notes

1. Pleck, "The Work-Family Role System"

Note: Revised version of a paper given at the 1975 Annual Meeting of the American Sociological Association. I would like to thank Artie Hochschild, Jeylan Mortimer, and Elizabeth Pleck for their comments on earlier drafts.

[1]Glazer-Malbin (1976) provides a useful analysis of current theoretical approaches to household work.

[2]The present analysis, it should be noted, omits consideration of children's family role performance. Walker and Gauger (1973) found that children aged 12–17 contribute an average of slightly over an hour a day to family tasks.

[3]Mortimer et al. (1976) have drawn attention to the extent to which wives can directly contribute to their husbands' work as an alternative to holding paid work of their own, a further indication of the demanding nature of the male work role.

[4]Safilios-Rothschild (1976) has analyzed in a somewhat different way the structural changes that may occur to accommodate families in which both parents have high status jobs.

3. Bernard, "The Good-Provider Role: Its Rise and Fall"

Note: This article was originally presented as the Invited Address at the meeting of the American Psychological Association, New York, September 1979.

[1]Rainwater and Yancey (1967), critiquing current welfare policies, note that they "have robbed men of their manhood, women of their husbands, and children of their fathers. To create a stable monogamous family we need to provide men with the opportunity to be men, and that involves enabling them to perform occupationally" (p. 235).

[2]Several years ago I presented a critique of what I called "extreme sex role specialization," including "work-intoxicated fathers." I noted that making success in the provider role the only test for real manliness was putting a lot of eggs into one basket. At both the blue-collar and the managerial levels, it was dysfunctional for families. I referred to the several attempts being made

even then to correct the excesses of extreme sex role specialization: rural and urban communes, leaving jobs to take up small-scale enterprises that allowed more contact with families, and a rebellion against overtime in industry (Bernard, 1975, pp. 217–239).

[3]In one department of a South Carolina cotton mill early in the century, "every worker was a grass widow" (Smuts, 1959, p. 54). Many women worked "because their husbands refused to provide for their families. There is no reason to think that husbands abandoned their duties more often than today, but the woman who was burdened by an irresponsible husband in 1890 usually had no recourse save taking on his responsibilities herself. If he deserted, the law-enforcement agencies of the time afforded little chance of finding and compelling him to provide support" (Smuts, 1959, p. 54). The situation is not greatly improved today. In divorce child support is allotted in only a small number of cases and enforced in even fewer. "Roughly half of all families with an absent parent don't have awards at all. . . . Where awards do exist they are usually for small amounts, typically ranging from $7 to $18 per week per child" (Jones, 1976, abstract). A summary of all the studies available concludes that "approximately 20 percent of all divorced and separated mothers receive child support regularly, with an additional 7 percent receiving it 'sometimes'; 8 percent of all divorced and separated women receive alimony regularly or sometimes" (Jones, 1976, p. 23).

[4]Even though the annals of social work agencies are filled with cases of runaway husbands, in 1976 only 12.6% of all women were in the status of divorce and separation, and at least some of them were still being "provided for." Most men were at least trying to fulfill the good-provider role.

[5]Although all the women in Lopata's (1971) sample saw breadwinning as important, fewer employed women (54%) than either nonemployed urban (63%) or suburban (64%) women assigned it first place (p. 91).

[6]Pleck and Lang (1979) found only one serious study contradicting their own conclusions: "Using data from the 1973 NORC [National Opinion Research Center] General Social Survey, Harry analyzed the bivariate relationship of job and family satisfaction to life happiness in men classified by family life cycle stage. In three of the five groups of husbands . . . job satisfaction had a stronger association than family satisfaction to life happiness" (pp. 5–6).

[7]In 1978, a Yankelovich survey on "The New Work Psychology" suggested that leisure is now becoming a strict competitor for both family and work as a source of life satisfactions: "Family and work have grown less important than leisure; a majority of 60 percent say that although they enjoy their work, it is not their major source of satisfaction" (p. 46). A 1977 survey of Swedish men aged 18 to 35 found that the proportion saying the family was the main source of meaning in their lives declined from 45% in 1955 to 41% in 1977; the proportion indicating work as the main source of satisfaction dropped from 33% to 17%. The earlier tendency for men to identify themselves through their work is less marked these days. In the new value system, the individual says, in effect, "I am more than my role. I am myself" (Yankelovich, 1978). Is the increasing concern with leisure a way to escape the dissatisfaction with both the alienating relations found on the work site and the demands for increased involvement with the family?

[8]Men seem to be having problems with both work and family roles. Veroff (Note 3), for example, reports an increased "sense of dissatisfaction with the social relations in the work setting" and a "dissatisfaction with the affiliative nature of work" (p. 47). This dissatisfaction may be one of the factors that leads men to seek affiliative-need satisfaction in marriage, just as in the 19th century they looked to the home as shelter from the jungle of the outside world.

[9]Among the indices of the waning of the good-provider role are the increasing number of married women in the labor force; the growth in the number of female-headed families; the growing trend toward egalitarian norms in marriage; the need for two earners in so many middle-class families; and the recognition of these trends in the abandonment of the identification of head of household as a male.

Reference Notes

1. Hesselbart, S. *Some underemphasized issues about men, women, and work*. Unpublished manuscript, Department of Sociology, Florida State University, Tallahassee, 1978.

2. Douvan, E. *Family roles in a twenty-year perspective*. Paper presented at the Radcliffe Pre-Centennial Conference, Cambridge, Massachusetts, April 2–4, 1978.

3. Veroff, J. *Psychological orientations to the work role: 1957–1976*. Unpublished manuscript, Survey Research Center, University of Michigan, Ann Arbor, 1978.

4. Shostak, A. *Working class Americans at home: Changing expectations of manhood*. Unpublished manuscript, Department of Sociology, Drexel University, Philadelphia, 1973.

5. Chafe, W. *The challenge of sex equality: A new culture or old values revisited?* Paper presented at the Radcliffe Pre-Centennial Conference, Cambridge, Massachusetts, April 2–4, 1978.

4. Voydanoff, "Unemployment: Family Strategies for Adaptation"

[1]Although existing research only examines the unemployment experiences of men, job loss for women, especially those whose income is critical to the family and whose identity is closely associated with a work role, can also be expected to produce considerable stress. The precise differences between men and women must await future research results and will not be discussed here.

[2]The analysis of sources of stress and mediating factors incorporates the work of Voydanoff (in press).

Reference Note

1. McCubbin, H. I., and Patterson, J. M. *Family stress and adaptation to crisis*. Paper presented at the annual meeting of the National Council on Family Relations, Milwaukee, Wisconsin, October 1981.

5. Rainwater, "Mothers' Contribution to the Family Money Economy in Europe and the United States"

Note: This article summarizes work carried out in collaboration with a number of people: Susan Anderson-Khleit, Mary Jo Bane, Richard Coleman, Martin Rein, and Joseph Schwartz. In addition to my reliance on their works cited in this article, I have benefited from regular discussions of changing family lifestyles with them and with Robert Weiss.

Our work has been supported by the Office of Income Security Policy, Department of HEW; the Ford Foundation; and the German Marshall Fund of the United States.

[1]The data for the United States comes from the Panel Study of Income Dynamics, conducted by the Institute of Social Research at the University of Michigan. The sample represents all households in the United States. We have selected a subsample of 2,816 families in which the head or the wife was in the 25–54 age range. Because the Panel Study involves reinterviews with the same families each year over a ten-year period, it has been possible to look at mother's labor force participation not only cross-sectionally, as in our comparison with the British and Swedish samples, but also longitudinally. The British sample comes from the General Household Survey (for the third quarter of 1973). There were not quite 1,573 households in our age range in that sample. The sample for Sweden comes from the 1968 Level of Living Survey; there are 2,735 households in the 25–54 age range.

We are indebted to the Central Statistical Office and the Office of Population and Census in Great Britain for permission to use the survey, and to Keith Hope and Phylis Thorburn for assistance in processing the data tapes. We are indebted to Sten Johanssen, Robert Erikson, and Miijan Vuksanovic of the Institute of Social Research at Stockholm University for many different kinds of help over the years that we have worked with the Level of Living Survey data. Joseph Schwartz was responsible for preparing comparable data tapes for the three countries.

[2]The European Community survey involved a sample of almost 10,000 men and women in the nine European Community countries. The sample includes nearly 5,000 women between ages of 18 and 64.

[3]Tabulations from the 1/100 Census Public Use tapes for 1960 and 1970 show no increase in the proportion of family income contributed by working wives (with or without children). Working wife-mothers contributed an average of 26.9 percent of family income in 1959 and 26.0 percent in 1969. In both years there is no clear pattern of difference in the proportionate contribution of working wives at different family income levels. But the Census tabulations do show a higher contribution in the lowest sextile than is true of our PSID sample. This may be a result of the tendency of the Census to show an excessive number of very low income families. The mean wife's contribution may consequently be distorted upward by a downward bias in the denominator.

[4]Of those who were in the labor force, a much smaller proportion would prefer to change their labor force status. There do not seem to be important differences between part-time and full-time workers in the proportion who say they would prefer not to be employed. Overall, about 14 percent of employed women would rather not be working.

[5]I have categorized those women who say they do not know whether or not they would prefer to work as preferring their present labor force status.

[6]Twenty percent of husbands were believed to want the wife to quit her job though she did not want to. Husbands were almost never (4 percent) believed to be opposed to a wife's wish not to go to work. Fewer than 15 percent of the husbands were believed to want wives to stay on the job even though they themselves would like to quit.

I did not find a strong effect of the number of children the couple had (or the wife's age) on husband's feelings about the wife working or not. I also tested whether total family income affected the likelihood that a woman would say that she does or does not prefer paid employment. There was no significant association between family income and her preferences, when she is in the labor force or when she is not.

[7]The data I reviewed for Europe does not allow me to address this issue directly. However, the high proportion of women in some countries who are part-time workers is consistent with this interpretation.

6. Vanek, "Housewives as Workers"

[1]U.S. Department of Labor, Bureau of Labor Statistics, *Handbook of Labor Statistics—1975*, reference ed., BLS Bulletin no. 1865 (Washington, D.C.: Government Printing Office, 1975), p. 46, table 9.

[2]Howard Hayghe, "Marital and Family Characteristics of the Labor Force," *Monthly Labor Review*, November 1975, p. 53.

[3]Cf. Barbara Ehrenreich and Deidre English, "The Manufacture of Housework," *Socialist Revolution*, October-December 1975, pp. 5–40; Heidi Hartman, "Capitalism and Women's Work in the Home, 1900–1930" (Ph.D. diss., Yale University, 1974); Ann Oakley, Woman's Work: *The Housewife Past and Present* (New York: Pantheon Books, 1974); Robert Smuts, *Women and Work in America* (New York: Schocken Books, 1971); Joann Vanek, "Time Spent in Housework," *Scientific American*, November 1974, pp. 116–20.

[4]This discussion is based on Robert Lynd and Helen Lynd, *Middletown* (New York: Harcourt, Brace and Company, 1956), pp. 93–180; Faith Williams and Anna-Stina Ericson, "The Homemaker's Job and the Home Scene" in *How American Buying Habits Change*, ed. U.S. Department of Labor (Washington, D.C.: Government Printing Office, 1959), pp. 83–101; and Smuts, *Women and Work*, pp. 6–13.

[5]Smuts, *Women and Work*, p. 13.

[6]U.S. Department of Commerce, Bureau of the Census, *Historical Statistics of the United States: Colonial Times to 1957* (Washington, D.C.: Government Printing Office, 1960), p. 510.

[7]U.S. Department of Commerce, Bureau of the Census, *Census of Housing*, vol. 11,

General Characteristics, Summary (Washington, D.C.: Government Printing Office, 1942), p. 20.

[8]Private correspondence with Marketing Research, Home Laundry Products Division, General Electric Company, Louisville, Kentucky, 1972.

[9]Siegfried Giedion, *Mechanization Takes Command* (New York: Oxford University Press, 1948), pp. 607–27.

[10]E. L. Kirkpatrick, *The Farmers' Standard of Living,* USDA Bulletin no. 1466 (Washington, D.C.: Department of Agriculture, 1926); J. O. Rankin, *Cost of Feeding the Nebraska Farm Family,* Nebraska Agricultural Experiment Station Bulletin no. 219 (Lincoln: University of Nebraska, 1927).

[11]Inez Arnquist and Evelyn Roberts, *The Present Use of Work Time of Farm Homemakers,* Washington Agricultural Experiment Station Bulletin no. 234 (Pullman: State College of Washington, 1929), p. 15.

[12]U.S. Department of Commerce, Bureau of the Census, *Population,* vol. 6, *Families* (Washington, D.C.: Government Printing Office, 1933), p. 25, table 32.

[13]Jeanne Ridley, "On the Consequences of Demographic Change for the Roles and Status of Women," in *Demographic and Social Aspects of Population Growth,* ed. Charles F. Westoff and Robert Parke, Jr., U.S. Commission on Population Growth and the American Future, Research Reports, vol. 1 (Washington, D.C.: Government Printing Office, 1972), p. 293.

[14]Smuts, *Women and Work,* p. 28.

[15]Calculated from the following sources: David Kaplan and M. Claire Casey, *Occupational Trends in the United States, 1900 to 1950,* Bureau of the Census Working Paper no. 5 (Washington, D.C.: Government Printing Office, 1958); *Handbook of Labor Statistics—1975,* table 6; U.S. Department of Commerce, Bureau of the Census, *Census of Housing: General Housing Characteristics, Summary* (Washington, D.C.: Government Printing Office, 1972), p. 53, table 10.

[16]George Stigler, "Domestic Servants in the U.S., 1900–1940," Occasional Paper no. 24 (New York: National Bureau of Economic Research, 1946).

[17]Smuts, *Women and Work,* p. 28.

[18]Ehrenreich and English, "Manufacture of Housework."

[19]Frank Gilbreth, Jr., and Ernestine G. Carey, *Cheaper by the Dozen* (New York: Thomas Y. Crowell Company, 1948).

[20]Lillian Gilbreth, *The Homemaker and Her Job* (New York: D. Appleton and Company, 1929).

[21]Wesley Mitchell, *The Background Art of Spending Money and Other Essays* (New York: McGraw-Hill Book Company, 1937), p. 11.

[22]Ibid., p. 22.

[23]Cf. Mary Pattison, *Principles of Domestic Engineering* (New York: Trow Press, 1915).

[24]Lita Bane, "What's New in Homemaking?" *Ladies Home Journal,* March 1930, p. 29.

[25]Benjamin Spock, *The Common Sense Book of Baby and Child Care* (New York: Duell, Sloan and Pearce, 1946).

[26]John Kenneth Galbraith, *Economics and the Public Purpose* (Boston: Houghton Mifflin Company, 1973).

[27]Staffan Linder, *The Harried Leisure Class* (New York: Columbia University Press, 1970).

[28]These include the following studies used in my analysis: Inez Arnquist and Evelyn Roberts, *The Present Use of Work Time of Farm Homemakers,* Washington Agricultural Experiment Station Bulletin no. 234 (Pullman: State College of Washington, 1929); May Cowles and Ruth Dietz, "Time Spent in Homemaking Activities by a Selected Group of Wisconsin Farm Homemakers," *Journal of Home Economics* 48 (1956): 29–34; Ina Crawford, *The Use of Time by Farm Women,* Idaho Agricultural Experiment Station Bulletin no. 146 (Moscow: University of Idaho, 1927); Dorothy Dickens, *Time Expenditures in Homemaking Activities by White and Negro Town Families,* Mississippi Agricultural Experiment Station Bulletin no. 424 (State College: Mississippi State College, 1945); Florence Hall and Marguerite Schroeder, "Time Spent on Household Tasks," *Journal of Home Economics* 62 (1970): 23–29; Hildegarde Kneeland, "What's New in Agriculture," in *Yearbook of Agriculture,* ed. U.S. Department of Agriculture

(Washington, D.C.: Goverment Printing Office, 1928), pp. 620–22; Marianne Muse, *Time Expenditures on Homemaking Activities in 183 Vermont Farm Homes*, Vermont Agricultural Experiment Station Bulletin no. 530 (Burlington: University of Vermont and State Agricultural College, 1944); Jessie Richardson, *The Use of Time by Rural Homemakers in Montana*, Montana Agricultural Experiment Station Bulletin no. 271 (Bozeman: Montana State College, 1933); U.S. Department of Agriculture, Bureau of Human Nutrition and Home Economics, *The Time Costs of Homemaking* (Washington, D.C.: Department of Agriculture, 1944); Jean Warren, *Use of Time in Its Relation to Home Management*, Cornell University Agricultural Experiment Station Bulletin no. 734 (Ithaca: Cornell University, 1940); Grace Wasson, *Use of Time by South Dakota Farm Homemakers*, Agricultural Experiment Station Bulletin no. 247 (Brookings: South Dakota State College of Agriculture and Mechanic Arts, 1930); Margaret Whittemore and Bernice Neil, *Time Factors in the Business of Homemaking in Rural Rhode Island*, Rhode Island Agricultural Experiment Station Bulletin no. 221 (Kingston: Rhode Island State College, 1929); Maud Wilson, *Use of Time by Oregon Farm Homemakers*, Oregon Agricultural Experiment Station Bulletin no. 256 (Corvallis: Oregon State Agricultural College, 1929).

[29]Joann Vanek, "Keeping Busy: Time Spent in Housework, United States, 1920–1970" (Ph.D. diss., University of Michigan, 1973).

[30]Ibid., chap. 4.

[31]Ibid.

[32]Ibid., chap. 5.

[33]Ibid., chap. 4.

[34]Kathryn Walker and Margaret Woods, *Time Use: A Measure of Household Production of Family Goods and Services* (Washington, D.C.: American Home Economics Association, Center for the Family, 1976).

[35]Ismail Sirageldin, *Non-Market Components of National Income* (Ann Arbor: University of Michigan, Survey Research Center, 1969).

[36]Galbraith, *Economics and the Public Purpose*, p.37.

[37]Ibid., p. 33.

[38]Discussed in Juanita Kreps, *Sex in the Marketplace: American Women at Work* (Baltimore: Johns Hopkins University Press, 1971), p. 67.

[39]Ibid., p. 73.

[40]Reported in Keith Love, "How Do You Put a Price Tag on a Housewife's Work?" *New York Times*, January 13, 1976, p. 39.

[41]Carolyn Shaw Bell, "Social Security: Society's Last Discrimination," *Business and Society Review*, autumn 1972, p. 46.

[42]*Handbook of Labor Statistics—1975*, p. 46, table 9.

[43]Ann Oakley, *The Sociology of Housework* (New York: Pantheon Books, 1974), p. 183.

[44]Bell, "Social Security," p. 46.

[45]William Chafe, *The American Woman* (New York: Oxford University Press, 1972), p. 222.

[46]Lois Hoffman, "Parental Power Relations and the Division of Household Tasks," *Marriage and Family Living* 22 (1960): 27–35.

[47]Robert Blood and Donald Wolfe, *Husbands and Wives* (Glencoe, Ill.: Free Press, 1960).

[48]Oakley, *Sociology of Housework*, p. 136.

[49]Ibid., chap. 8.

[50]Walker and Woods, *Time-Use*.

[51]Vanek, "Keeping Busy," chap. 4.

[52]Discussion of the research findings of M. Rutter and G. Brown, "The Reliability and Validity of Measures of Family Life and Relationships in Families Containing a Psychiatric Patient," *Social Psychiatry* 1 (1966): 38–53, quoted in Oakley, *Sociology of Housework*, p. 137.

[53]Vanek, "Keeping Busy," chap. 4.

[54]Helena Lopata, *Occupation: Housewife* (New York: Oxford University Press, 1971), p. 35.

[55]Discussed briefly in Colin Clark, "The Economics of Housework," *Oxford University Institute of Statistics Bulletin* 20 (1958): 205.

[56]Dorothea (Canfield) Fisher, *The Home-Maker* (New York: Harcourt, Brace and Company, 1924).

[57]Discussed in Smuts, *Women and Work*, pp. 135–36.

[58]Kreps, *Sex in the Marketplace*, chap. 4.

[59]Jean Grillo, "Wives Want Wages: Or the Great Housework War," *Soho Weekly News*, January 15, 1976, p. 13.

[60]Jessie Bernard, *The Future of Marriage* (New York: Bantam Books, 1972).

[61]Carolyn Shaw Bell, "A Full Employment Policy for a Public Service Economy: Implications for Women," *Social Policy*, September/October 1972, pp. 12–19.

7. Kanter, "Jobs and Families: Impact of Working Roles on Family Life"

[1]Information of the Family Impact Seminar, a program of the National Center for Family Studies, The Catholic University of America, is available from Theodora Ooms, Director, St. John's Hall, Suite 200, the Catholic University of America, Washington, D.C. 20064.

[2]Benjamin Zablocki and Rosabeth Kanter, "Differentiation of Life Styles," *Annual Review of Sociology*, 2, 1976.

[3]Joan Aldous, "Occupational Characteristics and Males' Role Performance in the Family," *Journal of Marriage and the Family*, November 1969.

[4]Paul E. Mott et al., *Shift Work: The Social, Psychological, and Physical Consequences*, Ann Arbor, University of Michigan Press, 1965.

[5]Laura Lein et al., *Work and Family Life*, Final Report to the National Institute of Education, Cambridge, Mass., Center for the Study of Public Policy, 1974.

[6]Rolf Meyersohn, "Changing Work and Leisure Routines," in E. Swigel (ed.), *Work and Leisure: A Contemporary Social Problem*, New Haven, Conn., College and University Press, 1963.

[7]David Riesman, "Work and Leisure in Post-Industrial Society," in E. Larrabee and R. Meyersohn (eds.), *Mass Leisure*, Glencoe, Ill., Free Press, 1958.

[8]Georg H. E. M. Racki, "The Effects of Flexible Working Hours," Ph.D. dissertation, University of Lausanne, 1975.

[9]Jean R. Renshaw, "An Exploration of the Dynamics of the Overlapping Worlds of Work and Family," *Family Process* 15, March 1976.

[10]John H. Scanzoni, *Opportunity and the Family: A Study of the Conjugal Family in Relation to the Economic Opportunity Structure*, New York, Free Press, 1970.

[11]See Melvin L. Kohn, "Social Class and Parental Values," *American Journal of Sociology*, January 1959; Melvin L. Kohn, "Social Class and Parent-Child Relationships: An Interpretation," *American Journal of Sociology*, January 1963; and Melvin L. Kohn, *Class and Conformity*, Homewood, Ill., Dorsey Press, 1969.

[12]Melvin Seeman, "On the Personal Consequences of Alienation in Work," *American Sociological Review*, April 1967.

8. Kohn, "The Effects of Social Class on Parental Values and Practices"

[1]This essay does not purport to be a systematic review of the entire research literature on social class and parent-child relationships. Instead, it focuses on my own research and that of my NIMH colleagues, as well as that of other investigators who have dealt with the same research issues. For a definitive review of the literature on social class and parent-child relationships through the mid-1950s, see Bronfenbrenner (1958). Research of the next decade or so is summarized in Kohn (1969). A seminal essay that reviews and assesses more recent work in the field, and also appraises the major interpretations of social class and parent-child relationships, is that by Gecas (1979).

[2]See Williams (1960, p. 98). See also Barber (1968, p. 292).

[3]See Kohn (1969, pp. 129–131). See also Kohn (1977).

[4]See Hatt (1950), North and Hatt (1953), and Reiss, Duncan, Hatt, and North (1961).

[5]See Gusfield and Schwartz (1963), Hodge, Siegel, and Rossi (1964), and Simmons and Rosenberg (1971).

[6]See Inkeles and Rossi (1956).

[7]See Tiryakian (1958), Svalastoga (1959), Thomas (1962), Hodge, Treiman, and Rossi (1966), and Haller and Lewis (1966).

[8]See Berelson and Steiner (1964). See also the references in Kohn (1969, p. 3, note 2).

[9]See Williams (1968, p. 283).

[10]See Kohn (1969, pp. 18–19, 47–48).

[11]See Kohn (1969, pp. 23–24).

[12]See Kohn (1969, pp. 20–21, 42–43, 50–51).

[13]See Kohn (1969, Chapters 2, 3, 4; 1977).

[14]See Kohn (1969, pp. 48–59, 68–69).

[15]See Kohn (1969, Chapters 2, 3, 4), Olsen (1971), Perron (1971), Platt (n.d.), Hynes (1977), Hoff and Grueneisen (1977a, b), Bertram (1976, 1977), Franklin and Scott (1970), Clausen (1974), Campbell (1977), Wright and Wright (1976), and Kohn (1976d). See also LeMasters (1975) and Sennett and Cobb (1973).

[16]See Kohn (1969, pp. 59–72), Wright and Wright (1976), Kohn (1976d), Kohn (1977).

[17]This is not to say that other major lines of social demarcation are unimportant for parental values. Race, for example, has a consistent effect on parental values at all social-class levels. But the effect of race on parental values is only about one-fourth as great as that of social class.

[18]This statement is based on my unpublished analysis of the data of the 1975 National Opinion Research Center's General Social Survey as compared to earlier studies cited above.

[19]See Erlanger (1974). Erlanger found that subsequent studies failed to confirm the pattern Bronfenbrenner had discovered in the earlier studies, particularly as regards working-class parents' allegedly greater propensity to use physical punishment.

[20]See Kohn (1969, pp. 92–95, 102–103).

[21]See Kohn (1969, Chapter 6) and Gecas and Nye (1974). Class differences in the conditions under which parents punish their children's misbehavior probably do not begin until the children are about 6 years old, but they seem to apply regardless of age thereafter, at least until the mid-teens.

[22]See Kohn (1969, pp. 120–122).

[23]See Kohn (1969, pp. 113–114).

[24]See Kohn (1969, pp. 120-122).

[25]The general picture of class differences in parental role-allocation sketched above appears to apply regardless of the age of the child, beginning at least as young as age 10 or 11 and probably earlier.

[26]See also Bronfenbrenner (1960) and Kohn (1969, p. 124, note 11).

[27]See Bronson, Katten, and Livson (1959) and Bronfenbrenner (1961).

[28]See Kohn (1969, Chapter 9), based on data from the United States and Italy. The generalization is also supported by Hoff and Grueneisen (1977a, b), using West German data; by Hynes (1977), using data from Ireland; by St. Peter (1975) using U.S. data; and by Scurrah and Montalvo (1975), using data from Peru; but not by Olsen (1971), using data from Taiwan.

[29]See Kohn (1969, pp. 161–163).

[30]See Kohn (1969, pp. 182–183 and Table 10-7).

[31]See Kohn (1969, pp. 152–164, 182–183).

[32]See Kohn (1969, pp. 143–152).

[33]See Olsen (1971) and Kohn (1977).

[34]See Scurrah and Montalvo (1975), Hoff and Grueneisen (1977a, b), Hynes (1977), and St. Peter (1975).

[35]In 1974, we conducted a 10-year follow-up to the 1964 study of employed men that is the basis of many of the findings presented in Kohn (1969). In the follow-up study, we not only reinterviewed the men, but this time we also interviewed their wives and children (see Kohn, 1977).

[36]See Kohn (1969, Chapter 9).

[37]See Kohn and Schooler (1973).
[38]Kohn and Schooler (1978).
[39]See Kohn (1969, p. 186).
[40]See Kohn and Schooler (1973).
[41]Kohn (1969, pp. 186–187).
[42]See Kohn (1973). Pertinent, too, are Kohn (1976a,b).

9. Hood and Golden, "Beating Time/Making Time: The Impact of Work Scheduling on Men's Family Roles"

Note: We wish to thank Joseph Pleck and two anonymous reviewers for their helpful comments on earlier versions of this article.

Reference Notes

[1]Hood, J. *Becoming a two-job family*. Unpublished dissertation, University of Michigan, Department of Sociology, 1980.

[2]Lein, L., Durham, M., Pratt, M., Schudson, M., Thomas, R., & Weiss, H. *Final report: Work and family life* (National Institute of Education Project No. 3-3094). Wellesley, Massachusetts: Wellesley College Center for Research on Women, 1974.

10. Gaylord, "Relocation and the Corporate Family: Unexplored Issues"

[1]"Why Moving Day Comes Less Often Now for Executives," *U.S. News & World Report,* January 13, 1975, p. 53.

[2]Vance Packard, *A Nation of Strangers* (New York: Pocket Books, 1974); Alvin Toffler, *Future Shock* (New York: Bantam Books, 1970); and "More Executives Refusing to Relocate," *New York Times,* November 7, 1975.

[3]Toffler, op. cit.; and "Why Moving Day Comes Less Often Now for Executives."

[4]See, for example, "Managers Move More But Enjoy It Less," *Business Week*, August 23, 1976, pp. 19–20; "For Lots of Reasons, More Workers Are Saying 'No' to Job Transfers," *U.S. News & World Report,* February 14, 1977, pp. 73–74; "Management: Helping the Transferred Employee," *New York Times,* November 11, 1977; "Why More Managers Are Refusing Transfers," *Nation's Business,* 64 (October 1976); and "More Executives Refusing to Relocate," *New York Times,* November 7, 1975.

[5]"More Executives Refusing to Relocate."

[6]Ibid.

[7]Myrna M. Weissman and Eugene S. Paykel, "Moving and Depression in Women," *Social Science and Modern Society,* 9 (July–August 1972), pp. 24–28.

[8]"Employee Transfers," *Wall Street Journal,* July 28, 1977.

[9]R. Paul Duncan and Carolyn Perrucci, "Dual Occupation Families and Migration," *American Sociological Review,* 41 (April 1976), pp. 252–261.

[10]See Weissman and Paykel, op. cit.

[11]Robert Seidenberg, *Corporate Wives—Corporate Casualties?* (Garden City, N.Y.: Anchor Press, 1975).

[12]As cited in ibid., p. 36. See also Robert A. Nisbet, *The Sociology of Emile Durkheim* (New York: Oxford University Press, 1974).

[13]Seidenberg, op. cit., p. 35.

[14]See Charles A. Reich, *The Greening of America* (New York: Random House, 1970), p. 80.

[15]See Weissman and Paykel, op. cit.

[16]Norma Upson, *How to Survive as a Corporate Wife* (Garden City, N.Y.: Doubleday & Co., 1974), pp. 77–78 and 72.

[17]Seidenberg, op. cit.

[18]Weissman and Paykel, op. cit.

[19]Seidenberg, op. cit.

[20]Patricia M. Barger, *The Family Move—Its Psychological Effects on Children,* a report from a symposium entitled "The Effects of Change of Environment on the Child," sponsored by Loyola University, Chicago, and Allied Van Lines, February 13–14, 1970 (Broadview, Ill,: Allied Van Lines, 1970); and ibid.

[21]Seidenberg, op. cit.

[22]Ibid.

[23]"Employee Transfers Costly," *Industry Week,* August 15, 1977.

[24]See Earl G. Witenberg, Janet MacKenzie Rioch, and Milton Mazer, "The Interpersonal and Cultural Approaches," in Silvano Arieti, ed., *The American Handbook of Psychiatry* (New York: Basic Books, 1966).

11. Moore and Sawhill, "Implications of Women's Employment for Home and Family Life"

[1]William Goode, "Family Disorganization," in *Contemporary Social Problems,* ed. Robert Merton and Robert Nisbet (New York: Harcourt Brace Jovanovich, 1971), pp. 467–544.

[2]E.g., Hugh Carter and Paul C. Glick, *Marriage and Divorce: A Social and Economic Study* (Cambridge: Harvard University Press, 1970).

[3]Heather L. Ross and Isabel V. Sawhill, *Time of Transition: The Growth of Families Headed by Women* (Washington, D.C.: Urban Institute, 1975), chap. 3.

[4]Stephen Bahr, "Effects on Power and Division of Labor in the Family," in *Working Mothers,* ed. Lois Hoffman and Ivan Nye (San Francisco: Jossey-Bass, Inc., Publishers, 1974), pp. 167–85.

[5]Robert Blood and Donald Wolfe, *Husbands and Wives: The Dynamics of Married Living* (New York: Free Press, 1960).

[6]David Heer, "The Measurement and Bases of Family Power: An Overview," *Marriage and Family Living* 25 (1963): 133–38; Constantina Safilios-Rothschild, "The Study of Family Power Structure: A Review 1960–1969," *Journal of Marriage and the Family* 32 (1970): 539–52.

[7]Otis Dudley Duncan, Howard Schuman, and Beverly Duncan, *Social Change in a Metropolitan Community* (New York: Russell Sage Foundation, 1973).

[8]Joann Vanek, "Time Spent in Housework," *Scientific American,* November 1974, pp. 116–20. . . .

[9]Mirra Komarovsky, "Cultural Contradictions and Sex Roles: The Masculine Case" in *Changing Women in a Changing Society,* ed. Joan Huber (Chicago: University of Chicago Press, 1973), pp. 111–22.

[10]Matina Horner, "Toward an Understanding of Achievement-related Conflicts in Women," *Journal of Social Issues* 20 (1972): 157–75.

[11]Kristin A. Moore, "Fear of Success: Antecedents, Consequences and Correlates of Fear of Success Imagery among Females in a Metropolitan Survey Sample" (Ph.D. diss., University of Michigan, 1975).

[12]Joseph Pleck, "Work and Family Roles: From Sex-patterned Segregation to Integration" (paper presented at the 70th American Sociological Association Meeting, San Francisco, August 1975).

[13]U.S. Senate, Committee on Finance, *Child Care Data and Materials* (Washington, D.C.: Government Printing Office, 1974).

[14]Lois Hoffman, "Effects on Child" in *Working Mothers,* ed., Lois Hoffman and Ivan Nye (San Francisco: Jossey-Bass, Inc., Publishers, 1974), pp. 126–66.

[15]Betty Friedan, *The Feminine Mystique* (New York: Dell Publishing Company, 1963).

[16]M. R. Yarrow, P. Scott, L. DeLeeuw, and C. Heinig, "Childrearing in Families of Working and Non-working Mothers," *Sociometry* 25 (1962): 122–40.

[17]Philip Goldberg, "Are Women Prejudiced against Women?" in *And Jill Came Tumbling After: Sexism in American Education,* ed. Judith Stacey et al. (New York: Dell Publishing Company, 1974), pp. 37–42.

[18]G. K. Baruch, "Maternal Influences upon College Women's Attitudes toward Women and Work," *Developmental Psychology* 6 (1972): 32–37.

[19]Inge Broverman, Susan Vogel, Donald Broverman, Frank Clarkson, and Paul Rosenkrantz, "Sex-Role Stereotypes: A Current Appraisal," *Journal of Social Issues* 28 (1972): 59–78.

[20]Ibid., p. 73.

[21]U.S. Department of Commerce, Bureau of the Census, "Fertility Expectations of American Women, June 1974," Series P-20, no. 277 (Washington, D.C.: Government Printing Office, 1975), p. 35, table 16.

[22]E.g., Jeanne Clare Ridley, "Number of Children Expected in Relation to Nonfamilial Activities of the Wife," *Milbank Memorial Fund Quarterly* 37 (1958): 227.

[23]Ritchie Reed and Susan McIntosh, "Costs of Children," in *Economic Aspects of Population Change*, ed. Charles Westoff and Robert Parke, Jr., Report of the Commission on Population Growth and the American Future, vol. 2 (Washington, D.C.: Government Printing Office, 1972), pp. 333–50.

[24]Linda Waite and Ross Stolzenberg, "Intended Childbearing and Labor Force Participation of Young Women: Insights from Nonrecursive Models," *American Sociological Review* 41 (1976): 235–52.

[25]Lester Thurow and Robert Lucas, *The American Distribution of Income: A Structural Problem* (Washington, D.C.: Government Printing Office, 1972).

[26]Martha W. Griffiths, "Requisites for Equality," in *Women and The American Economy: A Look to the 1980's*, ed. Juanita Kreps (Englewood Cliffs, N.J.: Prentice-Hall, 1976).

[27]Carol-Adaire Jones, Nancy M. Gordon, and Isabel V. Sawhill, "Child Support Payments in the United States," Working Paper no. 992–03 (Washington, D.C.: Urban Institute, 1976).

12. Gross, "Dual-Career Couples Who Live Apart: Two Types"

[1]We cannot know with any statistical certainty what proportion of married couples are choosing this lifestyle, nor can we determine whether the choice represents an increase, since we lack baseline comparison data. However, there is an index of change that supports the impression that this is an increasingly prevalent phenomenon. In recent months, journalists, who concern themselves professionally with what is new and different, have devoted considerable space to the lifestyle (see Baldridge, 1977; Drachman et al., 1976; Haddad, 1978; Rule, 1977; Saul, 1976).

[2]Note that it is impossible with these data to isolate the independent effects of dual-career, two-residence marriages from the other two-residence family arrangements. I am in the process of attempting to isolate these effects with a subsample of non-dual-career couples who live apart.

[3]Holmstrom (1972) found that, among the dual-career marriages she studied, the husband's career was typically considered more important by both spouses with the wife making the biggest occupational sacrifices and risks. For the related point that dual-career wives often believe that the husband's career goals supersede the wives', see Heckman et al., 1977.

14. Daniels and Weingarten, "Mother's Hours: The Timing of Parenthood and Women's Work"

*Four of these 6 women were early-timing mothers. Three continued to work full-time at clerical jobs after their babies were born because of pressing financial need; the fourth, a college graduate who had planned to stay home with her baby, changed her mind within the first few months of parenthood and found herself a job in the paid work force. The two late-timing mothers who continued to work away from home full-time did so for a combination of financial reasons and career reasons.

†The enrollment of older women in continuing-education programs in colleges and universities throughout the country accounts for the fact that in 1980, for the first time in history, more than 50 percent of American college students were women.

‡For most of the college-educated early-timing mothers who chose it, the sequential pattern has meant a single shift sometime in mid life from motherhood to paid work, since none of these women had been employed for long before the birth of her first child. Each has had to make a psychological transition from identifying herself primarily as a mother to identifying herself as a mother *and* a worker.

§The decrease in the number of years devoted solely to parenthood in the lives of both early-and late-timing mothers who adopted the sequential pattern corresponds with the national statistical picture. In 1950, when the children of our oldest group of mothers were preschoolers, only 11.9 percent of married women with preschoolers worked in the paid labor force; in 1960, 18.6 percent did; in 1970, 30.3 percent did; and in 1976, 39.4 percent of mothers with preschool children were in the paid labor force.[5]

[1]For a collection of personal accounts of the place of chosen work in women's lives, see Sara Ruddick and Pamela Daniels, eds., *Working It Out: 23 Women Writers, Artists, Scientists, and Scholars Talk about Their Lives and Work* (New York: Pantheon Books, 1977).

[2]Adrienne Rich, "Conditions for Work: The Common World of Women," Foreword to *Working It Out,* p. xvi.

[3]One of the engrossing themes in recent research and writing about women and work is the dilemma of combining family life with work outside the home. A seminal work on this topic is Alva Myrdal and Viola Klein, *Women's Two Roles: Home and Work* (London: Routledge & Kegan Paul, 1956). In *Woman's Place: Options and Limits in Professional Careers* (Berkeley: University of California Press, 1970), Cynthia Epstein points to the structure of professions as a source of strain for women, in view of the fact that our society considers "female and professional configurations" to be mutually exclusive.

Robert and Rhona Rapoport have spent more than a decade researching and writing about two-worker families. See especially *Dual-Career Families Re-Examined: New Integrations of Work and Family* (New York: Harper & Row, Colophon Books, 1977); their massive review of the literature, *Fathers, Mothers and Society* (New York: Basic Books, 1977); and their edited volume, *Working Couples* (New York: Harper & Row, Colophon Books, 1978).

Two reports that focus on the experience of "working mothers" are Lois Wladis Hoffman and F. Ivan Nye, *Working Mothers* (San Francisco: Jossey-Bass, 1974); and Mary C. Howell, "Employed Mothers and Their Families," *Pediatrics* 52 (1973): 252–63, 327–43.

Among the books of practical counsel written explicitly for women with children and jobs outside the home, see Jean Curtis, *Working Mothers* (New York: Simon and Schuster, 1977); and Jane Price, *How to Have a Child and Keep Your Job* (New York: St. Martin, 1979).

[4]See Pamela Daniels, "Dream vs. Drift in Women's Careers: The Question of Generativity," in Barbara Forisha and Barbara Goldman, eds. *Outsiders on the Inside: Women and Organizations* (Englewood Cliffs, N.J.: Prentice-Hall, 1981), pp. 285–302. For a thought-provoking discussion of the liability inherent in women's "disinclination to plan their lifelong work," see Caryl Rivers, Rosalind Barnett, and Grace Baruch, *Beyond Sugar and Spice: How Women Grow, Learn, and Thrive* (New York: Putnam, 1979), pp. 268–84.

[5]*Wall Street Journal,* September 15, 1978.

[6]See Erik H. Erikson, "On the Nature of 'Psycho-Historical' Evidence," *Life History and the Historical Moment* (New York: Norton, 1975), pp. 113–68; and "Pscyhological Reality and Historical Actuality," *Insight and Responsibility* (New York: Norton, 1964), pp. 161–215.

[7]See Sheila B. Kamerman and Alfred J. Kahn, "The Day-care Debate: A Wider View," *The Public Interest* 54 (winter 1979): 76–91; and also the work of James A. Levine and Michelle Seltzer and their colleagues, "The School-Age Child Care Project" (Wellesley College Center for Research on Women, 1980–1981).

[8]Robert J. Lifton, "On Becoming a Psychohistorian," *History and Human Survival* (New York: Random House, Vintage Books, 1971), p. 8.

[9]See the Working Family Project (Laura Lein, principal investigator), "Work and Family Life," *Final Report,* 1974 (Working Paper no. 13, Wellesley College Center for Research on Women).

[10]Daniel J. Levinson et al., *The Seasons of a Man's Life* (New York: Knopf, 1978), p. 91.

[11]Daniels, "Dream vs. Drift in Women's Careers: The Question of Generativity," pp. 288, 289.

[12]Ibid., p. 294.

[13]Arlie R. Hochschild, "Inside the Clockwork of Male Careers," in Florence Howe, ed., *Women and the Power to Change* (New York: McGraw-Hill, 1975).

[14]Joseph H. Pleck, "The Work-Family Role System," *Social Problems* 24 (April, 1977): 417–27.

[15]For a discussion of work/family overload, see Rapoport and Rapoport, *Dual-Career Families Re-Examined,* pp. 301–7.

15. Pleck, "Men's Family Work: Three Perspectives and Some New Data"

Note: The research reported here was conducted with support from the National Institute of Mental Health (MH 29143) and the U.S. Department of Labor (Contract J9M7-0119). Investigators conducting research under government sponsorship are encouraged to express their own judgment. The viewpoints expressed in this article do not represent the official policy or position of the sponsoring agencies or of the Wellesley College Center for Research on Women. I would like to thank Laura Lein, James A. Levine, and Pamela Daniels for their comments on an earlier draft; Linda Lang for her participation in the research discussed here; and Marguerite Rupp for her assistance in the preparation of the manuscript.

[1]Pleck (Note 1) first proposed this phrase as the generic term of these activities. This term stresses that these activities are work, and complements "paid work," the term for the other major form of productive work activity in our society.

[2]For readers interested in fatherhood, Fein (1978) has made a similar analysis of three different value perspectives in fatherhood research.

[3]These figures for average hours worked per day appear low because they average over all seven days each week, i.e., over both working and non-working days.

Reference Notes

1. Pleck, J. H. *Men's new roles in the family: Housework and child care*. Paper presented at the Ford Foundation/Merrill-Palmer Institute Conference on the Family and Sex Roles, Detroit, November, 1975.

2. Vanek, J. *The new family equality: Myth or reality?* Paper presented at the meeting of the American Sociological Association, Chicago, August, 1977.

3. Rapoport, R., & Rapoport, R. *Working women and the enabling role of the husband*. Paper presented at the 12th Family Research Seminar, International Sociological Association, Moscow, June, 1972.

4. Levine, J. Unpublished memorandum, October, 1978. (Available from Wellesley College Center for Research on Women, Wellesley, Massachusetts 02181.)

5. Pleck, J. H., & Lang, L. *Men's family role: Its nature and consequences*. Wellesley, Massachusetts: Wellesley College Center for Research on Women.

6. Pleck, J. H., Staines, G. L., & Lang, L. *Work and family life: First reports on work-family interference and workers' formal child-care arrangements, from the 1977 Quality of Employment Survey*. Wellesley, Massachusetts: Wellesley College Center for Research on Women.

16. Lein, "Male Participation in Home Life: Impact of Social Supports and Breadwinner Responsibility on the Allocation of Tasks"

Note: This paper describes work done by the Working Family Project, funded by the National Institute of Education and the National Institute of Mental Health. Principal Investigator: Laura Lein. Administrator: Janet Lennon. Research Collaborators: Kevin Dougherty, Maureen Durham, Gail Howrigan, Laura Lein, Michael Pratt, Michael Schudson, Ronald Thomas, and Heather Weiss.

Reference Notes

1. Doughtery, K. *Interactions between work and family life*. Unpublished manuscript, 1979. (Available from Department of Sociology, Harvard University, Cambridge, Massachusetts 02138.)

2. Working Family Project (Lein, L., Durham, M., Dougherty, K., Howrigan, G., Pratt, M., Schudson, M., Thomas, R., & Weiss, H.). *Final report: Work and family life*. Wellesley, Massachusetts: Wellesley College Center for Research on Women, 1977.

18. Skinner, "Dual-Career Family Stress and Coping: A Literature Review"

Reference Note

1. Portner, J. Impact of work on the family. Minneapolis: Minnesota Council on Family Relations, 1219 University Avenue SE, 55414, 1978, 13–15.

19. Keniston, "The Myth of the Self-Sufficient Family"

This article is based on an address that was delivered by Mr. Keniston at the Bicentennial Conference on Children, 2 February 1976, Washington, D.C., and appears in *Principal* with permission from the National Council of Organizations for Children and Youth.

*I should note that I although I am borrowing heavily from discussions of the Council on Children, the following comments are not necessarily a portrayal of the council's final views.

20. Schorr and Moen, "The Single Parent and Public Policy"

*As an example of recent confusion, in pressing their welfare reforms Presidents Nixon and Carter both said that welfare encourages family breakup. If the observation is accurate, which is doubtful despite the chorus to the contrary, both sets of proposals would still have provided an incentive to separation. That is, they would have allowed more income in total to a separated husband and mother with children than to the intact family.

[1]Allyson Sherman Grossman, "The Labor Force Patterns of Divorced and Separated Women," *Monthly Labor Review* 16 (1977), p. 50.

[2]Isabel Sawhill, Gerald E. Peabody, Carol Jones, and Steven Caldwell, *Income Transfers and Family Structure* (Washington, D.C.: The Urban Institute, 1975).

[3]Ruth Brandwein, Carol Brown, and Elizabeth Maury Fox. "Women and Children Last: The Social Situation of Divorced Mothers and Their Families," *Journal of Marriage and the Family* 36 (1974), pp. 488–489.

[4]William J. Goode, "Economic Factors and Marital Stability," *American Sociological Review* 16 (1951); Robert S. Weiss, *Marital Separation* (New York: Basic Books, 1975).

[5]Marvin B. Sussman, "Family Systems in the 1970s: Analysis, Policies and Programs," *The Annals of the American Academy* 396 (July 1971), p. 38.

[6]Martin Rein and Lee Rainwater, *The Welfare Class and Welfare* (Cambridge, Mass.: Joint Center for Urban Studies, 1977); Mary Jo Bane, "Marital Disruption and the Lives of Children," *Journal of Social Issues* 32, no. 1 (1976), pp. 103–109.

[7]Bane, ibid.

[8]Tamara Hareven, "Family Time and Historical Time," *Daedalus* (Spring 1977), pp. 57–70.

[9]Hugh Carter and Paul C. Glick, *Marriage and Divorce: A Social and Economic Study*

(Cambridge: Harvard University Press, 1970); Paul C. Glick, "A Demographer Looks at American Families," *Journal of Marriage and the Family* 15 (1975), p. 26.

[10]A. J. Norton and P. C. Glick, "Marital Instability: Past, Present and Future," *Journal of Social Issues* 32, no. 1 (1976), pp. 5–19.

[11]Greg J. Duncan, "Unmarried Heads of Households and Marriage," in Greg J. Duncan and James N. Morgan (eds), *Five Thousand American Families—Patterns of Economic Progress* (Ann Arbor, Mich.: Institute for Social Research, 1977).

[12]Daniel P. Moynihan, *The Negro Family: The Case for National Action* (Washington, D.C.: U.S. Department of Labor, 1965).

[13]Robert Moroney, *The Family and the State: Considerations for Social Play* (London: Longman, 1976).

[14]Lee Rainwater, *Welfare and Working Mothers* (Cambridge, Mass.: Joint Center for Urban Studies, 1977).

[15]Rein and Rainwater, op. cit.

[16]Dennis K. Orthner, Terry Brown, and Dennis Ferguson, "Single-Parent Fatherhood: An Emerging Family Life Style," *The Family Coordinator* (October 1976), pp. 429–437.

[17]Daniel D. Molinoff, "Life with Father," *New York Times Magazine* (May 22, 1977), p. 13.

[18]Isabel V. Sawhill, "Discrimination and Poverty Among Women Who Head Families," *Signs* no. 1–3 (1976), pp. 201–221.

[19]Brandwein, op. cit.; Orthner et al., op. cit.; Gasser and Taylor, op. cit.

[20]James Levine, *Who Will Raise the Children? New Options for Fathers (and Mothers)* (Philadelphia: J. B. Lippincott, 1976).

[21]Orthner, op. cit.; Gasser and Taylor, op. cit.

[22]Lucy B. Mallan, "Young Widows and Their Children: A Comparative Report," *Social Security Bulletin* (May 1975).

[23]J. Brubacher and W. Rudy, *Higher Education in Transition: A History of American Colleges and Universities, 1636–1968* (New York: Harper and Row, 1968), pp. 13–14.

[24]Benjamin Schlesinger, *The One-Parent Family: Perspectives and Annotated Bibliography* (Toronto: University of Toronto, 1975).

[25]Reynolds Farley and Suzanne Bianchi, "Demographic Aspects of Family Structure Among Blacks: A Look at Data a Decade After the Moynihan Report." Paper presented at the American Sociological Association; Chicago, Illinois; 1971.

[26]L. J. Weitzman, "To Love, Honor, and Obey: Traditional Legal Marriage and Alternative Family-Forms," *The Family Coordinator* 24 (1975).

[27]Edward Gross, "Plus Ca Change?: The Sexual Structure of Occupations Over Time," *Social Problems* 16 (1968), pp. 198–208.

[28]Erik Gronseth, "The Breadwinner Trap," in *The Future of the Family* (New York: Simon and Schuster, 1972), pp. 175–191; Erik Gronseth, "The Husband-Provider Role: A Critical Appraisal," in Andree Michel (ed.), *Family Issues of Employed Women in Europe and America* (Leiden: E. J. Brill, 1971).

[29]U.S. Department of Labor, *The Earnings Gap Between Women and Men* (Washington, D.C.: U.S. Government Printing Office, 1976).

[30]Greg J. Duncan and James W. Morgan, *Five Thousand American Families—Patterns of Economic Progress,* vol. V (Ann Arbor: Institute of Social Research, 1977).

[31]Saul Hoffman and John Holmes, "Husbands, Wives and Divorce," in Greg J. Duncan and James N. Morgan (eds.), *Five Thousand American Families—Patterns of Economic Progress,* vol. IV (Ann Arbor: Institute of Social Research, 1976).

[32]Grossman, op cit.

[33]Ibid. and Beverly Johnson McEaddy, "Women Who Head Families: A Socioeconomic Analysis," *Monthly Labor Review* (June 1976).

[34]Carter and Glick, op. cit.; Goode, op. cit.

[35]Heather Ross and Isabel Sawhill, *Time of Transition: The Growth of Families Headed by Women* (Washington, D.C.: The Urban Institute, 1975).

[36]S. G. Johnson, "The Impact of Women's Liberation on Marriage, Divorce, and Family Life-Style," in C. B. Lloyd (ed.), *Sex Discrimination and the Division of Labor* (New York: Columbia University Press); F. B. Santos, "The Economics of Marital Status," in C. B. Lloyd (ed.), *Sex Discrimination and Division of Labor* (New York: Columbia University Press).

[37]Sawhill, op. cit.

[38]Goode, op. cit.

[39]Alice S. Rossi, "A Biosocial Perspective on Parenting," *Daedalus* (Spring 1977).

[40]Suzanne H. Woolsey, "Pied Piper Politics and the Child Care Debate," *Daedalus* (Spring 1977), pp. 127–146; Arthur C. Emlen nd Joseph B. Perry, "Child-Care Arrangements," in Hoffman and Nye (eds.), *Working Mothers* (San Francisco: Jossey-Bass, 1974).

[41]Urie Bronfenbrenner, "Research on the Effects of Daycare on Child Development," in *Toward a National Policy for Children and Families* (Washington, D.C.: National Academy of Sciences, 1976).

[42]B. Caldwell, "Infant Day Care—The Outcasts Gain Respectability," in P. Roby (ed.), *Child Care—Who Cares? Foreign and Domestic Infant and Early Childhood Development Policies* (New York: Basic Books, 1973).

[43]Alice S. Rossi, "A Biosocial Perspective on Parenting," *Daedalus* (Spring 1977).

[44]Ruth Brandwein, Carol Brown, and Elizabeth Maury Fox, "Women and Children Last: The Social Situation of Divorced Mothers and Their Families," *Journal of Marriage and the Family* 36 (1974), pp. 488–489.

[45]Eleanor E. Maccoby, "Current Changes in the Family and Their Impact Upon the Socialization of Children." Paper presented at the American Sociological Association Meeting, 1977.

[45]Maccoby, op. cit.; Weiss, op. cit.

[47]Benjamin Schlesinger, "One-Parent Families in Great Britain," *The Family Coordinator* 26 (1977), pp. 139–141.

[48]John C. Condry and M. A. Simon, "Characteristics of Peer and Adult-Oriented Children," *Journal of Marriage and the Family* 36 (1974), pp. 543–554.

[49]Reuben Hill, "Social Stress on the Family," in Marvin Sussman (ed.), *Sourcebook in Marriage and the Family* (Boston: Houghton Mifflin, 1968).

[50]Jane K. Burgess, "The Single-Parent Family: A Social and Sociological Problem," *The Family Coordinator* 9 (1970), pp. 137–144.

[51]Maccoby, op. cit.

[52]Louis Kriesberg, *Mothers in Poverty* (Chicago: Aldine, 1970).

[53]Lee Burchinal, "Characteristics of Adolescents from Unbroken Homes and Reconstituted Families," *Journal of Marriage and the Family* 26 (1964), pp. 44–51; Judson Landis, "The Trauma of Children When Parents Divorce," *Marriage and Family Living* 22 (1960), pp. 7–13; F. Ivan Nye, "Child Adjustment in Broken and in Unhappy Unbroken Homes," *Marriage and Family Living* 19 (1957), pp. 356–361.

[54]Sheldon Glueck and Eleanor Glueck, *Family Environment and Delinquency* (Boston: Houghton Mifflin, 1962).

[55]Kenneth Keniston, *All Our Children* (Carnegie Council on Children, 1977); and *Toward a National Policy for Children and Families* (Washington, D.C.: National Academy of Sciences, 1976).

[56]William J. Goode, *Women in Divorce* (New York: Free Press, 1956); Dennis Marsden, *Mothers Alone: Poverty and the Fatherless Family* (London: Penguin, 1969).

[57]C. A. Brown, R. Feldberg, E. M. Fox, and J. Kohen, "Divorce: Chance of a New Lifetime," *Journal of Social Issues* 32 (1976), pp. 119–132.

[58]Brandwein et al., op. cit.

[59]Elsa Ferri, "Growing-Up in a One-Parent Family," *Concern* 20 (1976), pp. 7–10; Schlesinger, op. cit.

[60]Farley and Bianchi, op. cit.

[61]Ross and Sawhill, op. cit.

[62]Peter Moss and Ian Plewis, "Mental Distress in Mothers of Pre-School Children in Inner London." Undated paper from the Tomas Coram Research Unit, University of London.

[63]Alison Clarke-Stewart, *Child Care in the Family: A Review of Research and Some Propositions for Policy* (New York: Academic Press, 1977); J. A. Clausen and S. R. Clausen, "The Effect of Family Size on Parents and Children," in J. T. Fawcett (ed.), *Psychological Perspectives on Population* (New York: Key Book Services, 1972); N. Richman, "Depression in Mothers of Pre-School Children, *Journal of Child Psychology and Psychiatry* 17 (1976); Rossi, op. cit.

[64]Sawhill, 1977, op. cit.

[65]Irvin Garfinkel, "Testimony on Welare Reform to State Senate Human Services Committee," in Madison, Wisconsin: August 15 and 16, 1978.

[66]Heather Ross, "Poverty: Women and Children Last," in Jane Roberts Chapman and Margaret Gates (eds.), *Economic Independence for Women: The Foundation for Equal Rights* (Beverly Hills: Russell Sage, 1976).

[67]"Working America." A report of a special task force to the Secretary of Health, Education, and Welfare (Cambridge: M.I.T. Press, 1973).

[68]James Kent, *Commentaries on American Law,* vol. 2 (New York: Da Capo, 1826).

[69]Weiss, op. cit.

[70]Michael J. Smith and Beth Moses, "Social Welfare Agencies and Social Reform Movements: The Case of the Single-Parent Family" (Community Service Society of New York, 1976).

[71]Thelma Stackhouse, "Housing for One-Parent Families—Faddism or Favorable Options" (Community Service Society of New York, August 1975).

22. Sullivan, "Family Support Systems Paychecks Can't Buy"

Reference Notes

1. Pifer, A. *Women working toward a new society*. Unpublished manuscript, 1976. (Available from the Carnegie Corporation of New York, 437 Madison Avenue, New York, NY 10022.)

2. *Friendly Times Newsletter*, October, 1980. (Available from United Airlines, P. O. Box 66100, Chicago, IL 60666.)

3. Orton, J., & Sullivan J. *Long-distance marriage: Is it a viable lifestyle for couples?* Unpublished manuscript, 1979. (Available from Florida State University, College of Home Economics, Tallahassee, FL 36201.)

23. Bohen and Viveros-Long, "Balancing Jobs and Family Life"

[1]The opposing view that women are biologically more suited to rearing children than men has received new support in Rossi's recent biosocial research (1977); she argues that by virtue of childbearing, women have innate capacities for nurturant behavior that men can only be taught.

[2]But there are two additional groups of people without children who do not seem to be much helped by flexitime, namely both one- and two-earner men without children. They spend about three hours more a week on home chores than their standard-time counterparts (the difference is not statistically significant); but they do not have significantly less stress. For them, the slightly greater time on chores possibly explains the greater stress. On the other hand, for the two-earner women without children, who spend two hours a week more on chores and feel less stress, the reduced feeling of stress may be explained in terms of sex-role expectations. . . . In short, the men who do more home chores may feel more stress because they are not used to those responsibilities; whereas women who normally expect to carry the major home management and coordination responsibility may feel genuinely less stressed when they can leave work an hour or so earlier.

[3]As Joseph Pleck and his co-authors have pointed out (Sept. 1978, p. 7), a large part of what has been recently characterized as "work-family conflict" is really work-parenting conflicts. Labeling the problem as one involving specifically parenthood may help focus public attention on the problem in a more concrete way than the usual formulation.

24. Kamerman and Kahn, "Societal Learning"

[1]For example, in the United States, in one-third of all marriages in which the wife has earnings, she earns as much or more than her husband. U.S. Bureau of the Census, *Current Population Reports: Special Studies Series* P23, no. 77, "Perspectives on American Husbands and Wives" (Washington, D.C.: U.S. Government Printing Office, 1978).

[2]This may be occurring because (1) some marriages are not based on the woman's economic dependence on the male, her husband; and (2) some women may make a different marriage decision—or spouse selection—if they are in the labor force, and if they expect to stay in the labor force all their adult lives.

[3]Lois Hoffman, "Maternal Employment," *The American Psychologist* (October 1979), 34: 859–65.

[4]George Brown and Tirrell Harris, *Social Origins of Depression* (New York: Free Press, 1978); Ann Oakley, *Housewife* (London: Allen Lane, 1974); and Nickie Fonda and Peter Moss, eds., *Mothers in Employment* (Uxbridge, U.K.: Brunel University, 1976).

[5]Joseph H. Pleck and Linda Lang, *Men's Family Role: Its Nature and Consequences* (Wellesley, Mass.: Wellesley College Center for Research on Women, 1978). See also Sheila B. Kamerman, *Parenting in an Unresponsive Society: Managing Work and Family Life* (New York: Free Press, 1980).

[6]Sheila B. Kamerman, *Maternity and Parental Benefits and Leaves: A Comparative Review* (New York: Columbia University Center for the Social Sciences, 1980).

References

References

Abbott, S. Full-time fathers and weekend wives: An analysis of altering conjugal rules. *Journal of Marriage and the Family,* 1976, *36,* 165–173.

Abeles, R. P., Steel, L., & Wise, L. L. Patterns and implications of life-course organization: Studies from Project TALENT. In P. B. Baltes & O. G. Brim, Jr. (Eds.), *Life-span development and behavior* (Vol. 3). New York: Academic Press, 1980.

Aberle, D., & Naegele, K. Middle-class fathers' occupational role and attitudes toward children. *American Journal of Orthopsychiatry,* 1952, *22,* 366–378.

Aldous, J. Occupational characteristics and males' role performance in the family. *Journal of Marriage and the Family,* 1969, *31,* 707–712.

Aldous, J. From dual-earner to dual-career families and back again. *Journal of Family Issues,* 1981, *2,* 115–125.

Aldous, J., Osmond, M. W., & Hicks, M. W. Men's work and men's families. In W. R. Burr, R. Hill, F. I. Nye, & I. L. Reiss (Eds.), *Contemporary theories about the family* (Vol. 1). New York: Free Press, 1979.

Analysts see Americans staying at home more. *Wall Street Journal,* July 3, 1979, *1,* p. 1.

Anderson-Khleif, S. *Income packaging and lifestyle in welfare families* (Family Policy Note No. 7). Cambridge Mass.: Joint Center for Urban Studies of Harvard and M.I.T., 1978.

Anderson, R. N. Rural plant closures: The coping behavior of Filipinos in Hawaii. *Family Relations,* 1980, *29,* 511–516.

Angell, R. C. *The family encounters the depression*. New York: Scribner's, 1936.

Angrist, S. S., Lave, J. R., & Michelsen, R. How working mothers manage: Socioeconomic differences in work, child care, and household tasks. *Social Science Quarterly,* 1976, *56* (4), 631–637.

Axelson, L. J. The working wife: Differences in perception among Negro and White males. *Journal of Marriage and the Family,* 1970, *32,* 457–464.

Babcock, B. F., Freedman, A. E., Norton, E. H., & Ross, S. C. *Sex discrimination and the law: Causes and remedies*. Boston: Little, Brown, 1975.

Bahr, S. Effects on power and division of labor in the family. In L. W. Hoffman & F. I. Nye (Eds.), *Working mothers*. San Francisco: Jossey-Bass, 1974.

Bailyn, L. Career and family orientations of husbands and wives in relation to marital happiness. *Human Relations,* 1970, *23* (2), 97–113.

Bailyn, L. Career and family orientation of husbands and wives in relation to family happiness. In A. Theodore (Ed.), *The professional woman*. Cambridge, Mass.: Schenckman, 1971.

Bailyn, L. How much acceleration for career success. *Management Review,* 1979, *68,* 18–21.

Bain, A. The capacity of families to cope with transitions: A theoretical essay. *Human Relations,* 1978, *31,* 675–688.

Baker, S. H. Women in female-dominated professions. In A. H. Stromberg & S. Harkess, *Women working*. Palo Alto, Calif.: Mayfield, 1978.

Bakke, E. W. *Citizens without work*. New Haven, Conn.: Yale University Press, 1940.

Baldridge, L. For some, it's a tale of two home cities. *Chicago Daily News,* March 25, 1977.

Bane, M. J. *CPS data on labor force participation of mothers*. Unpublished memorandum, Dept. of Education, Wellesley College, Wellesley, Mass., 1975.

Bane, M. J. *Here to stay: American families in the twentieth century*. New York: Basic Books, 1976.

Barber, B. Social stratification. In D. L. Sills (Ed.), *International encyclopedia of the social sciences* (Vol. 15). New York: Macmillan Company and Free Press, 1968.

Barrett, N. S. Women in the job market: occupations, earnings, and career opportunities. In R. E. Smith (Ed.), *The subtle revolution: women at work*. Washington, D. C.: Urban Institute, 1979.

Bebbington, A. C. The function of stress in the establishment of the dual-career family. *Journal of Marriage and the Family,* 1973, *35,* 530–537.

Beckett, J. O. Working wives: A racial comparison. *Social Work,* 1976, *2,* 463–471.

Bell, C. S. The next revolution. *Social Policy,* 1975, *6,* 5–11.

Bell, R. The related importance of mother and wife roles among black lower-class women. In R. Staples (Ed.), *The black family: Essays and studies*. Belmont, Calif.: Wadsworth, 1971.

Benenson, H. *Family success and sexual equality: The limits of the dual-career family model*. Paper presented at the meeting of the American Sociological Association, Toronto, August 1981.

Berelson, B., & Steiner, G. A. *Human behavior: An inventory of scientific findings*. New York: Harcourt Brace Jovanovich, 1964.

Berger, B. M., Hackett, B. M., & Miller, R. M. Child-rearing practices in the communal family. In H. P. Dreitzel (Ed.), *Family, marriage, and the struggle of the sexes*. New York: Macmillan, 1972.

Berheide, C., Berk, S., & Berk, R. Household work in the suburbs: The job and its participants. *Pacific Sociological Review,* 1976, *19,* 491–581.

Bernard, J. *The future of marriage*. New York: Bantam Books, 1972.

Bernard, J. *The future of motherhood*. New York: Penguin, 1974.

Bernard, J. *Women, wives, mothers*. Chicago: Aldine, 1975.

Bernard, J. Homosociality and female depression. *Journal of Social Issues,* 1976, *32,* 207–224.

Bernard, J. The good-provider role: Its rise and fall. *American Psychologist,* 1981, *36,* 1–12.

Bertram, H. *Gesellschaftliche und familiäre Bedingungen moralischen Urteilens*. Unpublished doctoral dissertation, Universität Dusseldorf, 1976.

Bertram, H. Personal communication, 1977.

Best, F., & Stern, B. Education, work, and leisure: Must they come in that order? *Monthly Labor Review,* 1977, *100* (7), 31–34.

Bettelheim, B. *The children of the dream*. New York: Macmillan, 1969.

Bird, C. *The two-paycheck marriage*. New York: Rawson, Wade, 1979.

Blake, J. The changing status of women in developed countries. *Scientific American,* September 1974, pp. 137–147.

Blaxall, M., & Reagan, B. B. (Eds.). Women and the workplace: The implications of occupational segregation. *Signs,* 1976, *1* (3): Part 2 (Entire).

Blenkner, M. Social work and family relationships in later life. In E. Shanas & G. Streib (Eds.), *Social structure and the family: Generational relationships*. Englewood Cliffs, N.J.: Prentice-Hall, 1963.

Blood, R., & Wolfe, D. *Husbands and wives*. New York: Free Press, 1960.

Blood, R. O., & Wolfe, D. M. Negro-white differences in blue-collar marriages in a northern metropolis. In R. Staples (Ed.), *The black family: Essays and studies*. Belmont, Calif.: Wadsworth, 1971.

Bohannan, P. (Ed.). *Divorce and after*. New York: Doubleday-Anchor, 1970.

Booth, A. A wife's employment and husband's stress: A replication and refutation. *Journal of Marriage and the Family*, 1977, *39*, 645–650.

Bott, E. *Family and social network* (2nd ed.). New York: Free Press, 1971.

Boulding, E. Familial constraints on women's work roles. *Signs*, 1976, *1*, 95–118.

Brenner, M. H. *Mental illness and the economy*. Cambridge, Mass.: Harvard University Press, 1973.

Brenner, M. H. *Estimating the social costs of national economic policy*. Washington, D. C.: U. S. Government Printing Office, 1976.

Brenner, M. H. Personal stability and economic security. *Social Policy*, 1977, *8*, 2–4.

Brenton, M. *The American male*. New York: Coward-McCann, 1966.

Briar, K. H. *The effect of long-term unemployment on workers and their families*. Palo Alto, Calif.: R and E Research Associates, 1978.

Brim, O. G., Jr. Theories of the male mid-life crisis. *Counseling Psychologist*, 1976, *6* (1), 2–9.

Bronfenbrenner, U. Socialization and social class through time and space. In E. E. Maccoby, T. M. Newcomb, and E. L. Hartley (Eds.), *Readings in social psychology*. New York: Holt, Rinehart & Winston, 1958.

Bronfenbrenner, U. Freudian theories of identification and their derivatives. *Child Development*, 1960, *31*, 15–40.

Bronfenbrenner, U. The changing American child—a speculative analysis. *Journal of Social Issues*, 1961, *17*, 6–18.

Bronfenbrenner, U. *Two worlds of childhood: U. S. and the U. S. S. R.* New York: Russell Sage Foundation, 1970.

Bronfenbrenner, U. *The next generation of Americans*. Paper presented at the annual meeting of the American Association of Advertising Agencies, Dorado, Puerto Rico, March 1975.

Bronson, W. C., Katten, E. S., & Livson, N. Patterns of authority and affection in two generations. *Journal of Abnormal and Social Psychology*, 1959, *58*, 143–152.

Bryson, R., Bryson, J. B., & Johnson, M. F. Family size, satisfaction, and productivity in dual career couples. In J. B. Bryson & R. Bryson (Eds.), *Dual-career couples*. New York: Human Sciences, 1978.

Bryson, R., Bryson, J., Licht, M., & Licht, B. The professional pair: Husband and wife psychologists. *American Psychologist*, 1976, *31* (1), 10–16.

Burke, R. J., & Weir, T. Relationship of wives' employment status to husband, wife and pair satisfaction and performance. *Journal of Marriage and the Family*, 1976, *38*, 279–287.

Burke, R. J., & Weir, T. Marital helping relationships: The moderators between stress and well-being. *Journal of Psychology*, 1977, *95*, 121–130.

Burr, W. R. *Theory construction and sociology of the family*. New York: Wiley, 1973.

Cain, G. *Married women in the labor force: An economic analysis*. Chicago: University of Chicago, 1966.

Calavita, K. *Unemployed men and kinship interaction*. Paper presented at the annual meeting of the American Sociological Association, August 1977.

Campbell, J. D. The child in the sick role: Contributions of age, sex, parental status and parental values. *Journal of Health and Social Behavior*, 1978, *19*, 35–51.

Canon, B. Child care where you work. *Ms*. Magazine, April 1978.

Caplow, T. *The sociology of work*. Minneapolis: University of Minnesota, 1954.

Card, J. J., Steel, L., and Abeles, R. P. Sex differences in realization of individual potential for achievement. *Journal of Vocational Behavior*, 1980, *17*, 1–21.

Causey, M. The federal diary: More flexitime due. *Washington Post* December 21, 1976.

Causey, M. Part-time bill enacted, *Washington Post*, September, 28, 1978.

Cavan, R. S., & Ranck, K. H. *The family and the Depression*. Chicago: University of Chicago, 1938.

Cazenave, N. A. Middle-income black fathers. *Family Coordinator*, 1979, *28*, 583–593.

Chafe, W. H. Looking backward in order to look forward. In J. M. Kreps (Ed.), *Women and the American economy*. Englewood Cliffs, N.J.: Prentice-Hall, 1976.

Chodorow, N. *The reproduction of mothering*. Berkeley: University of California Press, 1978.

Clark, R. A., Nye, F. I., & Gecas, V. Work involvement and marital role performance. *Journal of Marriage and the Family*, 1978, *40*, 9–22.

Clausen, J. A. *Value transmission and personality resemblance in two generations*. Paper presented to the annual meeting of the American Sociological Association, Montreal, August 27, 1974.

Cobb, S., & Kasl, S. *Termination: The consequences of job loss*. Cincinnati: NIOSH, 1977.

Cochran, H., & Strasser, S. *The efficient home: The technology and ideology of housework in the early twentieth century*. Paper presented at the Second Annual Conference on Marxist Approaches to History, New Haven, Conn., February 23–24, 1974.

Cogswell, B. E. Variant family forms and life styles: Rejection of the traditional nuclear family. *Family Coordinator*, 1975, *24*, 391–406.

Cogswell, B. E., & Sussman, M. B. Changing family and marriage forms: Complications for human service systems. *Family Coordinator*, 1972, *21*, 505–516.

Cohn, R. M. The effect of unemployment status change on self-attitudes. *Social Psychology*, 1978, *41*, 81–93.

Coleman, R. *Husbands, wives and other earners: Notes on the family income assembly line* (working Paper No. 48). Cambridge, Mass.: Joint Center for Urban Studies of Harvard and M.I.T., 1978.

Coles, R. C. Statement. In *American Families: Trends and Pressures, 1973: Hearings before the subcommittee on children and youth, U. S. Senate*. Washington, D.C.: U.S. Government Printing Office, 1973.

Commission of the European Communities. *European Men and Women*. Brussels, 1977.

Corcoran, M., & Duncan, G. J. Summary of Findings. In G. J. Duncan & J. N. Morgan (Eds.), *Five thousand American families: Accounting for race and sex differences in earnings*. Ann Arbor: University of Michigan, Institute for Social Research, 1978.

Cowan, R. S. *A case study of technology and social change: The washing machine and the working wife*. Paper presented at the Berkshire Conference of Woman Historians, Douglass College, 1973.

Cowley, T. *Flexitime for increased productivity*. Mimeograph. Pay Policy Division, Office of Personnel Management, May 1976.

David, D. S., & Brannon, R. (Eds.), *The forty-nine percent majority: The male sex role*. Reading, Mass.: Addison-Wesley, 1976.

Davies, M. Women's place is at the typewriter: The feminization of the clerical labor force. *Radical American*, 1974, *8* (4): 1–37.

Davis, K. The American family in relation to demographic change. In C. F. Westoff & R. Parke, Jr., *Research reports, demographic and social aspects of population growth* (Vol.1). Commission on Population Growth and the American Future. Washington, D.C.: U.S. Government Printing Office, 1972.

DeFrain, J. Androgynous parents tell who they are and what they need. *Family Coordinator*, 1979, *28*, 237–243.

Demos, J. The American family in past time. *American Scholar*, 1974, *43*, 422–446.

Dizard, J. *Social Change in the Family*. Chicago: University of Chicago, Community and Family Study Center, 1968.

Doeringer, P. B., & Piore, M. J. *Internal labor markets and manpower analysis*. Lexington, Mass.: Heath, 1971.

Dougherty, K., Howrigan, G., Lein, L., & Weiss, H. *Work and the American family*. Working Family Project. Chicago: National Parent Teachers Association, 1977.

Douglas, J. (Ed.). *Dollars and sense: Employer-supported child care*. Washington, D.C.: Office of Child Development, 1976.

Douglas, M. *Purity and danger: An analysis of concepts of pollution and taboo*. Baltimore: Penguin Books, 1970.

Douglas, W. *Ministers' wives*. New York: Harper & Row, 1965.

Drachman, V., Schwartz, M. C., & Schwebs, C. Weekend marriage. *Vogue,* November 1976, pp. 278–280.

Duncan, G., & Hill, C. R. Modal-choice in child care arrangements. In G. Duncan and J. Morgan (Eds.), *Five thousand American families* (Vol. 3). Ann Arbor: University of Michigan, Institute for Social Research, 1975.

Duncan, G., & Morgan, J. N. (Eds.). *Five thousand American families—patterns of economic progress* (Vol. 4) Family Composition Change and other analysis of the first seven years of the Panel Study of Income Dynamics. Ann Arbor: University of Michigan, Institute for Social Research, 1976.

Duncan, O. D., Featherman, D. L., & Duncan, B. *Socio-economic background and achievement*. New York: Seminar Press, 1972.

Duncan, O. D., Schuman, H., & Duncan, B. *Social change in a metropolitan community*. New York: Russell Sage Foundation, 1973.

Duncan, R. P., & Perrucci C. Dual occupation families and migration. *American Sociological Review,* 1978, *41,* 252–261.

Dyer, W. The interlocking of work and family social systems among lower occupational families. *Social Forces,* 1956, *34,* 230–233.

Dyer, W. Family reactions to the father's job. In A. Shostak & W. Gomberg (Eds.), *Blue-collar world*. Englewood Cliffs, N.J.: Prentice-Hall, 1965.

Eisenberg, P., & Lazarsfeld, P. The psychological effects of unemployment. *Psychological Bulletin,* 1938, *35,* 358–390.

Elder, G. H., Jr. *Children of the Great Depression: Social Change in Life Experience*. Chicago: University of Chicago, 1974.

Elder, G. H., Jr. *Family history and the life course*. Paper presented at the Family Life Course in Historical Perspective Conference, Williams College, Williamstown, Mass., July 1975.

Elder, G. H. Jr., & Rockwell, R. C. Marital timing in women's life patterns. *Journal of Family History,* 1976, *1,* 34–53.

Engels, F. *The origin of the family, private property, and the state*. E. B. Leacock (Ed.), New York: International Publishers, 1972. (Originally published 1884.)

Entwisle, D., & Greenberger, E. *A survey of cognitive styles in Maryland 9th graders: views of women's roles* (Report No. 89), Baltimore: Center for the Study of Social Organization of Schools, John Hopkins University, 1970.

Epstein, C. D. Law partners and marital partners: Strains and solutions in the dual-career family enterprise. *Human Relations,* 1971, *24,* 549–563.

Erlanger, H. S. Social class and corporal punishment in childrearing: A reassessment. *American Sociological Review,* 1974, *39,* 68–85.

Farley-Maricq, C. *The support choices of female headed families*. Unpublished bachelor's thesis, M.I.T., 1979.

Farrell, M. P., & Rosenberg, S. *Men at midlife*. Boston: Auburn House, 1981.

Farrell, W. *The liberated man*. New York: Random House, 1974.

Farris, A. Commuting. In R. Rapoport & R. N. Rapoport (Eds.), *Working couples,* New York: Harper & Row, 1978.

Fasteau, M. F. *The male machine*. New York: McGraw-Hill, 1974.

Fein, R. Research on fathering: Social policy and an emergent perspective. *Journal of Social Issues,* 1978, *34* (1), 122–135.

Feree, M. M. Working class jobs. *Social Problems,* 1976, *23,* 431–441.

Ferman, L. A., & Gardner, J. Economic deprivation, social mobility, and mental health, In L. A. Ferman & J. P. Gordus (Eds.), *Mental health and the economy*. Kalamazoo, Mich.: W. E. Upjohn Institute, 1979.

Fiedler, L. *Love and death in the American novel*. New York: Meredith, 1962.

Finlayson, E. M. A study of the wife of the Army officer: Her academic and career preparations, her current employment and volunteer services. In H. I. McCubbin, B. B. Dahl, & E. J. Hunter (Eds.), *Families in the military system*. Beverly Hills, Calif.: Sage, 1976.

Fogarty, M. P., Rapoport, R., & Rapoport, R. N. *Sex, career, and family*. London: Allen & Unwin, 1971.

Foner, P. S. *Women and the American labor movement*. New York: Free Press, 1979.

Fowlkes. M. R. *Behind every successful man: Wives of medicine and academe*. New York: Columbia University Press, 1980.

Franklin, J. I., & Scott, J. E. Parental values: An inquiry into occupational setting. *Journal of Marriage and the Family,* 1970, *32,* 406–409.

Freeman, R. B. The work force in the future: An overview. In C. Kerr and J. M. Rosow (Eds.), *Work in America: The decade ahead*. New York: Van Nostrand Reinhold, 1979.

Freud, S. *Civilization and its discontents*. New York: Doubleday, Anchor, 1958. (Originally published 1930.)

Fried, M. The role of work in a mobile society. In S. B. Warner, Jr. (Ed.), *Planning for a nation of cities*. Cambridge, Mass.: M.I.T. Press, 1966.

Furstenberg, F. F., Jr. Work experience and family life. In J. O'Toole (Ed.), *Work and the quality of life*. Cambridge, Mass.: M.I.T. Press, 1974.

Gagné, J. Interview with Janet Zollinger Gielé. At the Vanier Institute of the Family, Ottawa, February 1975.

Garland, N. T. The better half? The male in the dual profession family. In C. Safilios-Rothschild (Ed.), *Toward a sociology of women*. Lexington, Mass.: Xerox, 1972.

Garson, B. *All the livelong day*. Baltimore: Penguin Books, 1977.

Gauger, W. Household work: Can we add it to the GNP? *Journal of Home Economics,* October 1973, pp. 12–23.

Gecas, V. The influence of social class on socialization. In W. R. Burr, R. Hill, F. Ivan Nye, & I. Reiss, *Contemporary theories about the family*. Vol.1: Research-based theories. New York: Free Press, 1979.

Gecas, V., & Nye, F. I. Sex and class differences in parent-child interactions: A test of Kohn's hypothesis. *Journal of Marriage and the Family,* 1974, *36,* 742–749.

Gerstel, N. R. The feasibility of commuter marriage. In P. J. Stein, J. Richman, & N. Hannon (Eds.), *The family: Functions and conflicts and symbols*. Reading, Mass.: Addison-Wesley, 1977.

Gerstel, N. R. *Commuter marriage: Constraints on spouses*. Paper presented at the annual meeting of the American Sociological Association, New York, September 1978.

Ghez, G. R., & Becker, G. S. *The allocation of time and goods over the life cycle*. New York: National Bureau of Economic Research, 1975.

Giele, J. Z. *Social change in the feminine role: A comparison of woman's suffrage and woman's temperance, 1870–1920*. Unpublished doctoral dissertation, Radcliffe College, 1961.

Giele, J. Z. Changing sex roles and the future of marriage. In H. Grunebaum & J. Christ (Eds.), *Contemporary marriage: Structure, dynamics, and therapy*. Boston: Little, Brown, 1976.

Giele, J., & Smock, A. *Women: Roles and status in eight countries*. New York: Wiley, 1977.

Gilman, C. P. *Women and economics*. C. N. Degler (Ed.). New York: Harper & Row, 1966, (Originally published 1898.)

Ginzberg, E. *The manpower connection*. Cambridge, Mass.: Harvard University Press, 1975.

Ginzberg, E. The professionalization of the U. S. Labor force. *Scientific American,* 1979, *240,* 48–53.

Glazer, N. Alternative lifestyles: Societal crises and personal solutions. *Alternative Lifestyles,* 1978, *1,* 423–433.

Glazer-Malbin, N. Housework. *Signs,* 1976, *1,* 905–922.

Glenn, E. N., & Feldberg, R. L. *Structural change and proletarianization: The case of clerical work*. Unpublished paper, Dept. of Sociology, Boston University, June 1976.

Glick, P. C. Demographic shifts: Changes in family structure. In C. D. Hayes (Ed.) *Work, family, and community: Summary proceedings of an ad hoc meeting*. Washington, D.C.: National Academy of Sciences, 1980.

Glueck, W. Changing hours of work: A review and analysis of the research. *Personnel Administrator,* 1979, *3,* 44–47.

Goldberg, H. *The hazards of being male*. New York: New American Library, 1976.

Goldman, N. Women in the armed forces. *American Journal of Sociology,* 1973, *78,* 892–911.

Goode, W. J. *World revolution and family patterns*. New York: Free Press, 1963.

Gordon, N. M. Institutional responses: The federal income tax system. In R. E. Smith (Ed.), *The subtle revolution: Women at work*. Washington, D.C.: Urban Institute Press, 1979. (a)

Gordon, N. M. Institutional responses: The Social Security system. In R. E. Smith (Ed.), *The subtle revolution: Women at work*. Washington, D.C.: Urban Institute Press, 1979. (b)

Gore, S. The effect of social support in moderating the health consequences of unemployment. *Journal of Health and Social Behavior,* 1978, *19,* 157–165.

Gore, S. *Social supports and unemployment stress*. Paper presented at the annual meeting of the American Sociological Association, August 1977.

Gould, R. E. Measuring masculinity by the size of a paycheck. In J. E. Pleck & J. Sawyer (Eds.), *Men and masculinity*. Englewood Cliffs, N.J.: Prentice-Hall, 1974. (Also published in *Ms.* Magazine June 1973, p. 18.)

Gove, W. R., & Geerken, M. R. The effect of children and employment on the mental health of married men and women. *Social Forces,* 1977, *58,* 66–76.

Grabill, W. H., Kiser, C. V., & Whelpton, P. K. A long view. In M. Gordon (Ed.), *The American Family in social-historical perspective*. New York: St. Martin's Press, 1958.

Granovetter, M. S. *Getting a job: A study of contacts and careers*. Cambridge, Mass.: Harvard University Press, 1974.

Greenblatt, B. *Responsibility for child care*. San Francisco: Jossey-Bass, 1978.

Greenwald, H. P. Politics and the new insecurity. *Social Forces,* 1978, *57,* 103–118.

Greiff, B. S., & Munter, P. K. *Tradeoffs: Executive, family, and organizational life*. New York: Mentor, 1980.

Griffiths, M. Can we still afford occupational segregation? In M. Blaxall & B. Reagan (Eds.), *Women and the workplace: The implications of occupational segregation*. Chicago: University of Chicago Press, 1976.

Gronseth, E. The husband-provider role: a critical appraisal. In A. Michel (Ed.), *Family issues of employed women in Europe and America*. Leiden: Brill, 1971.

Gronseth, E. The breadwinner trap. In L. K. Howe (Ed.), *The future of the family*. New York: Simon & Schuster, 1972.

Gross, H. E. Couples who live apart: Time/place disjunctions and their consequences. *Symbolic Interaction,* 1980, *3,* 68-82. (a)

Gross, H. E. Dual-career couples who live apart: Two types. *Journal of Marriage and the Family,* 1980, *42,* 567–576. (b)

Grubb, W. N. *Alternative futures for child care* (Working Paper No. 11, Childhood and Government Project). Berkeley: University of California, 1977.

Gusfield, J. R., & Schwartz, M. The meanings of occupational prestige: Reconsideration of the NORC scale. *American Sociological Review,*1963, *28,* 265–271.

Haddad, G. M. Married, but living apart. *Players,* 1978, *4,* 30, 32, 51.

Hall, D. T. A model of coping with conflict: The role behavior of college educated women. *Administrative Science Quarterly,* 1972, *4,* 471–486.

Hall, F. S., & Hall, D. T. Dual careers–how do couples and companies cope with problems? *Organizational Dynamics,* 1978, 55–77.

Hall, F. S., & Hall D. T. *The two-career couple*. Reading, Mass.: Addison-Wesley, 1979.

Haller, A. O., and Lewis, D. M. The hypothesis of intersocietal similarity in occupational prestige hierarchies. *American Journal of Sociology*, 1966, *72*, 210–216.

Handlin, O. *The uprooted*. Boston: Little, Brown, 1951.

Handy, C. The family: Help or hindrance? In C. L. Cooper & R. Payne (Eds.), *Stress at work*. New York: Wiley, 1978.

Handy, C. Going against the grain: Working couples and greedy occupations. In R. Rapoport & R. N. Rapoport (Eds.), *Working couples*. New York: Harper & Row, 1978.

Hansen, D. A., & Johnson, V. A. Rethinking family stress theory. In W. Burr, R. Hill, I. Reiss, & F. I. Nye (Eds.), *Contemporary theories about the family* (Vol. 1). New York: Free Press, 1979.

Hareven, T. K. Family time and industrial time: Family and work in a planned corporation town, 1900–1924. *Journal of Urban History*, 1975, *1*, 365–389.

Harris, L., & Associates. *Families at work: Strengths and strains*. The General Mills American Family Report, 1980–81. Minneapolis: General Mills, 1981.

Hartman, H. Capitalism, patriarchy, and job segreation by sex. *Signs*, 1976, *1*, 137–170.

Hatt, P. K. Occupation and social stratification. *American Journal of Sociology*, 1950, *55*, 533–543.

Havens, E. M. *The relation between female labor-force participation and fertility rates*. Paper presented at the American Sociological Association Annual Meeting. New Orleans, August 1972.

Havens, E. M. Women, work and wedlock: A note on female marital patterns in the United States. *American Journal of Sociology*, 1973, *78*, 975–981.

Hayghe, H. Families and the rise of working wives: An overview. *Monthly Labor Review*, 1976, 99 (5), 12–19.

Hayghe, H. Marital and family characteristics of the labor force, March 1977. *Monthly Labor Review*, 1978, *101* (2), 51–54.

Hayghe, H. Working wives' contributions to family income in 1977. *Monthly Labor Review*, 1979. *102*, 62–64.

Heckman, N. A., Bryson, R., & Bryson, J. Problems of professional couples: A content analysis. *Journal of Marriage and the Family*, 1977, *39*, 323–330.

Heclo, H., Rainwater, L., Rein, M., & Weiss, R. *Single-parent families: Issues and policies*. Prepared for the Office of Child Development. U. S. Department of Health, Education, and Welfare, 1973.

Hedges, J. N. Flexible schedules: Problems and issues. *Monthly Labor Review*, 1977, *100* (2), 62–65.

Hedges, J. N., & Barnett, J. K. Working women and the division of household tasks. *Monthly Labor Review*, 1972, *95*, 9–14.

Helfrich, M. L. *The social role of the executive's wife*. Columbus: Ohio State University, Bureau of Business Research, 1965.

Hill, R. *Families under stress*. Westport, Conn.: Greenwood, 1949.

Hill, R. Generic features of families under stress. *Social Casework*, 1958, *39*, 139–150.

Hochschild, A. R. The role of the ambassador's wife: An exploratory study. *Journal of Marriage and the Family*, 1969, *31*, 73–87.

Hochschild, A. R. Inside the clockwork of the male career. In F. Howe (Ed.), *Women and the power to change*. New York: McGraw-Hill, 1975.

Hodge, R. W., Siegel, P. M., & Rossi, P. H. Occupational prestige in the United States: 1925–1963. *American Journal of Sociology*, 1964, *70*, 286–302.

Hodge, R. W., Treiman, D. J., & Rossi, P. H. A comparative study of occupational prestige. In R. Bendix and S. M. Lipset (Eds.), *Class, status, and power* (2nd ed.). New York: Free Press. 1966.

Hoff, E. H., & Grueneisen, V. Arbeitserfahrungen, Erziehungseinstellungen, und Erziehungsverhalten von Eltern. In H. Lukesch & K. Schneewind (Eds.), *Familiäre Sozialisation: Probleme, Ergebnisse, Perspektiven*. Stuttgart: Klett, 1977. (a)

Hoff, E. H., & Grueneisen, V. *Personal communication*, 1977. (b)

Hoffman, L. W. Effects of maternal employment on the child: A review of research. *Developmental Psychology*, 1974, 204–228. (a)

Hoffman, L. W. Effects on child. In L. W. Hoffman and F. I. Nye (Eds.), *Working mothers*. San Francisco: Jossey-Bass, 1974. (b)

Hoffman, L. W. Effects of maternal employment on children. In C. D. Hayes (Ed.), *Work, family, and community: Summary proceedings of an ad hoc meeting*. Washington, D.C.: National Academy of Science, 1980.

Hoffman, L. W., & Nye, F. I. *Working mothers*. San Francisco: Jossey-Bass, 1974.

Holmstrom, L. L. Career patterns of married couples. In A. Theodore (Ed.), *The professional woman*. Cambridge, Mass.: Schenkman, 1970.

Holmstrom, L. L. *The two-career family*. Cambridge, Mass.: Schenkman, 1972.

Hopkins, J., & White, P. The dual-career couple: Constraints and supports. *Family Coordinator*, 1978, *27*, 253–259.

Hornblower, M. T. Divorce rate still spirals. *Boston Evening Globe*, 1973, p. 37.

Howe, L. K. *Pink collar workers: Inside the world of women's work*. New York: Avon Books, 1977.

Howell, J. T. *Hard living on clay street: Portraits of blue collar families*. New York: Anchor Books, 1971.

Howell, M. Employed mothers and their families (I). *Pediatrics*, 1973, *52*, 252–263. (a)

Howell, M. Effects of maternal employment on the child (II). *Pediatrics*, 1973, *52*, 327–343. (b)

Human Resources: Companies which come to the aid of employees with job-related emotional problems and find there is a bottom line pay-off. *Executive Magazine* (Los Angeles ed.), May 1980, pp. 55–75.

Hunt, J. G., & Hunt, L. L. Dilemmas and contradictions of status: The case of the dual-career family. *Social Problems*, 1977, *24*, 407–416.

Hunt, J. G., & Hunt, L. L. *The dualities of careers and families: New integrations or new polarizations*. Paper presented at the annual meeting of the American Sociological Association, 1981.

Hynes, E. Personal communication, 1977.

Inkeles, A., & Rossi, P. H. National comparisons of occupational prestige. *American Journal of Sociology*, 1956, *61*, 329–339.

Jones, C. A. *A review of child support payment performance*. Washington, D.C.: Urban Institute, 1976.

Kahn, A., & Kamerman, S. *Social services in international perspective*. New York: Columbia University Press, 1977.

Kamerman, S. *Work and family in industrialized societies*. Mimeograph. Cross National Studies of Social Services and Family Policy, Columbia University, September 21, 1978.

Kamerman, S. B. *Parenting in an unresponsive society: Managing work and family life*. New York: Free Press, 1980.

Kamerman, S. B., & Kahn, A. J. *Social services in the United States*. Philadelphia: Temple University Press, 1976.

Kamerman, S. B., & Kahn, A. J. The day-care debate: A wider view. *Public Interest*, 1979, *54*, 76–91.

Kanter, R. M. *Communes, the family, and sex roles*. Paper presented at the annual meeting of the American Sociological Association, New Orleans, August 1972.

Kanter, R. M. *Work and family in the United States: A critical review and agenda for research and policy*. New York: Russell Sage Foundation, 1977. (a)

Kanter, R. M. *Men and women of the corporation*. New York: Basic Books, 1977. (b)

Kasl, S. V., & Cobb, S. Some mental health consequences of plant closing and job loss. In L. A. Ferman & J. P. Gordus (Eds.), *Mental health and the economy*. Kalamazoo, Mich.: W. E. Upjohn Institute, 1979.

Keniston, K. *The uncommitted: Alienated youth in American society*. New York: Harcourt Brace Jovanovich, 1965.

Kirschner, B., and Walum, L. Two-location families: Married singles. *Alternative Lifestyles*, 1978, *1*, 513-525.

Kohn, M. L. *Class and conformity: A study in values*. Homewood, Ill.: Dorsey Press, 1969. (2nd ed. published 1977, by University of Chicago Press.)

Kohn, M. L. Social class and schizophrenia: A critical review and a reformulation. *Schizophrenia Bulletin*, 1973, *7*, 60–79.

Kohn, M. L. The interaction of social class and other factors in the etiology of schizophrenia. *American Journal of Psychiatry*, 1976, *133*, 177–180. (a)

Kohn, M. L. Looking back—a 25 year review and appraisal of social problems research. *Social Problems*, 1976, *24*, 94–112. (b)

Kohn, M. L. Social class and parental values. Another confirmation of the relationship. *American Sociological Review*, 1976, *41*, 538-545 (c)

Kohn, M. L. Occupational structure and alienation. *American Journal of Sociology*, 1976, *82*, 111–130. (d)

Kohn, M. L., & Schooler, C. Occupational experience and psychological functioning: An assessment of reciprocal effects. *American Sociological Review*, 1973, *38*, 97–118.

Kohn, M. L., & Schooler, C. The reciprocal effects of the substantive complexity of work and intellectual flexibility: A longitudinal assessment. *American Journal of Sociology*, 1978, *84*, 24–52.

Kohn. M. L., & Schooler, C. Job conditions and personality: A longitudinal assessment of their reciprocal effects. *American Journal of Sociology*, 1982, *87*, 1257–1286.

Komarovsky, M. *The unemployed man and his family*. New York: Dryden, 1940.

Komarovsky, M. *Blue-collar marriage*. New York: Random House, 1964.

Krause, N., & Stryker, S. *Job-related stress, economic stress, and psycho-physicological well-being*. Paper presented at the annual meeting of the North Central Sociological Association, May 1980.

Kreps, J. M., & Clark, R. *Sex, age, and work: The changing composition of the labor force*. Baltimore: Johns Hopkins University Press, 1975.

Kronholz, J. Women at work, management practices change to reflect role of women employees. *Wall Street Journal*, September 13, 1978, p. 1.

Kuviesky, W. P., & Obordo, A. S. A racial comparison of teenage girls' projection for marriage and procreation. *Journal of Marriage and the Family*, 1972, *34*, 75–84.

Ladner, J. *Tomorrow's tomorrow*. New York: Doubleday, 1972.

Lambert, W. E., Hamers, J. F., & Frasure-Smith, N. *Child-rearing values: A cross-national study*. New York: Praeger, 1980.

Land, H., & Parker, R. Family policy in the United Kingdom. In S. B. Kamerman & A. J. Kahn (Eds.), *Family policy: Government and families in fourteen countries*. New York: Columbia University Press, 1978.

Laslett, P. *Household and family in past time*. Cambridge, England: Cambridge University Press, 1972.

Leading two lives–women at work and home. *Newsweek*, May 19, 1980, pp. 72–78.

Lefkowitz, B. Life without work. *Newsweek*, May 14, 1979, p. 31.

Lein, L. Male participation in home life: Impact of social supports and breadwinner responsibility on the allocation of tasks. *Family Coordinator*, 1979, *28*, 489–495. (a)

Lein, L. Working couples as parents. In E. Corfman (Ed.), *Families Today* (Vol. 1). Bethesda, Md.: National Institute of Mental Health, 1979. (b)

Lien, L. Durham, M., Pratt, M., Schudson, M., Thomas, R., & Weiss, H. *Final report: Work and family life*. National Institute of Education Project No. 3-33094. Cambridge, Mass.: Center for the study of Public Policy, 1974.

Lekachman, R. On economic equality. *Signs*, 1975, *1* (Autumn), 93–102.

LeMasters, E. E. *Blue-collar aristocrats: Life-styles at a working-class tavern*. Madison: University of Wisconsin Press, 1975.

Levine, J. A. *Who will raise the children? New options for fathers (and mothers)*. Philadelphia: Lippincott, 1976.

Levine, J. *Day care and the public schools*. Newton, Mass.: Educational Development Corporation, 1978.

Levison, A. The working-class majority. *New Yorker,* September 2, 1974, pp. 36–61.

Levinson, D. J. Role personality and social structure in the organizational setting. *Journal of Abnormal and Social Psychology,* 1959, *58,* 170–180.

Levitan, S. A., & Alderman, K. *Child care and the ABC's too*. Baltimore: Johns Hopkins University Press, 1975.

Levitan, T. E., Quinn, R. P., & Staines, G. L. A woman is 58% of a man . . . on the American payroll. In C. Tavris (Ed.), *The female experience*. Del Mar, Calif.: CRM Books, 1973.

Liebow, E. *Tally's corner*. Boston: Little, Brown, 1966.

Little, C. B. Technical-professional unemployment: Middle-class adaptability to personal crisis. *Sociological Quarterly,* 1976, *17,* 262–274.

Litwak, E. Technological innovation and ideal forms of family structure in an industrial democratic society. In R. Hill & R. Konig, (Eds.), *Families in East and West*. Paris: Mouton, 1970.

Loeser, H. *Women, work, and volunteering*. Boston: Beacon Press, 1974.

Lopata, H. *Occupation housewife*. New York: Oxford University Press, 1971.

Lynn, D. B. *The father: His role in child development*. Monterey, Calif.: Brooks/Cole, 1974.

Maccoby, M. *The gamesman*. New York: Simon & Schuster, 1976.

Machlowitz, M. *Workaholics: Living with them, working with them*. New York: Mentor, 1980.

MacPherson, M. *The power lovers: An intimate look at politicians and their marriages*. New York: Putnam, 1975.

Mahoney, T. A. The rearranged work week. *California Management Review,* 1978, *20,* 31–39.

Mainardi, P. The politics of housework. In R. Morgan (Ed.), *Sisterhood is powerful*. New York: Vintage Books, 1970.

Margolis, L. H., & Ferran, D.C. Unemployment: The health consequences in children. *North Carolina Medical Journal,* 1981, *42,* 849–850.

Marks, S. R. Multiple roles and role strain: Some notes on human energy, time and commitment. *American Sociological Review,* 1977, *42,* 921–936.

Martin, V. H. Recruiting women workers through flexible hours. *S.A.M. Advanced Management Journal,* 1974 (July), pp. 46–53.

Martin, T. W., Berry K. J., & Jacobsen, R. B. The impact of dual-career marriages on female professional careers: An empirical test of a Parsonian hypothesis. *Journal of Marriage and the Family,* 1975, *37,* 734–742.

Mason, K. O., & Bumpass, L. L. U. S. women's sex-role ideology. *American Journal of Sociology,* 1970, *80,* 1212–1219.

Mason, K. O., Czajka, J., & Arber, S. Change in U. S. women's sex-role attitudes, 1964–1974. *American Sociological Recview,* 1976, *41,* 573–596.

McCubbin, H. Integrating coping behavior in family stress theory. *Journal of Marriage and the Family,* 1979, *41,* 237–244.

McCubbin, H., Dahl, B. B., & Ross, B. A. The returned prisoner of war: Factors in family reintegration. *Journal of Marriage and the Family,* 1974, *37,* 471–478.

McCubbin, H., Joy, C. B., Cauble, A. E., Comeau, J. K., Patterson, J. M., & Needle, R. N. Family stress and coping. *Journal of Marriage and the Family,* 1980, *42,* 855–871.

McKinley, D. G. *Social class and family life*. New York: Free Press, 1964.

Meade, E. *Role satisfaction of housewives*. Paper presented at annual meeting of Eastern Sociological Association, New York City, August 1975.

Meissner, M., Humphreys, E., Meis, S., & Scheu, W. No exit for wives: equal division of labor and the cumulation of household demands. *Canadian Review of Sociology and Anthropology,* 1975, *12,* 424–439.

Miller, D. R., & Swanson, G. E. *The changing American parent*. New York: Wiley, 1958.

Miller, H. P. A profile of the blue-collar American. In S. A. Levitan (Ed.), *Blue collar worker: A symposium on middle America*. New York: McGraw-Hill, 1971.

Miller, J., & Garrison H. H. Sex roles: The division of labor at home and in the workplace. *Annual Review of Sociology*, 1982, *8*, 237–262.

Miller, J., Schooler, C., Kohn, M., & Miller, K. Women and work: The psychological effects of occupational conditions. *American Journal of Sociology*, 1979, *85*, 66–94.

Mincer, J. Labor force participation of married women. In National Bureau of Economic Research (Ed.), *Aspects of labor economics*. Princeton, N.J.: Princeton University, 1962.

Ministry of Health and Social Affairs, International Secretariat. *Parental insurance in Sweden—some data*. Stockholm, Sweden, 1977.

Modell, J., & Hareven, T. K. Urbanization and the malleable household: An examination of boarding and lodging in American families. *Journal of Marriage and the Family*, 1973, *35*, 467–479.

Moen, P. Family impacts of the 1975 recession. *Journal of Marriage and the Family*, 1979, *41*, 561–572.

Moen, P. Developing family indicators. *Journal of Family Issues*, 1980, *1*, 5–30.

Moore, K. A. *Fear of success: Antecedents, consequences and correlates of fear of success imagery among females in a metropolitan survey sample*. Unpublished doctoral dissertation, University of Michigan, 1975.

Mortimer, J. T. Occupational value socialization in business and professional families. *Sociology of Work and Occupations*, 1975, *2*, 29–53.

Mortimer, J. T. Social class, work, and the family: Some implications of the father's occupation for familial relations and sons' career decisions. *Journal of Marriage and the Family*, 1976, *38*, 241–256.

Mortimer, J. T. Dual career families–a sociological perspective In S. S. Peterson, J. M. Richardson, & G. V. Kreuter (Eds.), *The two career family: Issues and alternatives*. Washington D.C.: University Press of America, 1978.

Mortimer, J. T. Occupation-family linkages as perceived by men in the early stages of professional and managerial careers. In H. Z. Lopata (Ed.), *Research in the interweave of social roles: Women and men* (Vol. 1). Greenwood: AIJ, 1980.

Mortimer, J., Hall, R., & Hill, R. Husband's occupational attributes as constraints on wives' employment. *Sociology of Work and Occupations*, 1978, *5*, 285–313. (Given as paper at the annual meeting of the American Sociological Association, 1976.)

Mortimer, J. T., & Kumka, D. A further examination of the "occupational linkage hypothesis." *Sociological Quarterly*, 1982 (Winter).

Mortimer, J. T., & Lorence, J. Occupational experience and the self-concept: A longitudinal study. *Social Psychology Quarterly*, 1979, *42*, 307–323.

Mortimer, J. T., Lorence, J., & Kumka, D. *Work and family linkages in the transition to adulthood: A panel study of highly educated men*. Paper presented at the annual meeting of the American Sociological Association, 1982.

Mosley, M. *Self-perception of roles of black and white female college students*. Unpublished manuscript, University of Cincinnati, 1976.

Mott, P., Mann, F.C., McLoughlin, Q., & Warwick, D. P. *Shift work: The social, psychological, and physical consequences*. Ann Arbor: University of Michigan Press, 1965.

Movius, M. Voluntary childlessness—The ultimate liberation. *Family Coordinator*, 1976, *25*, 57–62.

Moynihan, D. P. *The Negro family: The case for national action*. Washington D.C.: U.S. Department of Labor, 1965.

Myers, L. Black women: Selectivity among roles and reference groups in the maintenance of self-esteem. *Journal of Social and Behavioral Sciences*, 1975, *21*, 39–47.

Myrdal, A., & Klein, V. *Woman's two roles*. London: Routledge & Kegan Paul, 1968. (Originally published 1956.)

The new corporate wife goes to work. *Business Week*, April 8, 1979, pp. 88–90.

Nicholson, W., & Corson, W. *A longitudinal study of unemployment insurance exhaustees.* Princeton, N.J.: Mathematica, Inc., 1976.

Nollen, S. D., & Martin, V. H. *Alternative work schedules.* Part 1: *Flexitime, an AMA survey report.* New York: American Management Association, 1978.

North, C. C., & Hatt, P. K. Jobs and occupations: A popular evaluation. In R. Bendix & S. M. Lipset (Eds.), *Class, Status, and Power.* New York: Free Press, 1953.

Nye, F. I. Emerging and declining family roles. *Journal of Marriage and the Family,* 1974, *36,* 238–245.

Oakley, A. Are husbands good housewives? *New Society,* 1972, *112,* 377–379.

Oakley, A. *The sociology of housework.* New York: Pantheon, 1975.

O'Leary, V., & Harrison, A. O. *Sex role stereotypes as a function of race and sex.* Paper presented at the 83rd annual convention of the American Psychological Association, Chicago, August 1975.

Olsen, S. M. *Family, occupation, and values in a Chinese urban community.* Unpublished doctoral dissertation, Cornell University, 1971.

One job, two careers. *Working Women,* March 1981, pp. 79–80, 82, 84.

Oppenheimer, V. K. *The female labor force in the United States* (Population Monograph Series No. 3). Berkeley: University of California, 1970.

Oppenheimer, V. K. Women's economic role in the family. *American Sociological Review,* 1974, *42,* 387–406.

Oppenheimer, V. K. The Sex-labeling of jobs. In M. T. S. Mednick, S. S. Tangri, & L. W. Hoffman (Eds.), *Women and achievement.* Washington, D.C.: Hemisphere Publishing, 1975.

Orden, S. R., & Bradburn, N. M. Working wives and marriage happiness. *American Journal of Sociology,* 1969, *74,* 382–407.

O'Toole, J. Thank God. It's Monday. *Best of Business,* 1980 (Fall), pp. 23–28.

Pahl, J. M., & Pahl, R. E. *Managers and their wives.* London: Allen Lane, 1971.

Papanek, H. Men, women and work: Reflections of the two-person career. *American Journal of Sociology,* 1973, *78,* 852–872.

Parsons, T. The social structure of the family. In R. N. Anshen (Ed.), *The family: Its function and destiny.* New York: Harper, 1949.

Parsons, T., & Bales, R. F. *Family socialization and the interaction process.* New York: Free Press, 1955.

Pearlin, L. I. *Class context and family relations.* Boston: Little, Brown, 1974.

Perron, R. *Modèles d'enfants, enfants modèles.* Paris: Presses Universitaires de France, 1971.

Perrucci, C., & Targ, D. (Eds.), *Marriage and the family: A critical analysis and proposals for change.* New York: McKay, 1974.

Piotrkowski, C. S. *Work and the family system.* New York: Free Press, 1978.

Platt, J. *Social class and childrearing norms in Britain and the U.S.* Unpublished manuscript, University of Sussex, n.d.

Pleck, E. Two worlds in one: Work and family. *Journal of Social History,* 1976, *10,* 178–195.

Pleck, J. H. The work-family role system. *Social Problems,* 1977, *24,* 417–427.

Pleck, J. H. Men's family work: Three perspectives and some new data. *Family Coordinator,* 1979, *28,* 481–488.

Pleck, J., & Lang, L. Men's family role: Its nature and consequences. Wellesley, Mass.: Wellesley College Center for Research on Women, 1978.

Pleck, J. H., & Rustad, M. *Husbands' and wives' time in family work and paid work in 1975–76 study of time use.* Unpublished paper. Wellesley College Center for Research on Women, 1980.

Pleck, J. H., & Sawyer, J. (Eds.), *Men and masculinity.* Englewood Cliffs, N.J.: Prentice-Hall, 1974.

Pleck, J. H., Staines, G. L., & Lang, L. *Work and family life: First reports on work-family interference and workers' formal childcare arrangements, from the 1977 Quality of*

Employment Survey. Paper prepared under contract with U.S. Department of Labor. Rev., September 1978.

Pleck, J. H., Staines, G. L., and Lang, L. Conflicts between work and family life. *Monthly Labor Review*, 1980 (March), pp. 29–32.

Polatnick, M. Why men don't rear children: A power analysis. *Berkeley Journal of Sociology*, 1973–1974, *18*, 45–86.

Polit, D. F. Nontraditional work schedules for women. In K. W. Feinstein (Ed.), *Working women and families*. Beverly Hills, Calif.: Sage, 1979.

Poloma, M. M. Role conflict and the married professional woman. In C. Safilios-Rothschild (Ed.), *Toward a sociology of women*. Lexington, Mass.: Xerox, 1972.

Poloma M. M., & Garland, T. N. The married professional woman: A study of the tolerance of domestication. *Journal of Marriage and the Family*, 1971, *33*, 531–540. (a)

Poloma, M. M., & Garland, T. N. The myth of the egalitarian family. In A. Theodore (Ed.), *The professional woman*. Cambridge, Mass.: Schenckman, 1971. (b)

Poloma, M. M., Pendleton, B. F., & Garland, T. N. Reconsidering the dual career marriage. *Journal of Family Issues*, 1981, *2*, 205–224.

Pour-El, M. B. Spatial separation in family life: A mathematician's choice. In L. A. Steen (Ed.), *Mathematics tomorrow*. New York: Springer-Verlag, 1981.

Powell, D. H., & Driscoll, P. F. Middle-class professionals face unemployment. *Society*, 1973, *10*, 18–26.

Prather, J. When the girls move in: A sociological analysis of the feminization of the bank teller's job. *Journal of Marriage and the Family*, 1971, *33*, 777–782.

Preston, S., & Richards, A. T. The influence of women's work opportunities on marriage rates. *Demography*, 1975, *12*, 209–222.

Quinn, R., & Staines, G. *The quality of employment survey: 1977*. Ann Arbor: Inter-University Consortium for Political and Social Research, 1979.

Rainwater, L. Making the good life: Working-class family and lifestyles. In S. A. Levitan (Ed.), *Blue collar workers: A symposium on Middle America*. New York: McGraw-Hill, 1971.

Rainwater, L. *What money buys*. New York: Basic Books, 1974.

Rainwater, L. Work, well-being, and family life. In J. O'Toole (Ed.), *Work and the quality of life*. Cambridge, Mass.: M.I.T. Press, 1974.

Rainwater, L. *Women's employment preferences and participation in the EEC countries* (Family Policy Note No. 9). Cambridge, Mass.: Joint Center for Urban Studies of Harvard and M.I.T., 1977.

Rainwater, L., Coleman, R. P., & Handel, G. *Workingman's wife*. New York: Oceana, 1959.

Rainwater, L., & Yancey, W. L. *The Moynihan report and the politics of controversy*. Cambridge Mass.: M.I.T. Press, 1967.

Ramey, J. W. Intimate groups and networks: Frequent consequences of sexually open marriage. *Family Coordinator*, 1975, *24*, 515–530.

Rapoport, R. *Unemployment and the family*. Loch Memorial Lecture, Family Welfare Association, London, 1981.

Rapoport, R., & Rapoport, R. Work and family in modern society. *American Sociological Review*, 1965, *30*, 381–394.

Rapoport, R., & Rapoport, R. N. *Dual-career families*. Baltimore: Penguin Books, 1971.

Rapoport, R., & Rapoport, R. The dual career family: A variant pattern and social change. In C. Safilios-Rothschild (Ed.), *Toward a sociology of women*. Lexington, Mass.: Xerox, 1972.

Rapoport, R., & Rapoport, R. *The working woman and the enabling role of the husband*. Paper given at the XIIth International Family Research Seminar, International Sociological Association, Moscow, 1972. (b)

Rapoport, R., & Rapoport, R. N. *Dual-career families re-examined*. New York: Harper & Row, 1976.

Rapoport, R., Rapoport, R. N., and Thiessen, V. Couple symmetry and enjoyment. *Journal of Marriage and the Family*, 1974, *36*, 588–591.

Rapoport, R. N., & Rapoport, R. Dual-career families: Progress and prospects. *Marriage and Family Review*, 1978, *1*(5), 1–12. (a)

Rapoport, R. N., & Rapoport, R. *Working couples*. New York: Harper & Row, 1978. (b)

Reiss, A. J., Duncan, O. D., Hatt, P. K., & North, C. C. *Occupations and social status*. New York: Free Press, 1961.

Renshaw, J. An exploration of the dynamics of the overlapping worlds of work and family. *Family Process*, 1976, *15*, 143–165.

Rice, D. *Dual-career marriage: Conflict and treatment*. New York: Free Press, 1979.

Richardson, J. G. Wife occupational superiority and marital troubles: An examination of the hypothesis. *Journal of Marriage and the Family*, 1979, *41*, 63–72.

Ridley, C. A. Exploring the impact of work satisfaction and involvement on marital interaction when both partners are employed. *Journal of Marriage and the Family*, 1973, *35*, 229–237.

Ritzer, G. *Working, conflict and change*. Englewood Cliffs, N.J.: Prentice-Hall, 1977.

Robinson, J. *How Americans use time*. New York: Praeger, 1977.

Robinson, J., Juster, T., & Stafford, F. *Americans' use of time*. Ann Arbor, Mich.: Institute for Social Research, 1976.

Robinson, J., Yerby, J., Feiweger, M., & Sommerick, N. *Time use as an indicator of sex role territoriality*. Unpublished paper, Dept. of Communications, Cleveland State University, 1976.

Rodman, H., & Safilios-Rothschild, C. Weak links in men's worker-earner roles: A descriptive model. In H. Lopata & J. Pleck (Eds.), *Research in the interweave of social roles*. Vol. 3: *Families and jobs*. Greenwich, Conn.: JAI Press, 1983.

Roland, A., & Harris, B. *Career and motherhood: Struggles for a new identity*. New York: Human Sciences, 1979.

Root, K. *Workers and their families in a plant shutdown*. Paper presented at the annual meeting of the American Sociological Association, August 1977.

Root, K. A., & Mayland, R. L. *The plant's closing, what are we going to do?* Paper presented at the annual meeting of the National Council on Family Relations, October 1978.

Roper Organization. *The Virginia Slims American Women's Opinion Poll*. Vol 3: *A survey of the attitudes of women on marriage, divorce, the family, and America's changing sexual morality*. New York: Roper Organization, 1974.

Rosenberg, M. *Conceiving the self*. New York: Basic Books, 1979.

Rosenfield, C. Job search of the unemployed, May 1976. *Monthly Labor Review*, 1977, *100*, 39–43.

Rosow, J. M. The problems of lower-middle-income workers. In S. A. Levitan, *Blue collar workers: A symposium on middle America*. New York: McGraw-Hill, 1971.

Ross, H. L., & Sawhill, I. V. *Time of transition: The growth of families headed by women*. Washington D.C.: Urban Institute, 1975.

Rossi, A. S. A biosocial perspective on parenting. *Daedalus*, 1977, *106*, 1–31.

Rothman, S. Other people's children: The day care experience in America. *Public Interest*, 1973 (Winter).

Rubin, L. B. *Worlds of pain: Life in the working class family*. New York: Basic Books, 1976.

Rudd, N. *Dual-earner families: Issues and implications*. Paper presented at Dual Earner Family Symposium, Purdue University, October 21, 1981.

Rule, S. Long distance marriages on the rise. *New York Times*, Section M:31, October 31, 1977.

Ryder, N. B. A critique of the national fertility study. *Demography*, 1973, *10*.

Ryscavage, P. More wives in the labor force have husbands with 'above-average' incomes. *Monthly Labor Review*, 1979, *102* (6), 40–42.

Safilios-Rothschild, C. The study of family power structure: A review 1960-1969. *Journal of Marriage and the Family*, 1970, *32*, 539–552.

Safilios-Rothschild, C. Parents' need for child care. In P. Roby (Ed.), *Child care: Who cares?* New York: Basic Books, 1973.

Safilios-Rothschild, C. Dual linkages between the occupational and family systems: A macrosociological analysis. *Signs, 1976, 1* (3), 51–60.

Samuels, V. *Nowhere to be found: A literature review and annotated bibliography on white working-class women*. New York: Institute on Pluralism and Group Identity, 1975.

Sarason, S. B. *Working, aging, and social change*. New York: Free Press, 1977.

Saul, L. Living apart, but together. *New York Times,* Section 11:191, September 26, 1976.

Sawhill, I. Discrimination and poverty among women who head families. In M. Blaxall & B. Reagan (Eds.), *Women and the workplace: The implications of occupational segregation*. Chicago: University of Chicago Press, 1976.

Sawhill, I. V. Economic perspective on the family. *Daedalus,* 1977, *106* (Spring), 115–125.

Scanzoni, J. Resolution of occupational-conjugal role conflict in clergy marriages. *Journal of Marriage and the Family,* 1965, *27,* 396–402.

Scanzoni, J. *Opportunity and the family*. New York: Free Press, 1970.

Scanzoni, J. *Sexual bargaining*. Englewood Cliffs, N.J.: Prentice-Hall, 1972.

Scanzoni, J. Sex roles, economic factors, and marital solidarity in black and white marriages. *Journal of Marriage and the Family,* 1975, *37,* 140–144. (a)

Scanzoni, J. *Sex roles, life styles, and childbearing*. New York: Free Press, 1975. (b)

Scanzoni, J. H. An historical perspective on husband-wife bargaining power and marital dissolution. In G. Levinger & O. Moles (Eds.), *Divorce and separation in America*. New York: Basic Books, 1979.

Shaefer, E. S. A circumplex model for maternal behavior. *Journal of Abnormal and Social Psychology,* 1959, *59,* 226–235.

Schlesinger, B. Family life in the kibbutz of Israel: Utopia gained or paradise lost? In H. P. Dreitzel (Ed.), *Family, marriage, and the struggle of the sexes*. New York: Macmillan, 1972.

Schorr, A. L., & Moen, P. The single parent and public policy. *Social Policy,* 1979 (March/April), pp. 15–21.

Schlozman, K. L., & Verba, S. *The new unemployment: Does it hurt?* Public Policy, 1978, *26,* 333–358.

Schneller, D. P. Prison families: A study of some social and psychological effects of incarceration on the families of Negro prisoners. *Criminology,* 1975, *12,* 402–412.

Schrank, R., & Stein, S. Yearning, learning, and status. In S. A. Levitan (Ed.), *Blue collar workers; A symposium on middle America*. New York: McGraw-Hill, 1971.

Schwartz, J. *Three studies in stratification*. Unpublished doctoral dissertation, Harvard University, 1978.

Scurrah, M. J., & Montalvo, A. *Close social y valores sociales en Peru*. Lima, Peru: Escuela de Administracion de Negocios Para Graduados (Series: Documento de Trabaio No. 8), 1975.

Seidenberg, R. *Corporate wives–corporate casualties?* New York: Amacon, 1973.

Seifer, N. *The working family in crises: Who is listening?* Project in Group Life and Ethnic Americans, American Jewish Committee. New York: Institute on Pluralism and Group Identity, 1975.

Sennett, R., & Cobb, J. *The hidden injuries of class*. New York: Vintage Books, 1972.

Sewell, W. H., Hauser, R. M., & Wolfe, W. C. Sex, schooling, and occupational status. *American Journal of Sociology,* 1980, *86,* 551–583.

Seybolt, J. W. Work satisfaction as a function of person-environment interaction. *Organizational Behavior and Human Performance,* 1976, *17,* 66–75.

Sheppard, H, L., Ferman, L. A., & Faber, S. *Too old to work–too young to retire*.Washington D.C.: U.S. Government Printing Office, 1959.

Sidel, R. *Women and child care in China*. New York: Hill and Wang, 1972.

Sidel, R. *Urban survival; The world of working class women*. Boston: Beacon Press, 1978.

Sieber, S. D. Toward a theory of role accumulation. *American Sociological Review,* 1974, *39,* 567–578.

Silver, C. B. France: Contrasts in familial and societal roles. In J. Z. Giele & A. C. Smock (Eds.), *Women: Roles and status in eight countries*. New York: Wiley, 1977.

Simmons. R. G., & Rosenberg, M. Functions of children's perceptions of the stratification system. *American Sociological Review,* 1971, *36,* 235–249.

Skalka, P. What's good for the family is good for General Motors. *Passages* (magazine of Northwest Orient Airlines), 1979, *10,* 28–32.

Slote, A. *Termination*. New York: Bobbs-Merrill, 1969.

Smelser, N. J. *Social change in the industrial revolution*. Chicago: University of Chicago Press, 1959.

Smith, R. E. (Ed.), *The subtle revolution*. Washington D.C.: Urban Institute, 1979.

Smuts, R. W. *Women and work in America*. New York: Columbia University Press, 1959.

Snyder, L. The deserting, non-supporting father–Scapegoat of family non-policy. *Family Coordinator*, 1979, *38*, 595–598.

Sokolowska, M. Poland: Women's experience under socialism. In J. Z. Giele & A. C. Smock (Eds.), *Women: Roles and status in eight countries*. New York: Wiley, 1977.

Spenner, K. I. Occupational role characteristics and intergenerational transmission. *Sociology of Work and Occupations*, 1981, *8*, 89–112.

Stack, C. B. *All our kin: Strategies for survival in a black community*. New York: Harper & Row, 1974.

Statistical Abstract of the United States, 1973. Washington D.C.: U.S. Department of Commerce, Social and Economic Statistics Administration.

Stein, S. The company cares for children. In P. Roby (Ed.), *Child care: Who cares?* New York: Basic Books, 1973.

Steiner, G. *The children's cause*. Washington D.C.: Brookings Institute, 1976.

Steinfels, M. O. *Who's minding the children*. New York: Simon & Schuster, 1973.

Steinmetz, S. K., & Straus, M. A. (Eds.), *Violence in the family*. New York: Harper & Row, 1974.

St. John-Parsons, D. Continuous dual-career families: A case study. In J. B. Bryson & R. Bryson (Eds.), *Dual-career couples*. New York: Human Sciences, 1978.

St. Peter, L. G. *Fate conceptions: A look at the effects of occupational tasks on human values*. Unpublished doctoral dissertation, University of Nebraska, 1975.

Strober, M. H. Women and men in the world of work: Present and future. In L. A. Cater, A. F. Scott, & W. Martyn (Eds.), *Women and men: Changing roles, relationships and perceptions*. New York: Praeger, 1977.

Svalastoga, K. *Prestige, class and mobility*. Copenhagen: Glydendal, 1959.

Swart, J. C. Flexitime's debit and credit option. *Harvard Business Review*, 1979, *1*, 10–12.

Sweet, J. A. *The living arrangements of separated, widowed, and divorced mothers* (Working Paper #71-4). Madison: University of Wisconsin, Center for Demography and Ecology, 1971.

Szalai, A. *The quality of family life-traditional and modern: A review of sociological findings on contemporary family organization and role differentiation in the family*. Paper presented at the United Nations Interregional Seminar on the Family in a Changing Society: Problems and Responsibilities of Its Members, London, July 1973.

Taeuber, K. A., & Sweet, J. A. Family and work: The social life cycle of women. In J. M. Kreps (Ed.), *Women and the American economy*. Englewood Cliffs, N.J.: Prentice-Hall, 1976.

Talmon, Y. *Family and community in the kibbutz*. Cambridge, Mass.: Harvard University Press, 1972.

Taylor, M. G., & Hartley, S. The two-person career: A classic example. *Sociology of Work and Occupations*, 1975, *2*, 354–372.

Teague, C. H. Easing the pain of plant closure. *Management Review*, 1981, pp. 23–27.

Thomas, R. M. Reinspecting a structural position on occupational prestige. *American Journal of Sociology*, 1962, pp. 561–565.

Tiryakian, E. A. The prestige evaluation of occupations in an underdeveloped country: The Phillippines. *American Journal of Sociology*, 1958, *63*, 390–399.

Tocqueville, A. de. *Democracy in America*. New York: Langley, 1840.

Toffler, A. *The third wave*. New York: Morrow, 1980.

Turner, B. F., & McCaffrey, J. Socialization and career orientation among black and white college women. *Journal of Vocational Behavior*, 1974, *5*, 307–319.

Turner, C. Dual work households and marital dissolution. *Human Relations*, 1971, *24*, 535–548.

U.S. Bureau of the Census. *Employment status and work experience*. Washington, D.C.: U.S. Government Printing Office, 1970.

U.S. Bureau of the Census. Nursery school and kindergarten enrollment of children and labor-force status of their mothers: October 1967 to October 1976. *Current Population Reports* (Series P-20, No. 318). Washington, D.C.: U.S. Government Printing Office, 1978.

U.S. Bureau of the Census. *Child support and alimony: 1978* (Series P-23, No. 112). Washington D.C.: U.S. Government Printing Office, 1981.

U.S. Comptroller General. *Benefits from flexible work schedules—legal limitations remain* (report to the Congress; EPCD—78-62), Washington, D.C.: General Accounting Office, 1977.

U.S. Congress, House of Representatives. *A bill to authorize federal agencies to experiment with flexible and compressed employee work schedules*. Ninety-fifth Congress, 1st session, H. R. 7814, June 15, 1977.

U.S. Department of Labor. *The Dictionary of Occupational Titles*. Washington, D.C.: U.S. Government Printing Office, 1977.

U.S. Department of Labor. *Perspectives on working women: A datebook*. Bulletin 2080, Bureau of Labor Statistics. Washington, D.C.: U.S. Government Printing Office, 1980.

U.S. Senate Subcommittee on children and youth. *American families: Trends and pressures, 1973: Hearings*. Washington, D.C.: U.S. Government Printing Office.

VanDusen, R. A., & Sheldon, E. B. The changing status of American women: A life cycle perspective. In A. Skolnick and J. Skolnick (Eds.), *Family in transition*. Boston: Little, Brown, 1977.

Vanek, J. Time spent in housework. *Scientific American,* November 1974, 116–120.

Velle, L. Where have all the fathers gone? *Reader's Digest,* 1973, *102,* 155–157.

Voydanoff, P. *The influence of economic security on morale*. Unpublished thesis, Wayne State University, 1963.

Voydanoff, P. Unemployment and the family. In J. Sale (Ed.), *Readings*. Pasadena, Calif.: National Consortium for Children and Families, 1978.

Voydanoff, P. Unemployment and family stress. In H. Lopata & J. Pleck (Eds.), *Research in the interweave of social roles*. Vol. 3: *Families and jobs*. Greenwich, Conn.: JAI Press, in press.

Wade, M. *Flexible working hours in practice*. East Kilbride, Scotland: Gower, 1973.

Waldman, E., & McEaddy, B. Where women work: An analysis by industry and occupation. *Monthly Labor Review,* 1974, *95* (5), 3–13.

Wallston, B. S., Foster, M. A., & Berger, M. I will follow him: myth, reality, or forced choice—job seeking experiences of dual-career couples. In J. B. Bryson & R. Bryson (Eds.), *Dual-career couples*. New York: Human Sciences, 1978.

Walker, K. E. Time spent in household work by homemakers. *Family Economics Review,* 1969, *3,* 5–6.

Walker, K. E. Time spent by husbands in household work. *Family Economics Review,* 1970, *4,* 8–11.

Walker, K. E. Unpublished data, Dept. of Consumer Economics and Public Policy, Cornell University, 1974.

Walker, K., & Woods, M. E. *Time use: A measure of household production of family goods and services*. Washington, D.C.: American Home Economics Association, 1976.

Walker, K. E., & Gauger, W. Time and its dollar value in household work. *Family Economics Review,* 1973, *7,* 8–13.

Walshok, M. L. Occupational values and family roles: Women in blue-collar and service occupations. In K. W. Feinstein (Ed.), *Working women and family*. Beverly Hills, Calif.: Sage, 1979.

Warner, W. L., & Ablegglen, J. O. *Big business leaders in America*. New York: Harper, 1955.

Weinstein, F., & Platt, G. M. *The wish to be free*. Berkeley, Calif.: University of California Press, 1969.

Wheeler, K. E., Gurman, R., & Tarnowieski, D. *The four day week: An AMA research report*. New York: American Management Association, 1972.

White House Conference on Families. *Listening to American families: Action for the 80s*. Washington, D.C.: White House Conference on Families, 1980.

Whyte, W. H. *The organization man*. New York: Doubleday, 1956.

Wilensky, H. L. Work, careers, and social integration. *International Social Science Journal*, 1960, *12* (4), 543–560.

Williams, R. M., Jr. *American society: A sociological interpretation* (2nd ed.), New York: Knopf, 1960.

Williams, R. M., Jr. The concept of values. In D. L. Sills (Ed.), *International Encyclopedia of the Social Sciences* (Vol. 16). New York: Macmillan and Free Press, 1968.

Winston, M. P., & Forsher, T. *Nonsupport of legitimate children by affluent fathers as a cause of poverty and welfare dependence*. Santa Monica, Calif.: Rand Corporation, 1971.

Woolsey, S. H. Pied Piper politics and the child care debate. *Daedalus*, 1977 (Spring), pp. 127–146.

Word, C. Cross cultural methods for survey research in black urban areas. *Journal of Black Psychology*, 1977, *3*, 72–87.

Working Family Project. (Lein, L., Durham, M., Dougherty, K., Howrigan, G., Pratt, M., Schudson, M., Thomas, R., & Weiss, H.) *Final report: Work and family life*. Wellesley, Mass.: Wellesley College Center for Research on Women, 1977.

Working Famiy Project. Parenting. In R. N. Rapoport & R. Rapoport (Eds.), *Working couples*. New York: Harper & Row, 1978.

Wortis, R. P. The acceptance of the concept of the maternal role by behavioral scientists: Its effects on women. *American Journal of Orthopsychiatry*, 1971, *41*, 733–746.

Wright, J. D., & Wright, S. R. Social class and parental values for children: A partial replication and extension of the Kohn thesis. *American Sociological Review*, 1976, *41*, 527–537.

Yankelovich, D. The meaning of work. In J. M. Rosow (Ed.), *The worker and the job*. Englewood Cliffs, N.J.: Prentice-Hall, 1974.

Yankelovich, D. The new psychological contracts at work. *Psychology Today*, May 1978. pp. 46–47; 49–50.

Young, M., & Willmott, P. *The symmetrical family*. New York: Pantheon, 1973.

Zborowski, M., & Herzog, E. *Life is with people*. New York: Schocken Books, 1952.